Finance, Society and Sustainability

Nick Silver

Finance, Society and Sustainability

How to Make the Financial System Work for the Economy, People and Planet

palgrave
macmillan

Nick Silver
Cass Business School City
University London
London, United Kingdom

ISBN 978-1-137-56060-5 ISBN 978-1-137-56061-2 (eBook)
DOI 10.1057/978-1-137-56061-2

Library of Congress Control Number: 2017945670

© The Editor(s) (if applicable) and The Author(s) 2017
The author(s) has/have asserted their right(s) to be identified as the author(s) of this work in accordance with the Copyright, Designs and Patents Act 1988.
This work is subject to copyright. All rights are solely and exclusively licensed by the Publisher, whether the whole or part of the material is concerned, specifically the rights of translation, reprinting, reuse of illustrations, recitation, broadcasting, reproduction on microfilms or in any other physical way, and transmission or information storage and retrieval, electronic adaptation, computer software, or by similar or dissimilar methodology now known or hereafter developed.
The use of general descriptive names, registered names, trademarks, service marks, etc. in this publication does not imply, even in the absence of a specific statement, that such names are exempt from the relevant protective laws and regulations and therefore free for general use.
The publisher, the authors and the editors are safe to assume that the advice and information in this book are believed to be true and accurate at the date of publication. Neither the publisher nor the authors or the editors give a warranty, express or implied, with respect to the material contained herein or for any errors or omissions that may have been made. The publisher remains neutral with regard to jurisdictional claims in published maps and institutional affiliations.

Cover illustration: Photocase Addicts GmbH / Alamy Stock Photo

Printed on acid-free paper

This Palgrave Macmillan imprint is published by Springer Nature
The registered company is Macmillan Publishers Ltd.
The registered company address is: The Campus, 4 Crinan Street, London, N1 9XW, United Kingdom

To Carly, Izzy, Louis and Theo for putting up with me whilst I wrote this book.

Acknowledgements

I would like to thank Aimee Dibbens, Nicole Tovstiga, Magdalene Polan, David Boyle, Nick Edmonds, Peter Baker, Bruce Packard, David Pitt-Watson, Andrew Slater, Con Keating, Kenneth Orchard, Cynthia Williams, Hugh McNeill, Nico Aspinall, Helen Haworth, Irene Monasterolo, Abib Bocresion and Branco Milanovic, for help, advice or encouragement on the book, and Sepi Golzari-Munro for telling me that I should write the thing in the first place.

Contents

1	Introduction	1
2	Dramatis Personae	27
3	The Potemkin Market	53
4	The Sisyphus Savings System	77
5	La Grande Illusion	101
6	A Kind of Magic	133
7	The Economy's Helminths	159
8	Collateral Damage	191
9	On Value and Values	221
10	A Financial Renaissance?	247
11	Epilogue: Twilight of the Gods of Finance	279
Index		287

About the Author

Nick Silver is an actuary and economist whose expertise includes pensions and insurance, risk management and sustainable finance, in particular working in developing economies. He is managing director of Callund Consulting Limited which for 40 years has advised developing economy governments on pensions, social protection and developing capital markets.

Nick is a founder and director of Climate Bonds, which works with governments and investors to transition to a low carbon economy. He has advised the UN, UK and EU on the carbon markets, climate finance in developing countries and managing risk from climate change. He is also a founder and director of Radix, the think tank of the radical centre.

Nick is a visiting fellow at the London School of Economics and Cass Business School and lectures at Trinity College Dublin, City University. He is a freeman of the City of London and until recently, and was a member of council of the Institute and Faculty of Actuaries.

List of Abbreviation

AFP	Administradoras de Fondos de Pensiones
AGM	Annual general meeting
AI	Artificial Intelligence
ALM	Asset liability del
BP	British Petroleum Plc
CalSTRS	California Public Employees' Retirement System
CAPM	Capital asset pricing model
CDO	Collateralised debt obligation
CEO	Chief executive officer
DB	Defined benefit (pension scheme)
DC	Defined contribution (pension scheme)
EMH	Efficient market hypothesis
ESG	Environmental, social and governance
FinTech	Financial technology
FTSE	Financial Times Stock Exchange (index)
FTT	Financial transaction tax
GDP	Gross domestic product
GHG	Greenhouse gas
GSE	Government-Sponsored Enterprises
HFT	High-frequency trader
IMF	International Monetary Fund
IPO	Initial public offering
LBO	Leveraged buy-out
LIBOR	London Interbank Offered Rate
MPT	Modern portfolio theory
NEST	National Employment Savings Trust
NFC	Non-financial corporation

NGO	Non-governmental organisation
OECD	The Organisation for Economic Co-operation and Development
OPEC	Organization of Petroleum Exporting Countries
OTC	Over-the-counter (derivatives)
PAYGO	Pay as you go (pension system)
QE	Quantitative easing
SRI	Socially responsible investment
SWF	Sovereign wealth funds
UAE	United Arab Emirates

List of Figures

Fig. 1.1	Pyramid of the Magician, Uxmal, Mexico	2
Fig. 1.2	Temples of finance	2
Fig. 1.3	Finance, economy, society and the environment	4
Fig. 1.4	GDP share of US financial sector	10
Fig. 1.5	Finance sector profits as proportion of total US profits	11
Fig. 1.6	Size of OTC global derivate market (Notional amounts outstanding $trillion)	12
Fig. 1.7	UK Bank lending by sector in 2015	13
Fig. 1.8	Real income growth in USA	14
Fig. 2.1	Global invested capital split by asset class	40
Fig. 3.1	Real yields on UK government bonds on 3 January 2017	67
Fig. 3.2	Selected government bond yields	68
Fig. 4.1	Projections of support ratio for the UK	81
Fig. 4.2	Percentage of total tax relief on individual and employee pension contributions by income decile (2009/10)	84
Fig. 4.3	FTSE 100 index	94
Fig. 5.1	Asset allocation by pension funds	103
Fig. 5.2	UK bond market split by sector	106
Fig. 5.3	History of UK government net borrowing	107
Fig. 5.4	CEO to worker compensation ratio	119
Fig. 5.5	Ratio of investment compared to funds returned to shareholders	120
Fig. 6.1	UK Bank lending by sector in 2015	142
Fig. 6.2	Total UK debt levels	146
Fig. 6.3	Ratio of house prices compared to income	149
Fig. 6.4	Mortgage payments as proportion of income	150
Fig. 7.1	GDP share of US financial sector	161
Fig. 7.2	Finance sector profits as proportion of total US profits	167

List of Figures

Fig. 7.3	Size of OTC global derivate market (Notional amounts outstanding $trillion)	169
Fig. 8.1	Global human population 10,000 BC to present	195
Fig. 8.2	Population projections to 2100 by region	196
Fig. 8.3	Global Economic growth compared with carbon emissions and population	199
Fig. 8.4	Planetary Boundaries	201
Fig. 8.5	Global temperature over last 100,000 years	202
Fig. 8.6	Real income growth in USA	208
Fig. 8.7	Change in real income between 1988 and 2008 at various percentiles of global income distribution (calculated in 2005 international dollars)	211
Fig. 8.8	Proportion of global population living in extreme poverty	212
Fig. 9.1	How values translate to economic outcome	224
Fig. 9.2	The price of sugar and spice in Sugarscape	232
Fig. 9.3	GDP growth of USA, UK, Japan and France	236
Fig. 10.1	Towards a flourishing finance system	250

List of Tables

Table 2.1	Characterisation of deposit and savings channels	28
Table 2.2	World's 20 largest asset owners	31
Table 2.3	World's largest 10 pension funds	34
Table 2.4	World's 10 largest sovereign wealth funds	37
Table 2.5	Summary of asset owners	39
Table 2.6	World's largest asset managers	45
Table 3.1	World's largest 20 pension funds	57
Table 3.2	US bond market – outstanding issuance	62
Table 4.1	What are pensions for?	79
Table 4.2	Contributions required to achieve two-thirds pension	87
Table 4.3	Estimates of annual fees of equity funds	93
Table 5.1	Annual government subsidy of finance	108
Table 5.2	Proportion of pension fund investment that is productive	113
Table 11.1	Recent tech-firm takeovers	282

1

Introduction

The Archaeology of Finance

In 1750 a small group of Spanish explorers, cutting their way through the jungles of Central America, came across the ruins of what was once a vast city. In the centre of this city, they discovered the ruins of monumental structures such as the Pyramid of the Magician in Uxmal (Fig. 1.1). Being unable to decipher Mayan glyphs, they must have wondered for what purpose the long-disappeared inhabitants had built these magnificent and alien structures.

The ruins we see now were the peak of Mayan civilisation. Why did the Mayans devote so much of their precious resources to building these temples just before their civilisation collapsed?

We now know that Mayan pyramids were used by an elite caste of priests to carry out arcane rites, often involving human sacrifices, based on sophisticated mathematical calculations. The purpose of these rites was to keep the gods happy so that the crops would grow. They didn't work; a mixture of over-farming and climate change caused crop yields to decline, resulting in the collapse of the classical Mayan civilisation and abandonment of cities like Uxmal in about the ninth century AD.[1]

When I come out of Canary Wharf Station, London's financial district, and am confronted with monumental, temple-like structures (Fig. 1.2), I often wonder what a future archaeologist would make of the ruins of these buildings. Why did the twenty-first-century civilisations devote such a large amount of scarce resources to constructing these buildings? What were they for?

This book is an attempt to answer these archaeological questions: What are these contemporary temples for? How do they impact on the society that

© The Author(s) 2017
N. Silver, *Finance, Society and Sustainability*,
DOI 10.1057/978-1-137-56061-2_1

Fig. 1.1 Pyramid of the Magician, Uxmal, Mexico
Uxmal Pyramid on Yucatan Peninsula, Mexico

Fig. 1.2 Temples of finance
As viewed from Cabot Square in London's Docklands development

supports them and how does this society, directed by the priests who inhabit the temples, impact the environment? Is their purpose the same as the Mayan temples, albeit they are not directly used for human sacrifices any more, and will our civilization go the way of the Mayans?

If we visualise the finance sector, we picture a roomful of men – it is nearly always men – surrounded by computer screens with columns of numbers flashing up at them. It is not obvious how this relates to the day-to-day cares of ordinary folk and even less so to man's impact on the natural world, as manifest by such phenomena as climate change and biodiversity loss.

Finance sits within the human economy. I think of finance as the control centre of the economy directing where our capital is allocated; finance is a social technology which allocates economic surplus back into the economy. The economy itself is situated in human society, it is reliant on social institutions, rules and norms by which people behave and interact. When these rules and norms break down, now in war-torn Syria or Somalia for example, or historically after the collapse of the Roman Empire, these societies are unable to maintain much of an economy.

Society itself relies on the natural world, for example for energy, water, clean air and a favourable climate. The Mayan civilisation collapsed because of changes to the natural world, some of which they caused. This relationship is captured by Fig. 1.3, which shows finance embedded in the economy, which is embedded in society which in turn is embedded in the natural world.[2]

1.1 What Is Sustainability?

I started thinking about this book when I was working on trying to get the finance sector to invest in a way to avoid dangerous climate change. As a by-product of human activity, we are producing carbon dioxide and other gasses which cause global warming. The impact of global warming is uncertain, but increased temperatures will cause the Greenland and Antarctic ice sheets to melt, leading to sea level rises of many metres which, amongst other things, could cause the flooding of most of the world's major cities.

The technology exists to go about our activities without producing these gasses, and it is not even more expensive to deploy renewable energy than fossil fuels, but our existing capital is locked into the fossil-fuel economy. If we could shift this capital quickly into the low-carbon economy, catastrophic global warming could be avoided. The financial system allocates our capital – can it be utilised to solve this problem? Or is it the cause of the problem?

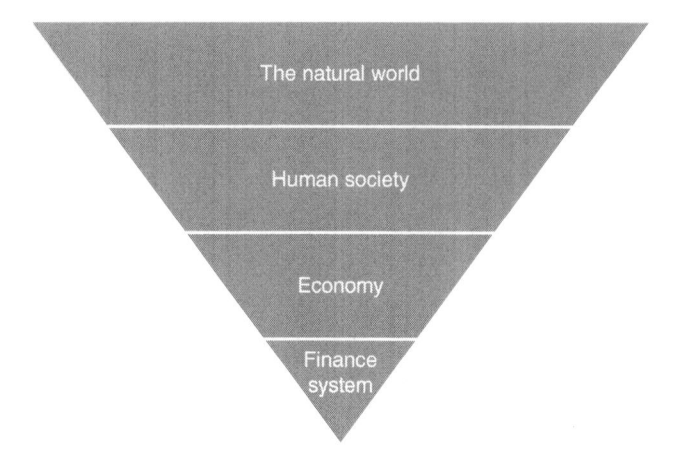

Fig. 1.3 Finance, economy, society and the environment

There are many other serious environmental and social problems facing us today. Humanity's impact on nature is immense: for example, the population of non-human vertebrates has declined by 60% over the last 40 years,[3] and we have already breached three planetary boundaries of the planet's self-regulating biophysical processes.[4] What has the financial system to do with these problems, can it be used to solve these problems or is it making them worse?

We appear to be seeing the outbreak of populism in many Western countries, as embodied by the election of Donald Trump as President of the USA, the Brexit vote in the UK and the "illiberal" democratic governments of Poland, Hungary and Turkey. In many countries, real wages have stagnated and inequality has grown over an extended time period. Finance allocates capital – to what extent, if any, has finance caused this?

If we look at the global picture of income distribution, whilst some countries have been rapidly developing, others are still mired in poverty. With the number of billionaires increasing rapidly, there are still 3 billion people (out of a global population of 7 billion) living on less than $2.50 per day and 1 billion living on less than $1.25.[5] Yet capital is being shifted, by the financial system, from the poorer world to the richer world rather than the other way round, why is this?[6]

Let's start with an underpinning definition. I define the sustainability of a system as: *The ability of a system to maintain itself indefinitely without a high risk of it dropping to a lower level of complexity.*

From what we know about Classical Mayan civilisation, it had a high level of complexity. It was able to support a large population, had developed sophisticated mathematics and was capable of building impressive monuments such as the Magician's Pyramid. After the collapse, it was no longer capable of maintaining a large population or high culture. The difference between the civilisation before and after it collapsed is encapsulated in this idea of complexity.[7]

It is useful to split up sustainability into three levels when we think about finance:

1. Self-sustainability: Can the financial system keep going indefinitely?
2. Economic sustainability: Does the finance system contribute to sustainability of the economy?
3. Ecological and societal sustainability: Does the system contribute to environmental or social sustainability – how does it impact on resource use, environmental damage and social well-being?

When it comes to the first level of sustainability, the financial system proved not to be sustainable in 2007–08, when the global financial system would have collapsed, had it not been rescued by coordinated action by governments. The global financial crisis, its aftermath or whether the whole thing will happen again, has been dealt with extensively and exhaustively elsewhere[8] and this book will only incidentally concern itself with this first level.

The financial system is embedded within a "real", physical economy, the economy that makes goods and provides services. There is a complex relationship between the real economy and the financial system, which I hope will become apparent during this book. The second level of sustainability is whether the financial system leads to a sustainable real economy or undermines its sustainability. Take the Weimar Republic, for example, which governed Germany after the First World War: its financial system collapsed in the 1930s and was replaced by the different political, social and economic system of the Nazi regime.

Of course, financial crises have important implications for the sustainability of the real economy. The immediate cause of the collapse of the Weimar Republic was the Wall Street Crash of 1929, and the recent financial crisis almost plunged the world into a depression too. But there are also underlying factors which contribute to whether or not the economy is sustainable. The ultimate cause of the economic collapse of the Weimar Republic was the burden of having to pay unaffordable reparations for the First World War, which made it particularly vulnerable to a financial shock.

Just as the financial system is embedded in the real economy, the real economy is embedded within the natural world. The natural world provides us with our life support system; without the natural world we would not have air, water or food. Does the financial system drive the destruction of the natural environment, and how could finance be used for sustainable investment to avoid ecological damage?

1.2 What Has Finance Ever Done for Us?

The headmistress of my daughter's school is a very impressive lady. She is in charge of dozens of staff overseeing hundreds of school children. Obviously the job the school is doing is highly useful to society. I know a lot of people who work in financial services, myself included. It is often not obvious even to me, to understand what it is exactly that they do. Many of these people get paid ten times what my daughter's headmistress earns. Surely, they must be doing something frightfully useful to be so highly remunerated? And where does the money come from to pay them?

The genesis for this book came when I was dumbfounded by a statement in the Kay Review. John Kay had been commissioned by the UK's business department to investigate the impact of the equity market on the long-term economic performance of the economy.[9] The report says that: "UK equity markets are no longer a significant source of funding for new investment by UK companies." If this is the case, then what on earth are the equity markets for?

The review then finds that the asset managers who dominate the market are not actually doing the job that they are supposed to be doing (more of this in Chapter 5), yet the people who work in this field are highly paid to not do their job. How has this happened?

Equity markets are not a source of new investment. It would not take you long to find an article in the newspapers or on the web bewailing the fact that banks are not lending into the "real" economy. The recent global financial crisis proves that the system is not managing risk properly.

If the financial system is not lending or investing into the real economy or managing risk, how can it be expected to finance a sustainable economy? In fact, what it is it actually doing?

Finance is a social technology which allocates economic surplus back into the economy; finance directs where capital is allocated. For the end user:

1. it manages the payment system,
2. it allows people to manage risk,
3. it allows people to smooth lifetime consumption and
4. it allocates savings into useful investment.

How well does it do these? This question requires a value judgement. Let's start with my own experience as a user. From my computer, I can make a payment to almost anyone in the world who has a bank account, at no or relatively low costs. Or when I was in Dushanbe in Tajikistan, I could put my debit card into an ATM and withdraw Somoni notes debited directly from my UK account. These are really amazing achievements. For me, at least, the payment system works perfectly well.

How about risk management? I face a plethora of risks just from going about my daily life, some of which I just have to bear myself or risk manage through my behaviour, for example not walking across a motorway or not picking a fight with aggressive drunken people. But I am also able to buy an array of financial products which help me to manage risk. Primarily among these is a simple bank account. I can store surplus income with my bank, and I can transfer this surplus into an almost limitless choice of assets. This means that if my house is robbed, or burns down or London is hit by a severe drought, then my surplus assets are unaffected. Yet this isn't true of everyone; if I were an African subsistence farmer without a bank account, I would have to store any surplus income as a physical asset in my possession, such as a cow. The cow could die in a drought or could be stolen or get ill, in which case I have lost my asset.

Beyond my bank account, I can purchase insurance against a range of unfortunate events that might befall me, for example if I were to get ill, die, live for a long time or if my house gets burgled or burns down. The financial system also provides more esoteric forms of risk management, which as an individual I am unlikely to use. For example, if I need to make a purchase in the future in a foreign currency, I can purchase a financial product to lock the exchange rate at a future date, so I am not at risk from fluctuations in the currency. Similarly, if I need to buy a commodity in the future, such as oil or grain, I could also lock in the price that it is at today.

So, for me the finance system provides a wealth of risk management tools, which I can generally rely on.

Smoothing lifetime consumption requires a bit more explanation. At the start of a typical lifetime, we are unable to earn a living, but we still need money to be spent on our behalf, for food, shelter, nappies and education. This phase of our lives end at some point, when hopefully we get a job and our income exceeds our expenditure, a period of our lives that continues until we get too old or ill, at which time we will again have expenditure and no earned income. Even in the working period, there may be times when your expenditure exceeds income, for example you might need to make a big purchase such as a house or a car, you might get ill or unemployed or take time off for education, or you might want to buy something a few days before you get your pay-check. To facilitate all of this, the finance system offers a range of products; saving into a pension helps defer income till retirement, a loan can be used to finance a house purchase or a car. We have credit cards for smaller payments which we can pay when we get paid.

For any money that I save, there is a range of financial vehicles in which I can invest, and I am confident that the intermediaries or ultimate beneficiaries are not criminals and will not run off with my money, so all I have to worry about is whether the investment is good or not. This too is a remarkable achievement and should not be underrated.

Smoothing lifetime consumption is a non-trivial task and the financial system does provide all of the products I could possibly need to carry this out. How well these products work will be explored in detail in Chapters 4 and 5.

From my perspective, the finance system appears to perform the first three tasks that it is there for. But I do belong to a specific and favourable demographic. I am relatively affluent, in work, financially literate, have a good credit rating and live in the financial centre (London) of a developed country. If I was a subsistence farmer living in a developing country earning less than $2.50 a day, the current situation of 3 billion people, none of the products and services provided by the global financial system would be available to me.[10] And there are far more people in this situation than in mine. Even in the UK, there are far fewer products available to people who are in a less fortunate position than myself, and those products that are available will be much less favourable to the client, for example pay-day loans targeted at the poor; very short-term loans with very high interest rates.

What of the fourth function? Does the finance system allocate savings into useful investments? I can put my excess earnings into a bank account or a pension, or the money markets, or a range of other financial products, and hopefully access at a later date when I might need them. What does the finance system do with these savings? As well as a saver, I could also be a user of capital. If I want to buy a house, for example, I could get a mortgage from a bank to do so. To fund the loan, the bank is using other peoples' savings. The bank as an intermediary is investing these savings by funding my purchase of a house.

It is very easy for me to get a mortgage on a house and it is also easy for me to borrow money on a credit card to fund consumer purchases. But if I want to set up my own business, or if I run a small company, it is more difficult for me to borrow or raise money. This is despite all the advantages that I might have as a borrower. And this could be a problem, because if I and others like me have collectively borrowed large amounts to purchase assets, this in itself could push up the price of these assets. Loans which are made to fund consumer spending have to be paid back with interest.

For borrowers *en masse* to payback loans plus interest, our income has to grow, which means that the economy has to grow – which in turn means that businesses have to have access to finance to expand and to employ people. Without this growth of companies and employment, the economy will be unable to grow.

It is also a problem that I can very easily and cheaply access finance, currently at very favourable terms, for an asset purchase, whereas someone not in my favourable situation cannot. This means that it makes sense for me, and others like me, to borrow money cheaply and buy property or other assets, which because good finance terms are available, increase in value, making me wealthier. A person on a low income will find it extremely difficult to do so, can only borrow money at higher interest rates or is trapped at a low consumption level, especially as small- and medium-sized companies can't access finance to expand and employ these people.

Some aspects of the financial system appear to be working satisfactorily, but where it is choosing to allocate finance resources looks problematic. The system appears to be directing resources towards asset purchases and consumption rather than to productive purchases, such as to a new business, to meet the needs of wealthier and more affluent people only.

1.3 All Is Well in the House of Finance?

Although I can purchase an array of risk management products, the financial system crashed in 2008 convincingly demonstrated that, as a system, it was not doing risk management well. The only reason that the money in my bank account and my other financial assets did not disappear was because governments stepped in to save the system. Since then, the financial system has been living on borrowed time. Furthermore, the reason that the system crashed, and has done so in the past, was not because of the risks that actually matter to normal people; it did not crash because lots of people got ill, or died, or many of their houses burned down. It was crashed from risks generated by the finance system itself.[11]

The reason the 2008 crash could have such a dramatic impact was because the finance sector had grown so large (see Fig. 1.4 for the USA).

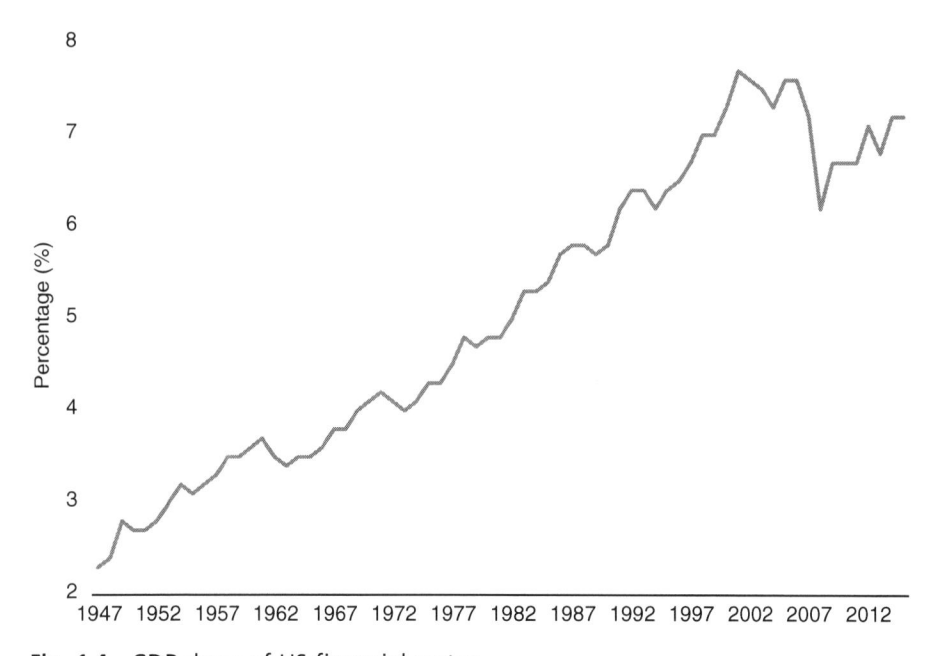

Fig. 1.4 GDP share of US financial sector
Source: US Bureau of Economic Analysis
From https://www.bea.gov/industry/gdpbyind_data.htm accessed 16 January 2017

Since the 1940s, the size of the finance sector has almost quadrupled relative to the size of the economy, with an almost doubling in size between the 1980s and 2007. The absolute increase in size is much larger as the economy has grown significantly in that period. This is a trend mirrored in a number of countries, such as Australia, UK and Ireland. Countries such as the UK show an even more dramatic increase, where the finance sector increased by more than 50% in just 10 years.

Technological developments and globalisation have caused the finance sector to have increased substantially in size during this period, but such a large increase seems suspicious.

This suspicion is reinforced by Fig. 1.5. The proportion of corporate profits in the USA attributable to the finance sector has approximately doubled since 1980, added to this average compensation in finance was similar to other sectors in the 1980s, but has increased to four times as high.[12]

Such a large relative increase in size, wages and profits in the finance sector should set alarm bells ringing. Unlike most other industries, the finance sector does not produce goods that people want. The financial sectors are intermediates that facilitate the production of these goods. For example, a car

1.3 All Is Well in the House of Finance? 11

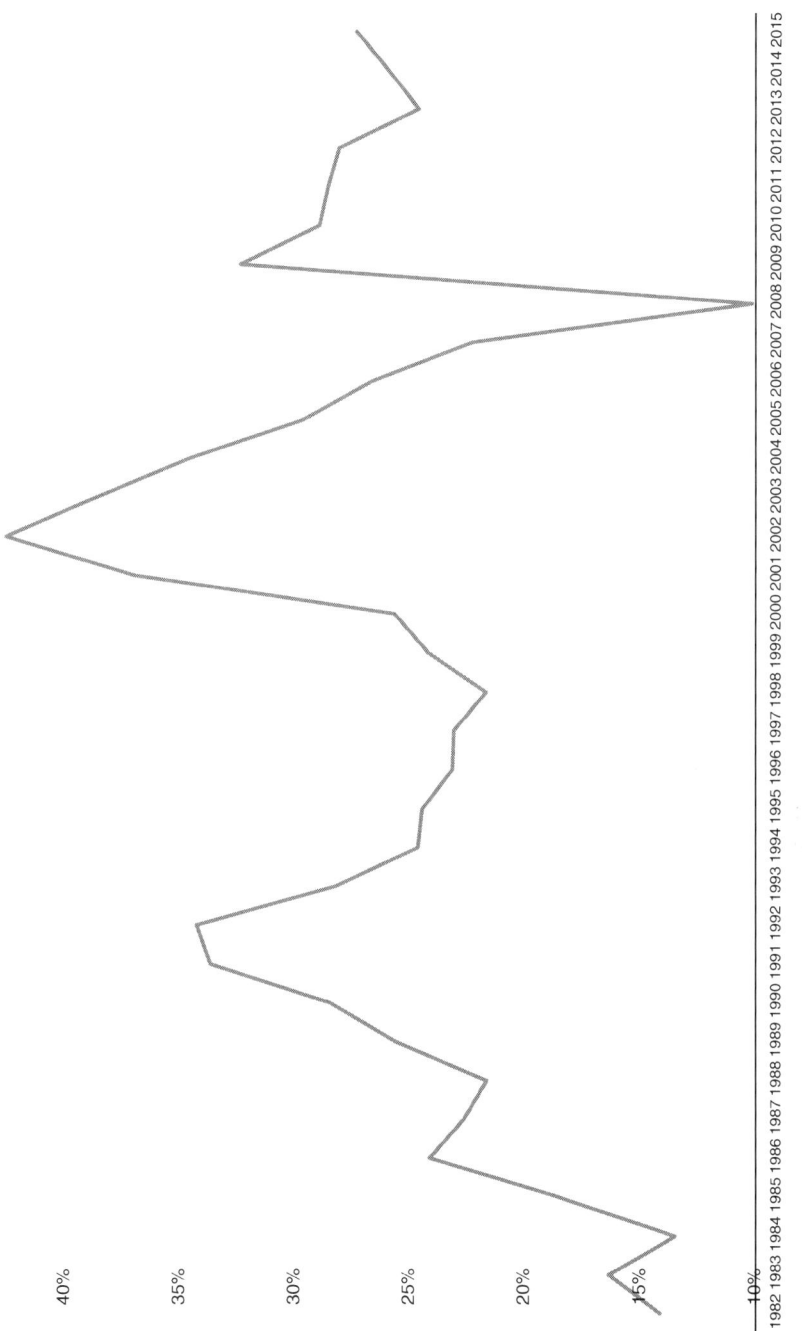

Fig. 1.5 Finance sector profits as proportion of total US profits

Source: US Bureau of Economic Analysis
From National industry data, NIPA table 6.16 https://www.bea.gov/national/nipaweb/downss2.asp accessed 16 January 2017

manufacturer might need to raise finance and part of the costs will be for finance. The growth of technology just reflects that people are buying different goods, but the increase in size of the finance sector means that an increasing proportion the profits of goods that people want is being diverted to finance. With better technology and increasing amounts of capital, the opposite should happen, the cost of finance should be decreasing.

Alongside this disproportionate increase in salaries and profits, there is evidence to suggest that the finance sector is largely engaged in activities which are of little use or even harmful to the real economy.

The number of financial transactions has massively increased over the last 20 years, with little apparent need for them to do so. Figure 1.6 shows the growth in the size of the derivatives market. There may be good reasons why the volume has increased because of better technology and globalisation. But this does not really explain the massive explosion in the size of the market, which has increased 100-fold in the last 25 years, before plateauing; with a size now of approximately 10 times global GDP.[13] Derivative contracts are not new they have been around for at least a century – so why the sudden

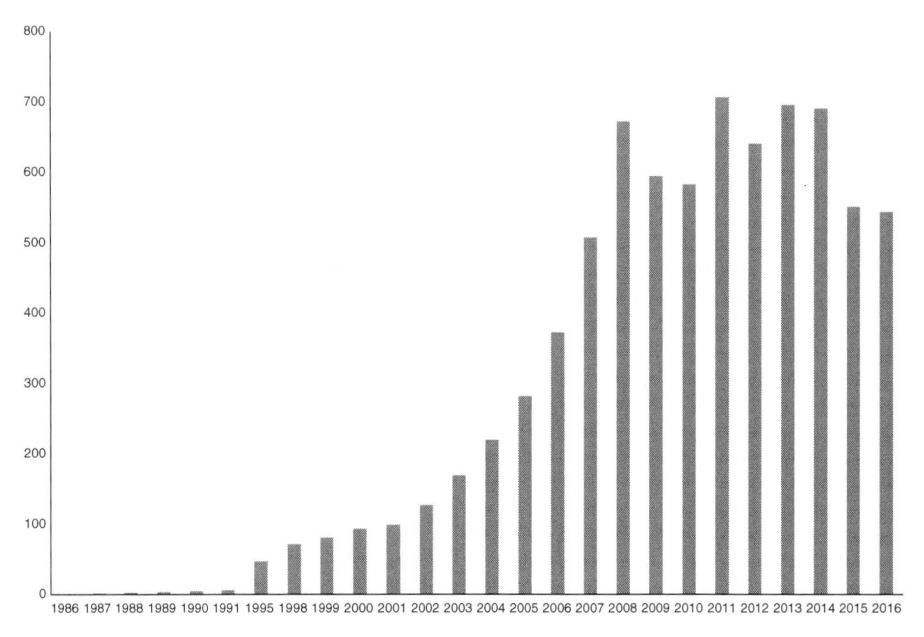

Fig. 1.6 Size of OTC global derivate market (Notional amounts outstanding $trillion)

Source: Bank for International Settlements
Semiannual OTC derivatives statistics http://www.bis.org/statistics/about_derivatives_stats.htm; pre 199 data was quoted in Remolona (1992) *The Recent Growth of Financial Derivative Markets* Federal Reserve Bank of New York accessed 16 January 2017

1.3 All Is Well in the House of Finance?

explosion? Also, derivatives are inherently risk management products, the explosion in the size of the market coincided with the global financial crisis, not exactly a vindication of their ability to manage risk.

The finance sector has a crucial role to play in allocating capital. Figure 1.7 shows UK banks' lending split by sector. It shows that only a small proportion of lending is going into non-financial corporations, with a far larger proportion going to finance itself. The combined biggest sector is property. People need to borrow against housing, but why so much? And how will the economy grow if such a small proportion is lent to the productive economy?

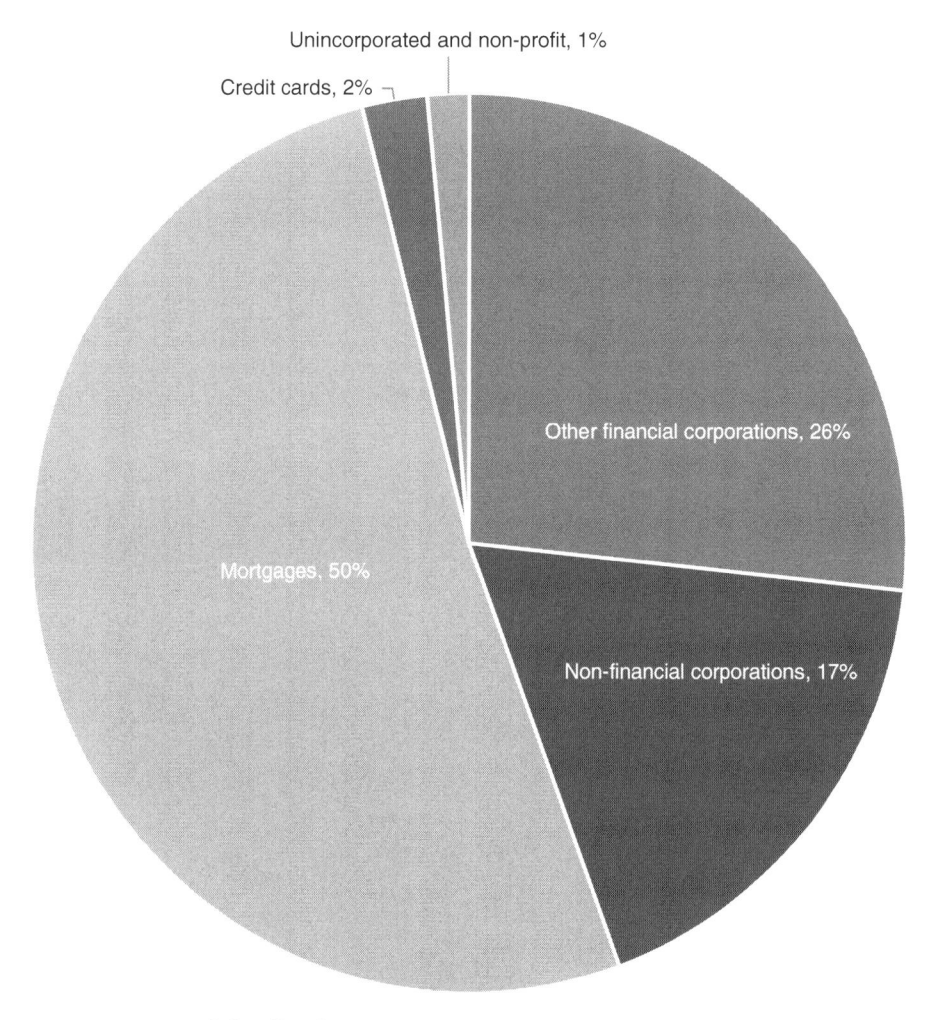

Fig. 1.7 UK Bank lending by sector in 2015
Source: Bank of England Bankstats table A4.1

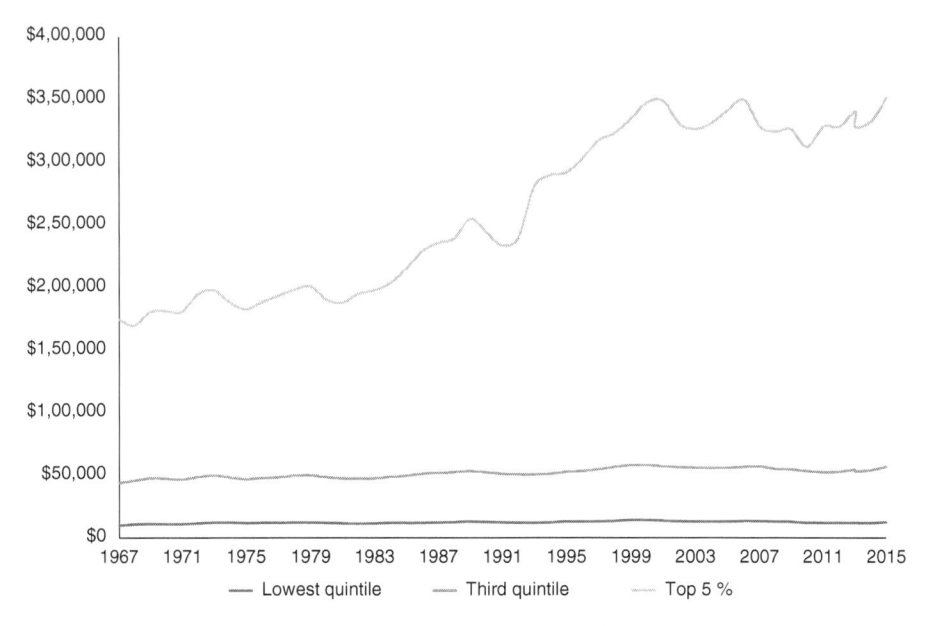

Fig. 1.8 Real income growth in USA

Source: United States Census Bureau
The chart shows the mean within each quintile band so the 3rd quintile is approximately the population's median in 2015 prices. Table A-2 from http://www.census.gov/data/tables/2016/demo/income-poverty/p60-256.html accessed 22 January 2017

Economies of many developed countries have become increasingly unequal in recent years. Figure 1.8 shows that the income of the top 5% has increased dramatically over the last 50 years in the USA, whereas the poorest people, or even the "average" person has barely increased at all. The finance system is the means by which we allocate capital, and while it is not the finance system alone that will be the cause of this increased inequality, is it coincidental that the growth of the finance sector has happened at the same time as the growth in inequality?

1.4 Conducting the Economy

Where the finance system allocates capital changes everything. Where capital is directed shapes the structure and future course of the economy.

If capital is directed towards clean energy, we could avoid dangerous climate change, whereas if it is directed towards fossil-fuel infrastructure, we will be locked into a carbon-intensive industrial structure. If finance is directed towards health and education, we will end up with a healthier and well-educated population, whereas if it were directed into tobacco and the drinks industry, we will not. It would not be right to put all the blame on finance, if there was a high and credible carbon price it would be more profitable and less risky to invest in clean energy and so more capital would flow into this sector, but the decisions made by the financial sector do have a crucial role to play.

This impact of the financial system on the economy is a by-product of its four functions as outlined earlier. Because I need to save to meet future expenses, I buy a financial product. My savings are combined with others who have bought similar products and are invested by the financial services industry. Where these savings are invested impacts the economy, yet the decision is based on whatever motivates the intermediary who invests the money.

There are essentially two channels by which savings are invested which are institutionally very different. The **deposit** channel, essentially bank accounts, is where I leave some cash which I might want at short notice. The bank can lend this money out because depositors won't all want to withdraw their money at the same time. The **savings** channel is used for longer term savings. If I save money into a pension scheme, this is invested in the capital markets by an intermediary on my behalf, which might be a pension fund, an asset manager or a mutual fund.[14]

How savings are invested shapes the future direction of the economy. It is not the job of the intermediary to invest in something that is good or useful. His job is to earn income for his company by getting a good return. Whether this investment is for the good of the economy or not is incidental.

The intellectual justification for capital to be allocated in this way is essentially the theory of free markets. People are free to invest their savings where they want. Resources will therefore be directed towards investments which make the most efficient use of capital, as this will give the best return. The information provided by the price mechanism ensures that the market will optimally allocate capital to those who will use it in the most efficient way.

If this wasn't the case – if a company could use capital efficiently but wasn't getting enough of it – it could pay a higher return as it could make more money from getting more capital. Because it can make a higher return, it can pay investors a higher return for the use of capital and therefore if financial markets were free and complete, investors would invest in this company until it had enough capital at which point it could no longer pay excess returns.

Even though investments are made by financial intermediaries who are not paid to invest in the best interests of the economy, there is a built-in system that encourages them to invest efficiently. Because they want to maximise their returns, capital will be directed to the most efficient users as these users will help them do that. The economy will be optimised if capital is allocated by the free market. That is the theory.

1.5 Thesis

Some variant of the free-market argument provides the intellectual justification for capital markets; a free-market allocation of capital is the most efficient way of allocating resources. This justification is used as a reason for governments to support the markets, and as we saw in 2008, to bail them out when things go wrong.

Capital markets are not free, they are what I call **Potemkin markets** (Chapter 3); the main buyers and sellers are governments who are also the main influence on the price at which financial assets are traded.

People are encouraged or forced by governments to save via a finance system which is shaped by governments. Governments do this through regulation and legislation, by providing the enabling environment, by deciding who can or cannot be a financial intermediary, determining the design of investment vehicles and by providing many of the financial products. Governments also set the interest rate which is the most important price in the market. The finance system is carrying out the will of the state in a way prescribed by the state.

One of the objectives of governments is to get people to save so that they can have a decent income when they retire. By encouraging people to save via what I call the **Sisyphus savings system** (Chapter 4), interest rates have been driven to virtually zero, making savings products such as pensions unaffordable, exacerbated by high charges from the financial sector and hence this objective has been a total failure.

The role of the financial sector at the macro level is to invest society's excess earnings. The finance sector fails to do this; under **La Grande Illusion** (Chapter 5), financial intermediaries intercept these savings and manage them in a way that maximises their own revenue. The finance sector can do this because governments have in effect given mandates to a small group of private sector actors to manage society's assets. This mandate gives rise to a huge concentration of power, for example $24 trillion of assets, a quarter of the world's assets, is managed by just 20 asset management companies.

Banks have also been given a powerful mandate by the state, **a kind of magic** (Chapter 6); the ability to create money. Money is created by banks who decide where it gets distributed in the economy; and where it goes is important. It is predominantly used to fund real estate purchases, and this causes the price of real estate to increase, so banks can lend more into the sector. Only a derisory amount of lending is directed to the real economy.

Though the financial sector is a creation of the state, the agents who populate it are very much private actors, whose objective is to maximise their own revenue. Power has been concentrated in a very few organisations, be they asset management companies, banks or investment banks. The agents in the financial system manage the capital stocks and flows in the economy in such a way as to generate revenue for themselves. The outcome for the economy, society and the environment is incidental to the financial agents, whom I call the **economy's helminths** (Chapter 7).

The helminth employs a set of tools to maximise its revenue. **Leverage** allows financial agents to increase their revenue from a given set assets. A key mechanism is the interest rate, which the finance system has pushed down to virtually zero, increasing asset prices and thereby increasing the revenue that the finance sector can generate from these assets.

Financial innovation involves creating new financial products, the purpose of which is to leverage further existing assets or to create virtual assets which can be bought and sold out of which financial intermediaries receive fees.

Colonisation is the process whereby the finance sector takes over non-financial corporations and governments, so that these institutions are increasingly financialised themselves and act in the interest of the finance sector. For example, asset managers invest in public companies and influence how those companies are managed. The companies are incentivised to take short-term decisions to boost their own share price, to the detriment of the economy. This involves reducing investment in research and development, reducing staff costs via redundancy, driving down wages and offshoring and distributing funds back to shareholders. Executive pay has exploded as executives are rewarded based on a company's share price in the interests of the finance sector, but not in the interests of the company or the economy.

The final tool is **hegemony**, where the logic of finance theory dominates society's discourse. The hegemonic view is that the purpose of companies is to maximise shareholder value, and markets are efficient so companies should be run to maximise their share price. In maximising their own revenue, corporations are acting in the best interest of society; in reality it is mainly in the interest of the finance sector. Hegemonic theories are employed by regulators, central banks and finance ministries, so regulation and government action aids and abets financial agents to extract value.

1.5.1 What Goes Wrong

It has been observed that people in finance get well paid, so they must be doing something very important. And indeed they are; they are in charge of allocating societies' resources, which requires a great deal of skill, so the best ones get very well paid.

What is not true is that they allocate capital in a way that is good for society or even that they are doing a very good job at what they are paid to do. This is not because they are stupid, unskilled or corrupt but is because they are incentivised to earn revenue by controlling financial flows, which is at odds with the needs of society and their clients.

The system we have does have certain merits. I do have access to most of the financial services I need, as I set out above. Does the way capital is allocated really make a big difference to our lives?

Countries with an "Anglo-Saxon"-style finance system, such as the USA and the UK, have experienced the growth of financialisation since the 1970s, the rapid growth of the financial services sector as a proportion of the economy and the increasing importance of finance in the non-financial sectors.

This period has seen impressive economic growth, but it has also been characterised by **Collateral damage** (Chapter 8): real wage stagnation, rising debt levels and increased inequality. All of these are detrimental to society and at least partly caused by the financial system. Finance is directed towards existing assets, leading to the boosting of asset prices. Those that have assets, the richest segment of the population, get richer, whereas the majority of the population, which has few or no assets, does not, leading to increased inequality. This is not because rich people are creating wealth, but simply because they have assets. This process is leveraged; if you are wealthy and want to buy an asset you can borrow money cheaply, and because finance is available, this boosts the value of these assets. If you are poor, you can't and remain poor.

The increased level of debt in the economy is a problem created by our financial system. Debt has to be repaid with interest, meaning the economy has to grow. When it does not grow, things go badly wrong, causing unemployment and financial hardship. High levels of personal debt are associated with high stress, anxiety and mental illness. High levels of government debt mean that the government has to raise taxes or is less able to fund social programmes.

The assets of our economy are invested by professional asset managers; who exert a great deal of influence on the way the companies that they invest in are run. Asset managers are incentivised to boost short-term returns, which means that, in turn, the management of companies are incentivised by asset managers to boost short-term earnings by linking executive pay to share price. They can boost earnings by reducing staff costs which results in the stagnation of long-term wages for the majority and a massive increase in earnings for the very rich. They can reduce investment in research and development, undermining future growth. Increasing debt levels is another way of boosting earnings.

The natural environment is damaged as a result of decisions made in the financial sector. Because the financial system encourages companies to make increasingly short-term decisions, they are more inclined to use up resources then invest in longer term efforts to make processes more resource efficient. Because of the narrow concern for maximising shareholder value, companies will look to pass on externalities, such a pollution, on to the rest of society. Lobbying to lessen environmental laws achieves extraordinarily high financial returns for companies, as does offshoring production to countries with weaker environmental laws. Other ways of boosting short-term profits involve advertising spending; getting people to buy stuff they don't need and can't afford; the creation and distribution of this stuff uses up natural resources and causes pollution.

The increase in debt levels generated by the financial system requires the economy to grow to payback this debt. This leverages up the social damage done if the economy does not grow, and it therefore leverages up the requirement to use more resources and generate more pollution to payback this debt.

However, finance's main environmental crime is that it is blind to environmental destruction and it has no concern about it. To transform the global economy into a resource-efficient, low-carbon economy will require a new, global industrial revolution much greater in size than previous industrial revolutions. The required investment is immense. The finance sector is too busy directing investment to itself to notice, when these intercepted savings are desperately required to transform the global economy into a sustainable economy.

Finally, most of the people I know who work in finance are smart and talented people. The world has lots of problems that need tackling, a few of which I have elucidated. These people are desperately needed to do important, useful work but instead are working in finance.

1.5.2 Antithesis

The financial services industry is changing. Since the financial crisis, there has been more legislation brought in to try and stop another financial crisis from happening and there has also been a raft of lawsuits and fines imposed on banks and other financial institutions. Though this legislation is wholly inadequate for its purpose, the net effect is that financial institutions have had to reduce much of their activities which have reduced the range of financial activities, institutions' appetite to take risks and their profitability.

In generating past profits for itself, the finance sector aided and abetted by governments has forced down the interest rate and hence has increased asset prices. But the interest rate has been driven down to zero, which means that the finance sector can no longer make so much money.

At the same time, new technologies have been emerging that allow new entrants into finance to outcompete existing incumbents. For example, to change money into a different currency, I use an internet company who charge a fraction of the cost of my bank. I hold my short-term savings via a marketplace lending platform rather than a bank as it offers me a better rate of interest. On the other side of the platform is a borrower, who would previously have borrowed from a bank.

My pension is invested in a passive index-tracking fund. This is a fund invested in the stock market by a computer, which simply buys and sells shares in the same proportion of the overall market. The fees of this are much lower than an actively managed fund, because they do not have to pay the computer as much as expensive human beings.

These innovations are all outcompeting current incumbents on price, mainly because they don't have to employ large numbers of highly paid finance professionals. They vary in size, so marketplace lending platforms are tiny compared to traditional banks, whereas some passive funds are enormous – one, Vanguard, is the second largest fund manager in the world.

New financial technologies, called FinTech, are attracting enormous quantities of investment. It is not guaranteed that a finance system dominated by FinTech will be better than the current system we have. Current financial institutions are still large and powerful and could take a long time to die off and many will adapt themselves to the new world.

Yet a FinTech world will be quite different to our current world. Although there will be some very highly paid finance people in a FinTech world, there will be far less than now. Technology industries tend to be winner-takes-all, so you get one dominant player in a market (like Airbnb, Uber or Facebook) with a small number of employees making a huge profit. This is not necessarily a good thing, but it does mean that most of the relatively large number of highly remunerated people working in financial services will have to find something else to do.

The current financial system is based on an implicit set of values. These are based around the free market allocating capital in the most efficient way, so that the economy can grow at an optimal rate, and everyone is materially better off. Ironically, though capital markets are Potemkin markets not free markets, governments have set them up to try and replicate free markets in the hope of achieving this efficiency. In **On value and values** (Chapter 9) I argue that the finance system is operated on the premise that all ethical values can be distilled into the concept of financial value. I argue that this ethical basis is not logically coherent and works neither in theory nor in practice. I outline an alternative ethical basis on which finance should be premised, based on human flourishing. It is up to democratic society to decide what values it wishes finance to embody and set the rules of the system to achieve these values.

As financial markets are government created, and the current set up is not working, it is up to governments to put right the mess. The first solution I propose in a financial renaissance? (Chapter 10) is for governments to stop supporting the current damaging system. I then suggested how we could reinvent finance to deliver the products and services that the economy needs to operate, and further how finance could be applied to deliver a flourishing, sustainable society.

1.6 What This Book Is Not About

This book is of finite length, and the finance system is large and diverse, so I have had to make choices in which aspects to cover in the book.

1.6.1 Different Forms of Capitalism

Shareholder capitalism is where people save via the financial system and their savings are used to buy shares of publicly listed companies, which make up a large proportion of the economy. Countries such as USA, UK, Ireland, Australia, Chile and Holland are examples of countries which are set up in this way. Shareholder capitalism is often contrasted with stakeholder capitalism, as practiced in many continental European countries such as Germany. In these economies there are often have cross-holdings between companies and banks, and workers and other stakeholders have a far greater say in the way companies are run.[15] Another model of capitalism is the developmental state model. This is often employed by developing countries which have sought rapid industrialisation; it was employed by Japan after the Second World War, the Asian tiger economies in the 1980s and China now. In these countries, the financial system appears private but is largely directed by the state towards favoured industries.[16] And of course there is socialism, whereby the state directly allocates capital. In reality, no country precisely follows any one model, all economies have some elements of the different system.

This book focuses on the financial system of countries which are seen as practicing shareholder capitalism and mainly draws on examples from the USA and UK, which I will call shareholder finance. The other forms of capitalism are different in nature and have different strengths and weaknesses. Shareholder finance has intellectual dominance, and the global financial system is very much in its image. Much of the management of international flows takes place in the centres of shareholder finance such as London and New York. Shareholder finance is much greater than the shareholder capitalist economies, countries which could in no way be described as shareholder capitalist participate in financial markets as described in this book. For example countries issue government bonds which are bought and sold on international financial markets and the savings of most of the world's countries are invested via the same financial markets.

In describing the ideas in this book to people, I have often been accused of being some kind of socialist or communist or even a new Karl Marx (I should be so fortunate enough to have a fraction of his influence). This could not be further from the truth. Part of the misunderstanding is that many people seem to equate shareholder finance with capitalism in general. One of the main themes of this book is that the current flavour of shareholder finance is largely the creation of governments, who are its major participants. My proposed solutions are that governments should first stop supporting this damaging form of finance. I then go onto suggest that they could undo the damage that they have done and set up different institutions for capitalism to work better, and then largely step away; the resulting capitalist system will have less state involvement then the current one. If this makes me a Marxist, well so be it.

1.6.2 The Financial Crisis

The risks generated by the financial system itself can cause damage to the global economy as manifested in the 2008 crisis. We are still living on borrowed time, with a partially reformed system with worries that it could topple back into crisis mode if there was another shock. I do not intend to cover this directly, if the reader wants to read about risk in the financial system or the cause behind the Great Financial Crisis of 2008, there is a whole library of books on this subject.[17]

The risks that books on the Crisis discuss are generally the risk that the finance system will collapse, causing huge economic and social damage. This book considers the risk that it survives, only to cause huge economic, social and environmental damage. Is this system, currently on life support, one that we should keep, or is it a monster that we need to radically re-engineer before it wreaks more damage?

1.6.3 The Deposit and Savings Channel

The library of books that have come out since the Crisis are mostly on the banking system, and this has also been the focus of regulators and governments. Banks are obviously important, and they are briefly dealt with in Chapter 6, but the focus of this book is mainly about the savings channel via capital markets, which is at least as important as the deposit channel via banks.

Banks were publicly listed companies before and during the financial crisis, until some of them were directly taken over by governments. Their ownership had been delegated to professional asset managers. Part of these asset managers' job is stewarding the companies they own, making sure public companies' management operate under the right incentives, and striking the right balance between short and long-term investment, between risk and profit. Instead we got the financial crisis, where asset managers were "asleep at the wheel".[18]

1.6.4 Bank-Bashing

Some scandal involving the appalling behaviour of banks, bank employees or other financial service firms hits the headlines with high frequency. The culture, values and incentives within the financial system are a key theme of this book. The culture certainly seems to give rise to the bad eggs who engage in criminal behaviour. Yet the damage done by these illegal or semi-legal acts are very minor compared to the system as a whole functioning normally. It is easy to direct opprobrium and moral outrage at these acts, but it is a distraction from the real problem. In the words of Bertolt Brecht, "Why rob a bank when you can found one?"[19]

1.6.5 Gender and Diversity

I believe that diversity is important, because if you have an organisation which is run by as diverse a range of people from as many cultural and gender backgrounds, you usually get a wider range of ideas, a more objective view of risks and values and less groupthink. It is fashionable to use the female article to promote gender equality. But I have deliberately not done this and stubbornly use "he" because I want to reflect that financial services are male dominated, so asset managers and bankers usually are men. If there were more women working in financial services, there would be more overpaid women, as well as men, doing socially useless activities. I would rather both women and men were paid for their contribution to society and did something useful.

1.6.6 Economics

The Institute and Faculty of Actuaries recently published a literature review of academic journal papers on sustainability and the financial system.[20] The review analysed papers from all the leading economics journals going back 30 years, covering 355,000 articles. I remember the first economics textbook I ever picked up at school described economics as the study of the allocation of scarce resources, so you would have thought this was a core subject of economics journals. Yet there were only 40 articles on this topic and these only dealt with relatively peripheral issues. All 40 were critical of the way mainstream economics treated sustainability, for example in the way they measured success via GDP. Academic literature is not much help in answering the questions set by this book. My approach is to look closely at how the financial system actually works in practice. I have cited some economic theory, where I have used economic theories I have attempted to use them illustratively and non-dogmatically; my arguments work whether or not the economic theory is correct.

I have tried to write the book so no prior knowledge of finance is required, but I hope that someone with expertise in finance will find the book enjoyable, thought provoking and infuriating.

Notes

1. Diamond, J (2006) *Collapse* Viking Press.
2. For an in-depth discussion of this, see Gleeson-White, J (2014) *Six Capitals* Allen & Unwin.
3. WWF (2016) *Living Planet Report 2016.*
4. Steffen, W., Richardson, K., Rockström, J., Cornell, S.E., Fetzer, I., Bennett, E.M., Biggs, R., Carpenter, S.R., Vries, W. de, Wit, C.A. de, Folke, C., Gerten, D., Heinke, J., Mace, G.M., Persson, L.M., Ramanathan, V., Reyers, B. and Sörlin, S (2015) *Planetary boundaries: Guiding human development on a changing planet* Science 347:6219.
5. World Bank data: http://www.worldbank.org/en/topic/poverty/overview
6. Buttonwood (2016) *The Wrong Kind of Savings* The Economist 21 April 2016.
7. Tainter, J (1988) *Collapse of complex societies* Cambridge University Press.
8. See for example Wolf, M (2014) *The Shifts and the Shocks* Penguin, Turner, A (2015) *Between Debt and the Devil* Princeton University Press, King, M (2016) *The End of Alchemy* Little.
9. Kay, J (2012) *The Kay review of UK equity markets* UK Government.
10. Although technology is now making this possible through monetary transfers via mobile phone networks.
11. Kay, J (2015) *Other People's Money* Public Affairs.
12. Cohen, S and DeLong, B (2016) *Concrete Economics* Harvard Business Review Press.
13. The figures in the table are OTC only, if exchange traded contracts are included, this increases the amounts by about 10%.
14. Kay, J (2015) *Other People's Money* Public Affairs.
15. See for example Brandt, F and Georgiou, K (2016) *Shareholder vs Stakeholder Capitalism* Penn Law: Legal Scholarship Repository.
16. Leftwitch, Adrian (1995) *Bringing politics back in: Towards a model of the developmental state* Journal of Development Studies, Volume 31, Issue 3 February 1995, pages 400–427.
17. As note 9.
18. Words of Lord Myners, former City minister; quoted in http://www.standard.co.uk/business/time-for-shareholders-to-get-a-grip-6747570.html
19. From the *Threepenny Opera* (1928).
20. N. G. Aspinall, S. R. Jones, E. H. McNeill, R. A. Werner, T. Zalk (2015) *Sustainability and the finance system* Institute and Faculty of Actuaries.

2

Dramatis Personae

An Introduction to the Savings Channel, Investment Management and Capital Markets

There are two channels through which people save via the financial system, which allocates these savings back into the economy. The **deposit channel** is where savings are left in a bank which lends money out against these deposits. The other is the **savings channel**, for example a pension, where the saver pays money into a pension, which is invested on their behalf by a series of intermediaries in capital markets.[1]

The two channels are very different. People use bank deposits when liquidity is important; funds can be withdrawn at short notice and the money doesn't lose its nominal value. Your bank account is normally at least as big as the money you put in, perhaps with some interest. The bank stands between the lender and the borrower, deposits are claims on the bank and loans are assets of the bank.

In contrast, the assets of the savings channel are ultimately owned by the saver, the intermediary's role is more like a steward who is looking after the saver's money. This is obviously a simplification of all the many types of arrangement, but in general, some form of vehicle is used to aggregate many peoples' savings and is run on behalf of the savers. The difference is summarised in Table 2.1. The savings channel typically represents longer term savings than the deposit channel, where liquidity is less important because savers may not need to get at the money for a long time. So, for example, the funds in a pension are not touched until you are old, the aim of the pension is to make sure the value of assets can meet your spending requirements when you retire. On a day-to-day basis, the value of your

Table 2.1 Characterisation of deposit and savings channels

	Deposit channel	Savings channel
Intermediary	Bank	Asset manager, trustee
Term	Short	Long
Liquidity	Liquid	Illiquid
Ownership	Call on bank	Direct or indirect own assets

pension can go up and down, and in theory you should not have to worry too much about this.

Chapters 2–5 focus on the savings channel, or investment management in the capital markets. This is not to say the banks are somehow less important, and I discuss banks in Chapter 6. Following the financial crisis, there has been a panoply of books and articles about banks and what went wrong with them, but there have been very few about asset management. Yet asset management is arguably at least as important in shaping our economy as the banks, and I want to redress the balance.

The case of banks demonstrates for the importance of investment management. In 2008, a number of large banks failed and many of them had to be bailed out by governments. Nearly all these banks were publicly listed companies, meaning that their shares were traded on public markets, such as the London Stock Exchange. The bulk of these bank shares were owned by institutional investors, that is pension funds, insurance companies and sovereign wealth funds (SWFs).

Institutional investors, which are amalgamations of savings, invest them on behalf of savers, with the investment decision delegated to professional investment managers. Some of these savings are used to buy shares of large banks. Thus banks are ultimately owned by savers, with the ownership rights delegated to professional asset managers. These asset managers therefore have a great deal of influence on how the banks are run. They can vote at Annual General Meetings (AGMs), they have regular meetings with senior management, they can vote against the pay packages of directors, they can, in theory, approve or disapprove the appointment of directors. If they don't like the way a company is run, they can sell its shares, causing the value of these companies to fall. All of this has a great deal of influence on the behaviour of the banks' management, especially as the directors' remuneration is usually related to the company's share price.

What did these professional asset managers do in the run up to the financial crisis? Did they encourage banks to take less risk so as not to prejudice their investments? Unfortunately, according to former City minister Lord Myners, they were "asleep at the wheel".[2] The financial crisis was just one example where asset managers had a role to play and were conspicuous by their absence.

Finance is characterised by complexity, so this chapter tries to look through the noise by explaining who the end users of the savings channel are. It asks: what are they using capital markets for? What are they buying and who do they employ to help them achieve their aims? Chapters 4 and 5 discuss how well these aims are fulfilled.

There are a large number of people working in finance whose existence is apparently not explained by this chapter – the young men surrounded by computer screens. These people are mostly traders, who are buying and selling financial instruments, ultimately to the institutional investors who I describe in this chapter. Their job is either to help institutions fulfil their function (by buying and selling financial instruments on their clients' behalf) or to make money for their employer by buying or creating financial instruments and selling them on to someone else at a profit. That someone else is normally another intermediary, but there will be a chain of intermediaries which will ultimately end with an institutional investor as these are the guys with the money.

Asset managers are entrusted with savers' assets, and their job is to get the best returns for those savers. The economy as a whole can only generate returns if investment is usefully deployed. The economic function of asset managers is to make ensure that savings are converted into useful investments.

The job of the asset manager, and how they get compensated, is therefore different to their economic function. But the circle can be squared. The asset manager is a skilled professional who assesses where he can achieve the best return for a given level of risk and assigns investments accordingly. To generate a good return, the investment, almost by definition, must be doing something useful that is generating an income. And because asset managers are skilled professionals, they can assess which investments generate the best returns.

Through the savings channel, savings should therefore be converted into the optimum useful investments, which will generate economic growth, so that the economy as a whole can generate returns for savings, and individuals will get the best returns from their investments.

My contention over the next few chapters is that savings are not invested in the best way for their savers, in order to generate returns. Savings are not converted into useful investments that the economy needs in order to grow and pay back these savings. This non-useful investment is not sustainable and it can be harmful to society.

In saying this, I don't believe that the people who work in investment management are bad or stupid. Quite the contrary, most of them are highly educated, thoughtful and many of them are my friends. It is the structure of the investment system, with incentives that causes the system to malfunction in this way.

First, we need to look at how the savings channel operates.

2.1 Asset Owners

The basic model of institutional investment is that an individual puts money aside for the purpose of meeting future spending requirements. Institutions aggregate many individuals' savings and invests those savings in financial assets such as equity or bonds. There is a great deal of variation, though, in terms of the requirements of the saver, what the future spending requirement is, whether it is specific or not, the structure of the institution and its relationship with the individual and what it invests in.

A common theme is that governments often encourage people to save via these institutions, through compulsion, tax breaks, auto-enrolment or providing an enabling regulatory environment. The way these institutions behave is also heavily determined by government and regulation, which will be discussed further in Chapter 3. The largest asset owners in the world are very large indeed, as is shown by Table 2.2. The total funds of these 20 asset owners are $11 trillion, an astonishingly large number.

2.1.1 Pension Funds

A pension is where someone decides, or is made to decide, to save some of her earnings whilst she works, so that she can receive an income when she is too old to work. There are two basic designs of pension scheme: defined benefit (DB)[3] and defined contribution (DC),[4] although many schemes are a mixture of the two. A pension scheme is typically a legal-trust arrangement whereby the savings are aggregated and overseen by a board of trustees, who have a fiduciary duty to manage the scheme responsibly.

A DB pension is where the benefits you get when you retire are calculated according to a formula, depending on how long you have been contributing to the scheme and your salary. A DC scheme is where your contributions are

Table 2.2 World's 20 largest asset owners

	Fund	Country	Type	Total assets
1	Government Pension Investment Fund	Japan	PF	$1,394,320
2	Abu Dhabi Investment Authority	UAE	SWF	$841,120
3	AXA Insurance	France	IF	$813,694
4	MetLife Insurance	United States	IF	$677,302
5	Allianz	Germany	IF	$612,793
6	Government Pension Fund Global	Norway	SWF	$574,335
7	Prudential Financial Inc.	United States	IF	$557,687
8	AIG	United States	IF	$556,451
9	General Insurance	Italy	IF	$536,208
10	Aviva	United Kingdom	IF	$531,632
11	Legal & General Group	United Kingdom	IF	$492,465
12	SAMA Foreign Holdings*	Saudi Arabia	SWF	$464,800
13	General Organization for Social Insurance (GOSI)	Saudi Arabia	PF	$448,000
14	Nippon Life Insurance Company	Japan	IF	$437,673
15	CNP Assurances	France	IF	$406,946
16	Aegon	Netherlands	IF	$406,752
17	ING Group	Netherlands	IF	$403,683
18	Prudential (UK)	United Kingdom	IF	$373,390
19	China Investment Corporation*	China	SWF	$372,281
20	SAFE Investment Company*	China	SWF	$368,872
	Total			$11,270,404

Data from Asset International's Chief Investment Officer on 2 December 2016 http://www.ai-cio.com/aiGlobal500.aspx?id=3100

invested until you retire, when you receive whatever the proceeds of those investments are.

DB schemes are typically sponsored by a company (the employer) or the government. The scheme is liable to pay the defined benefits, whether or not it has enough money to pay them. If it doesn't have enough money, it can call on the sponsor to pay the shortfall. A DB scheme is in deficit when the value of its assets is less than the estimated value of its future payments that it has to make. This is a problem if the sponsor goes bankrupt, in which case the pensions will not be paid in full, as has recently happened in the case of the bankrupt retailer BHS. For this reason, many countries have some form of mandatory insurance for DB schemes. It is also a problem for the sponsor or employer if investments do badly or the estimated value of the future payments goes up. The sponsor or employer then has to stump up the money to pay for the shortfall. In a DB scheme, the sponsor bears the investment risk, with the saver or beneficiary only bearing the risk if the scheme goes into deficit and the sponsor can't meet the shortfall. The job of the trustees is to make sure the scheme has enough money in it to pay the benefits.

By contrast, a DC scheme is a pot of money which gets invested and is basically all owned by the saver. The saver, maybe supplemented by the employer or the government, pays into the DC scheme, his funds get invested and the value of the DC pot is whatever is the value of the underlying investments. The saver bears all of the risk of poor investment performance. Even if such a scheme is set up by the saver's employer, the scheme is entirely separate from the employer, so it makes no difference to the DC pension whether the employer goes bankrupt or not. A DC scheme can't go into deficit because it doesn't promise to pay anything out besides the underlying value of the fund. The job of the trustees is simply to choose how the funds get invested and make sure the administration runs smoothly.

DB schemes are, or should be, favoured by the employee because they take no investment risk, whereas DC schemes are favoured by employers for the same reason. Generally, DB schemes are shutting down and being replaced by DC schemes.

The popularity of DB schemes with employers in the past was because they were set up in a period of high returns and high inflation (the 1960s and 1970s), when they looked like a cheap way of providing pensions for staff. But as the schemes matured, inflation and interest rates reduced (meaning the cost of future payments increased), and life expectancy increased (meaning you had to pay pensions for longer), combined with tighter regulation (guaranteeing more expensive pensions benefits). It became mandatory in the UK to give inflation-linked benefits, which meant that it became more and more expensive to provide these benefits and, because of tougher reporting standards, DB pensions appear more expensive in company accounts.

DB schemes ultimately have to pay an explicit stream of payments – the payment of pensions, which are predefined – whereas DC pensions have an implicit stream of payments: their aim would be to pay the saver a pension which is big enough to live off and increases with inflation. Sometimes DC pensions are used to buy an annuity, that is, the pensions pot is exchanged for a guaranteed stream of payments for the lifetime of the pensioner.

The pensions industry is massively supported and regulated by government. Governments often legislate mandatory contributions into a pension, as they do in countries as diverse as Sweden, Chile, Nigeria and Australia. A lesser compulsion, which is fashionable at the moment, is called auto-enrolment. That means you are automatically opted-in to a scheme unless you chose not to be. This is the situation in the UK and New Zealand, but a lot of other countries are looking at this option too.

Governments normally provide incentives to contribute into a pension, usually in the form of tax benefits, a typical example being that your contributions and interest earned are tax exempt. Some governments even provide direct contributions into schemes.

Finally, pensions are massively regulated. There are a number of reasons for this, for example if the government mandates people into a pension, they will look very bad if things go wrong. It is also because governments are contributing in the form of tax rebates, and they would like reassurance that people are not using pensions for tax evasion. And because the contracts are very long term (if you start contributing in your 20s and live until you are in your 90s, that is a 70 year contract), which creates many problems. Most organisations, like a sponsoring employer, don't last for 70 years. There is also an information asymmetry: if you don't start getting your pension for a long time, you don't know how well it is being managed in the interim. And people often have a limited understanding of finance, especially pensions because of all of the complicated legislation, so savers don't have as much information as the provider. Hence heavy government involvement is justified to protect the saver.

These government incentives and regulations shape the structure of the pensions industry, which will be discussed over the next three chapters.

The structure of pension schemes is important. A company pension fund is typically governed by a set of trustees. They are often amateurs, and might only meet four times a year, to run an entity which can be worth tens of billions of dollars. They are advised by actuaries who tell them how much money the scheme needs to have in it. Investment management is delegated to one or more asset managers, who either manage the whole portfolio, or are charged with managing a proportion of the fund in a certain way. The actuary will advise the scheme of the optimal mix of assets, so different fund managers might be charged with investing bonds or equities.

There are many variations on this model. DC schemes don't require an actuary to assess the funding level, although they may take advice on how large members' pensions will be. They will also choose what investment options are available to members. This could vary from only offering one fund, to allowing beneficiaries to choose between investments and asset managers.

Typically, larger schemes might do some of the investments in house, only outsourcing more specialised functions. Also, I have described a model of one

34   2 Dramatis Personae

Table 2.3 World's largest 10 pension funds

	Pension fund	Country	Value (US$ billions)
1	Federal Old-age and Survivors Insurance Trust Fund	United States	$2,645
2	Government Pension Investment Fund	Japan	$1,370
3	Government Pension Fund of Norway	Norway	$856
4	Civil Service Retirement and Disability Fund	United States	$850
5	Military Retirement Fund	United States	$474
6	National Pension Service (NPS)	South Korea	$422
7	Stichting Pensioenfonds ABP (ABP)	Netherlands	$388
8	Thrift Savings Plan (TSP)	United States	$407
9	California Public Employees' Retirement System	United States	$289.8
10	National Social Security Fund	China	$247.4

OECD (2015) *Annual Survey of Large Pension Funds and Public Pension Reserve Funds 2015*

employer; many countries have multi-employer schemes or quasi-government schemes which workers are enrolled into. And some schemes, typically for public sector workers, are unfunded, which means the government pays pensioners out of tax revenue. These therefore do not require any investment at all.

The structure of the industry is highly unequal. Table 2.3 shows the largest ten pension funds in the world by size. Just in this table, the largest pension fund is ten times the size of the tenth pension fund. In the UK, there are about 44,000 occupational pension schemes, with total assets of £2 trillion, meaning the mean average pension scheme in the UK would be valued at £48 million.[5] This is compared to the largest in the UK the Universities Superannuation Scheme at £43 billion (£43,000 million), a thousand times larger than the average.

If we were to look at the behaviour or influence of pension funds as a whole, it would be dominated by a few extremely large funds.

2.1.2 Insurance Companies

Insurance is usually divided between life insurance and non-life insurance.[6] Life insurance is insurance against dying, getting ill, surviving (an endowment is where you save and get a payment if you survive) or living a long time (a pension annuity, as described above). These are longer term contracts and are events that will definitely happen: everyone will die; it is the date that is unknown. Non-life insurance are products for individuals, such as motor or home insurance or for corporates, such as product liability or insuring an oil rig. These contracts are typically annual, often each contract has a small probability of a loss, but from the insurer's perspective, there can be a relatively predictable number of claims each year. You would be very unlucky if your house burned down, but there will be a few house fires in a typical insurance portfolio every year and, from an insurance company's perspective, they hope that this number is stable.

Insurance companies often have large reserves which are invested in financial assets and are one of the main groups of institutional investors or asset owners, which is why I am including them here. Life insurance is a form of savings: you put money aside against a possible, and often inevitable, contingency such as dying. It is more of a moot point whether non-life insurance is a form of saving, but insurance companies form an important part of the institutional landscape. Life insurance companies also often act as asset managers on behalf of other institutions such as pension funds.

The relationship between insurance companies to the saver or policyholder is different from the pension arrangement (unless you have a pensions product with a life insurance company, in which case it is exactly the same). Many insurance companies used to be mutuals, owned by their policyholders, but nowadays most are public companies.[7] In both life and non-life contracts, the policyholder has a contract with the firm.

Insurance companies form some of the largest asset owners: Table 2.2 shows that the 13 of the world's 20 largest asset owners are insurance companies.

Insurance companies are highly regulated. This is because there is asymmetric information between a policyholder and the insurance company. When I buy insurance, it is very hard for me to assess how capable the insurance company of paying out a claim, should it occur. There is also asymmetric information the other way round: if I buy health insurance, for example, I have a better idea of how healthy I am than the insurer.

Insurance company regulation differs by country but, this year, an overarching regulatory framework came into effect in the EU called Solvency 2. Regulation in other major markets, such as USA and Japan, is similar to Solvency 2, and smaller developing markets, such as Nigeria, are looking to replicate Solvency 2 to assure policyholders and international investors that their insurance sectors are safe.

Solvency 2 is split into three pillars. Pillar 1 is how much capital the insurer has to hold, Pillar 2 how the companies should be governed and run, and Pillar 3 the disclosure requirements. Pillar 1 sets out that the insurance company has to hold enough assets to cover its liabilities, which are the claims that it is estimated it will have to pay out. It also has to hold an extra reserve. This amount, the Solvency Capital Requirement (SCR), should be enough that the company has a 99.5% probability of meeting its claims. For investment purposes, if the assets are volatile and go down a lot, the reserve will fall and the company might face regulatory intervention, hence Solvency 2 implies investment in assets which hold their nominal value. As well as the SCR, companies often have an extra free reserve, which gives them more flexibility in how to invest.[8]

Life insurance products which resemble savings will have a different investment profile from non-life products. The expected payout on an endowment policy might be much larger than the guarantee, which makes it part of the "profit" of investment which goes to the policyholder. In this sort of product, the SCR only covers the guaranteed part, so the insurance company can be more flexible in what they invest in. But, for a guaranteed product, such as an annuity, the insurance company has to hold capital to meet the future payments and therefore will have to hold mainly bond-like assets to meet the payments.

The sizes of the insurance companies in Table 2.2 are somewhat misleading. Much of this money is actually pension fund money, either from occupational pension funds as described above or individual savers which has been given to insurance companies to invest. It also includes the companies' own insurance funds, and management of funds on behalf of other, smaller insurance companies.

Monoline insurance is a particular niche form of insurance which is important in capital markets. Monolines insure bonds which pay out in the event that a bond defaults, which makes investing in a bond apparently less risky. The problem is that the circumstances that cause one bond to default, such as a recession, are likely to cause many bonds to default, so a monoline which has insured lots of these bonds is prone to default too. The monolines mostly went bankrupt in the financial crisis, although some have subsequently reopened.

2.1.3 Sovereign Wealth Funds

Table 2.2 shows that the 2nd, 6th, 12th, 19th and 20th largest asset owners in the world are SWFs. Table 2.4 shows the largest SWFs.[9] These are usually separate companies or legal entities wholly owned by their parent government, but often managed at arm's length.

Table 2.4 World's 10 largest sovereign wealth funds

	Fund	Country	Origin	Total assets (USD – billion)
1	Government Pension Fund	Norway	Oil	$850
2	China Investment Corporation	China	Non-commodity	$814
3	Abu Dhabi Investment Authority	UAE	Oil	$792
4	SAMA Foreign Holdings	Saudi Arabia	Oil	$598
5	Kuwait Investment Authority	Kuwait	Oil	$592
6	SAFE Investment Company	China	Non-commodity	$474
7	Hong Kong Monetary Authority Investment Portfolio	China	Non-commodity	$442
8	Government of Singapore Investment Corporation	Singapore	Non-commodity	$350
9	Qatar Investment Authority	Qatar	Oil and gas	$335
10	National Social Security Fund	China	Non-commodity	$236

Data from Sovereign Wealth fund institute http://www.swfinstitute.org/sovereign-wealth-fund-rankings/downloaded on 28 September 2016

The majority of all SWF assets relate to oil and gas ($4.3 trillion of $7.5 trillion).[10] The government gets revenue from the country's oil reserves, either from a national oil company (for example in the case of Abu Dhabi, the Abu Dhabi National Oil Company), or from licenses to exploit reserves from private or foreign companies. The government uses this revenue to meet its annual spending budget, with the excess transferred into the SWF.

Besides the Government of Singapore Investment Fund, the other SWFs in the top 10 are all Chinese funds that have been built up by the Chinese government's policy of immunising its exchange rate. China produces an increasing proportion of the world's goods. As this causes China to run a trade surplus, this should mean that the Chinese currency appreciates, as the demand for the Renminbi increases, which would make Chinese goods less competitive. The People's Bank of China therefore buys foreign currency, predominantly US dollars, to put downward pressure on the Renminbi. One of the results is that China has built up large reserves of foreign currency, so it has set up SWFs to invest these reserves.

SWFs are not governed by any external rules, as pension funds and insurance companies are, and there is always the risk that they will be used for political purposes. The IMF (International Monetary Fund) has developed a set of voluntary standards, the Santiago Principles, which basically set out that SWFs should be invested in line with a market-based approach, and disclose what they are doing.[11]

As SWFs usually have no fixed liabilities, this gives them much more investment freedom than pension funds and insurance companies. SWFs don't have to meet specified payments on any given date, and if their investments go down, this won't affect a funding or solvency position.

2.1.4 Endowments, Foundations and Family Offices

These are private individuals' or institutions' wealth. A family office is an organisation which manages the wealth of an individual, or family or group of people or families. As you can imagine, these individuals or families are generally very wealthy. It is hard to get data on single family offices – a company that manages the money of one ultra-high net worth individual. Multifamily offices are essentially asset managers, either independent or part of a bank or fund management company. The largest is HSBC Private Bank, managing $169 billion.[12]

An endowment could be a charity or an institution such as a religious or educational foundation, which normally gets donations. For example, the Harvard University endowment is the largest, at $32 billion.[13] A foundation is often the charitable funds of one individual or organisation; the largest is the Bill and Melinda Gates Foundation with $42 billion.[14]

Compared to the other groups of investors, this class is relatively small. But it isn't trivial: the 334 families managed by HSBC Private Bank hold more assets than the pensions savings of all employees in Chile or Malaysia, or all South African civil servants.

The other reason that this class is interesting is that it is innovative. Like SWFs, there are no fixed liabilities. Family offices will need to pay various expenses of their families – these people are too rich to need a pension, but they might want to buy a house or a yacht from time to time, and these payments are not predefined and guaranteed. Endowments and foundations are supposed to distribute their earnings to good causes, but the minimum is quite low (5%) and again there is no predefined commitment. They are not operating under any solvency requirements.

The result has been that many of the most famous and successful investors have come from this category, think of Warren Buffett, John Maynard Keynes (who managed the assets of King's College, Cambridge) and David Swensen who manages the Yale University endowment and who pioneered an investment style named after him. Unlike other institutions, these people are not chasing short-term returns, matching an index or having to meet solvency requirements. They have been given more freedom to take large positions, often in illiquid investments which are therefore underpriced.

Table 2.5 Summary of asset owners

	Pension funds	Insurance company	Sovereign wealth fund	family office	Foundation and endowment
Liability	Pension payment	Claim payment	Future government expenditure	Future expenditure of family	Charitable donations, funding of institution
Source of funds	Individual savings	Insurance premiums	Excess government revenue – often from natural resource	Income of individual above needs	Donations, excess income
Structure	Trust	Corporate	Corporate or trust	Corporate or trust	Trust

Because of their mission or views, many foundations and endowments are also interested in impact investing, which means making investments that have social or environmental benefits Table 2.5 summarizes the different classes of asset owners.

2.2 Investments

The total capital invested by the asset owners described above is approximately $100 trillion. Figure 2.1 shows which asset classes this is invested into.

I will explore the investment in each category in detail in later chapters, for now I will just summarise their characteristics:

2.2.1 Bonds

This is the largest asset class with 46% of overall capital. A bond is a specific type of tradable debt security. The issuer, normally a government or large corporation, agrees to pay specified fixed amounts to the holder of the bond. These amounts are usually quarterly interest payments, plus the repayment of the capital at the end of the term. So a 10-year £100 million bond with a coupon of 5% means that the issuer will pay £5 million every year, usually payable quarterly, for 10 years and then repay the £100 million at the end of 10 years.

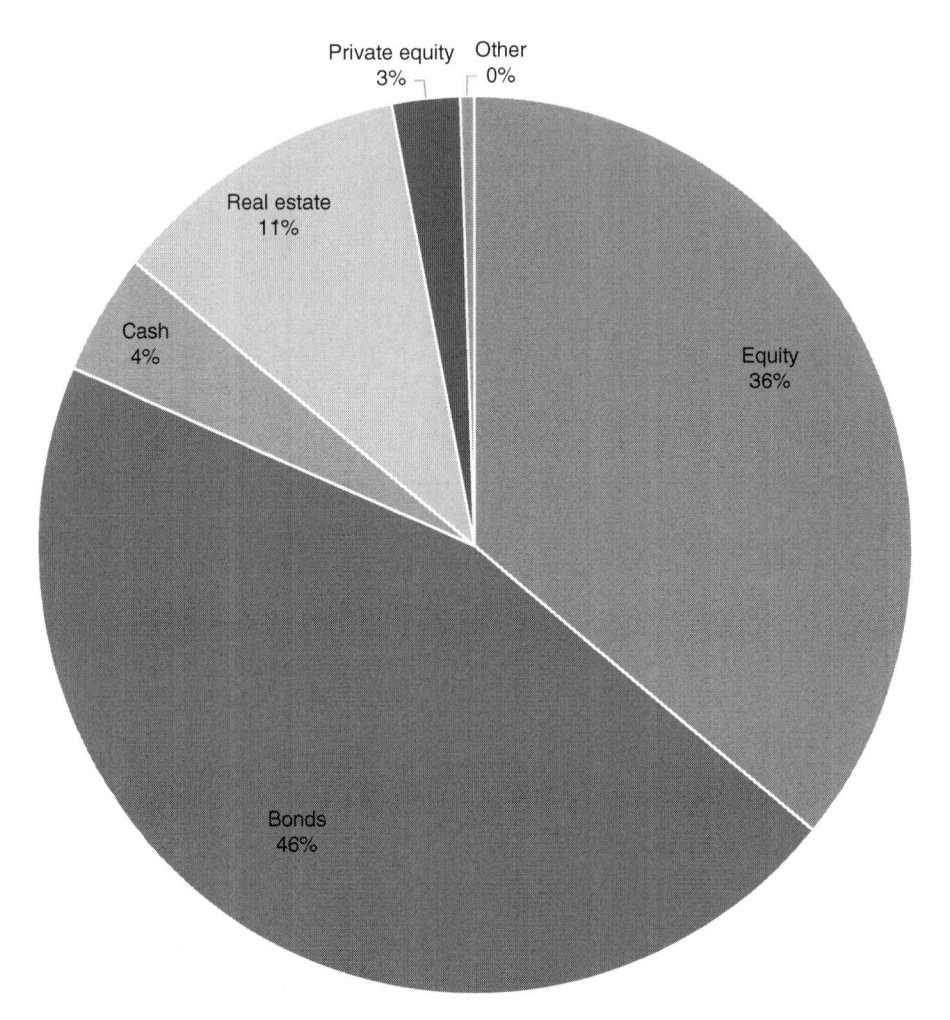

Fig. 2.1 Global invested capital split by asset class
Source: Hewitt EnnisKnupp Survey
Hewitt (2014) *Global invested capital market* Hewitt EnnisKnupp

Publicly traded bonds are rated by supposedly independent ratings agents, the largest and most well-known of which are Standard and Poor's, Moody's and Fitch. Each bond is given a rating, depending on how likely the issuer is to meet all the payments that are due. Canadian and German governments have Standard & Poor's highest rating of AAA (the USA only has a AA+ and the UK AA), which means that the bond is very unlikely to default. Standard & Poor's lowest rating is C, which would mean the issuer is highly likely to default. The example bond I gave in the previous paragraph had a par value of £100 million, but this is not the price at which the bond will be bought and sold. The price is set by the market, and will be determined by the bond's credit rating and prevailing interest rates, as well as many other factors, such as market sentiment.

2.2.2 Equity

About 36% of capital is invested in equity, into the shares of publicly listed companies. These shares can be bought and sold on stock exchanges. Companies can raise money through an Initial Public Offering (IPO), when the owners of a private company can sell their shares to the public or institutional investors, transforming the company into a public company, whose shares are traded publicly. The owners can raise more money by selling more shares, or the companies can raise finance through a rights issue, creating more shares and selling them via the exchange. This waters down the shareholdings of existing investors, and so it usually reduces the share price.

Companies distribute revenue to shareholders, either through dividends – paying a portion of earnings to shareholders, or through share buy-backs – purchasing shares from shareholders.

2.2.3 Real Estate

This is investment in residential, or more usually, commercial property. It can be in the form of equity or debt, either through direct or shared ownership of a property, or through lending money to a company to buy a property where the debt is secured against the property being purchased. Investment can be via a fund, or a real estate investment trust (REIT). The REIT owns a selection of properties, and its shares are traded on commercial exchanges, the value of the shares reflects the underlying assets.

2.2.4 Private Equity

These are funds which buy private companies, or buy public companies and take them out of public ownership, then try to improve their performance. The funds attempt to make money by selling them later either to a private buyer or on a public exchange.

2.2.5 Cash

This means holdings in money market funds, which maintain their nominal values, are paid interest, and can be withdrawn at any time for spending or investment in other assets.

2.2.6 Hedge Funds

The list of the wealthiest funds (Figure 2.1) shows no holdings of hedge funds, which might be a surprise given the amount of publicity they get. This is because hedge funds are invested in one of the other asset classes. The proportion invested in hedge funds is approximately 2.4%. The term hedge funds covers a vast range of different investment strategies but can be defined as what they are not – they are not a traditional fund.

A traditional non-hedge fund, also known as a "long-only", generally invests against an index (more of this later). A UK equity fund might invest against the FTSE All share index, for example. A hedge fund can be different from a normal fund in one or more of the following ways:

- It might make more use of derivatives, options to buy or sell stock. Derivatives allow leverage, the hedge fund can make a higher profit if a stock goes up than it would do from just holding the stock. Long-only funds can only make money if an asset goes up, but hedge funds can short a stock by using derivatives and make a profit when the stock goes down in price as well.
- Hedge funds might invest on a total returns basis, trying to achieve a level of return whatever the market does.
- Hedge funds might invest in alternative assets, such as derivatives or commodities.
- They might try to make use of trading strategies, such as arbitrage (using price differences of one or similar assets).
- Hedge funds often charge a performance fee, historically 2/20, which is an annual management fee of 2% of the funds invested plus 20% of any excess return the hedge fund makes. The charges are much higher than a traditional long-only fund, which typically charge 1% or less, with no performance fee. The hedge fund does particularly well if it performs spectacularly in any given year.

2.3 The Intermediaries

We have looked at the asset owners and what they invest in. Practically all of the people who work in the finance sector are intermediaries.

2.3.1 Actuaries and the Investment Decision

An actuary is a financial professional who is crucial to the management of financial institutions. They are at the crux of the financial system. Actuaries have to be members of a professional body, and by far the two largest are the Institute and Faculty of Actuaries in the UK and the Society of Actuaries in the USA. The actuary has a statutory role: pension funds and insurance companies have to have their funding level assessed by an appointed actuary, and actuaries also advise the institutions on investment.[15] Actuaries are regulated by governments, which set out codes of conduct, professional standards and guidance notes to help them go about their business.

The actuarial consulting market is highly concentrated. The three largest firms in the UK advise 80% of the pensions market by asset size.[16] This means that these firms have a huge amount of influence on how capital is invested in the economy. Also, as all actuaries are members of the same professional body, they sing for the same hymn sheet – their methodology is aligned and is set by the regulator because of their statutory role.

Investment decisions are made like this: Asset owners with liabilities, which means pension funds and insurance companies, have to first work out their solvency level – whether they have enough money to make the future payments which they are committed to paying. This is normally a calculation carried out by an actuary. If the institution doesn't have enough funds to meet its future liabilities, it has to get higher contributions from its employer (in the case of a pension fund) or raise capital or close business lines (in the case of an insurer). The actuary also calculates how much the institution has to collect to make sure they stay in business.

Once they have worked out the funding level, actuaries often carry out an asset liability model (ALM). This looks at a range of possible ways to allocate the assets between bonds, equities, or other asset classes. They estimates the cost of meeting the institution's liabilities with each different asset mix – and how likely they are to get there. This helps institutions to optimise their allocation of assets, depending on how much risk they are prepared to take. One investment might have a higher expected pay-off than other investments, but be more risky. An institution has to decide the balance between risky assets which make the expected cost lower and less risky assets which increase the expected cost, but lower the risk. A pension fund might be more willing to take risks with investment if it has a strong employer backing it, like a government, which will always be there to bail the scheme out if things go wrong. If the institution is well funded, it can take more risks as it has a buffer of excess reserves to call on if things go wrong.

This description applies to DB schemes, which have defined liabilities. But a similar analysis can be carried out for DC schemes, because it will tell the institution how likely it is that particular asset mixes will meet members' expectations. Similarly, the SWFs, family offices, endowments and all the rest don't usually have fixed liabilities, but they can still have future projected spending requirements, which would provide a basis for deciding which will be the best asset mix to invest in.

The asset owner then appoints asset managers to invest these different asset classes, in the agreed proportion. There could be just one asset management firm or many firms, and the allocation could be more or less broad brush. One manager could be given an equity portfolio, or the equity portfolio could be split between the UK, the USA, Europe, emerging markets, passive, active or any number of combinations.

A very large institution, such as the ones listed in Table 2.2, might invest most of the assets themselves, perhaps delegating specialist mandates where they had little in-house expertise, for example to private equity and hedge fund managers. At the other end of the extreme, a small pension fund might delegate all of the investment decisions to one investment manager with a balanced mandate, to invest in an asset mix of a typical pension fund.

The actuary, or investment consultant, also sets a target or benchmark for the investment manager and then monitors their performance against this benchmark. An investment manager might be awarded a mandate to invest in UK equity. The target might be to beat the FTSE All share index. The investment manager will produce performance figures every 3 months, and the investment consultant will compare the manager against other asset managers who invest in UK equity. If the manager consistently does worse than their peers, the investment consultant might suggest appointing a different asset manager.

2.3.2 Investment/Asset Managers

This class is often mistaken for asset owners. They are not. You and I are asset owners, as are the various categories of institutions described above. Investment managers manage our assets on our behalf.

Table 2.6 World's largest asset managers

	Pension fund	Home country	Value (US$ billions)
1	Black Rock	United States	$3,844
2	Vanguard Asset Management	United States	$2,557
3	State Street Global Advisors	United States	$2,023
4	Fidelity Investments	United States	$1,595
5	BNY Mellon Invest	United States	$1,407
6	J.P. Morgan Asset Management	United States	$1,267
7	Capital Group	United States	$1,167
8	PIMCO	United States	$1,163
9	Pramerica Investment Management	United States	$968
10	Amundi	France	$866
11	Goldman Sachs Asset Management Int.	United States	$846
12	Northern Trust Asset Management	United States	$772
13	Wellington Management	United States	$755
14	Natixis Global Asset Management	France	$736
15	Franklin Templeton Investments	United States	$727
16	Deutsche Asset & Wealth Management	Germany	$722
17	TIAA-CREF	United States	$704
18	Invesco	United States	$655
19	Legal & General Investment Management	UK	$643
20	AXA Investment Managers	France	$623
	Total		**$24,040**

Data from Investment and Pensions Europe as at 31/12/2104 https://www.ipe.com/Uploads/2015/06/16/c/l/l/IPE-TOP-400-List-2015.pdf accessed on 2 December 2016

Table 2.6 shows the world's 20 largest asset managers. It is interesting to compare this table with 2.2, which presented asset owners. The largest investment manager, Black Rock, is nearly three times larger than the biggest asset owner. The total assets under management from the top 20 asset managers, a staggering $24 trillion, are twice the size of the 20 largest asset owners combined. There is an incredible concentration of assets with these investment managers, almost a quarter of the world's assets are managed by the largest 20. There is a great deal of geographic concentration too: the largest asset owners are spread throughout different countries, whereas the largest are nine asset managers are from the United States. The asset manager is usually remunerated as a proportion of funds under management, a fee might be 1% of funds under management. That is if the mandate is $100 million, the asset manager would receive $1 million every year that they managed the money.

There could be a number of reasons why there is such a concentration of funds with a small number of asset managers. The asset management industry benefits from economies of scale – it does not cost much more to manage $1,000 billion than $100 billion, yet as they charge a proportion of funds, the revenue from the former is 10 times as large as the latter. This means that the larger you are the more you can spend on marketing and hiring top managers, but there is very low marginal cost from winning new business.

2.3.3 Investment Styles – Active and Passive

An investment manager has to stick to the asset class that they are mandated to invest in. For a UK equity portfolio, the asset manager will have to buy shares in listed UK companies. How good the manager is depends on their ability to pick which companies' shares will perform well and buy and sell them at the right time to maximise their profits.

This is where the distortions begin to creep in. In this sort of mandate, the investment manager is heavily constrained in what he can do by the mandate itself and how he is incentivised. The manager is given a benchmark to invest against, this is usually some index like the FTSE All share – a weighted average of the value of all of the companies that make up the market. An investment manager who is given such a benchmark will typically invest in all of the companies that make up the index, which is all the companies in the market, and try to beat the index by taking small positions against that index. So for example, if British Petroleum (BP) makes up 2% of the index, the manager might hold 1 or 3% of his portfolio in BP shares, depending on whether he felt BP looked expensive or cheap.

The way the manager is rewarded also strongly affects his behaviour. The annual management charge (AMC) means that the manager does well if he attracts lots of mandates and keeps them, but badly if he loses lots of mandates. The incentive is to consistently outperform the index by a small amount; if he takes big long-term positions against the index, there is the risk that he will do very badly and get fired. If he only takes small deviations from the index, he will never be bad enough to fire, and if he consistently beats it by small amounts, he might be rewarded by attracting more funds.

The mandate I described is the most basic one, but more specialist mandates get awarded too. A small fund might give all their assets to one investment manager, who then has to decide on which asset class to invest in. A very large asset owner might delegate a small portion of assets to specialist mandates, for example which take big positions in a few stocks, or to a hedge fund which invests in alternative assets.

Different asset managers promote themselves on having different styles of investment. The two traditional main styles are value and growth. A value investor buys stocks which he thinks are undervalued for some reason, for example they may be unfashionable and have been overlooked by the market, or the market may be mispricing the risk of a stock. A growth manager is one who looks for stocks which will be high fliers in future. Apple or Google might have seemed expensive a few years ago, but they have continued to grow rapidly. There are a number of variations on these themes and other variants.

A more significant distinction is between active and passive management. What we have described above is active management, which is the traditional form of investment management. The investment management company employs humans, who do detailed research on the companies they invest in and then decide which stocks to invest in based on their research and professional judgement. The alternative, which is attracting increasing amounts of money, is called passive, or index-tracking, management, which means that a computer buys all of the shares in the index in the same proportion as the index.

The original idea of passive management came from an economic theory – the efficient market hypothesis (EMH). This states that all relevant information is reflected in the market price. The corollary is that it is impossible to beat the market, because the market price will only change if a new piece of information comes along. Any investor would be as much in the dark about this as anyone else, unless she had insider information, which is illegal.[17]

So, if it's impossible to beat the market, you can't do better than buying all the stocks in the market in line with an average of all investors, which is what passive investment does. Even if you are somewhat sceptical about EMH, which you probably should be, lots of research has shown that the market index beats the average asset manager, especially when you include asset management fees. A passive manager is much cheaper than an active manager, because the humans that it employs to make investment decisions, are paid more than the passive manager's computers. As we have seen, active managers are only able or willing to take small positions against an index and are therefore quasi-passive managers, but with higher fees. The argument in favour of passive management is pretty strong.

It is very hard to know which investment management company is best, other research has shown that past performance of a manager is no guide to future performance for a whole range of reasons. The investment management company may have a star employee who leaves, their strategy might work under one set of economic circumstances but not others, the managers' very success might be the cause of his downfall, in that the assets he has bought have appreciated and are now expensive. Any asset owner, aware that he can't predict the future or assess the competence of asset managers, might conclude that the logical option would be to invest with a passive manager.

2.3.4 Investment Banks/Brokers

I have described the asset owners, what assets they invest in and who they employ to make these decisions. The final piece of the jigsaw is the intermediaries in the buying and selling process.

Investment banks and brokers used to be separate institutions, and there are still many independent brokers, but many have merged or been taken over by banks, so I will treat them together. The asset owners and investment managers are described as the "buy-side": they are buying assets with people's savings. Investment banks and brokers are described as the "sell-side", because they are selling assets to the buy-side.

Investment banks mediate access to financial markets. If a government or company wants to issue a bond, they employ one or a series of investment banks to advise them, to issue the bond and to underwrite the sale. If a company wants to make a public offering of its shares, it will employ an investment bank to do so.

When an investment manager wants to buy a financial asset, he will do so via a broker. This is not as simple as it sounds. If Black Rock, with $4 trillion assets, decides to buy an asset, it will have to purchase a large quantity of the asset, indeed so much that there is probably not enough of it in the market at any one time to buy. Making this happen will be a complicated process, which could take a while, by which time the asset may have changed price from when the decision was made to buy it in the first place.

The very fact that Black Rock makes a decision to buy, or sell, an asset will change the market price, first because there will suddenly be increased demand on the market and secondly because – if it is known that Black Rock is buying an asset – then other agents will try and buy the same asset knowing that the price will go up. This is a complex business which means that brokers have to hold stock of the asset so they can try to smooth out the buying and selling process.

This implies a passive role, but in reality, investment banks and brokers actually play a highly active role and have a great deal of market power. As well as simply executing orders, brokers compete with each other and actively try to sell stock. As part of this process, they provide research for investors on the stock that they sell. This practice has become increasingly controversial. If you were to buy a car you wouldn't trust the car salesman to provide independent research on how good the car was. Hence, there has been an attempt by the regulator to separate research from orders.

Investment banks actively create products to sell to investors. The large growth in the mortgage-backed security market was due to investment banks packaging mortgages into bonds and selling them to investors. This is because investment banks spot opportunities in the market, create products and sell them – asset owners were not demanding mortgage-backed securities. I think of the relationship as like the one between horse racing stables and punters: the investment banks train the horses and enter them in the races, the asset owners, via asset managers, just bet on which horse will win.

Investment banks also don't just act on the order of their clients. A government or a company may employ an investment bank to tell them how best to raise finance, the investment bank provides analysis and advice on this before they do it. This is aided and abetted by the fact that finance directors, and finance ministers, often come from a finance world dominated by investment banks. They speak the same language and have similar world views – part of the phenomenon of financialisation.

This crucial position in the financial system occupied by investment banks means that they have a great deal of power. Knowledge is power and they know who is buying and selling, be it investment managers buying a stock via their brokerage function or via their advice to their clients about raising finance. It is for this knowledge that clients employ them, but this it also enables them to profit. If you know which financial assets are being bought and sold, you can make money by trading on your own account. Regulators have clamped down on this activity, but because of the brokerage function you cannot eliminate it. A broker has to hold stock to perform a function, and so they can make money just by holding more of one stock then another. This knowledge is called "the edge". There have been a stream of examples of top traders leaving banks to set up on their own, but mysteriously losing "the edge" when they do so.

The information advantage is employed more subtly then just trading on their own account, known as "trading on principle". Investment banks sit on a network of information and relationships which they can exploit for financial gain.

2.4 Summary

In this section I have outlined the main actors in financial markets, and what it is they are buying and selling. I have missed out large and important parts of the financial system, such as financial advisors and financial exchanges, because a full description would require a book in itself. But these are the main actors, and it explains why there is a problem. The owners of the assets are heavily directed in what they do by investment consultants, where there is a great concentration of influence as the majority of the market is controlled by a few firms. The investment consultants advise on the allocation of assets between asset classes, but the allocation between assets is delegated to investment managers. There is another concentration of power here, as just 20 firms control a quarter of all of the world's assets. A further power centre is with investment banks, who mediate access to the markets and therefore sit at a fulcrum of relationships and information which they can exploit for financial gain.

In the next chapter, I look at how much the capital markets described in this chapter are actually free markets, and how much they are extensions of the state. After that, I investigate how well the financial intermediaries are delivering what savers, government and society want and need.

Notes

1. Kay, J (2015) *Other People's Money* Public Affairs.
2. Quoted in Evening Standard 22 May 2009 http://www.standard.co.uk/business/time-for-shareholders-to-get-a-grip-6747570.html
3. Also referred to as final salary.
4. Also referred to as money purchase or savings account.
5. Pensions Policy Institute data accessed on 28 September 2016.
6. Also known as general insurance.
7. There are many exceptions to this, for example Lloyd's syndicates have a different corporate structure; there are some lines where mutual are common, such as marine insurance, and there are also captive insurers – subsidiaries which provide insurance to their parent firms.
8. See European Commission http://ec.europa.eu/finance/insurance/solvency/index_en.htm
9. Note there is a difference between 2.2 and 2.4 in relative positioning, this is because they are at different dates.
10. As at March 2015; Sovereign Wealth Fund Institute http://www.swfinstitute.org/sovereign-wealth-fund-rankings/ downloaded on 28 September 2016.

11. International Working Group of Sovereign Wealth Funds (2008) *Santiago Principles* http://www.ifswf.org/sites/default/files/santiagoprinciples_0_0.pdf
12. Bloomberg Markets 13 November 2015 http://www.bloomberg.com/news/articles/2015-11-13/for-fast-growing-family-office-it-s-perks-that-seal-the-deal accessed on 29 September 2016.
13. Endowments.com The Endowment 500: http://endowments.com/funds/ on 29 September 2016.
14. Bill and Melinda Gate Foundation, foundation factsheet http://www.gatesfoundation.org/Who-We-Are/General-Information/Foundation-Factsheet accessed on 29 September 2016.
15. Although this is often referred to as investment consultant.
16. Investment and Pensions Europe March 2015 https://www.ipe.com/reports/special-reports/europes-pension-consultants/room-for-smaller-players-in-uks-oligopolistic-pension-consulting-market/10006892.fullarticle accessed on 30 September 2016.
17. There are various forms of EMH, in the stronger form the market price reflects even insider information.

3

The Potemkin Market

Are Capital Markets Free Markets or an Extension of the State?

A few years ago, I holidayed in the Caribbean island of Cuba, still one of the last remaining communist countries in the world. Havana is a beautifully crumbling city, full of very talented but poor musicians, artists, dancers and mixologists.

When economists talk about markets, you envision something like a bazaar, where you have a bunch of sellers selling something like carpets or spices, which are pretty much uniform, with buyers wandering around haggling over the price. None of the buyers and sellers are large enough to affect the price in the market. Most real markets diverge from this ideal, because they have large buyers or sellers, and much of the work of economists is looking at how monopolies or oligopolies diverge from free markets. Real markets, made up of profit-making companies, whether they are small, oligopolies or monopolies, are what capitalism is.

Cuba does have shops and money, but these are very different to a bazaar. There are shops for tourists which sell stuff like cigars, rum, souvenirs and art, and there are shops for locals which sell cheap clothes, tinned food – actually not much at all. The shops are all owned by the Cuban government, which employs almost all its citizens and sets the prices of the goods and wages.

In the eighteenth-century Russia, Prince Grigory Potemkin, general, politician and lover of Catherine the Great reputedly built a mobile village populated by his own men dressed as peasants, to fool Catherine and foreign ambassadors to believe that Russia had extensively rebuilt the recently conquered Crimea.[1]

A contemporary example of a Potemkin economy is Abu Dhabi, the capital of the United Arab Emirates (UAE). UAE is a merger of previous Emirates

© The Author(s) 2017
N. Silver, *Finance, Society and Sustainability*,
DOI 10.1057/978-1-137-56061-2_3

(principalities), which maintain a good deal of autonomy. If you visit Abu Dhabi, it looks very much like a modern capitalist economy. You can fly there by Etihad, the national airline, take a taxi to your luxury hotel from the modern airport, buy Gucci bags from a Gucci shop in one of Abu Dhabi's numerous malls and have dinner in a Gordon Ramsey restaurant. You can even shop at Waitrose. Abu Dhabi looks like a modern city, the opposite of Havana, with lots of high rise buildings, a huge amount of construction going on, and wide traffic-filled boulevards. But it is not as it seems.

Abu Dhabi has the world's sixth largest oil reserves,[2] but it has a native population of less than 500,000. The government, which is controlled by the Abu Dhabi royal family, receives practically all its revenue from oil exports. All businesses must have a majority ownership of an emiratee. Waitrose, Gordon Ramsey and Gucci are all partnerships where a local owns a majority share.[3] And the only locals with enough cash to own large businesses are members of the extended royal family. Etihad, the airport and the taxi are all government owned, controlled by the royal family. The hotel is owned by the royal family, the banks that lend money to build the hotel are owned and controlled by the royal family, and the royal family-controlled government decide on what gets built where. All of the emiratees, and most of the guest workers, who make up over 80% of the population, are employed by the government or the royal family.[4]

Abu Dhabi is a façade which looks like a capitalist economy, which is actually entirely owned and controlled by one extended family. True, some of the prices are outside their control, crucially the international oil price, but also the price of Gucci handbags and the like, but wages, rents, taxi fares are all government controlled. Although Abu Dhabi might look more like Huston than Havana, in terms of economic organisation it is much closer to Cuba, despite the Gucci bags.

When we talk about living in a capitalist economy, where the means of production are owned by private individuals, we are presuming our economy is not like Cuba or Abu Dhabi. The academic discipline of economics as studied in Western universities does carry out research on the state, and there are still some Marxist economists left, but most economic research concerns the workings of capitalism. Economics would be mostly useless when it comes to explaining why there are so many hotels in Abu Dhabi, and the price of taxi fares.

When we think about financial markets, which category do they fall into? Surely these are the epitome of capitalism? In this chapter, I look at who the end users are of finance and find that financial markets are more like a Potemkin economy than the bazaar.

This question is of crucial importance. If all of the actors in the financial system have got together to buy and sell stuff, if our economy is doing pretty well and if they are earning themselves a good living, then who am I to criticize? If this were the case, it could be argued that the state has a role to play in regulating the markets to ensure the financial system is safer, that it does less damage to the economy in a financial crisis and ordinary folk are not being ripped off by sharks.

On the other hand, if financial markets are extensions of the state, then the emphasis is very different. It becomes up to the state to justify why it is supporting them, for the actors in the financial system to justify their social use and for governments to explain why they are not using better alternatives to achieve their objectives if the current system is not working.

Economic theory argues that free, competitive markets are efficient; regulation is designed to make markets more free, more competitive and more complete.[5] Generally, economic theory does not have much to say about the efficiency of artificial markets which are largely determined by the actions of governments or the public sector.

Finally, if the market is almost free, new models and entrants can outcompete inefficient incumbents. If Tesco was selling oranges for £10, I could find another fruit seller who was selling oranges for less, meaning that Tesco would lose money on the oranges and have to reduce the price or stop selling them. But if the Cuban government decides to sell oranges at £10, you can either pay the price, not eat oranges, or buy them on the black market.

If finance is doing something crucial, but only a select oligopoly is allowed by the government to do this, then there is a great deal of room for them to make economic rents.

I just want to add one qualification. The government, the state or the public sector is not one unified body. The public sector's influence over or control of the financial markets is often in the hands of public sector bodies who are separate from the central government. However, these bodies are given their power and mandate from the central government, although they often end up becoming a separate power base or body of influence. So, for example central banks often have a mandate from central government to oversee the money supply and set short-term interest rates, often targeting a level of inflation set by central government. The power, though, ultimately lies with the central government who can withdraw or change that mandate, as has happened many times in the past.

Also, much of the influence of government on a financial market is where that market resides, so the most important influential governments in this respect are the UK and USA. However, the action of other governments is often highly influential on the price of some financial assets, in particular the actions of the Chinese government and the oil exporting countries, as described below.

3.1 The Buyers

In financial markets, the buyers are the asset owners described in Chapter 2. Who are they?

3.1.1 Sovereign Wealth Funds

The name is a bit of a giveaway; these are government funds normally built up from excess oil revenue. The largest sovereign wealth fund is the Abu Dhabi Investment Authority, with $841 billion assets.[6]

3.1.2 Pension Funds

Table 3.1 shows the largest 20 pension funds in the World. Of the top 10, the Federal Old-age and Survivors Insurance Trust Fund, The National Pension Service and the National Social Security Fund of China are all social security funds, and the rest are pension funds for government employees (civil servants, teachers and the like), except for the Government Pension Fund of Norway which is actually a sovereign wealth fund. The make-up of 11–20 is similar.

What this table shows us is that all of the world's largest pension funds are effectively government entities. So, for example CalSTRS, the California Public Employees' Retirement System, is run by the State of California's Government Operations Agency. The Administradoras de Fondos de Pensiones (AFP) in Chile, at number 17, are privately run funds. But they receive mandated contributions from all Chilean workers: if you work in Chile you and your employer are obliged by the government to pay part of your salary into an AFP. The Government also specify what the AFP can invest in, how it charges, and the AFP has to be approved by the regulator. If the government changed its mind on any of these issues, as it has done in the past, the AFPs would be very different.[7] If the government decided not to

Table 3.1 World's largest 20 pension funds

	Pension fund	Country	Value (US$ billions)
1	Federal Old-Age and Survivors Insurance Trust Fund	United States	$2,645
2	Government Pension Investment Fund	Japan	$1,370
3	Government Pension Fund of Norway	Norway	$856
4	Civil Service Retirement and Disability Fund	United States	$850
5	Military Retirement Fund	United States	$474
6	National Pension Service (NPS)	South Korea	$422
7	Stichting Pensioenfonds ABP (ABP)	Netherlands	$388
8	Thrift Savings Plan (TSP)	United States	$407
9	California Public Employees' Retirement System	United States	$289.8
10	National Social Security Fund	China	$247.4
11	Canada Pension Plan and CPP Investment Board	Canada	$209
12	Central Provident Fund	Singapore	$208
13	Stichting Pensioenfonds Zorg en Welzijn	Netherlands	$183
14	California State Teachers' Retirement System	United States	$189.1
15	Employees Provident Fund	Malaysia	$185
16	Caisse de dépôt et placement du Québec	Canada	$176
17	AFP	Chile	$160
18	Ontario Teachers' Pension Plan	Canada	$150
19	Government Employees Pension Fund (GEPF)	South Africa	$112
20	Employees' Provident Fund Organisation (EPFO)	India	$128
	Total		$9,649

OECD (2015) *Annual Survey of Large Pension Funds and Public Pension Reserve Funds 2015*

impose mandatory contributions, workers may decide to invest their excess savings elsewhere, maybe investing in their sister's business or buying a new car, or anything else, really.

I am not saying it is right or wrong that governments decide to set up and run these large schemes, or that they are run and invested in a good or bad way. I am simply observing that all of the largest pension funds in the world are set up and run directly or indirectly by the government or public sector.

These are organisations with huge economic clout. Total pension fund assets are $36 trillion.[8] Just the funds listed above total almost $10 trillion. As these are the largest funds, they are also the leaders. They can employ the top managers and exert market power.

The majority of smaller pension funds are not directly government entities, but they are massively influenced by governments. There are a number of reasons why governments might want to intervene in the pensions markets; what I present here is from the research justifying government intervention, not necessarily my own views.[9] People are thought to be myopic, they favour short-term consumption over the long term and hence tend not to save enough. A pension is a long-term contract; you pay in now and your pension still has to be there in as long as 60 years' time, beyond the life of most companies. Also, they are generally complex and most people don't understand finance. Hence, the pension requires protection from something that is going to be around for 60 years' time. If people fail to save, the state is going to be left with lots of poor old people, which is not an attractive proposition. Many countries don't have sophisticated capital markets which could support a pension system, and the population may lack the financial education to realise the needs and means to save. Because of this perceived lack of demand for pensions, governments usually accept that no effective market will develop spontaneously, without state intervention.[10] For some or all of these reasons, governments generally intervene heavily and strongly support the pensions market.

This intervention varies from country to country and changes through time, as countries experiment with different policies. International institutions, in particular the World Bank, are very influential. Governments often have little internal expertise in pensions, so they rely on expertise learnt in other countries. That tends to mean that reforms often follow fashions influenced by the World Bank.

Intervention can take many forms. Most countries offer a tax incentive to contribute into a pension, usually income tax relief on contributions and the interest earned is not taxed. Some countries make contributions into a pension mandatory, or the latest fashion is for auto-enrolment (all workers in a country automatically join a pension scheme unless they choose not to).

Pension schemes are highly regulated as the government has incentivised, encouraged or mandated that its citizens contribute money into a pension, which makes it to some extent responsible if things go wrong, and also to protect savers giving over their money to people for a long period of time with little ability to oversee what happens to their savings.

Governments therefore spend a lot of effort developing an enabling environment for pensions through regulation. This includes defining what a pension looks like, how it is legally structured, what it is invested in, who is allowed to manage a pension, what level of contributions go in, what and when it can and can't pay out. Sometimes the regulation can be quite restrictive, for example specifying that the value of the pension has to be greater than the contributions at given points in time, and that pensions have to be linked to inflation.

Because of the principle/agent problem, pensions are often run under trust law – trustees are appointed to oversee pensions. A trustee has a fiduciary responsibility to act as if he were a prudent person. There has been a lot of argument over what actually constitutes a "prudent person". To me, this does not suggest a red-blooded profit-maximising capitalist. There is a subtle difference to looking after someone else's money as a prudent person and looking after your own money.

Governments have often taken other actions so that people can save through financial markets, perhaps by issuing bonds or sponsoring the development of capital markets.

Governments provide implicit or explicit guarantees for pensions. The Pension Protection Fund in the UK and the Pension Benefit Guarantee Corporation in the USA are companies set up by their respective governments to insure company pension funds. This introduces even more government intervention, specifying the funding levels of the pension schemes that are insured. In some countries (e.g. Poland and Kazakhstan), the private system was deemed by the government not to be working and was too important to fail, so it is being nationalised.

In summary, theory suggests that a pensions market would not exist without government intervention.[11] Governments encourage or force people to save into a pension, through regulation governments define what a pension contract looks like, who is allowed to manage it, what are the level of benefits and contributions and – if things go wrong – the government will bail the system out, either ex-ante (by setting up an insurance system) or ex-poste. A free market this isn't.

3.1.3 Insurance Companies

Here, we have a group of institutional investors who are genuinely in the private sector. Table 2.2 shows the world's largest asset owners. The majority of these are insurance companies. Large insurance companies are usually publicly listed companies, and therefore these might be considered capitalist enterprises. Their shares are traded on the stock market and owned by private institutions and individuals.

Insurance companies often manage the money of others, and that is often pension fund money. The pension fund money is either the money of savers or annuitants. The first of these is simply the funds of pension funds as described above, except it will be biased towards smaller entities. So, for example AXA insurance will be managing the money of individual savers or small pension funds, although it could also be winning mandates from the large, mostly government funds of Table 3.1. The annuity phase of a pension is when savers reach retirement they might buy an insurance product which pays them an income until they die.

So many of the assets managed by insurance companies of Table 2.2 are actually pension fund money, as described in the previous section, which means that it is either run by a government entity and outsourced to the insurance company, or it is mandated by a government and managed by the insurer.

Insurance companies do have other business besides pensions. Yet, pensions are disproportionately large, as these are funds built up over many years. Much of the rest of insurance is annual business, where the insurer collects premiums on insurance contracts and holds the assets as a contingency to pay the premiums. Each year, the premiums are renewed, so the insurer only has to hold assets to cover one year's potential losses, plus a buffer of reserves in case of unexpected events.

Some insurance policies are compulsory by law – for example motor insurance in most countries, household in some countries (e.g. France) and liability insurance for many enterprises. So, private insurers are actually often writing policies that the government insist that people buy.

Insurance companies also suffer from the same asymmetric information problems that pensions or banks do; insurance companies are highly complicated entities so, when you buy an insurance policy, it is very hard to assess how solid the insurer is and so they are massively regulated as well.[12]

There has been a long history of insurers going bankrupt and unable to make their claims. In fact, in the early 1990s a whole market went bankrupt – when Lloyd's of London was hit by unexpectedly large claims from asbestos poisoning. The individual companies (called syndicates) in the markets thought they were covered, as they had purchased reinsurance, but it turned out they had purchased reinsurance with each other, so the losses were concentrated in a few syndicates, who could not settle their claims, which then spiralled through the market – the so-called LMX spiral.[13]

To try and stop insurance companies from failing, governments have increasingly developed insurance regulation which has culminated in Solvency II. This is an EU regulation for insurance companies within the EU, but many other countries have adopted Solvency II regulation as well. Solvency II sets the amount of capital that insurers have to hold, how these companies can be governed and risk managed, and what they have to disclose. They are typically overseen by a national regulator, who checks their compliance with Solvency II.[14]

There is a lot of discretion under Solvency II for how insurance companies operate. But the regulation defines how much capital the insurance company has to hold. This capital is held in the form of financial assets and, because the risk is defined by Solvency II, this in turn guides the make-up of those assets.

In summary, insurance companies are more like private agencies than pension funds are, even though their shares are partly owned by institutional investors, which as we have seen are dominated by government entities, much of the assets they manage is pension fund money (see above), and many lines of their business are mandated by government. Insurance companies are highly regulated which means much of their activity is determined by regulation.

3.2 The Sellers

The previous section identified the buyers of assets in capital markets. This section looks at what they buy. The main asset classes globally are publicly traded equity (approximately 36% of assets) and bonds (approximately 43%), the rest being private equity, real estate and a few other alternative asset classes such as infrastructure and commodities, as we saw in Figure 2.1.[15,16] I shall look at the two main asset classes.

3.2.1 Bond Market

Approximately 45% of outstanding global issuance of bonds is government bonds.[17] That means governments borrowing from financial markets. The next largest categories, globally, are financial corporate debt (38%) and non-financial corporations (12.8%).[18]

It is quite difficult to get a grip on what this financial debt actually is, but about half of all debt is issued in the USA, and the USA does provide a good breakdown of that debt. Table 3.2 shows us that government represents

Table 3.2 US bond market – outstanding issuance

Category	Amount (US$ billion)	Percentage
Treasury	$13,418	33
Corporate debt	$8,433	20.7
Mortgage related	$8,783	21.6
Municipal	$3,826	9.4
Money markets	$2,536.1	7
Agency securities	$2,005	4.9
Asset backed	$1,398	3.4
Total	$40,713	100

Securities Industry and Financial Markets Association (SIFMA) statistics, as of Q2 2016

about 47% (treasury, agency securities and municipal) of outstanding issuance, in line with the global proportion.

By comparing Table 3.2 with Bank for International Settlements data, we can work out that about half of the "corporate debt" category is financial and about half non-financial. Financial corporate debt is essentially banks borrowing money from the capital markets to finance loans. I will deal with banks in Chapter 6, in particularly how separate or not they are from the state.

Besides government debt, the main category is "mortgage-related" debt, which makes up over a fifth of the US bond market. This is where loans to individuals for housing are packaged up and sold into the financial markets. It was this category that sparked the financial crisis in 2008.

Without commenting on whether or not mortgage backed securities are a good idea, I want to note here that mortgage-related bond market was first set up and heavily supported by the so-called government-sponsored enterprises (GSEs), the Federal National Mortgage Association (Fannie Mae) and the Federal Home Loan Mortgage Corporation (Freddie Mac). The GSEs were set up by the US government to fund home purchases for Americans and, although they were nominally independent of government, they always had an implicit guarantee form the US government. In the financial crises, the GSEs were bailed out by the US government to the tune of $187.5 billion.[19]

The GSEs invented the mortgage backed security, supported the market, and underwrote a great deal of issuance, which is why they were so badly hit in the financial crisis.

The vast majority of the bond market is made up of government borrowing, or a market largely created by quasi-government entities or borrowing by banks, who as we shall see are mandated and guaranteed by governments.

3.2.2 Equity Market

Surely now we are coming to a purely private sector market – the shares in publicly listed companies? Well, not quite. The *Financial Times* list companies' share prices traded on the London Stock Exchange by industry. Going through these categories in alphabetical order, the first category is **aerospace and defence**. If we take a company like BAE systems, this is an arms manufacturer, whose only clients will be governments (or so we hope). Moreover, the British government decides who BAE systems can sell to. Okay, you might say I have picked on a particularly government-related sector, which just happens to start with the letter A.

Many other sectors may not have governments as their only customer but still have the heavy hand of government controlling or heavily constraining what they do or are highly dependent on government. **Banks** are too big to fail and hence have an implicit government guarantee, as well as have a licence to create money (see Chapter 6). **Utilities** are told by their regulator how much they have to invest and how much profit they can make, and **mining** and **oil and gas** rely on licenses being granted by governments so they can go about their business, and the price of oil is largely determined by the Organization of Petroleum Exporting Countries (OPEC), a cartel of oil exporting governments. Even sectors which would appear to be more independent of government, such as **food and beverages**, are heavily regulated, agriculture is heavily subsidised by the taxpayers (e.g. via Common Agricultural Policy) and rely on international, government-negotiated tariff regimes to operate.

Finally, a stock or a share it is not a physical product like an apple or a car, but one that is defined legally. The structure of a company share or bond was designed by governments and perpetuated and supported by the law and regulations. The legal structure of companies, and what the company can and can't do, is also defined by legislation and regulation.

3.3 The Price: The Interest Rate

Like any other market, the price of a financial asset is determined by how much a buyer is willing to pay for it and how much a seller is willing to sell it for. However, in financial markets, how much the buyer and seller are willing to buy and sell a financial asset for is largely determined by what the public sector does.

Any financial asset's price depends on what investors think about the idiosyncrasies of that asset. So, for example Apple Inc.'s share price will depend on what investors think future sales of iPhones will be and what else Apple is up to. But the price of **all** financial assets depend on the interest rate.

The public sector to a large extent determines the interest rate. The short-term interest rate is set directly by the central bank. The longer term interest rate is influenced by a variety of factors; one of the major ones being what central banks will do in the future. The way governments have chosen to save and intervene in the financial system also has a large influence on the level of interest rates, as do governments' fiscal and monetary policies. In this section, I will describe the direct impact of government or central bank policy on interest rates. In the next chapter, I will explain the indirect impact via the savings channel, which has driven down interest rates to near zero levels. The purpose of this section is to establish that governments, via monetary policy, have a major influence on the price of financial assets, I am not arguing whether or not these policies are correct or a good thing.

The value of a financial asset is the present value of a stream of future payments. For example, shareholders expect that Apple's sales of iPhones in the future will generate a stream of income, some of which will be paid to shareholders in the future. The adjustment to the price of this future revenue, to translate it into present day terms, is called the discount rate.

To put it mathematically, the value of a financial asset is the sum of the discount value of future cash flows. So, for a stock with future dividends $d(n)$, its value is given by the following equation:

$$\sum_{n=0}^{\infty} d(n)/(1+i)^{\wedge} n \qquad (3.1)$$

To calculate the value of a financial asset, you add up all the future cash flows that you expect will be paid to you, discounted by the interest rate from now until the time when the particular cash flow is paid. The pattern of cash flows will vary greatly between assets: a bond may pay a fixed payment, called a coupon, every quarter and then repay the redemption value at the end date. A share in Apple Inc., on the other hand, may not pay any dividend, so the present value is the amount that you think that you will sell the share for, discounted to today.

The discount rate is the price you use to convert a future payment into a value now. The easiest way of thinking about it is how much would you give

3.3 The Price: The Interest Rate

me if I promised to pay you £100 in a year's time? If the annual discount rate was 10%, then you would pay me £90.91 (100/(1 + 10%)). If the payment was in 2 years' time, and the rate was fixed at 10%, you might give me £82.64 (100/(1 + 10%)^2).

The discount rate you offer me is actually made up of three parts:

Inflation– £100 in a year's time will be worth less than £100 today.
Risk – there is a risk that I will run off with your money or go bankrupt and be unable to pay you.
Impatience – how much you value £100 now compared to how much you will value it in a year's time.

If we strip out risk and inflation, we get the real risk-free discount rate, which is a measure of your impatience.

In theory, the discount rate is equivalent to the interest rate. This is the return that you can get instead of lending me money. If you invest in a Greek bond, you may not get your money back, and the payment will be affected by inflation as well. But there are certain forms of investment that are considered risk free, such as a UK government bond (called a gilt). This is because the UK government has the ability to print money to repay the bond, so never needs to default. You can also buy inflation-linked UK government bonds – if you buy one of these, you are guaranteed to get paid your investment plus inflation. The inflation-linked gilt yield is therefore the same as the risk-free real interest rate. The market's inflation expectation can be calculated by comparing the yield on inflation-linked bonds to a normal bond of the same term.

The risk-free interest rate is equivalent to the discount rate allowing for impatience alone. Your or my impatience may be different from the market but if you were the market, the risk-free discount rate would be the gilt rate. That is because, if the market's preference was different, the price of bonds would be bid up or down until it reached the level of the discount rate.

For example, if the market was more impatient then the interest rate suggested, it could borrow money to spend now. But this would reduce demand for bonds, driving the price down and the interest rate up until it was equivalent to the discount rate, reflecting people's impatience.

Of course, the market doesn't really have human emotions, such as impatience. Yet the buyers and sellers in the market are humans, the market really means an average of all the buyers and sellers.

This is how a free market would work if we had one – but we don't. This is because the interest rate is set by the central bank. About 30 years ago, central banks had the idea (not all of them, but they all copied each other) to target inflation. They did this by using the interest rate as a tool. If the demand in the economy is greater than its full-employment potential, this will drive up prices and hence cause inflation. If the central bank puts up interest rates, this will dampen activity because it will be more expensive for people to borrow money to spend or invest, until the economy comes back to its potential.

There is not just one interest rate. The interest rate that the central bank controls is the short-term interest rate, but longer term interest rates are decided by "the market" which is linked to short-term interest rates in complex ways. The market determines the long-term rate through its demand for government bonds. If the yield on, say, a 10-year government bond is 5%, and there is high demand, this will increase the price of the bond and reduce the yield and hence the interest rate. (This is a very simple piece of arithmetic – if a bond's price is 100, but it is paying 5, the yield is 5%. If the price goes up to 125, the bond still pays 5, so the yield and hence the interest rate is 5/125 = 4%.)

The idea of different yields of bonds by term is called the yield curve. This charts the relationship between the term of a bond and the discount rate. In the explanation of discount rates above, I set the rate for borrowing at 10% for both 1 and 2 years, hence the 2-year rate was 21% (1 + 21% is 1 + 10% squared). But this is not necessarily the case, the discount rate from year 0–1 is not necessarily the same as the rate of year 1–2. To illustrate, Figure 3.1 shows the current yield curve of UK government bonds.

Figure 3.1 shows that real yields are below –2% on very short-dated bonds, but this gradually increases for longer dated bonds, reaching –1.5% for 25-year bonds.

The left-hand side of the yield curve is the short-term rate which is set by the central bank. To a certain extent this anchors the yield curve. Since the financial crisis, central banks have been using "unconventional" monetary policy. This means trying to reduce longer interest rates by buying longer term bonds.

Bond yields have been falling in most developed countries for a long time. Figure 3.2 shows that 10-year bond yields were very volatile up until the mid-1990s, with some yields peaking at over 15%. In the mid-1990s, the volatility was massively reduced and so was the spread between the yields. And since then these yields have progressively reduced, with a blip during the financial crisis in 2008, most yields are now around 0%. To some extent, this is mirrored by central banks' rates which have steadily declined from around 6% to around 0% today.

Why is this? Unfortunately, I don't know, but neither does anyone else. There is a current debate within the finance and economic communities about what the

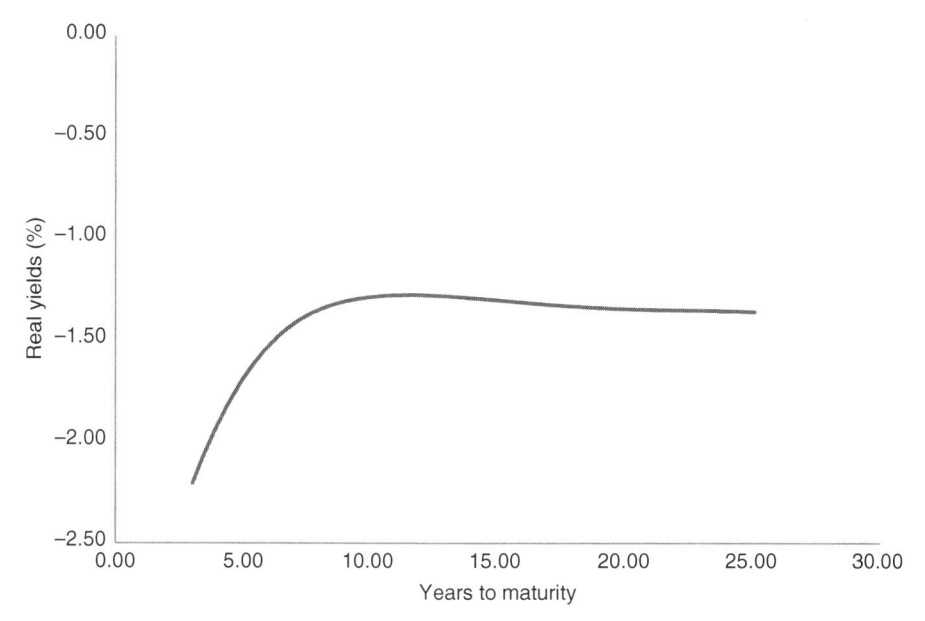

Fig. 3.1 Real yields on UK government bonds on 3 January 2017

Source: Bank of England http://www.bankofengland.co.uk/statistics/pages/yieldcurve/default.aspx downloaded 16 January 2017

causes are. One argument is that the cause is structural: the structure of the global economy has changed which has caused interest rates to drop. The other is that it is central banks' doing.[20] Clearly, the answer lies somewhere between the two, central banks and other government policies have some influence over the long-term level of the interest rate, and the structure of the economies also has an influence. In the next chapter, I will argue that nearly all of the structural reasons that have been proposed as explanations for the decline in interest rates have been caused by government decisions, in particular the way they have chosen to encourage people to save via the financial system.

It is clear that central banks have some influence on interest rates. In the 1980s and 1990s, central banks introduced inflation targeting: they were given the mandate of keeping inflation at a predetermined target level, usually around 2% a year in the advanced economies, (higher in EMs, or countries with history of high inflation), and used the interest rate as their major tool to do this. This policy was largely successful, and hence people's expectations of wage increases were brought down, as central banks were generally trusted to meet their target inflation, which in turn controlled inflation as wages were not being bid up.[21] If you buy a long-dated government bond, your main risk

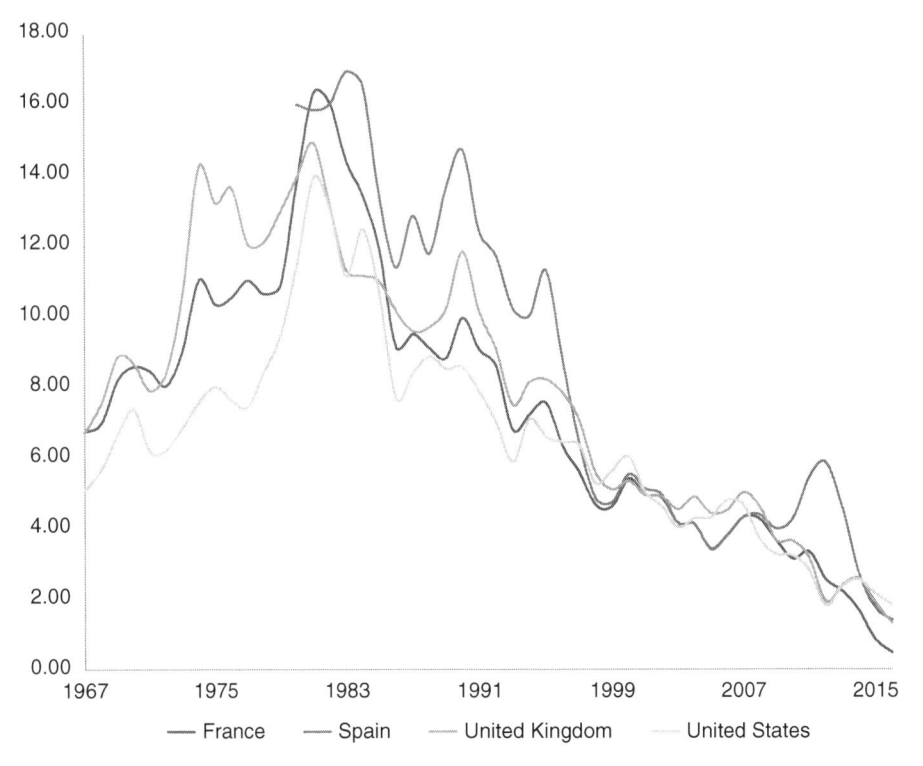

Fig. 3.2 Selected government bond yields

Source: OECD
Dataset: Monthly Monetary and Financial Statistics (MEI) http://stats.oecd.org/OECDStat_Metadata/ShowMetadata.ashx?Dataset=MEI_FIN&ShowOnWeb=true&Lang=en accessed 16 January 2017

is high inflation. If inflation is high, then you need a higher yield to compensate. Also, if inflation is volatile and uncertain, you would demand an even higher yield as compensation for the risk. But as investors and the market believed that central banks had brought inflation under control, this reduced investors need for higher yields, and they were more willing to buy bonds at lower yields.[22]

There were also structural reasons why inflation was brought under control. The industrialisation of China and other developing countries meant a huge number of new workers who could make stuff cheaply. As demand increased, this didn't push up the price of stuff because more of it could be made cheaply by Chinese peasants migrating to cities. The Chinese central bank also intervened in this process by buying foreign currencies so that Westerners' purchase of Chinese goods did not drive up the Renminbi and make them more expensive, which would have caused inflation.[23]

We must add the Greenspan Put. For ideological reasons, the very influential chairman of the Federal Reserve (the US Central Bank, known colloquially as the "Fed") between 1987 and 2006, Alan Greenspan felt that it was his responsibility to bail out capital markets after an economic shock by reducing interest rates. He did this on a number of occasions, such as after the collapse of the hedge fund LTCM in the late 1990s and the bursting of the dot-com bubble of the early 2000s. Normally, when a central bank reduces interest rates, this causes inflation, but because of the expectations of low inflation and because of the Chinese situation, this did not do so. This means there was always an asymmetric pressure on interest rates downwards.[24] Also, because the USA was the dominant world economy, all other countries had to follow suit otherwise their currency would appreciate in value, which would make them less competitive.

Another impact of the Greenspan Put was that investors knew that if things went bad, the Fed would reduce interest rates. This meant that it was safer to buy long-dated bonds, driving down yields again. Because yields were so low, this meant that people could borrow money cheaply, which caused a wall of liquidity, meaning there was a load of money chasing assets, which drove down interest rates even more.[25]

This situation blew up in the financial crisis. But since then, central banks have been engaged in unconventional policies, continually reducing interest rates to zero, and buying up longer assets to reduce these rates as well. These unconventional measures are supposed to be temporary but have lasted 8 years so far and, as Keynes said, "in the long run we are all dead".

Central banks are not the only cause of low interest rates, there are also what are termed structural causes. My contention in chapter 4 is that these structural causes are endogenous to the financial system, which has been ultimately caused by governments' decisions to get people to save via the finance sector and to set the rules by which the financial system operates. If the interest rate is not directly set by the central bank, it is indirectly set by government through their influence on the savings channel.

3.4 Oil Cartels and Currency Manipulators

The influence on financial markets by governments is not solely by the domestic government which happens to host the financial market in question. The actions of many countries' governments have an impact on some crucial prices and variables.

First of all there is OPEC which has had a large or often determining influence on the price of oil over the last 50 years. OPEC is a cartel of governments, the most powerful of which is Saudi Arabia. Oil is by far the world's most traded commodity and is therefore, in itself, the most important commodities future market and has an indirect effect on many other financial markets; for example if the price of oil increases, this can cause inflation leading to an increase in interest rates.

By forming a cartel to often artificially keep the price of oil high, OPEC countries have attracted a great deal of wealth to themselves; 5 of the 10 largest SWFs of Table 2.4 are oil related. The money earned from oil is mostly ploughed back into the financial markets via SWFs and the private wealth of the oil barons. Many OPEC governments are the major purchasers of defence equipment for the listed companies described above.

Another group of government actors are the Asian countries pursuing export-led growth strategies, in particular China. Of the remaining top 10 SWFs of Table 2.4, 4 are Chinese and 1 is Singaporean, which pursues the same policy as China. In addition to this the Chinese central bank is the world's largest holder of US treasuries.[26] The way this works is that China, or another Asian country, sells goods to an importing country, the largest market being the USA. As China is running a persistent trade surplus with the USA, this should mean that the Renminbi appreciates compared to the dollar, which would mean that Chinese goods are becoming more expensive. Instead, the Chinese central bank purchases US assets, mostly US treasuries, which pushes upside pressure on the dollar and keeps the exchange rate the same.

The result is that the price of US treasuries is increased and hence the US interest rate is suppressed, the exchange rate between the world's two largest economies is fixed by the Chinese government, and China has built up a huge supply of financial assets, and the world's pool of savings is greatly increased – all the result of Chinese government policy.

3.5 Some Implications

The end user of a financial market might be a government agency, such as Abu Dhabi Investment Authority or the California Public Employees' Retirement System, and the other end user is another government agency, such as the US Treasury issuing a US treasury bond. Or the buyer might be an entity that wouldn't exist unless a government had set it up, and it looks the way it does because of regulatory design, such as a Chilean AFP.

The nearest activity to a free market in financial markets is where a highly regulated entity buys equity or bonds from another, very highly regulated entity. Even in those circumstances, what they both do and how much money they make is to a large extent determined by a regulator.

The financial system is global, so financial markets are more like bazaars of governments purchasing stuff from other governments. They are not like the Abu Dhabi economy which is all in the control of one royal family. I happen to sit in London, which is exceptionally international, but many markets are much more insular. This is even true of large markets, such as Japan and USA, where – because of the size of their economies – most of the activity is domestic – and small markets, such as most emerging markets, as their savings often have to invest domestically, and most of the buyers of domestic instruments are local.

If we go back to the BAE systems example, here is a description of what financial markets do. The defence department decides that it needs a new weapons system, agreed by Treasury. The government then issues a bond to fund this purchase, which is bought by investors, for example a local government pension scheme. The government pays BAE systems for the weapons system. BAE systems is owned by institutional asset owners, who receive a portion of the profits from this deal via dividends. Some of these asset owners are government pension schemes, some of them are SWFs, and one is NEST, the company set up by the government to invest auto-enrolled pensions. The price of BAE systems shares and government bonds is to some extent determined by the central bank's interest rate policy.

3.5.1 Reality Check

Is really true that financial markets are so dominated by governments? Surely they are the epicentre of private enterprise?

Government spending in proportion to GDP in developed countries ranges from 34% (in Switzerland) to 58% (in Finland).[27] This is an understatement of government influence, as the impact of regulation and laws are not included in the spending statistics. In any economy, the government is the biggest player: it employs most people, raises the most debt and therefore is the most likely to use financial markets. A large part of any economy consists of small- and medium-sized enterprises, and much economic activity will be between individuals. The 34–58% of GDP is a proportion of all economic activity, which includes me paying my cleaner or buying a coffee from an independent coffee store. Neither my cleaner, the coffee store nor I can raise money on the capital markets – the number of companies that can do is very small. The proportion of government activity in capital markets is therefore much higher than in the economy as a whole. And these enterprises come and go, whereas governments are around forever. So, Google might be big now and able to raise debt, but it has only been able to do so for 10 years, whereas you can still buy UK government bonds dating back to the Second World War.

The history of capital markets is also biased towards government activity. The bond market in the UK was created to raise money to fight the French in the eighteenth century.[28] The most successful early joint stock company was the East India Company, which ended up governing India and was the forerunner of the British Empire.[29]

So, given the size and longevity of governments compared to the rest of the economy, and the history of financial markets, it should be no surprise that they are government-dominated.

3.5.2 Summary

The activities in financial markets can be categorised as follows:

1. Enacting the will of the government: For example, auto-enrolled or mandatory pension funds where the government decides that workers should save for a pension and sets up laws and institutions to encourage or compel people to do so.
2. Perform services for governments: An example of this would be to raise money for government debt. Another would be that the California government decides to pay part of its public teachers' salaries via a funded pension scheme.
3. Perform a function of government: Banks issue legal tender on behalf of the government as will be described in Chapter 6.
4. Behave in a way specified by government: Governments or regulators specify how much capital institutions have to hold, who can manage money, the structure of the market, what they are allowed to buy and sell, how they communicate with the investor and strongly influence the price securities are traded at through the interest rate.

Governments are not unitary institutions, so the central government outsources the running of different aspects of the financial markets to other bodies, such as the central bank or the regulator, who can have a greater or lesser level of independence. Also, the architecture of financial markets is the product of domestic governments, but many of the actors in these markets are foreign governments who are the ultimate buyers and sellers of financial assets. The countries that host these markets, most notably the UK and USA, receive large revenues from the fees that they earn from the transactions and management of assets of foreigners, and therefore have incentives to promote themselves as centres of financial services.

As well as all these, governments, central banks and public international institutions such as the IMF or World Bank provide a back-stop insurance for banks, financial institutions and financial markets when things go wrong. They reduce interest rates following a market crash, suspend trading in times of difficulty, bail-out important institutions or arrange emergency takeovers. Just the knowledge that something is too big, important or complex to fail has a significant impact on prices, because it limits the downside risk of any activity.

The point of this chapter is to show that financial markets are in no sense free markets that have sprung up independently, where capital is allocated efficiently by the private sector. They are largely the creation of governments, they fulfil certain services for governments and they run in a way that is specified by governments. The actors within the financial system – the intermediaries – are private sector, but they have been delegated by governments to do their bidding. The buyers and sellers of goods are governments, but they often get private sector agents to do the buying and selling on their behalf.

Financial markets are a creation of society to do something. The next two chapters look at what society wants them to do and how well they perform in achieving their objectives.

Notes

1. Montefiore, S (2005) *An Affair to remember* New York Review of Books February 24 2005 Issue.
2. See UAE trade and commerce office http://www.uaetrade-usa.org/index.php?page=economic-sectors-in-uae&cmsid=48 accessed 5 December 2016.g
3. See UAE trade and commerce office http://www.uaetrade-usa.org/index.php?page=uae-economy&cmsid=105 accessed 5 December 2016.

4. BQ magazine http://www.bq-magazine.com/economy/socioeconomics/2015/04/uae-population-by-nationality accessed 5 December 2016.
5. Turner,A (2013) *Economics after the crisis* MIT Press.
6. Data from Asset International's Chief Investment Officer on 2 December http://www.ai-cio.com/aiGlobal500.aspx?id=3100 – 31 August 2016.
7. OED (2011) *Chile review of the Private Pensions System* OECD.
8. Towers Watson (2015) *Global Pensions Assets Study 2015.*
9. Holzman, R and Hinz, R (2005) *Old-Age Income Support in the twenty-first Century* World Bank.
10. Holzman, R and Hinz, R (2005) *Old-Age Income Support in the twenty-first Century* World Bank.
11. Holzman, R and Hinz, R (2005) *Old-Age Income Support in the twenty-first Century* World Bank.
12. There is also asymmetric information the other way, when you buy a policy, you often know more about how good a risk you are than the insurer does.
13. Kay, J (2007) *Same old folly, new spiral of risk* Financial Times 13 August 2007.
14. See European Commission http://ec.europa.eu/finance/insurance/solvency/index_en.htm
15. In Chapter 5, I will delve into more detail.
16. Hewitt (2014) *Global invested capital market* Hewitt EnnisKnupp.
17. Bank for International settlements (2016) *BIS Quarterly Review, September 2016.*
18. Bank for International settlements (2016) *BIS Quarterly Review, September 2016.*
19. http://www.nytimes.com/2016/05/22/business/how-freddie-and-fannie-are-held-captive.html
20. Wolf, M (2016) *Monetary Policy in a low rate world* Financial Times September 13 2016.
21. See for example, Mishkin, F and Posen, A (1998) *Inflation Targeting: Lessons from Four Countries* NBER Working Paper No. 6126.
22. See for example Fouejieu A and Roger, S (2013) *Inflation Targeting and Country Risk: an Empirical Investigation* International Monetary Fund Working Paper.
23. See for example Krugman, P (2010) *Chines rumbles* New York Times February 4, 2010.
24. Stiglitz, J (2010) *Freefall: America, Free Markets, and the Sinking of the World Economy* WW Norton & Co.
25. Stiglitz, J (2010) *Freefall: America, Free Markets, and the Sinking of the World Economy* WW Norton & Co.
26. Bloomberg 16 November 2016 *China Holdings of U.S. Treasuries Decline to Lowest Since 2012.*

27. OECD date https://data.oecd.org/gga/general-government-spending.htm downloaded 27 September 2016.
28. Ferguson, Nial (2012) *The Ascent of Money: a Financial History of the World* Penguin.
29. Robins, N (2006) *The Corporation That Changed the World: How the East India Company Shaped the Modern Multinational* Pluto Press.

4

The Sisyphus Savings System
Does the Savings Industry Do What It Is There for?

In Greek mythology, Sisyphus was punished by the gods to be condemned for eternity to push a boulder up a hill, only to see it roll down again. This is exactly what happens to your savings.

In the last two chapters, I introduced the capital markets and described how they are largely determined by governments.

In the next two chapters, I shall focus on one part of the savings system in detail – the pensions industry in the UK and investigate if it achieves the purpose for which it was created. As we saw in Chapter 2, pensions represent one of the largest classes of asset owners. I have chosen the UK which, along with the USA, has one of the most developed pensions systems and relies heavily on capital markets to provide pensions. In countries such as Germany and France, the state is much more directly involved; so these countries do not rely on the private sector to deliver pensions.

It is generally assumed that it is beneficial for people to save for a pension, both for their own good and for the good of the economy. If you save for a pension, your money is entrusted to the financial services industry; so it makes sense to think about whether that is a good idea. This chapter considers whether the finance industry delivers benefits to savers that they might reasonably expect in return for entrusting the industry with their savings. Chapter 5 will look at whether the industry delivers benefits to the economy as a whole.

The purpose of a pension is to provide savers with an income when they are too old to work, smoothing lifetime consumption by deferring your income from when you receive a salary till when you are no longer earning. Pensions are also a form of insurance against living a long time. If you have enough savings to last you to, say 80, but you actually live till 120, you will run out of money; your pension is supposed to protect you against this happening. Many people save for a pension partly because they don't trust the state to provide a large enough income to comfortably live on in retirement. If they trust the private sector, is it delivering the benefits?

Most governments encourage people to save for a pension, through financial incentives and other forms of encouragement, such as marketing and setting up enabling regulatory environments. They do this because as a society, we believe that citizens shouldn't fall below a certain poverty level, and that it is the government's job to make sure they don't. This is especially true of vulnerable or older people. All developed countries and many developing countries therefore provide at least a basic level of pension and encourage people to save for themselves.

The more people save for themselves, the less of a financial burden they will be on the state when they get old. This need is particularly acute in countries faced with ageing populations, where there is a declining proportion of people of working age compared to people who have retired. In this case, it will be more difficult to fund people's pensions through taxation, as there will be fewer working people to pay tax; so if the economy has savings to call on, it will be better able to afford to pay pensions. Currently, most countries in Europe and Asia have rapidly ageing populations because they have declining fertility rates and increasing life expectancies; less people are being born to replenish the stock of workers and there are more old people as they are not dying off.

From an individual's perspective, saving for a pension might make sure that they have enough income in retirement to live comfortably and not have to rely entirely on the state. From the government's point of view, they need to make sure that the economy has a savings pool to draw on to supplement tax when there are an increasing proportion of older people who need a pension.

Governments also encourage savings because the economy needs money for investment which is essential for economic growth. Increased standards of living require economic growth, and this in turn requires investment into the economy; savings are the source of this investment. A larger economy is required to pay a larger pool of pensioners, hopefully with a higher standard of living than previous generations. If the pension is paid out of savings or by the government, the economy still needs to grow to afford to pay the pensions; in the former the economy has to generate income to pay savers' pensions, in the latter it has to generate enough tax revenue for the government to pay pensions.

If you save for a pension, your money is supplemented by a government subsidy, in the form of tax relief, and entrusted to the management of the financial services industry. This chapter looks at how well this industry fulfils the needs of the saver and the state as discussed above and described and summarised in Table 4.1.

It is a huge boon for financial services that governments encourage people to save for their pension, because the industry collects a substantial fee for these funds under its management. On top of this, every time an asset held by a pension fund is bought or sold, a broker takes a fee. And also pension funds provide a "buy side" for financial transactions. This provides a market for the "sell side", typically investment banks, who create financial products to sell to the buy side. By encouraging people to save for a pension, the government creates a large flow of funds into the welcoming arms of the financial services industry.

To work out how well the pension system fulfils its purpose, I consider three questions:

(1) Do people who save for a pension help the government, specifically by reducing the financial burden that the state will face when current savers retire?
(2) Does saving ensure that an individual will receive a decent pension?
(3) Are savings invested in a way that is beneficial to the economy? (see Chapter 5 for this one).

Table 4.1 What are pensions for?

Individual	State
Smooth lifetime consumption	Reduce future fiscal burden from elderly
Reduce dependency on government	Encourage people to take responsibility for own savings
Manage longevity risk	
Meet future expenses (e.g. higher medical expenses in old age)	Manage risk of ageing population
	Increase long-term investment to facilitate economic growth
	Develop domestic financial services industry

4.1 What Your Pension Does for Your Country

4.1.1 Funded Schemes, PAYGO and the Ageing Population

Do governments reduce their future fiscal burden by encouraging people to save for a pension?

There are two possible ways that the economy can manage savings before retirement. The first is where your savings are put aside and invested in a fund, which is then used to pay your pension when you retire and is normally managed by the private sector. The alternative is an unfunded pension, also known as pay-as-you-go (called PAYGO for short), which are mostly state systems. In return for your contributions, the government promises to pay you a pension when you retire; your contributions are used to pay current pensioners or go into the government's general revenue. Most countries have a mixture between these two systems.

One of the reasons that pension savings are particularly important is because Western countries, and much of Asia as well, have ageing populations. These countries have low or declining fertility rates. For example an extreme case is Taiwan, where on average each woman has only 1.1 child over her lifetime.[1] This is far too few to maintain the size of the population without immigration. The result of low or declining fertility is that at some point there will be a smaller proportion of working-age people compared to post-retirement people. This puts pressure on PAYGO systems as there are fewer workers to collect the tax required to pay an increasing number of pensioners.

The problem that the UK government has to solve is illustrated in Figure 4.1. At the moment, there are nearly four workers for every pensioner (this ratio is called the support ratio), but over the next 25 years or so this number is likely to reduce to around two, although somewhat mitigated as the retirement age is increasing. If the government is going to have to finance this out of spending, taxation of workers will have to increase considerably to pay the increased number of retirees a pension, with all of the associated social, political and economic consequences this will entail. The government has therefore outsourced part of this process to the financial sector.

Most Western and Asian countries face similar challenges, some countries such as Taiwan or Italy would face a more dramatic reduction in the support ratio than the UK because of very low fertility rates and lower inward migration, whereas some, like the USA, face a better situation because of higher fertility rates and immigration.

4.1 What Your Pension Does for Your Country

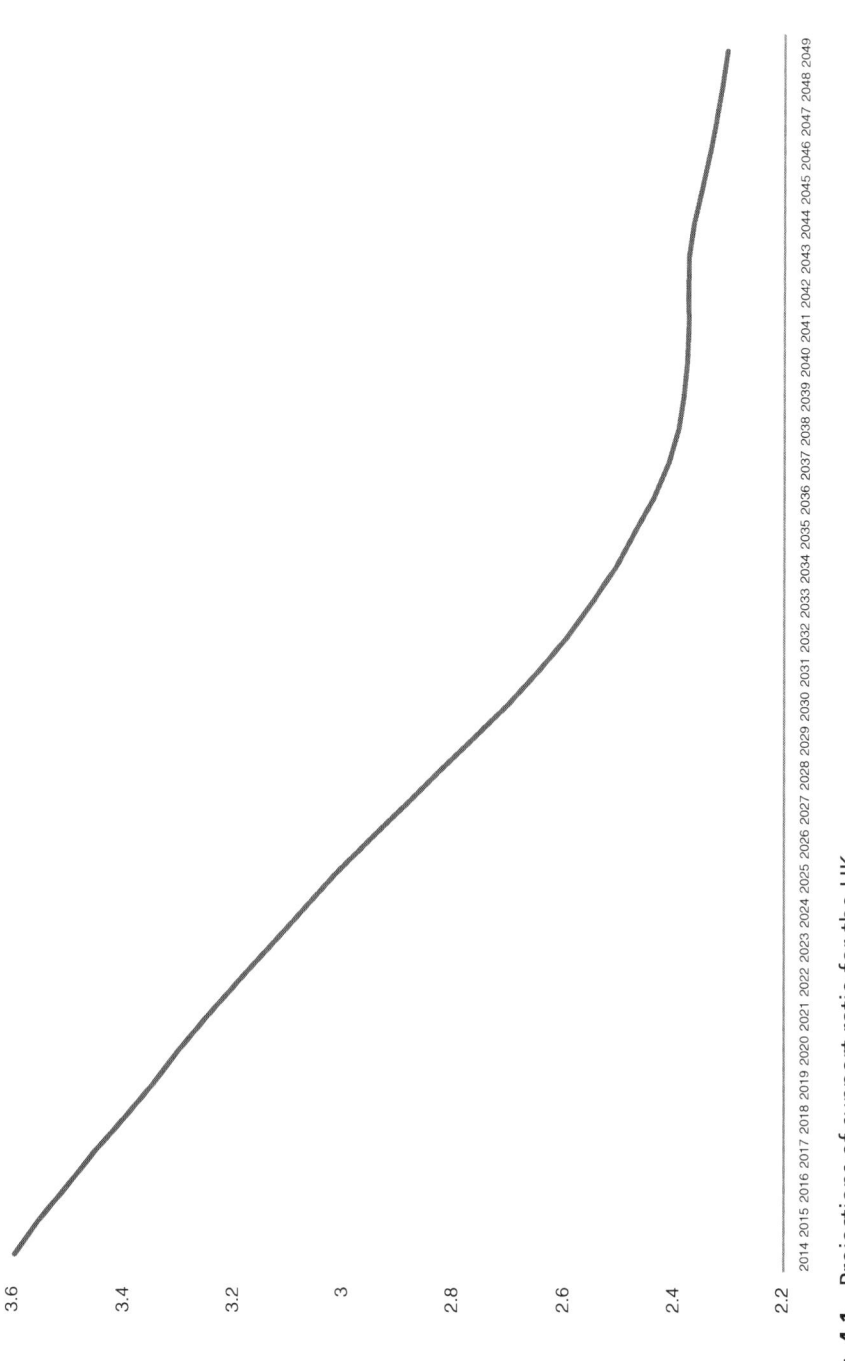

Fig. 4.1 Projections of support ratio for the UK

Source: Office National Statistics

Number of people over 65 compared to people between 16 and 64. The state pension age is increasing, which should increase the support ratio, although this does not always correspond to people retiring later. 2014-Based National Population Projections, accessed 16 January 2017

Under a funded system, savings need to be put to good use, ensuring that each worker is more productive so that they can produce enough output to afford to look after the increasing number of pensioners.

4.1.2 The Case for Government Intervention

Governments around the world use a number of methods to encourage people to save for their pension. The first is to use financial incentives, usually in the form of tax relief on pension contributions. Governments also encourage people to save through auto-enrolment, which is where you automatically join a pension unless you opt-out. The most extreme measure is compelling workers to join a pension scheme by law. Governments also provide a facilitating environment in the form of specific pension regulation, to make sure, for example, that people understand what they are buying and that pension providers are properly qualified to manage pension funds.

Even if the state has no PAYGO system, most societies think that it is socially unacceptable for there to be hoards of poor old people, and therefore, governments feel compelled to look after these people. If workers can save enough for a pension then they can look after themselves, reducing the future burden on the state. Many countries have means-tested pensions; if someone retires and has assets below a certain threshold, the government guarantees them a minimum income – so if people don't save for a pension, there is a direct cost to the government.

Other reasons are often cited for government intervention in favour of pensions. The main one is paternalistic, because people need encouragement to do what's good for them. People tend to be myopic, or so the argument goes: they might be aware that they should save for a pension, but they underestimate how much they need to save or other more immediate spending needs get in the way. The result is that people generally save too little. This is a similar argument for taxing tobacco and alcohol – most people know what they should or should not do, but there is a gap between awareness and action, and people need to be encouraged to make choices that are good for them.[2]

Finally, market failure is often cited as a reason for government intervention. Left to their own devices, people may not demand a pension, so a pensions market could hardly develop by itself. It is beneficial for a country to have a market in pensions, so the government should encourage people to save for a pension so that a market will develop.[3]

I will now see if the pensions market reduces the burden of the aging population on the state in the UK.

4.1.3 The Unseen Counter-Revolution

Peter Drucker in his influential 1976 book, *The Unseen Revolution* observed that much of the means of production in a capitalist economy was no longer owned by a rentier-capitalist class, as identified by Karl Marx, but by the workers themselves, via their pension funds.[4] The situation has changed since Drucker's time. Now nearly all pension savings is made by the richest sections of society. These people are wealthy enough to look after themselves in retirement, so the fact that they save for a pension will not reduce the burden on the state at all. It also means that ownership of the economy is not democratised, which might have been an added extra benefit, as the small minority of the population people who own shares are by and large the same people who save for a pension.

Figure 4.2 shows the earnings distribution of the tax savings benefit on pensions in the UK. The top 10% of earners receive 58% of the tax relief, and the top 20% get 75% of the total tax relief on pensions. This means that approximately three quarters of pension savings are made by the richest fifth of the population; the people most likely to save anyway. Rather than help people to look after themselves in retirement, most of the benefits from pension tax-relief goes to the wealthiest people in society. The tax rebate is highly regressive, the rich benefit from it but the poor do not. By simply abolishing this rebate, worth £40 billion per year,[5] the government would increase tax revenue by the same amount, which could instead be spent on reducing tax for poorer people, reducing the deficit or boosting public spending and hence increasing poorer people's income, some of which they might choose to save.

It is true that there are other ways that governments can expand savings into pensions across the income groups. For example, the British government has introduced an initiative called National Employment Savings Trust (NEST). This is an auto-enrolment scheme – you have to join NEST unless you specifically choose not to. Auto-enrolment schemes have very high participation rates, so in time NEST will change the distribution of Figure 4.2. What is won't do is change the distribution by very much. The default contribution rates of NEST are very low – on their own they won't earn you a large enough pension to live off. Other countries, like Australia, have introduced mandatory pensions: Australian workers are compelled to save for a pension, which has succeeded in increasing coverage across income groups.

We will see in the rest of this chapter that these policies are increasing coverage of an inherently faulty system. Improving the coverage will increase net contributions into the system, which will channel more money to the

84   4 The Sisyphus Savings System

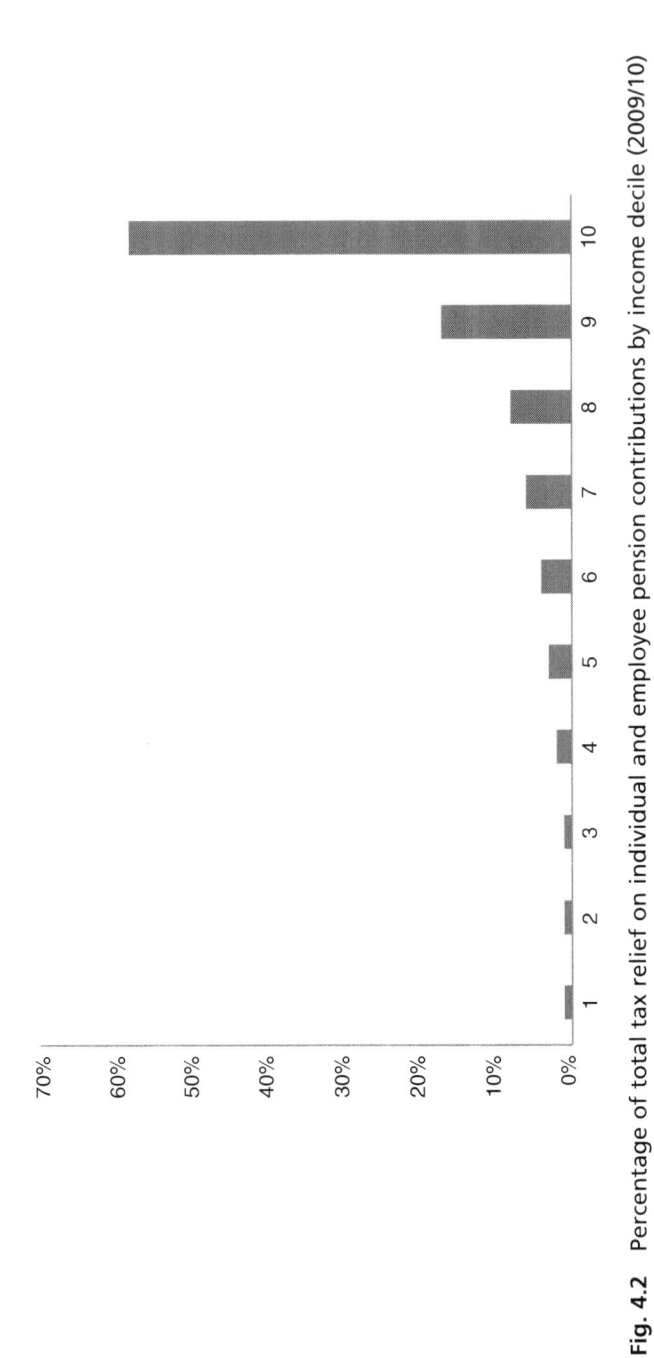

Fig. 4.2 Percentage of total tax relief on individual and employee pension contributions by income decile (2009/10)

Source: Pensions Policy Institute
PQ Rachel Reeves, House of Commons *Hansard 6 July 2011* Column 1247 W, sourced from PPI website http://www.pensionspolicyinstitute.org.uk/pension-facts/pension-facts-tables/private-pensions-table-29 accessed 5 December 2016

financial services industry. Yet – as we will see later – the industry uses the power that it gains by virtue of managing these funds to generate revenue for itself whilst incidentally damaging the economy.

4.2 Where Have All Your Savings Gone?

There are two determinants measuring the cost of a pension, life expectancy and our old friend the interest rate. Over the last 40 years, the interest rate has gone down to historic lows, which makes buying a pension more expensive, and life expectancy has gone up achieving historic highs, which also makes buying a pension more expensive.

There has been some confusion over the impact of low interest rates on pensions. A pension is a stream of payments which are paid until you die. The formula for calculating the value of a pension is similar to Formula (3.1) in Chapter 3:

$$\sum_{yearofdeath}^{n=ageatretirment} pensionpayment(n)/(1+i)(n-\widehat{currentage}) \qquad (4.1)$$

What this formula means is that the value of your pension is the sum of the future payments you will receive valued at today's date. The higher the interest rate, the lower the value of this pension.

So, if you already have a pension, its value has gone up as interest rates have gone down. For a DB pension scheme (the difference between DB and DCs was described in Chapter 2), the value of the pensions it has to pay has increased, so its liabilities have increased, which means that it will go into deficit, or its deficit will have increased. Yet, its assets would also have increased: Formula (3.1) explained that a financial asset is a stream of discounted future payments. If the pension fund is holding bonds, the price of bonds is inversely correlated with interest rates. So a reduction in interest rates means that the price of bonds will have increased as well.

We would hope that the reduction in interest rates would have increased the assets and liabilities of pension schemes. Unfortunately, although under this reduction in rates, both have indeed increased, for most pension funds the assets have not increased as much as the liabilities. The total deficit on UK DB schemes, that is how much the cost of providing the promised pensions exceeds the assets held to meet the costs, has been estimated as £384 billion.[6] This in turn puts a huge burden on companies which have DB pension schemes, which have to make up the shortfall.

The case of DC pension is not so clear cut: when you retire, you get paid out of whatever you have in your DC pot, so there are no liabilities as usually understood. Because interest rates have reduced, the value of your pot will have increased. But the cost of buying an annuity will also have increased, and – like DB schemes – your assets will probably not have increased as much as the cost of the annuity. But your employer is not obliged to make up the shortfall, so the result will be a lower pension.

Another complication is that you are no longer obliged to purchase an annuity. A pension is an income that you receive after you retire. If you don't buy an annuity, you have to convert your own pension yourself, that is by keeping it invested and taking out an income from it, which will reduce the size of your pot. If interest rates are still low when you retire, you will not earn a large return, unless you take large risks which you won't want to do with your pension. So even if you don't buy an annuity, your income will still be reduced, because of low interest rates.

What I've said here is confined to existing pensions. The real problem is the increased cost of your pension in the future. When you retire, you will probably want a pension that is the same order of magnitude as your salary when you retire, but you will probably make do with a slightly lower income to reflect that work entails costs which you no longer have (like travel costs), you will hopefully have paid off your mortgage and your kids no longer have to be supported. You will probably be entitled to some state benefits which supplement your private pension.

The replacement rate is the proportion of your pension immediately after you retire compared to your salary when you retire. A desired replacement rate might be two-thirds of your salary.

Figure 4.1 tells us that from the government's perspective, the support ratio, the proportion of workers to retirees, will be at its worst from 2040, that means it is most important for people who are currently 40 and younger to save to alleviate the worst of the problems. So how expensive is it for these people to buy a pension?

The best way of measuring the cost is to take a targeted replacement rate and calculate what proportion of your salary you would have to put aside to achieve that targeted pension. So if the replacement rate is two-thirds – if you would like a pension that is two-thirds of your salary when you retire – Table 4.2 compares what proportion of your salary you would have had to put in to get this pension 25 years ago compared to today. This is true for

Table 4.2 Contributions required to achieve two-thirds pension

Year	Contribution rate (%)	Contribution on £20,000 salary	£40,000 Salary
1991	7	£1,300	£2,700
2016	39	£7,800	£15,600

Author's own calculation. Assuming male starting to contribute from age 25, retiring at 65. In 1991, I have used a pre-retirement real interest rate of 6% and a post-retirement rate of 4%, with PA90 mortality. For 2016 I have used 1% and –2%, respectively, and PMA92 Long mortality tables.

DB or DC pensions; the cost is the same the difference between the two is who bears the shortfall when things go wrong.

Table 4.2 shows the contributions you would have to make to your pension if you started contributing at age 25 and continued until you retired at age 65. You would have had to contribute 7% of your salary every year till you retired if you started back in 1991. But because of lower interest rates and higher life expectancies, to get the same pension now you would have to contribute over five times as much – 39%. Nearly all of this increase is due to reduced interest rates.

Imagine a 25-year-old earning £25,000. In 1991 circumstances, she would only have to pay in £1,300, and if her salary increased to £40,000 just before she retired, her contributions would have had to increase to £2,700. She could then achieve a pension of £27,000 per annum, two-thirds of £40,000, increasing with inflation. By contrast, in current conditions you would have to contribute £7,800 per year from the age of 25, increasing to £15,600 at age 65, to achieve the same pension.

So, over the last 25 years, the amount you have to save to achieve the same pension has increased massively – and almost entirely due to the reduction in real interest rates. To expect a 25-year-old to put away 7% of a salary into a pension is feasible, but nearly 40% just isn't realistic. Even to achieve a pension of half of your salary – a 50% replacement ratio – you have to contribute 30% of your salary into a pension. The current system is therefore unable to deliver an affordable pension. What has caused this damaging reduction in interest rates?

4.3 Interest Rate – Revisited

This section argues that interest rates are low because of the actions of government and the savings' industry; by encouraging people to save for their pension and their subsequent actions, governments have ensured that pensions have become unaffordable; the whole exercise has been futile.

Figure 3.2 showed that the yield on government bonds has dropped from around 10% to 15% in most advanced economies in the 1980s to around zero today. The rates in this chart are nominal rates; the payment on the interest rate is fixed in monetary terms. Most pensions are inflation linked; the price of a pension is related to the inflation linked, or "real", interest rate. The rate on these kinds of bonds is even lower, currently at −2%.

What has caused this decrease in interest rates? It is time to go back to the discussion in Chapter 3 in a bit more detail. Economists who study this sort of thing distinguish between the actual interest rate and the natural rate. The actual rate is heavily influenced by central banks, whereas the natural rate is what interest rates would be without central bank intervention.

There are a number of explanations that have been put forward by economists for the decline in interest rates; I will go through each of these explanations in turn and show that nearly all of them have either been caused by government action or are endogenous to the savings' system; the way governments have determined how people save. I will not take a view on whether any of the explanations are correct or incorrect, because it is likely that a combination of factors has caused the decline, but whatever the explanation or the combination of explanations – the ultimate cause of the reduction in interest rates has been the interaction between government policy and the financial system.[7]

4.3.1 Central Bank Rate

Conventional central bank policy has been to adjust the short-term interest rate, and over the last 20–30 years before the financial crisis, they had been using this policy to target inflation. Long-term bond yields are affected by inflation because inflation will erode the value of a bond. This applies both to the level of inflation and to the uncertainty of what the level will be. The policy of central banks has been a success. It has been in place for a long time and therefore is credible, and inflation has indeed been bought under control in all developed countries. The effect is self-reinforcing: because inflation is under control, people's expectations of inflation reduce, and therefore, workers' wage demands go down too, which reduces inflation even more.[8] This explains the reduction in nominal bond yields, not real bond yields, which are inflation proofed.

In Chapter 3, I also mentioned the Greenspan Put, where the former Chairman of the Federal Reserve, Alan Greenspan, consistently reduced interest rates after asset price problems but didn't increase them in the same way during asset bubbles. He was in part able to do this because globalisation – plus the action of the Chinese Central Bank – had stabilised prices of goods, which meant that inflation didn't increase when the Fed reduced its rates. His policy coincided with a large increase in savings by central banks in emerging markets increasing the supply of money and further putting downward pressure on interest rates.

Finally, since the financial crisis, central banks have been engaged in what they call "unconventional monetary policies". Their main weapon of choice has been Quantitative Easing (QE), where they have injected money into the economy, by buying financial assets, mainly government bonds, with newly created money. The scale of QE has been enormous. The US central bank, the Federal Reserve, alone has increased the size of its balance sheet by $3 trillion dollars.[9] The result of this has been to reduce long-term interest rates.

Why have central banks intervened to reduce interest rates and to engage in unconventional policies, beyond their inflation-targeting mandate? The Greenspam Put was employed to contain damage from financial markets. For example, in 2000 the dotcom bubble burst and the equity market crashed. The Fed reduced interest rates to reduce the impact of the crash on the wider economy. So this decline in rates was caused firstly by the "irrational exuberance" of the markets which led to the bubble and subsequent crash, and because the Fed thought that this warranted a reduction in interest rates.[10] This chapter and the previous chapter have been arguing that savings, which make up the investments in the equity markets, are either from government institutions or are there because of encouragement from governments. It is those savings which were invested in an irrationally exuberant way which caused the bubble, the subsequent crash and the reduction in interest rates.

The incidence of QE post the financial crash of 2008 essentially has the same causation writ large. The story of this chapter and the previous one has been that governments have directly saved or encouraged their citizens to save and then defined the way that they do so. These savings were invested by professional asset managers into mortgaged backed securities, which led to the financial crisis when they blew up. That in turn has led to QE and ultra-low interest rates. The investment banks which sold those securities, and the banks which created the mortgages, were publicly listed companies owned by the same asset owners and invested in these banks on their behalf by the same asset managers.

In summary, governments have employed the private sector to reduce the fiscal burden of an ageing population, but this has been rendered impossible by ultra-low interest rates. If these ultra-low interest rates are the fault of the central bank, it is because of deliberate government inflation-targeting policy, or because of the central bank reacting to the poor decisions made by the same finance sector which is managing these savings as delegated by governments.

4.3.2 The Natural Rate

Some economists have suggested that central banks are not wholly responsible for declining and low interest rates; the natural interest rate has been on the decline as well. In this section, I shall run through the explanations given by economists for this low natural interest rate, showing that by and large these are ultimately caused either directly by government policies or indirectly by governments' decision to save via the financial sector.

The argument goes that there are various structural reasons in the global economy that has caused the interest rate to reduce over time. A recent paper by the Bank of England works through the possible structural reasons put forward for the reduction of the natural interest rate.[11] These can be summarised as follows:

- *Low global growth*: The expected rate of future global growth has reduced. This is because there will be a lower increase in the labour supply and a reduction in the pace of technological progress. These reduce the interest rate because – if people are expecting lower future growth – they have to save more to smooth consumption.

  Savings glut: There is an increase in global savings; all things being equal more savings push up the demand for financial assets which reduces their yield and hence interest rates. The following factors are suggested as causes of the savings glut:
  Demographics: There is currently a large number of working age people compared to dependents, but that population is ageing, people are living longer and having less children. This means that people save more for their retirement.
  Inequality: Within countries there is increased inequality. If poor people's income increases, they spend more of this income as they need to buy basic necessities and luxuries that they could not afford before. But if rich

people's income increases, they already have all these things, so save more of this increased income than poor people do.

Emerging markets savings glut: Many emerging market countries were burned by the Asian crisis of 1997. Since then many emerging market countries have adopted policies to increase the savings rate and build up reserves to make sure that they are not hit by future crisis.

- *Reduced investment*: The interest rate is also affected by the level of investment. More investment will increase demand for capital, which will increase the level of the interest rate. The following factors have been suggested that have reduced demand for investment:

  Capital goods: The relative price of capital goods has reduced due to mechanisation. This means the same amount of output has been achieved for less investment, causing the level of investment to drop.

  Government investment: There has been a trend of reduced investment by government.

  Increased spread: Though the risk-free rate on government bonds has dropped, the rate at which companies can borrow has decreased by less. The difference between the two rates, the yield spread, has increased.

These are the reasons given by economists why interest rates have been going down. All are plausible, and I am sure that a combination of the above has caused this reduction, although it is difficult to know which is the most important.

There are some themes running through the explanations: demographic factors, namely the ageing population, are cited as a cause of low economic growth and high savings. But the literature suggests, as described above, that people are myopic and save too little, which is why governments intervene to get people to save, in an attempt to avert demographic problems. This demographic situation contributes to the reduction in interest rates, increasing the cost of a pension, which implies that encouraging people to save via the financial system is self-defeating.

The second group of explanations involves excess savings. The argument is the same here: the excess savings has caused the interest rate to go down, making savings via the financial system ineffective. This is either because governments have forced savings for their own reason (the emerging market savings glut) or in a futile attempt to solve the ageing population problem.

The other explanation within this group is inequality; in Chapter 9 I will argue that this is an outcome of financial system. The finance system has driven pay inequality, has caused a reduction in interest rates which increases the wealth of the wealthy, has transferred huge resources to itself and rations the access to cheap finance.

The final group of explanations involves low investment. I shall deal with the ultimate cause of low investment in Chapter 5, which is because savings are not allocated to investment but instead are diverted into financial assets.

In summary, governments have employed the private sector to reduce the fiscal burden of an ageing population, but this has been rendered impossible by ultra-low interest rates. These ultra-low interest rates are caused by governments' policies to encourage or enforce savings via the financial system, which has led to a savings glut; these savings have not been soaked up by investment, which is not surprising when we investigate where savings are invested in Chapter 5.

The next section considers the bill for this unaffordable pension, the amount that you pay to financial intermediaries.

4.4 A Disappearing Pension

A saver benefits from tax relief on contributions- she doesn't pay income tax on her contributions paid into her pension, the investment return that the fund makes is not taxed and, when she retires, she can take some of her fund tax free.

On the other hand, the fund manager charges a fee for managing the money. An annual charge might be, say, 1.5% of the fund, which does not sound very much at all. Yet, you don't buy a pension fund for just a year. You are in the system until you die, which could be another 50 years, and a fee is paid every year. Assuming a saver starts contributing at age 25, retires at 65 and is paid a pension for another 20 years, then a 1.5% annual fee would represent 37.5% of the fund. Her pension would be 60% higher if there were no fees.[12]

How does this happen? If she contributes £1,000 per year, rising with inflation, by the time she retires, her pension pot would be worth £248,170, which would translate into an inflation-linked pension of £16,080 per annum – if there were no fees associated with her pension. But when the fees are taken out, the fund would only be worth £174,556, purchasing her a pension of £9,901 per year.[13]

The figures I have just quoted were published in a report by the RSA. This report was heavily criticised by the pensions industry, mainly because typically AMCs are less than 1.5%. A subsequent report found that both savers and providers think (incorrectly) that the AMC represents the total annual costs of a pension fund.[14] Because this 1.5% figure is indeed wrong: the real cost of a pension is actually much greater.

A pension fund is invested in a variety of assets, as described in Chapter 2. A fund buys and sells these assets constantly and, every time it does so, there are transaction costs. For example, a fund invested in equity has an average turnover of 60%. This proportion of any given pension fund is bought and sold in any given year. When every transaction is made, there is a commission, a bid/offer spread, an impact on the price of the security and stamp duty to pay and other related costs.

The expert in the subject, David Pitt-Watson, estimates that there are 16 different agents "to shepherd our money from an account…there are money management fees which most of us see, but also marketing fees, transfer agent fees, sub-transfer agent fees, custodial fees, sub-custodial fees, audit fees, mutual fund board fees, valuation agent fees, proxy advisory fees, trading costs, broker fees, administration fees…the list goes on and on".[15]

What is the actual total annual cost of financial intermediation? Amazingly no one seems to know.[16] Even investment managers seem to be in the dark.[17] I have compared estimates in Table 4.3.

Railpen are a large DB scheme, which carried out possibly the most detailed study of fees. It is hard to use their results, because their AMC was quite low (they are a large scheme), so it isn't whether typical charges would be three to four times a higher fee or the additional fees are the same whoever the investor is. Therefore, taking an average of the other studies, we get a rough estimate of 2.7%.

These are all estimates of the fees on (public) equity funds. The overall fees in some form of assets will be higher than this, and in others lower. If we use this figure of 2.7% a year, we get the shocking figure that over 60% of a pension is eaten up by costs.[18] A typical pension would be nearly twice as large if there were no charges.

Table 4.3 Estimates of annual fees of equity funds

Source	Fee estimate
Railpen (2014)[23]	3–4 times annual management charge
Sier and Norman (2011)	3.1%
Khorana, Servaes and Tufano (2009)[24]	2.28%
True and Fair Campaign (2014)[25]	2.7%
Edelen, Evans and Kadlec (2013)[26]	2.63%

Not all fees are so large. If you are a member of a company pension scheme, or the Government's new auto-enrolment scheme the NEST, for example the annual charge will be lower. Fees on "tracker" funds, which are managed by a computer programme which follows an index, are also lower. Furthermore, the government has attempted to cap the annual charge at 0.75% for workplace pensions.

From the saver's perspective, you have to ask whether she is really smoothing lifetime consumption by contributing to a pension, when over half of her money is instead helping to fund her asset manager's consumption.

4.4.1 Things Fall Apart

It may be quite reasonable for fund managers to be paid. They are providing a service after all. But I would question whether they are offering value for money. Figure 4.3 shows the performance of the index of the leading shares on the UK equity market over the last 30 years.

Figure 4.3 shows that between 1984 and 2000, the market increased in value by six times, approximately 11% per year. In that time, fees of 2.7% per annum would have been masked by the performance of the market. The annual return would simply be reduced by fees, but if you invested in an average fund in the market you would still get a nice return of around 8% a year. Since that time, the market has fluctuated, but there has been only a small upward trend.[19] In such a situation, the 2.7% costs will actually reduce the value of the fund, unless fund managers can consistently beat the market and produce returns in excess of charges. Study after study has shown that, on average, managers don't outperform the market.[20] In fact, a recent survey found that 99% of actively managed funds underperformed the market over the last 10 years.[21]

Historic good performance was down to the market, not the skill of the fund manager. It is true that there are some good fund managers, but it is not possible to predict in advance who will be good in specific circumstances. Often a fund manager who performs well under one set of circumstances does badly when the economic environment changes.

If we have entered a new norm of low returns, then our pensions will dwindle because of fees. Not saving for a pension in this context would seem to be a wise choice, especially for less affluent people for whom the tax advantage is not so valuable. By introducing mandatory pension schemes or auto-enrolment type arrangements such as NEST, governments are not

4.4 A Disappearing Pension 95

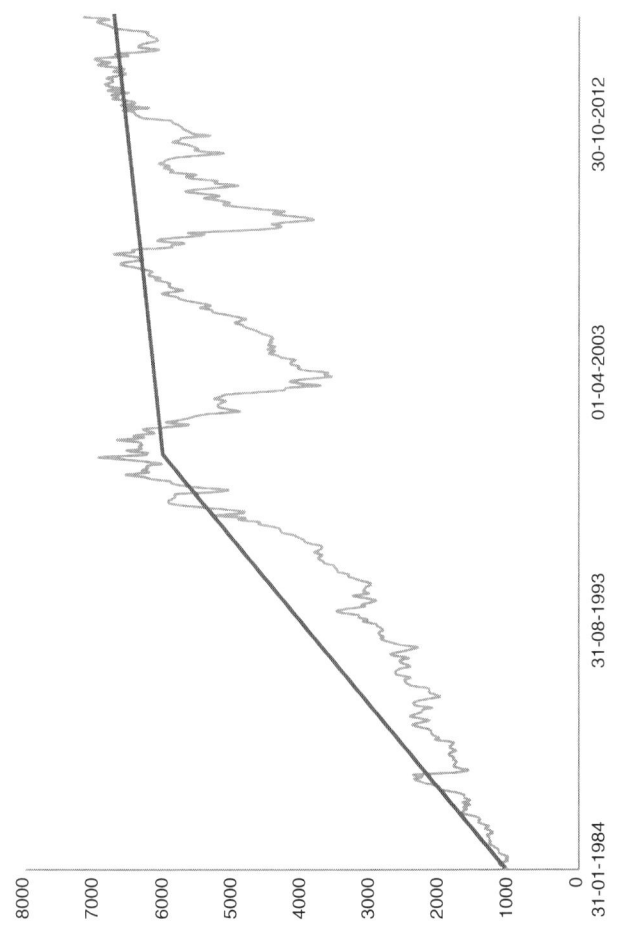

Fig. 4.3 FTSE 100 index

Source: FTSE

helping people to help themselves but are helping the financial services industry make more money at the expense of savers.

The irony is that in driving down interest rates to near zero, the savings industry has rendered its own business model unviable. As returns are driven lower and lower, costs become more apparent and are squeezed and it becomes harder for asset managers to outperform. Savers will withdraw their money and governments will be put under pressure to justify why they are forcing or encouraging people to save in a system which is patently not working.

4.5 Where Do We Go from Here

Governments encourage people to save for a pension, to reduce the future fiscal burden from an ageing population. This clearly isn't working, because they have only managed to persuade rich people to save, the very section of society who would not be a burden when they retire as they can afford to look after themselves.

The problem is the result of the savings glut, caused by governments encouraging people to save, in combination with the way that central banks are acting to try and repair the damage done by the same savings being mismanaged. Together, this combination of factors has driven down interest rates below zero, making pensions unaffordable.

At least in failing to persuade non-rich people to save for a pension, the majority of the population are safe from the clutches of the financial services industry. The current pensions industry makes your pension disappear in charges, so it is people who do not save for a pension that are the sensible ones. In the absence of a functioning pensions system, it is actually very difficult for people to know what to do. I discuss possible alternatives in Chapter 10. The government are trying to correct the accidental good outcome of the failure to get people to save by introducing auto-enrolment pensions and defaulting people into a pension fund.

If the corrosion by the financial services industry of our pensions is larceny, the scale is huge. The UK manages £6.2 trillion.[22] If 2.7% disappears as fees, that is £167 billion every year. If half of that ends up as fees over its lifetime, that is £3.1 trillion.

The alternative, PAYGO systems, has been widely criticised. But if they are well governed, with appropriate checks and balances, they provide a much cheaper and more efficient alternative, which can provide pensions which meet people's needs. In Chapter 10, when I discuss remedies for our current financial travails, I describe such a system in more detail.

This chapter dealt with the UK pensions sector. What about the other classes of asset owners (insurers, SWFs, endowments and all the rest of them)? And what about non-UK pensions? Like pension funds, insurance companies do have fixed liabilities. But they do tend to be more short term, so they are more likely to be invested in more liquid instruments, where the costs will be lower. Also, insurance companies often invest their own assets, so can keep a handle on fees. On the other hand, they suffer from low interest rates as they cannot make a return on their assets, and any investment outsourced to investment managers will suffer from the same charges as pension funds.

The other asset owners do not have fixed liabilities, but they do have implicit liabilities. At some point, they will be converted to spending. In which case, because of low interest rates, they will suffer from the same inability or expense of earning a return. They will also be eroded by the high charges.

The UK pension system is characterised by much of the provision being outsourced to the private sector, which is typical of Anglo Saxon types of economies, such as the USA and Australia. There are some countries, such as Holland and Denmark, which have done a much better job of controlling fees than the UK. But all countries suffer the same low interest rates and hence expense of paying a pension. The alternative model, the PAYGO system, is typically favoured in continental Europe. A functioning PAYGO system is not a given: France is one of many countries which has a PAYGO system which, in its way, is just as disastrous as the UKs pension system.

The economy requires people to save so that the country has a capital pool with which it can usefully invest facilitating future economic growth. As we have seen, this capital allocation is entrusted to the financial sector, which extracts such a large fee for its services. The next chapter will investigate how well it does this, or indeed if it does this at all.

Pensions form part of the larger assets management industry. Pension funds and other savings are invested for the long term by professional asset managers. These asset managers should exercise a benign stewardship of the companies that their funds own, where they oversee and set incentives so that the companies they invest in are managed in the long-term interests of their beneficiaries. In the next chapter, I shall investigate how the industry sets incentives for company management to enrich themselves and the investment management industry, to the detriment of the companies and the rest of society.

Notes

1. Index Mundi: http://www.indexmundi.com/taiwan/total_fertility_rate.html accessed as at 5 December 2016.
2. See for example Robert Holzmann and Richard Hinz (2005) *Old-Age Income Support in the Twenty-First Century: An International Perspective on Pensions and Reform* World Bank.
3. See for example Robert Holzmann and Richard Hinz (2005) *Old-Age Income Support in the Twenty-First Century: An International Perspective on Pensions and Reform* World Bank.
4. Drucker (1976) *The Unseen Revolution: How Pension Fund Socialism Came to America* (New York: Harper & Row).
5. Pensions Policy Institute: http://www.pensionspolicyinstitute.org.uk/pension-facts/pension-facts-tables/private-pensions-table-27 accessed on 5 December 2016.
6. Data from Pension Protection Fund, quoted in This is Money http://www.thisismoney.co.uk/money/pensions/article-3686601/Total-deficit-final-salary-schemes-soars-90bn-384bn-Brexit-hits-funds.html
7. I have used the summary provided by Rachel, L and Smith, T (2015) *Secular drivers of the global real interest rate* Bank of England Staff Working Paper No 57.
8. Mishkin, F and Posen, A (1998) *Inflation Targeting: Lessons from Four Countries* NBER Working Paper No. 6126 and Fouejieu A and Roger, S (2013) *Inflation Targeting and Country Risk: an Empirical Investigation* International Monetary Fund Working Paper.
9. The Economist 9 March 2015 "What is quantitative easing?": http://www.economist.com/blogs/economist-explains/2015/03/economist-explains-5
10. Shiller, R (2000) *Irrational exuberance* Princeton University Press.
11. I have used Rachel, L and Smith, D (2015) *Secular Drivers of the global real interest rate* Bank of England Working Paper number 571 as a good summary.
12. My example is taken from a recent report: RSA (2010) *Tomorrow's Investor: Pensions for the people: addressing the savings and investment crisis in Britain* Royal Society of Arts. When this report came out, it was heavily criticised for using a figure of 1.5%, as most annual management charges are less than this. However, the average Total expense ratio on UK equity funds is actually higher, so this figure is conservative.
13. RSA (2010) *Tomorrow's Investor: Pensions for the people: addressing the savings and investment crisis in Britain* Royal Society of Arts
14. RSA (2012) *Seeing through Britain's pensions* Royal Society of Arts.
15. Value Edge Advisors *Nell Minow Interviews the Authors of "What They Do With Your Money"* https://valueedgeadvisors.com/2016/06/22/nell-minow-

interviews-the-authors-of-what-they-do-with-your-money/ accessed 5 December 2016.
16. Financial Services Consumer Panel (2014) *Investment Costs – More than Meets the Eye* http://www.trueandfaircampaign.com/wp-content/uploads/2014/11/financial-services-consumer-panel-discussion-paper-investment-costs.pdf
17. Lane Clark & Peacock (May 2013) *LCP Investment Management Fees Survey 2013.*
23. Professional Pensions http://www.professionalpensions.com/professional-pensions/news/2362085/railpen-to-reduce-external-managers-over-fee-concerns accessed 5 December 2016.
24. Total charges in UK from Khorana, A., H. Servaes and P. Tufano (March 2009), "Mutual Funds Fees Around the World", Review of Financial Studies, Vol. 22, Issue 3, 1279–1310.
25. True and Fair Campaign (2014) *2nd Anniversary Report – Legalised Looting* http://www.trueandfaircampaign.com/wp-content/uploads/2014/03/true-and-fair-campaign-2nd-anniversary-report-legalised-looting-march-2014.pdf
26. I have added the paper's estimate of average trading cost to expense ratio Edelen, R. Evans, R. & Kadlec, G. (2013) *Shedding Light on Invisible Costs: Trading Costs and Mutual Fund Performance.*
18. I have differed in my approach here from RSA; RSA compares funds at retirement; however, fees continue to be deducted after retirement which I have included.
19. I must admit that I have been somewhat selective in my choice of index here, for example at the time of writing the main US index, the S&P 500 is soaring because of the "Trump effect", which says a lot about the rationality of the markets.
20. For example, see Lipper (2012) *Beating the Benchmark.*
21. Financial Times 24 October 2016 *99% of actively managed US equity funds underperform* https://www.ft.com/content/e139d940-977d-11e6-a1dc-bdf38d484582 accessed 5 December 2016.
22. UKTI (2015) *Fund management in the UK* https://www.gov.uk/government/uploads/system/uploads/attachment_data/file/478378/UKTI_Asset_mgmt_broch_B5_RC_AW_DIGIAL.pdf accessed 5 December 2016.

5

La Grande Illusion

How the Financial System Does Not Invest Savings

An individual saves into a pension to smooth lifetime consumption so that she can have an income after she stops working, paid for by accepting lower consumption when working. From a government's point of view, the purpose of encouraging saving into a private pension is to reduce the future fiscal burden of an ageing population – when there will be less workers to support more pensioners. Chapter 4 showed that the current system is failing as saving for a decent pension has become unaffordable because of low interest rates, the fiscal burden is not reduced because only the rich, who will look after themselves anyway, save for a pension and the savings industry takes a large chunk, perhaps the majority, of savings as fees.

There is another reason for outsourcing the allocation of capital to the private sector, which I call the **pensions deal**. Society encourages and subsidises people to save via the financial sector. In return the financial sector allocates those savings efficiently, so that those savings are invested with those who can best make use of it. This efficient investment enables the economy to grow, ensuring that the economy becomes large enough to pay decent pensions when the savers retire. The private sector seeks the best returns, as this is how it makes a profit for itself, ensuring that investments are placed with enterprises that are able to generate these returns. The savings/investment market ensures that capital is being used efficiently to generate economic growth.

This need is crucial when societies are faced with an ageing population, when there is a declining proportion of workers to retirees, the remaining workers have to be more productive, and this increased productivity can only be achieved by effective investment. This chapter investigates whether this occurs in practice.

Chapter 4 dealt with UK pensions; in this chapter I will continue to use UK pensions as my example. However, the analysis of this chapter applies generally to all the asset owners described in Chapter 2; these institutions delegate the management of their assets to professional asset managers, with the aim to achieve long-term sustainable returns.

5.1 What Your Pension Doesn't Do

The economy needs people to save so that it has a pool of long-term investment, which in turn is required to generate economic development. When people retire, the economy can then afford to pay people a decent pension. This is particularly important in the case of an ageing population, where a shrinking number of people of working age will have to generate enough income to pay an increasing number of elderly dependents. If these workers are more productive, each worker could produce a larger amount of economic output to compensate for there being fewer workers.

Let's take a very basic economic model, where economic output is a function of labour and capital, so if the labour stock decreases, output can be kept up by increasing the capital stock through savings. When people retire *en masse*, they will take their money out over time and the capital stock will no longer increase either. However, if savings are wisely invested, productivity will increase so that by the time people retire, the economy will still be able produce enough output with a shrinking workforce.

The ability of the economy to be able to afford to pay decent pensions depends on savings being put to productive use; it has to be invested in such a way that future workers will be more productive. If savings were being used to pay people to dig holes and fill them up again, this would not increase productivity. However, we do not even have to consider whether investments made by the financial system are productive or not, because it turns out that most savings are not actually invested at all.

Figure 5.1 shows how pensions are invested by asset class in the seven largest pension fund markets: 52% is invested in equity, that is stocks and shares of publicly listed companies, 29% is invested in bonds, that is traded debt of governments and companies, 18% is invested in alternatives – mainly

5.1 What Your Pension Doesn't Do 103

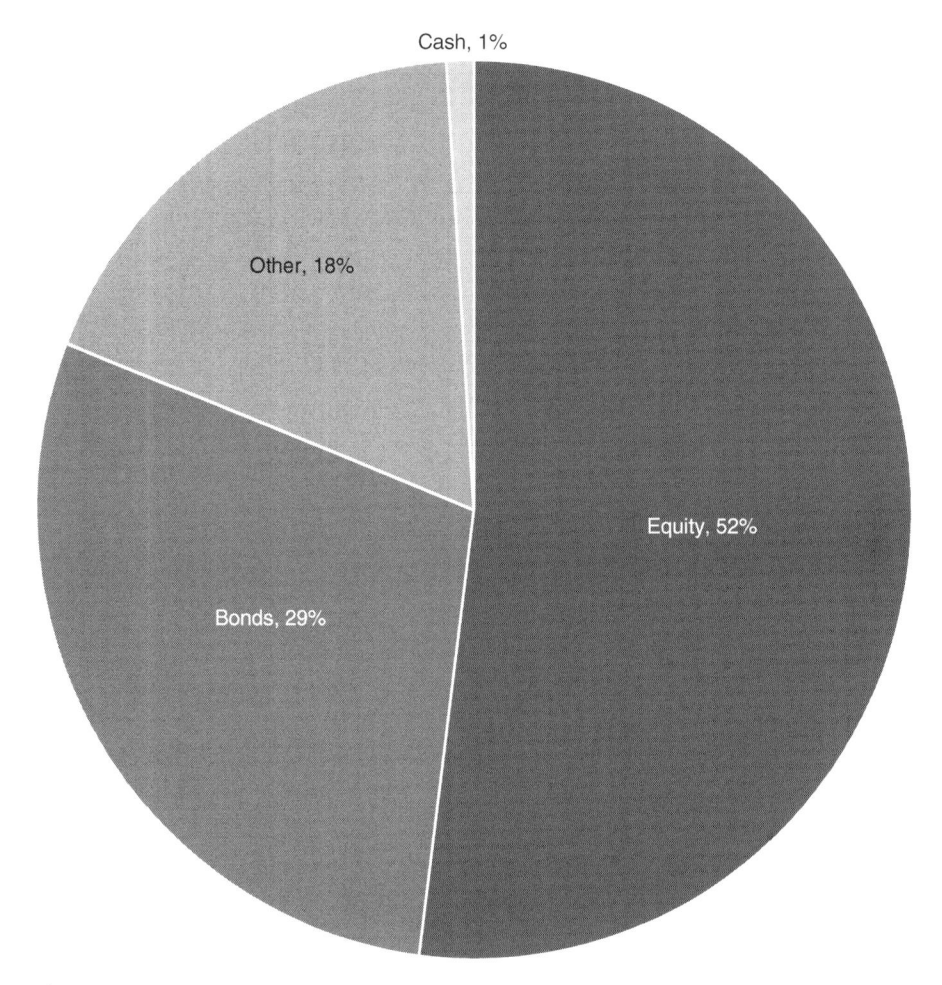

Fig. 5.1 Asset allocation by pension funds
Source: Towers Watson
P7 countries; Source: Towers Watson (2014) *Global Pensions Asset Study*

hedge funds, property, private equity and commodities and 1% is in cash. I shall deal with each of these in turn, investigating whether any of these investments contribute to the future productivity of the economy.[1]

5.1.1 Equity Investment

Fifty-two per cent of pension fund investment is into equity, that is, into the shares of publicly listed companies. Investing in the shares of these companies contributes to the future development of the economy in two ways.

Companies can directly use the money to invest in "real" assets, for example factories, call centres or research and development. Secondly, the prospect of listing encourages entrepreneurs like Mark Zuckerberg to build companies which they can then sell and get richly rewarded.

Equity has come to be perceived as being an expensive form of finance and is only used as a last resort by companies. There are two methods by which companies can raise finance from equity – rights issues and IPOs or placements. A rights issue is where companies create new shares and ask existing shareholder to buy them. This is unpopular with shareholders as it dilutes existing holdings and is therefore hardly ever done. For example, if a company has 100 million shares which are worth £1 each, the company's market capitalisation (the total value of its shares) would be £100 million. If it then issues another 100 million shares at 75 pence (this has to be below £1 to induce people to buy it) then its market capitalisation is £175 million (the £100 million plus the extra £75 million raised), and each share is now worth 87.5 pence (£175 million market capitalisation divided by 200 million shares). Existing shares are reduced in value from £1 to 87.5 pence, and the shareholders will not be happy about this as they will lose money – so a rights issue is seen as a desperate measure when companies really are in trouble and it's difficult for them to raise money from other sources.

An IPO is where a company offers shares to the market – this could be a company which is listing for the first time, like Facebook in 2012, or an existing company. An IPO differs from a rights issue as new shares are not created; for example, Manchester United Football Club was owned approximately 90% by the Glazer family and listed on the New York Stock Exchange. Recently, one of the family members decided to sell approximately 10% of the stock, a pension fund could buy this and the Glazer family would own 80% of the shares[2] – unlike a rights issue, no new shares have been created, so the rest of the Glazer family's existing holding has not been diluted. Placements are alternatives to IPOs, where one or a group of institutions agree to buy all of the issuance.

Rights issues and IPOs/Placements can be used by companies to raise cash to invest. IPOs, but not rights issues, reward investors or management for building up the company.

The market capitalisation of the London Stock Exchange, that is the total value of the UK's publicly listed equity market (including international listed), was £3.9 trillion at the end of 2015. The total issuance on the London Stock exchange, including rights issuance, placements and IPOs in 2015 was £28 billion, that is 0.7% of the market.[3]

We can think of the equity market as a stock of capital – a portion of the nation's saving that could potentially be used by publicly listed companies for useful investment. This stock of capital is valued at £3.9 trillion. However, only 0.7% a year is actually drawn down by companies and used for investment. About 99.3% of the equity stock remains as virtual assets, circulating the financial system – with estimates that around 90% are being churned every year by an average equity portfolio.[4]

Rather than investing, many companies are engaged in returning money to shareholders, either through share buy-backs; that is purchasing shares from shareholders, or by acquiring companies for cash in takeovers. This is a disinvestment by companies; they are returning investment to the shareholders and reducing the amount of equity, the opposite of a rights issue or IPO. When you net-off this against new issuance, the result is that there has been a negative investment in companies via the equity market in 8 of the last 11 years.[5]

For the economy to grow, investment is required in "real" assets. Most real assets decline in value with time through depreciation and obsolescence, and the economy requires investment in research and development, new infrastructure and new products and services to grow and enhance standards of living. In aggregate, the equity markets are a place where companies liquidate real assets to pay shareholders.

5.1.2 Bond Investment

The next largest asset class is bond investment at 29% of the average portfolio. A bond is a specific type of tradable debt security. The issuer, normally a government or large corporation, agrees to pay specified fixed amounts to the holder of the bond, as was described in Chapter 2.

Corporates and governments can borrow money via the bond market, the proceeds of which can then be used for investment. Hopefully, this investment will be invested in the economy, which will provide sustainable growth so that the economy will be able to pay pensions.

Figure 5.2 shows the current split of the UK bond market between different sectors. By far, the majority, 79%, of the bond market is government or quasi-government debt.

The government debt is an accumulation of past deficits, each year if the spending of the government is higher than its revenue, the resultant government deficit has to be funded, usually through the issuance of government bonds. In 2015, the UK government's deficit was £74 billion,[6] which is the amount that the government funds through debt issuance in the year, much of which is bought by pension funds. The deficit over the last few years has been anomalously high

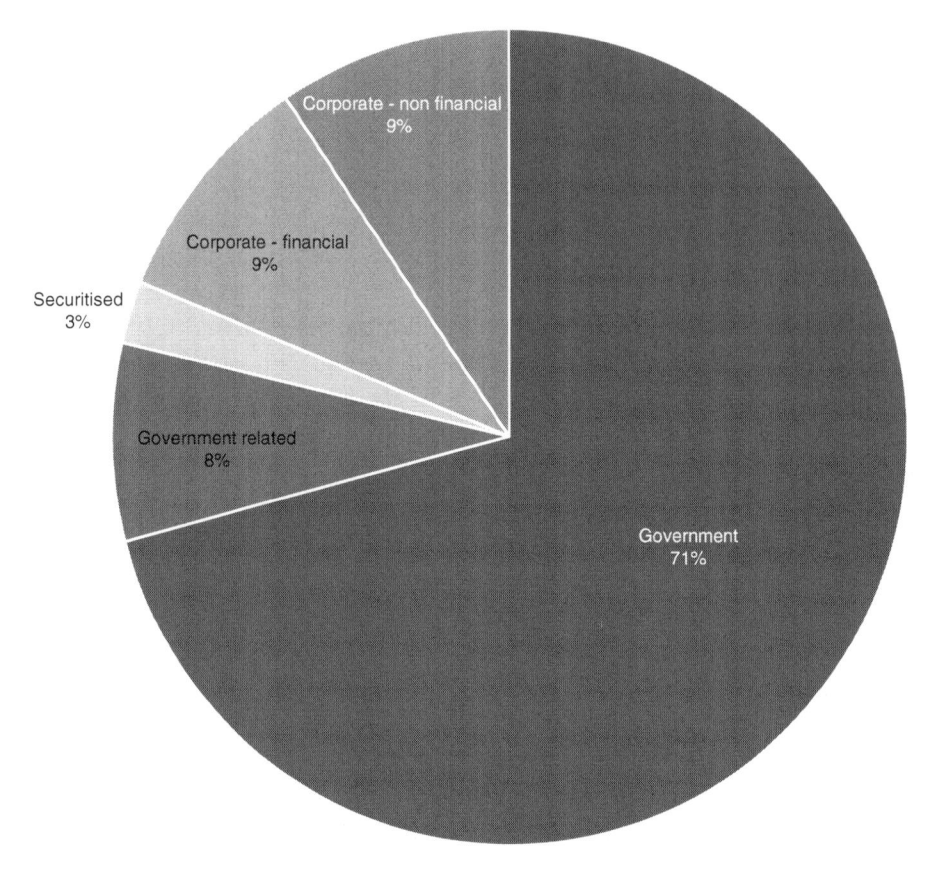

Fig. 5.2 UK bond market split by sector
Source: Barclays
Data from Bloomberg/Barclays UK aggregate index, with corporate bonds split approximately 50/50 between financial and non-financial from as suggested by https://www.youinvest.co.uk/market-research/LSE:IBCX?tab=13

because of the financial crisis (which incidentally was largely the fault of the financial services industry). Figure 5.3 shows the history of government deficits.

In many years, the government could eliminate the deficit by abolishing direct subsidies to the financial sector, which this book argues are damaging to the economy. For example, to encourage people to save for a pension, the government gives tax rebates and other incentives, which are estimated to be worth £40 billion per year (Table 5.1). If these tax incentives are abolished, this extra tax would go directly into the government's coffers, reducing the current deficit to £34 billion. These ignore implicit subsidies – for example, the value to banks of the implicit guarantee that they will be bailed out

5.1 What Your Pension Doesn't Do   107

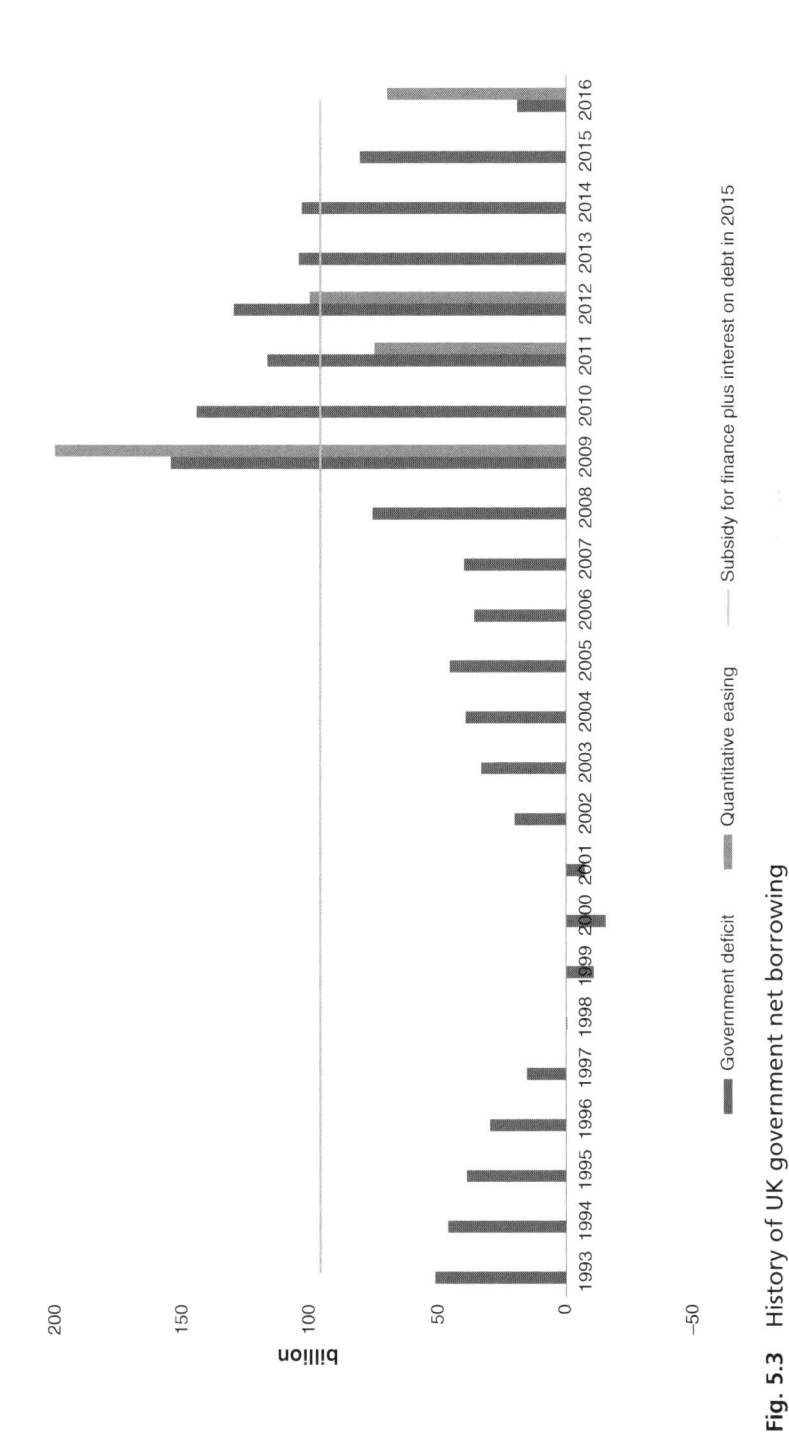

Fig. 5.3 History of UK government net borrowing

Source: Office for National Statistics and Bank of England
Quoted in House of Commons Library (2016) *Quantitative Easing* Debate Pack Number CDP 2016/0166, 14 September 2016

5 La Grande Illusion

Table 5.1 Annual government subsidy of finance

Subsidy	Amount (£ billion)
Pension tax relief[a]	36
ISA, VCT and EIS[b]	3
Capital gains tax (CGT) relief for entrepreneur's business disposal[c]	3
Annual exempt amount CGT[d]	4
Total subsidies	**46**
Plus interest on existing debt[e]	50
Total	**96**

[a]Pensions Policy Institute: In 2013/2014 http://www.pensionspolicyinstitute.org.uk/pension-facts/pension-facts-tables/private-pensions-table-27 Accessed 7 December 2012.
[b]Tax Research UK http://www.taxresearch.org.uk/blog/2014/02/06/enough-of-the-cost-of-benefits-what-do-subsidies-to-higher-rate-taxpayers-cost/ Taken from the UK government figures.
[c]Tax Research UK http://www.taxresearch.org.uk/blog/2014/02/06/enough-of-the-cost-of-benefits-what-do-subsidies-to-higher-rate-taxpayers-cost/ Taken from the UK government figures.
[d]Tax Research UK http://www.taxresearch.org.uk/blog/2014/02/06/enough-of-the-cost-of-benefits-what-do-subsidies-to-higher-rate-taxpayers-cost/ Taken from the UK government figures.
[e]UK Public Spending: http://www.ukpublicspending.co.uk/breakdown Accessed 7 December 2012.

should they fail which could be worth as much as £100 billion,[7] and their government-granted mandate to create money, to be covered in Chapter 6, but these do not obviously directly affect the government's ability to reduce its deficit.

Historical and projected deficits are much lower than the current deficit, which is anomalously high due to the fallout from the financial crisis, which is a manifestation of the government's implicit subsidy of the banks and the financial system. As well as the government running a large budget deficit, the Bank of England has reacted to stimulate the economy through QE, that is, buying up financial assets, mostly government bonds, to inject money into the economy. It has been convincingly argued that this has largely been ineffective, a much more effective way would have been for the government to have created money and spent it; although there are governance dangers to this approach.[8] That is in this exceptional time where the UK government deficit has increased, instead of QE, the government could have boosted its spending through money creation.

In "normal" times, by abolishing the subsidy to finance, the government can mostly eliminate its deficit, and in exceptional times, if the government is going to use unconventional monetary policy, it would be better used to eliminate its deficit. Cumulative deficits give rise to unnecessary interest alone on this debt of around £50 billion a year,[9] without this and the direct support that the government gives to finance, it would almost never need to run a deficit.

To be clear, this is not an argument for austerity; without tax rebates supporting finance, we would not have to worry about austerity because government debt levels and deficits would be low or non-existent.

If the government did not give tax incentives on pensions and other financial support for the financial system, it would hardly ever run a deficit and would therefore not need savings from pensions to fund this non-existent deficit. However, even if governments were running large deficits, the idea of funding government debt via pension funds is nonsensical. The government is effectively forcing, encouraging or bribing people to save so that it can borrow money from them. This is very inefficient as there are lots of middlemen, all of whom are taking a cut.

By issuing bonds, the government is effectively borrowing money from future generations. This is all very well if future generations would be much richer than us, but we have seen that because we have an ageing population, there will be less workers in the future who will have to pay back this debt on top of the pensions of the baby boomers. We have previously argued that governments encourage people to save for a pension because it takes the fiscal burden off the government of an ageing population – when pension funds invest in government debt, savers are lending money back to the government and the whole exercise is pointless; the state is simply paying pensioners interest rather than a pension and therefore not reducing the burden of an ageing population at all.

Finally, if funding the government deficit is the main reason for encouraging people to save for their pension, then this would be dishonest; the government is claiming that people should save to help themselves and the economy, when in fact the purpose of this saving is to fund deficit spending.

Government debt represented 79% of the bond market – what about the other 21%? Of this 9% is financial, which I will discuss further in Chapter 6, and 3% is securitised or collateralised. This means that the debt is backed by an asset, and this asset is invariably property. We will also show that this is not a useful investment in Chapter 6. We are therefore left with the remaining 9%. If this 9% is to contribute to future economic growth, how these proceeds are actually used is vitally important.

There is evidence that companies issue debt so that they can return money to pay shareholders,[10] rather than for investment. If companies can borrow money cheaply, they have issued bonds and then engaged in share buy-backs to return this borrowed money to shareholders. There is a correlation between issuance of corporate debt and episodes of share buy-backs in the USA.[11] I am going to ignore this and unrealistically assume in favour of the financial services industry again and assume that this is all put to productive use by the issuers of the debt, even though this seems highly unlikely.

5.1.3 Alternatives

From Figure 5.1, we have seen that alternatives only represent 18% of all pension fund investment, so I will consider these only briefly. Alternatives encompass an array of different assets, the largest being property, hedge funds, commodities, private equity and infrastructure. I shall deal with each in turn.

5.1.3.1 Property

We will consider lending against property in Chapter 6 and concluded that this is no better than a pyramid-selling scheme. Institutional investment in property is slightly different as it is mainly into commercial not residential property, that is offices, retail and industrial. Property funds are mostly invested in already built property and therefore are not contributing productively to the economy.

5.1.3.2 Hedge Funds

Hedge funds are investment funds invested in securities. By definition they differ from normal investment funds in that they can "short" a stock, this means that they can effectively sell a stock that they do not own and hence can get positive returns if that stock's price is going down. This is in contrast to normal pension fund investment which is "long only", which only gets a positive return if the stock increases in value.

A bit of an explanation is required. An option is a contract that you can buy which gives you the right to buy an asset at a certain date for a certain price. So, if you have an option to buy shares in Facebook on 1 January 2018 for $100, this means that if on 1 January 2018, Facebook shares are worth less than $100, your option is worth nothing, but if they are worth more, your option is valuable. So for example, if the price of Facebook is $120, you could buy shares at $100 and immediately sell them for $120, making a $20 profit. In reality you do not have to do this, you just cash in your option, making $20. This is called a call option, a put option is where you have the right to sell your option at the stated price. So, if you have a put option to sell Facebook shares at $100, and Facebook's value is only $80, you would make $20.

A future is the other side of the contract, if you own a future of to sell at $100 on 1 January 2018, you have to sell at this price, whatever the price of the underlying stock.

The original purpose of options and futures is to "hedge" risk (hence "hedge" fund), so if you are a farmer, for example, and want to guarantee the price of your crop against a sudden crash in the market, you could buy put options to protect your position; this would guarantee a minimum price that your produce would achieve when it comes to market. Options are still used for this purpose, but the main use of options nowadays is for speculative purposes.

Typically, hedge funds deal a lot more in options than non-hedge funds, and unlike non-hedge funds they are able to buy "uncovered" put options or futures, contracts to sell a stock without holding the underlying stock. For example, I might buy an option to sell Marks and Spenser's shares for £5.00 on 31 October. If the price of the shares is £4.50 on this date, the option would be worth 50 pence (as I can buy the shares for £4.50 and immediately sell them for £5.00, making a 50-pence profit). This is a highly leveraged position, if the option cost me 10 pence, I could lose all my investment if the share was priced higher than £5.00 on 31 October or I could multiply my investment many times (500% in the example).

Hedge funds tend to take bigger positions than normal "long only" pension fund investment and tend to be more short term and are more opaque as to their modus operandi. They can also offer more specialist services such as liability-driven investment where they tailor the profile of the fund using options. They typically charge more for their services – a hedge fund often charges on the 2/20 model – that is an annual management fee of 2% and 20% of any profits. In terms of where the money goes, they are like equity investment, but more so. Hedge funds are more abstracted from the actual "real" operation of the economy, money invested in a hedge fund is even less likely to find its way into "real" assets, hedge funds are even more absentee than other asset owners (although we will see later that there is a subgrouping of hedge funds which are activist owners).

5.1.3.3 Private Equity

Private equity is where companies are taken out of public ownership and held privately. The aim of private equity is to increase the return on capital of the company and normally, at some point, the company is sold on. The weapon of choice of private equity is the leveraged buy-out (LBO).

Say a company is worth £100 million, and makes £10 million profit – its price/earnings (PE) ratio is 10 (100 divided by 10). A private equity firm might buy this company, with say £20 million of equity and £80 million debt. If the firm can then increase the profit, to say £15 million, net of interest, and if the company can be sold at a PE of 10, it is now worth £70 million (£15 million profit times PE of 10 less debt of £80 million). But the private equity firm only paid £20 million, so its investment has multiplied by 350%.

If you think this is some kind of trick, you would be right. Like hedge funds, private equity employs leverage to increase returns. Rather than leverage at the share level, private equity leverages the companies that it owns. Private equity can be highly profitable to private equity investors, but it does not represent investment into the real economy.

5.1.3.4 Commodities

I find it hard to find an argument against why investments in commodities will increase the economy's productivity, because I cannot think of any argument justifying why they could possibly be a productive investment. When institutional investors invest in commodities, they do not buy the physical commodities but they buy a future in the commodity. So, for example, if a pension fund decided to invest in oil, it would not take physical possession of tankers of oil. What it would do is buy an exchange traded fund (ETF) on the price of oil. This is a financial construct which shadows the price of oil, based on options/futures contracts. So, if you bought an ETF at $60 per barrel, and the price of oil went up to $100, you could sell the ETF and make $40 profit. I find it hard to differentiate between this form of investment, speculation and gambling.

5.1.3.5 Infrastructure

At last – an investment class which is unambiguously investment in the future of the economy! Without differentiating between sustainable and unsustainable infrastructure, for argument sake I shall accept all infrastructure investment, uncritically, as contributing to the future development of the economy, that is all 1% of it.[12]

5.1.3.6 International Investment

Investment in each of the asset class described above is either in the home economy or a foreign economy. For example, UK pension funds invest nearly 60% of their equity investment in foreign assets, whereas nearly

90% of bond investment is domestic.[13] This is reciprocal, as 41% of the UK equity market is owned by foreign investors.

There is going to be a qualitative difference between equity investment in emerging market and developed economies. The figures quoted above for IPOs and rights issues for the UK market are broadly similar in developed markets.[14] Emerging markets, on the other hand, are by definition less developed and therefore are more likely to be directly investing. However, only a small proportion of investment is actually into emerging markets (13% in 2011 from UK investors).[15]

The fact that a large proportion of investment is international does not therefore change the situation.

5.1.4 The Reckoning

Governments want and need people to save for a pension to build up a capital pool which is then invested in the economy, which is essential for economic growth. This is one of the reasons why governments encourage people to save for a pension, which in turn is a great boon to the financial services industry. The maximum proportion of pension fund investment that might be being used productively is summarised in Table 5.2.

Thus, 3.85% of pension fund investment is actually used by the economy, and this is a maximum figure, we have not investigated whether this investment is actually put to productive use. The figure is almost definitely an overestimate, as companies are returning money to shareholders via share buy-backs, so the equity figure should be negative, and much of the corporate bond issuance is to fund this share buy-back activity. The pension fund industry is there to invest people's money, yet it actually invests less than 4% in the "real" economy.[16]

Table 5.2 shows that almost all pensions savings go into secondary financial markets, which do serve an important economic function. Investors should be willing to provide cheaper capital to primary

Table 5.2 Proportion of pension fund investment that is productive

	Proportion of pension fund invested
New issuance in the equity market: 0.5% of 52% (invested in equity)	0.25%
Non-financial corporate bonds: 9% of 29% (invested in bonds)	2.6%
Infrastructure investment	1%
Total	**3.85%**

investments, such as new businesses or infrastructure, knowing that they can sell on into liquid capital markets. But the balance is wrong – this on–selling is minuscule. Secondary markets also ensure a market price, so that assets, including primary investments, are allocated efficiently; but if these are not real market prices, for example if the market interest rate merely reflects investors anticipating what central banks will do, then this is not exactly useful information which will ensure efficient capital allocation. An argument that governments should support savings merely to ensure secondary market liquidity seems very weak.

5.2 What Your Money Does Do

La Grande Illusion of investment is that at least 96% of investments by pension funds are not used for investment. The pension deal is that society supports pension savings into the private sector as these contribute to the development of the economy. The money is not being used for investment so it does not directly contribute to the development of the economy.

Pension funds own assets which make up a large proportion of the economy and because of this ownership they exert a strong influence on how underlying companies are managed. If they exert a benign influence on the companies that they own and ensure that publicly listed companies are well managed and make wise investments, then they will contribute to the future development of the economy and hence its ability to pay pensions.

Company securities and government bonds are traded in financial markets. Because the market knows best, companies are given a signal through the price of their shares. When a company makes the right choices, it will be rewarded by the market and its share prices will go up, if it makes the wrong choices, its share price will go down. It is not easy to define what the criteria for right/wrong choices are without getting into a circular argument along the lines of the right choice is doing something that increases the value of the company. But we might say that increasing the share price means increasing expected returns for shareholders, which in turn means that companies are making good investment decisions, increasing efficiency and generally being well managed.

We have seen that funds invested in a company's shares are not used by the company itself, so there is no obvious reason why company management should care what the share price is, unless management is rewarded in some way related to the share price.

Of the two main asset classes, bonds and equity, the influence on the underlying asset is different. The impact of the bond market has been much debated. For example, former US President Bill Clinton once famously said, "You mean to tell me that the success of the economic program and my re-election hinges on the Federal Reserve and a bunch of *($&ing bond traders?".[17] However, except when things go dramatically wrong, bonds have little direct leverage on the bond issuer. A bond is effectively a loan to a company or government, whereas equity bestows ownership of the underlying company and therefore, in theory at least, the equity owner has some direct control over the underlying company. The rest of this section concentrates on equity, which as we have seen accounts for over half of pension fund investment.

Through their equity holdings, pension funds, along with other institutional asset owners, own a large proportion of listed companies, which make up most of the large enterprises in the economy. How these asset owners exercise their ownership rights has a large impact on how the economy runs. It also has implications for society as a whole, how people behave and our values. I shall explore these more in Chapter 9.

Although individual savers are the beneficial owners of the underlying assets, this ownership is distributed widely and the ownership function is effectively delegated to asset managers. As we saw in Table 2.5, this is highly concentrated in a few asset managers, the largest 20 control a quarter of the world's capital. It is up to the asset manager to oversee that the underlying companies are run in the interests of the beneficiaries. The tools available to the investment manager are to vote at AGMs, to engage with company management and ultimately to buy and sell the shares of the company if it is not managed in a way the asset manager approves. Buying and selling shares affect the share price, thus sending a signal to the company.

If companies are better run because of this stewardship by investment managers, and invest their assets so that the economy grows; this would indeed be beneficial for the future development of the economy as this investment by companies would mean that the economy is better able to pay pensions. The Kay Review states that "promoting good governance and stewardship is therefore a central, rather than an incidental, function of UK equity markets."[18]

Even so, this is a much weaker argument than if the economy actually utilised invested savings directly, these companies would have to be run a damn sight better to justify so much government munificence. The onus of proof should be on asset managers to demonstrate that they are making such a big positive impact that governments should be diverting resources their way on such a large scale.

There are three possible benefits from companies being owned by pension funds. Firstly, and most crucially to the ability of the economy to pay pensions, the owners of companies should encourage and incentivise companies to make long-term investments. Only then can the economy grow and become able to afford to pay future pensions. Furthermore, because pension funds are universal owners, they own large chunks of the economy, they should be encouraging companies to consider the wider social impacts of their decisions. Finally, it has often been argued that because of pension funds, the ownership of large companies is widely distributed amongst the population, thus democratising ownership of the means of production. We saw in Chapter 4 that this might have been true in the 1970s but is no longer true, most of pension fund money is in the hands of the wealthy. The rest of this chapter deals with the other two supposed benefits.

5.2.1 "Asleep at the Wheel"

The deal between society and pension savers is that the economy makes productive use of savings, so when people retire, the economy will be able to afford to pay the pensions. As we have seen, with an ageing population, the workers that there are need to be more productive, and they could achieve higher productivity if they are working with better infrastructure and technology.

To some extent, the lack of direct investment is not entirely surprising; we live in a mature economy, so we already have extensive existing infrastructure, we already have a network of roads, railways and water supply. These might need refurbishment and upgrading, but, in contrast to developing countries, it does not need to be built from scratch. Also, in a modern economy, much of economic growth comes from the knowledge economy, which does not need a great deal of physical infrastructure.[19]

Even so, we do need some investment, and as we have seen, this is not coming via the equity markets. The investment that is made by the private sector is at company level. Rather than using equity investment to fund expansion, companies either use retained earnings or some other form of finance, and it is company management who decide where this is invested. Therefore, the role of the owners of these companies is important, as the owners should be ensuring that the companies are well managed and making the right investment decisions. Specifically, if the economy is going to be in a position to pay the pensions of an ageing population, then companies have to be making long-term investments.

There should be an alignment of interest between pension funds and long-term investment. Pension funds need to pay pensions a long time in the future, so they should be encouraging the firms that they own to invest in the long term, rather than taking short-term profits. Whilst the ownership of companies via the beneficiaries of pension funds is diverse and large, these holdings are aggregated and managed by a relatively few number of asset managers, who have been delegated the crucial ownership function.

These managers are professionals and disinterested, so they should be acting in the best long-term interest of the beneficiaries, which is aligned with the interest of the economy as a whole. According to the Kay review, "The asset management industry can benefit its customers – savers – taken as a whole, only to the extent that its activities improve the performance of investee companies,"[20] this is their main function which justifies their fees.

However, investment managers are not acting in this way, and it is to do with their incentives; I will quickly recap on how a pension fund is run to explain why they are so badly run.

The purpose of a pension fund is to pay people an income at retirement. Different investment classes have different characteristics, the theory goes, when you are young you want to invest in equity which is linked to the growth of the economy so you benefit from higher returns. However, as you approach retirement, you want to lock in your investments to a less volatile asset class with a guaranteed return and so you should switch your assets into bonds. Occupational or company pension funds have to be advised by an actuary as to how the assets of the fund are allocated. They might specify that x% should be in equity, y% in bonds and z% in alternatives, depending on the age profile of the fund. The fund then selects an asset manager, either to manage all of the assets in the way set out by the actuary, or different managers are given different portfolios. For example one manager might be given 20% of the fund and instructed to invest in UK equity which would be his speciality. The asset manager would also be given a benchmark against which he measures his performance, so for example the UK equities might be measured in relation to the performance of the FTSE All share index; a weighted index of all UK shares. To earn her keep, the scheme's investment consultant monitors the fund manager's performance. She does this by looking at the manager's quarterly returns and comparing it to the manager's peers.

Private and personal pensions do not have quite the same structure, it is often up to the individual to choose which funds to invest in. But most arrangements have a default fund, which essentially invests along the lines I have just outlined, that is equity when younger and moving to bonds when older, the manager investing against a benchmark and being judged on quarterly performance.

An asset manager is not at all disinterested – he is generally rewarded by being paid a proportion of funds under management, so the more money he can attract, the more fees he gets. As he is being constantly monitored by an investment consultant, he can attract funds based on relatively short-term performance, so basically if he beats the benchmark and does well against his peers he will attract more funds and earn higher fees. The manager is normally monitored on his quarterly performance – that is every 3 months. If he were to outperform the benchmark three or four quarters in a row he would be doing well and start to attract more money, if he were to perform poorly over four quarters, he would start to get worried about being sacked.

The purpose of investing for a pension is to meet people's retirement earnings aspirations, which could be 20 or 30 years away, so the fund's performance over 3 months should be of little interest. Famous successful investors, such as Warren Buffett and John Maynard Keynes (who in his spare time did some work on economics), adopted a rather different approach, they picked stocks of companies that were well managed but undervalued; if they went down 50% over a couple of years so be it, as long as they increase in the long term. These guys would be fired if they were asset managers being monitored on a quarterly basis. This situation is exacerbated by accounting rules; pension schemes have to be accounted on a mark-to-market basis. This means that the market value of the assets on the accounting day is used. So even if the shares that the scheme owns happened to go down in value on the accounting day, and then returned to their original value the next day, the anomalously low market value would have to be used.

The purpose of this section is not to judge if funds are making the best returns, but how they are influencing the companies that they own to make long-term investment decisions. Incentives are doing the opposite – asset managers are judged on quarterly performance. If a company does something that boosts its short-term share value, for example by paying out large dividends or buying back its shares, this would be in the interest of the asset manager, but not in the interest of the ultimate beneficiaries who would want the company to be prospering when they retire.

Engaging with companies, lobbying management and researching how you should vote at AGMs are expensive, with little measurable reward for the asset manager, so the asset managers do as little of it as possible – this would eat into the manager's profits or increase his fees, and hence make his short-term performance worse. This activity is therefore left to shareholder activists, the fund manager prefers to sit behind a computer buying and selling shares. For example, one of the largest UK asset managers said that "engagement with investor companies requires investment of time and resource which can be seen as an encumbrance in a situation where mandates are being awarded based on fees".[21]

Public companies are owned by a diffuse group of shareholders, with the ownership function delegated to an asset manager with little incentive to perform

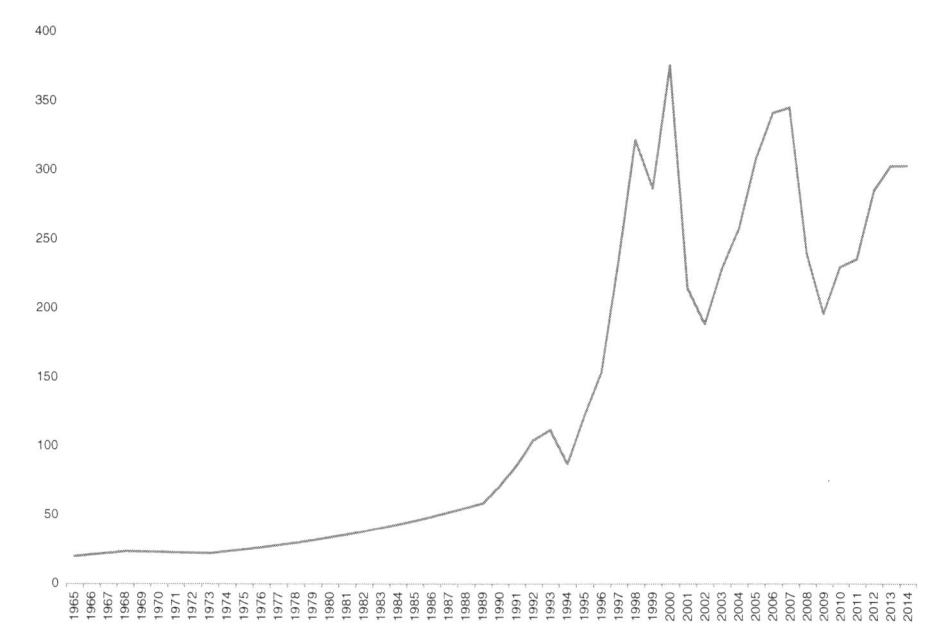

Fig. 5.4 CEO to worker compensation ratio

Source: Economic Policy Institute
This is based on the average within firm ratios. Mishel, L and Davis, A (2015) *Top CEOs Make 300 Times More than Typical Workers* Economic Policy Institute 21 June 2015

this role. We would expect company management to have a free reign with the company. If company management's interest is aligned with asset managers, as opposed to the underlying beneficiaries, we would expect companies to reduce investment and boost shareholder value. Where institutional investors do exercise the ownership powers that they have been delegated, they vote with management at AGMs because of business ties with corporations.[22]

If company management was given free reign and acting in their own interest rather than that of the company, we would expect executive pay to increase. Figure 5.4 shows the dramatic increase in CEO pay in the USA; CEO's pay has increased by 1,000% since 1978 compared to the average worker of about 10%. Also, the increase in CEO's pay has outstripped the increase of other very high earners, indicating that they are able to extract rent.[23] Similarly in the UK, executive pay has increased from 47 times more than a full-time employee 15 years ago to 120 today.[24]

The large increase in the ratio of executive pay to average wages described in Figure 5.4 has been ascribed to executive compensation being linked to company share price.[25]

120   5   La Grande Illusion

Because companies do not finance themselves from equity, the company management should not have much interest in what its share price is doing. However, it is in asset managers' interest for companies to be incentivised to make decisions which boost short-term share prices. This is achieved through executive compensation – the people within companies who make decisions which affect the share price are compensated in relation to the company's share price. This form of compensation package was unknown 30 years ago but is now common practice. This linkage between pay and share price performance, unsurprisingly championed by investors, has a low correlation with company performance.[26]

Long-term investment is often loss making in the short term, but starts to pay off in the long term. If companies reduce long-term investment and instead distribute the funds to shareholders, they will boost the company's short-term share performance. This is what we would expect to see if asset managers, who are judged on short-term performance, are exerting influence on company management who are paid in relation to the share price of their companies. And this is what Figure 5.5 shows is increasingly occurring, with

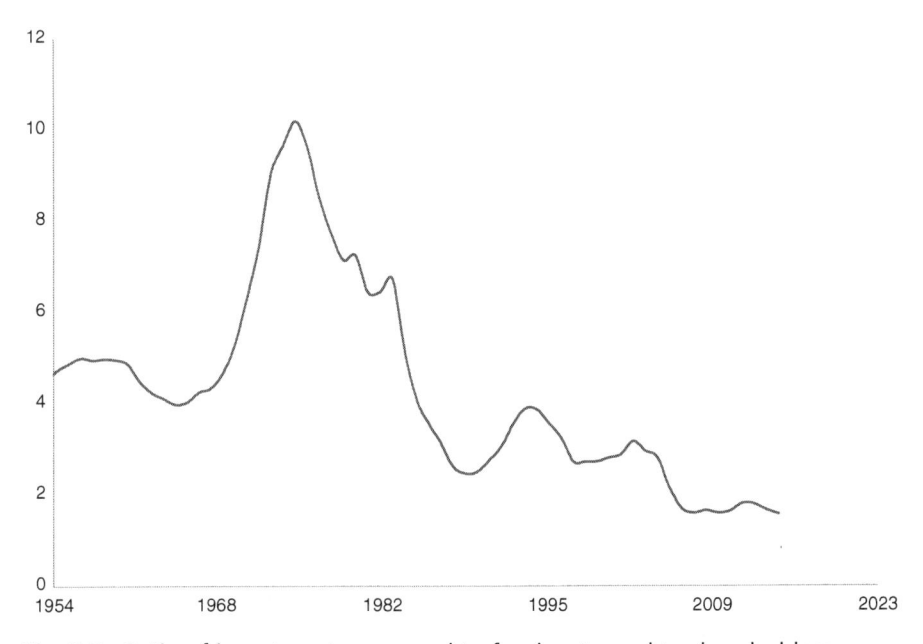

Fig. 5.5 Ratio of investment compared to funds returned to shareholders

Source: US Federal Reserve
The table's design is based on one produced in The Economist 3 October 2013 *The Profits Prophet*, which was in turn based on work done by Andrew Smithers
This table uses US Flow of Fund Accounts, published by the Board of Governors of the Federal Reserve System, table Z1 F.103. The ratio is non-financial corporate gross fixed investment to: equity liability plus dividends

the ratio of cash spent on investment compared to distributed to shareholders falling from over 10 in 1970 to less than 2 today. This does not augur well for the ability of the economy to pay future pensions.

Recent research has shown that private firms, which are not faced with the incentives from institutional investors, have a much higher level of investment and make long-term investment decisions compared to publicly listed companies.[27]

The UK government has commissioned two reviews in recent times to look into these issues. In 2001 the government commissioned Paul Myners, a city grandee, to carry out a review of Institutional Investment in the UK.[28] Lord Myners concluded that "institutional investors are asleep at the wheel".[29] In 2011, the Government commissioned another review, this time by John Kay, a leading economist and columnist for the Financial Times. Kay is much politer than Lord Myners but came to similar conclusions.[30]

Kay identifies examples of short-term thinking leading to bad long-term decision-making, "Companies may not invest sufficiently, especially when the costs of such investment must in part or in whole be charged to current profits, as with expenditure to maintain a good safety record or reputation with customers for value for money."[31]

A good example of this is the case of BP PLC, the UK-based energy multinational. My friend Raj Thamotheram has catalogued how BP, over a number of years, reduced expenditure on safety and used this reduction to boost profits. This behaviour was encouraged and rewarded by institutional investors, but resulted in a series of highly damaging accidents, culminating in the Deepwater Horizon spill, which cost the company billions of dollars, in addition to the destruction to the environment and local communities in the Mississippi River Delta.[32]

A paper by the Bank of England quantitatively investigated short termism in equity markets. They found that share prices reflected an excessive discounting. The paper concludes that "First, some projects with a positive net present value might be rejected because future cash flows are discounted too heavily, reducing investment and ultimately growth. Second, long-duration cash flows and projects are penalised particularly severely by excess discounting."[33]

Chapter 5 showed that 96% of pension savings is not actually invested at all and therefore do not directly contribute to the long-term development of the economy. In considering asset managers' role as delegated owners of publicly listed companies, the long-term development of the economy is actually harmed, as companies are encouraged to boost short-term performance at the expense of long-term investment. This view is not mine alone

5.2.2 Principles of Irresponsible Investment

Pensions are long-term savings, for the pension deal to work, your pension has to be invested in a way so that the economy can pay it back between 30 and 50 years – that is between when you retire and die. Up to now I have discussed the need of the economy to increase productivity. However, there are also negative long-term trends which reduce the ability of the economy to pay pensions. Climate change is a prime example; greenhouse gasses (GHGs), which are produced as a by-product of industrial activity, released into the atmosphere now, causes global warming which will result in future damage to human society and the environment. There are many other long-term trends which will impact our ability to pay future pensions, for example the ageing population will put a future strain on our medical systems, there is an increasing risk of pandemics as pathogens are becoming increasingly resistant to antibiotics.

For the pension deal to work, investment now has to be sustainable, in the framework I introduced in Chapter 1; level 3 or ecologically sustainable. Investment should not only increase productivity but also increase the resilience of the economy. Aligned to this is the concept of the universal investor; a pension fund owns a wide variety of assets, so if an individual company does something that increases its own profitability but does harm to the economy, it will negatively impact the rest of the portfolio. In economics parlance, the portfolio is impacted by externalities arising from an investee company's activities. These externalities could be positive or negative.

BP's aforementioned reduced expenditure on safety is an example of a negative externality; not only was BP harmed, but other assets have been impacted from the resultant environmental damage, some of which may be owned by pension funds. It is therefore in pension funds' interest for BP to increase expenditure on safety, beyond what BP might do for its own benefit, as any safety failure has a negative impact on the rest of the economy, even if increasing expenditure on safety impacts BP's short-term profits. An example of a positive impact is education and training; companies are conflicted about training as their staff can leave and get a job with a competitor. However, from the universal investor's point of view education and training are unambiguously beneficial as the overall economy will be boosted, from which all assets will benefit, so it should encourage its investee companies to spend more on education and training than they might otherwise do.

A pension fund has an interest in using its influence to get companies to reduce their negative externalities and increase their positive ones. For the pension deal to work, pension funds should be encouraging their investee companies to make investments which increase the long-term resilience of the economy.

There is a long-established investment style, termed socially responsible investment (SRI), which attempts to take environmental, social and governance (ESG) factors of the kind we have been discussing into consideration in the investment process. SRI funds represent approximately 11%[34] of total investment, so while still a small minority, it is not insignificant.

ESG has to some extent influenced mainstream or non-SRI investors. Most large investors have an ESG policy, a department or employees with an ESG or SRI role. There are also a number of initiatives between investors, probably the most substantial is the United Nations Principles of Responsible Investment (UNPRI) which has an impressive 1,335 signatories, who, combined, have assets under management of $45 trillion. To become a signatory, you need an ESG policy and report on your performance in this area.[35]

Whilst SRI has made a lot of progress over the last decade, in reality SRI investing has little, if any, influence on investment management. In our example of BP, investors actually rewarded BP for their reduction in safety expenditure.[36] The UNPRI has researched its signatories' behaviour in relation to selecting and evaluating asset management. UNPRI signatories are the asset owners who care most about ESG issues which is why they became signatories. Yet, less than 20% of signatory asset owners assign specific weighting to ESG factors in manager selection,[37] which means that 80% of fund managers employed by the leading asset owners are not incentivised at all to take ESG issues into consideration.

Using climate change as a weather vane for long-term sustainability issues, on the face of it institutional investors seem particularly concerned about climate change. In December 2014, 364 investors representing $24 trillion of assets under management issued a statement which starts that "We, the institutional investors that are signatories to this Statement, are acutely aware of the risks climate change presents to our investments. In addition, we recognise that significant capital will be needed to finance the transition to a low-carbon economy and to enable society to adapt to the physical impacts of climate change" and continues in this manner.[38]

To do something about climate change, investors signed up to the Montreal Climate Pledge, organised by the UNPRI. In it investors pledged to "commit, as a first step, to measure and disclose the carbon footprint of our investments annually". Notice this is not to actually do anything, but just to report on GHG emissions in their portfolio. About $10 trillion of assets under management have been willing to make this pledge.[39]

Recently at an AGM of ExxonMobil, The US-based energy company, a resolution to "stress test its business model against the international goal of holding global warming below 2C"[40] was defeated by shareholders. Many of the shareholders, such as Vanguard and Blackrock, voted against the resolution, despite being UNPRI signatories and despite the pathetically low bar for requesting disclosure, the investment managers were not even prepared to request this, which you would have thought was relevant information to their investment decision.

Meanwhile, the companies that these funds own spent $674 billion in 2013 before oil price crashed on finding and developing new reserves of fossil fuels,[41] 49% of all the capital expenditure of listed companies. Even though the amount of expenditure is eye wateringly high, in reality there is not so much that investors could do to stop fossil fuel companies developing reserves, only governments can set energy policies which make alternative fuels more competitive than fossil fuel. However, these same fossil fuel companies spend over $200 million a year in the USA and EU on lobbying[42] to ensure that governments maintain the profitability of fossil fuels, so that it pays for them to continue to develop these reserves. It has been estimated that the return on money spent by companies on lobbying is 5,800%.[43] Whilst it is clearly in fossil fuel companies' interest to keep lobbying, it is not in pension funds' interest for them to do so. By developing fossil fuels, the economy is locked into a high GHG emissions pathway, which will result in future damage, undermining the economy's ability to pay pensions, and this is ignoring moral issues of damage to planet, which I will return to in Chapters 8 and 9.

Another example is corporate tax avoidance. Many large multinational corporations minimise their tax bills by shifting profits to jurisdictions with low tax regimes, rather than where they do business. Recently, there was a big public outcry when it was discovered that Starbucks, Amazon and Google were hardly paying any taxes despite huge profits.[44] The groups that remained largely silent were pension funds and other institutional investors. It is not in the interest of a pension fund for a company to avoid tax, as it means that other companies that it owns will have to pay more tax, the government, whose bonds it owns, will become less credit worthy or have to cut back on spending, or workers will have to pay more tax, all of which harm the economy and hence the pension funds' other assets.

Yet the institutional asset owners who own these companies exert no influence on curtailing lobbying or tax avoidance, and other such activities. Asset owners have the ability to hire and fire company directors, and set and approve the pay structure and hence incentives of these directors. By not intervening, asset managers are colluding with companies' senior management, to the detriment of pension fund beneficiaries and society as a whole. But non-intervention contributes to their own personal gain as these asset managers benefit from the resultant enhanced short-term returns on the companies' shares.

5.2.3 Activist Investors

There is the hope that SRI investors might be activist investors, to engage with companies to influence investee companies to change behaviour. This is the whole *Raison d'être* of one very laudable NGO called Share Action who are "concerned with highlighting those business practices that are negligent or harmful to people or the environment, and catalysing action to change them."[45]

Given that most investors are "asleep at the wheel", the activist investors have disproportionate amount of influence in changing company behaviour. The most famous and probably successful of these is not Share Action but Carl Icahn. In the 1980s he was described as being a "corporate raider" and was probably the inspiration behind Gordon Gekko in the film *Wall Street*.[46] Activist investors like Icahn's concern is not to persuade the businesses that he invests in to improve the lot of the people and environment on whom they have an impact on, but to increase the short-term value of these companies' shares and hence his own wealth. They do this by encouraging companies to distribute value to shareholders, for example by share buy-backs,[47] which as we have seen occur at the expense of long-term investment.

There are a number of hedge funds which specialise in activist investment, the majority of activism is to improve "general undervaluation" through distributing money to shareholders, or to induce investee companies into increasing debt or for the company to agree to be purchased so that the investor can make a short-term profit.[48]

In conclusion, there are laudable initiatives which try to mobilise institutional investors to influence investee companies to reduce their negative impacts on society. Many mainstream institutional investors support these initiatives on paper, as it makes them look good. The reality is that these initiatives have virtually no influence and are greatly outweighed by active shareholders who seek to get companies to give money back to shareholders, rather than making long-term investment decisions.

The reason that asset managers and pension funds are not effective in encouraging ESG behaviour is because asset managers are rewarded for short-term performance, expenditure on ESG would reduce companies' profits. In fact, if companies can pass on costs and risks to society, so much the better as internalising these costs would reduce share value. As we saw in the case of BP and the whole banking sector during the financial crisis, ignoring ESG issues can result in long-term value destruction.

5.2.4 Capitalism in the Twenty-First Century

Companies are managing to maintain and increase their value whilst reducing investment. Reducing investment can boost short-term profits, as I have described before. But investors are not stupid, they will not buy shares in a company just because it is distributing profits, it has to have some long-term prospects. What is more, the corporate word is doing very well, the share of profits as a proportion of the economy is increasing, for example in the USA it has more than doubled since 2000, from below 5% to over 10%.[49] The way to increase profit share in the economy, as opposed to profits increasing along with the economy, is to take some of the value of economic activity away from other stakeholders. For example, one way of increasing profitability is to reduce staff costs by reducing staff benefits (such as pensions), cap pay increases or make people redundant. This inherently increases income inequality as real wages stagnate. Other methods that companies can employ are to reduce supplier costs, charge customers more or lobby governments against legislation, all of which pass externality costs onto the rest of society.

I do not want to overstate my case here; it is difficult to say how much influence investors actually have in practice on company behaviour. But, where they do have an influence, it is to encourage companies to boost short-term profitability. Governments are encouraging people to save for a pension, and in doing so, they are funnelling cash, and hence power, to the financial services industry. The industry uses these funds to enrich itself. One of its tools to enrich itself is to use the management of these funds to incentivise companies to take decision which undermine the economy's ability to pay pensions. For example reducing staff costs, which increase inequality and undermining peoples' ability to save; by passing on externality costs to society which increase governments' fiscal burden and reduce the economy's resilience, or by persuading people to buy goods that they do not need and cannot afford, thus increasing consumer debt. I shall deal with these issues more fully in Chapter 8.

5.3 Conclusion

The state encourages people to save for a pension, so that the economy can invest this money in order to develop and be able to afford to pay savers a pension when they retire. By encouraging people to save, the government helps people to help themselves, so that they will not be a burden on future generations. People tend to need encouragement to save because they are myopic, and by encouraging people to save a market for pensions develops which might not otherwise have come into being. The asset allocation decisions of the economy are managed by the private sector, it is in the hands of disinterested professional investors who ensure that the economy is well run.

Unfortunately, this only occurs only on planet economics but bears no relation to the world we live in. Less than 4% of the savings that people make are actually invested at all. Professional managers undermine the ability of the companies they are supposed to oversee to create long-term value. Companies boost share price by passing on externalities to society, which will ultimately undermine the ability of the economy to pay pensions. The distribution of pensions savings and hence the tax rebate is highly unequal, massively favouring the rich and there is no democratisation of ownership in the economy as the same people who own companies have a pension. The affluent will look after themselves anyway, so the state is not reducing the burden on itself by encouraging pensions. The majority of savings are eaten up by charges, so people are entirely sensible, not myopic, in not saving for a pension.

This market is in no sense a free market in which people have the right to be ripped off by the financial services industry. The market is a Potemkin market, created, overseen and run by governments; the government is bribing people to contribute to a pension through tax incentives, they are constantly dreaming up schemes, the latest being auto-enrolment, to encourage people to save for their pension. Many of the largest pension funds who invest in the system are government or quasi-government, such as the Norwegian Pension fund of the Californian Teachers' Pension Fund.

The pensions industry might not even exist if it were not for government intervention, more likely because people are not stupid rather than because they are myopic. The savings industry might still exist, but even this is largely government influenced. Governments set the regulation which determines the incentive structure within the markets, and the government directly or indirectly sets the most important price, the interest rate, and governments often intervene in the markets, normally in investors' favour. Many large participants in financial markets are public sector, such as central banks and SWFs.

As I have shown, the structure of the market causes collateral damage to the economy for which society has to pick up the tab. The structure of the economy is determined by the actions of the financial services industry. Wealth is highly unequal because some people are paid much more than others; as we have seen, CEOs are paid 120 times more than employees within companies. This is because asset managers have an interest in CEOs pay being linked to share price, the result being that CEOs pay themselves so much whilst capping other employees' salaries, contrary to the interests of society and the company itself. These well-paid company executives, along with people who work in the financial services, are "high net worth individuals" who make up the bulk of the savings pool that owns these companies.

The pension/savings industry as is does not create value, it does not create new products or innovate in a way which contributes to economic growth or development. Fund management is a zero sum game, unless the stewardship of the assets leads to an improved performance of the underlying assets. We have seen that the opposite is true, the industry is net value destroying.

It is easy to criticise, but it is harder to come up with solutions. To do so we should first ask what we want pensions to do and then to design a system which delivers what we actually want. We might want a pension system which pays people a liveable income when they can no longer work, addresses the challenge of an ageing population and provides productive investment in our economy. All of these are achievable and there are some countries that have developed solutions to these problems which actually work, as described in Chapter 10.

The financial services industry which currently manages our pensions delivers none of the above, instead enriching itself whilst wreaking havoc on our economy and society. It has grown up under a set of benign economic circumstances, but it looks like those days are over. We have reached a time for change.

Notes

1. Note that this is a different proportion to Figure 2.1 as that dealt with global assets combined, whereas Figure 5.1 is for UK pension funds only.
2. BBC website 9 December 2014 *Manchester United will keep spending, says share prospectus* http://www.bbc.co.uk/sport/0/football/30391487

3. Financial Times 1 April 2011 *The hidden cost of portfolio turnover* https://www.ft.com/content/11cd09d6-5c80-11e0-ab7c-00144feab49a
4. Taken from London Stock Exchange Main Market Factsheet for December 2015 http://www.londonstockexchange.com/statistics/historic/main-market/main-market-factsheet-archive-2015/dec-15.pdf I have summed UK Listed and International listed, so Market capitalisation = £2,183 billion (UK) + £1,693 billion (international) and equity raised = £22,036 million (UK) + £6,224 million (international).
5. Kay, J (2012) *The Kay review of UK equity markets* UK Government and Bank of England (2015) and *Trends in Lending January 2015*.
6. Office for National Statistics for year 2015–16.
7. Noss, J and Sowerbutts, R (2012) *The implicit subsidy of banks* Bank of England.
8. See Turner, A (2015) *The Case for Monetary Finance – An Essentially Political Issue* Paper presented at the 16th Jacques Polak Annual Research Conference and Jackson, A (2013) *Sovereign Money* Positive Money.
9. UK Public spending: http://www.ukpublicspending.co.uk/breakdown accessed 7 December 2012
10. Financial Times 21 April 2015 *Bond investors grumble at buyback bonanza* https://www.ft.com/content/3f1e310a-e7a8-11e4-8e3f-00144feab7de
11. Van Rixtel, A and Villegas, A (2015) *Equity issuance and share buybacks* BIS Quarterly Review, March 2015.
12. From National Association of Pension Funds (2013) *Trends in defined benefit asset allocation* http://www.napf.co.uk/PolicyandResearch/DocumentLibrary/-/media/Policy/Documents/0314_Trends_in_db_asset_allocation_changing_shape_UK_pension_investment_NAPF_research_paper_July_2013_DOCUMENT.ashx
13. In 2012: from UBS Pension Fund Indicators 2012.
14. IPOs in Europe in 2014 were €40 billion compared to €9 trillion, making 0.4% a similar proportion than in the UK. PriceWaterhouseCoopers (2015) IPO Watch Europe http://www.pwc.co.uk/deals/publications/ipo-watch-europe.jhtml.
15. IMA(2012) *The IMA Annual Survey Asset Management in the UK 2011–2012* Investment Management Association http://www.investmentfunds.org.uk/assets/files/research/20120907_IMAAssetManagementSurvey2012.pdf
16. My figures here could be construed as being a bit misleading: the total assets are a stock, as are the bond and infrastructure figures, whereas the equity figure is a flow; the 0.5% of equity is the amount being drawn down every year by companies. However, as the net flows in equity are actually negative, that is more money is being returned to shareholder every year, and I have ignored this, in reality this 3.85% figure is a massive overestimate.
17. Quoted in New York magazine http://nymag.com/nymetro/news/bizfinance/columns/bottomline/199/ accessed 7 December 2016.

18. Kay, J (2012) *The Kay Review of UK Equity Markets and Long-Term decision Making* UK Department for Business, Innovation and Skills.
19. Although it does need some, such as widespread, fast internet. To educate the population to participate in a knowledge economy requires a great deal of infrastructure.
20. Kay, J (2012) *The Kay Review of UK Equity Markets and Long-Term decision Making* UK Department for Business, Innovation and Skills.
21. Kay, J (2012) The *Kay review of UK equity markets and long-term decision making* UK Department for Business, Innovation and Skills.
22. Dasgupta and Zacharaidis (2011) *Delegated activism and disclosure* LSE.
23. Mishel, L and Davis, A (2015) *Top CEOs Make 300 Times More than Typical Workers* Economic Policy Institute 21 June 2015.
24. Financial Times 5 January 2015 *Executive pay: hand over the cash* http://www.ft.com/cms/s/3/0238538c-94f2-11e4-b32c-00144feabdc0.html?siteedition=uk#axzz3O1UDGMOb
25. Bebchuck, L and Grinstein, Y (2005) *The Growth of Executive Pay* NBER Working Paper Series.
26. CFA Society UK *Measuring and rewarding performance: theory and evidence in relation to executive compensation.*
27. Asker, J, Farre-Mensa, J and Ljungqvist, A (2015) *Corporate Investment and Stock Market Listing: A Puzzle?* Review of Financial Studies 28, no. 2: 342–390.
28. Myners, P (2001) *Institutional Investment in the UK: A Review* HM Treasury.
29. Quotation of Lord Myners, quoted in Evening Standard 22 May 2009 *Time for shareholders to get a grip* http://www.standard.co.uk/business/time-for-shareholders-to-get-a-grip-6747570.html
30. Kay, J (2011) *Kay review of UK equity markets and long-term decision making* UK Department for Business, Innovation and Skills.
31. Kay, J (2011) *Kay review of UK equity markets and long-term decision making* UK Department for Business, Innovation and Skills.
32. Preventable Surprises website http://www.preventablesurprises.com/wp-content/uploads/2011/09/The-BP-Crisis-as-a-Preventable-Surprise_June-1-2012_plus-reviews.pdf
33. Haldane, A and Davis, R (2011) *The Short Long* Bank of England.
34. Forum for Sustainable and Responsible Investment http://www.ussif.org/content.asp?contentid=82
35. See UNPRI website: https://www.unpri.org/
36. Raj Thamotheram and Maxime Le Floc'h (2012) *The BP Crisis as a "Preventable Surprise": Lessons for Institutional Investors* Rotman International Journal of Pension Management Volume 5, Issue 1 Spring 2012.
37. UNPRI *Reporting on Progress 2014.*
38. See: http://montrealpledge.org/ accessed 7 December 2016.
39. See: http://montrealpledge.org/ accessed 7 December 2016.

40. Climate Change News 6 September 2016 http://www.climatechangenews.com/2016/09/06/named-and-shamed-the-top-funds-blocking-climate-action/
41. Carbon Tracker (2013) *Unburnable carbon.*
42. Desmog blog *Fossil Fuel Lobby Spent $213 Million Last Year to Influence US, EU Politicians* http://www.desmogblog.com/2014/10/18/fossil-fuel-lobby-spent-213-million-last-year-influence-us-eu-politicians
43. Oil Change International *Fossil Fuel Funding to Congress: Industry influence in the U.S.* http://priceofoil.org/fossil-fuel-industry-influence-in-the-u-s/
44. See foe example BBC News 21 May 2016 *Google, Amazon, Starbucks: The rise of "tax shaming"* http://www.bbc.co.uk/news/magazine-20560359
45. Share Action websitehttp://shareaction.org/
46. The Independent 22 September 2010 *Whatever happened to the real Gordon Gekkos?* http://www.independent.co.uk/arts-entertainment/films/features/whatever-happened-to-the-real-gordon-gekkos-2086842.html
47. Financial Times 1 October 2013 *Activist investor Carl Icahn steps up push for Apple buyback* http://www.ft.com/cms/s/0/4bdc4e02-2ac3-11e3-8fb8-00144feab7de.html#axzz3Nw8Ar7G5
48. Brav, A., W. Jiang, and H. Kim, (2010) *Hedge fund activism: A review* Foundations and Trends in Finance.
49. Federal Reserve Bank of St Louis: http://research.stlouisfed.org/fred2/graph/?g=cSh

6

A Kind of Magic

Banks, Property and Money

Chapters 2–5 have described the savings channel, where money is managed on behalf of savers by asset managers in capital markets. People also save through the deposit channel, which is the subject of this chapter.

More of this book deals with the savings than the deposit channel The main reason, really, is because there are countless numbers of books on banks, the banking crisis and banking reform, by much more eminent people than myself, such as the former Governor of the Bank of England, the former chairman of the Financial Services Authority and the former Chairman of the Federal Reserve amongst others. Banks are where all the attention and effort has been directed in trying to fix the financial system. But the savings system is at least as important as banks. Large banks are almost entirely publicly listed companies; hence, their shares are ultimately owned by asset owners, with the ownership function delegated to professional asset managers, as described in Chapter 2.

In the run-up to the 2008 financial crisis, during the financial crisis and its aftermath, with the excess risk taking, insolvency of banks, bailout by governments and the much publicised bad behaviour of banks resulting in billions of dollars of fines; this sorry period in banking history was all during a time when asset managers were supposedly overseeing the management of the banks.

In the previous chapters, I argued that the savings channel did not lead to savings being invested into the economy. That investment could potentially come via the deposit channel; as well as saving via capital markets through their pension and the like, people also store some of their excess income with banks. The banks then lend this out to individuals and businesses, who hopefully use the loans productively.

This chapter describes the money system; how money is created and allocated in practice and why it is mostly allocated to the wrong places. Money is created by the private banking system during the process of lending. This has implications in that the sectors of the economy which grow fastest are those that have access to finance from banks, as determined by the decisions of bank mangers. The chapter outlines the importance of this process to the economy.

Banks have been much in the news for a while. Variations on the themes "too big to fail, greedy bankers risking tax-payers money whilst paying themselves huge bonuses and abusing their position to manipulate markets" are in newspapers most days. Arcane terminology such as Basel III, LIBOR and leverage ratios now form part of the popular lexicon. This chapter considers banks from a different perspective; what are they for, what do they do and what role do they play in the modern economy? Whilst banks do some of the things that we might want them to do, they have evolved in such a way that they are harmful to the economy. This is not because of the nefarious activities by individual bank employees that make the media headlines, but because of the aggregate daily decisions of decent hard-working bank managers, who are working in an environment with the wrong incentives.

So, what are banks for?

6.1 So, What are banks for?

6.1.1 Payments System

Banks effectively run the payments system, which is a crucial part of the infrastructure of the economy, and which generally works. If I want to access my own money and use it for a payment, this is facilitated by a bank. So, for example if I want to make a payment to someone in another country and currency, I can organise a SWIFT transfer via my bank to do so. The payment system is utility-like in nature. For the economy to run smoothly requires everyone to have access money, the main means of exchange as well as other essentials such as water, power and heating. If one of these functions were to break down, there would be a disproportionate impact, so utilities are normally either highly regulated or provided by the state.

There are criticisms of the payment system that it could be more efficient. I can draw money out of a cash machine from my UK bank account almost everywhere in the world, which really is remarkable. Unlike the savings system described in previous chapters which really does not do what it is supposed to, the payments system may not be perfect but it does work.

During the financial crisis, if the banks had been allowed to collapse, the payment system would have stopped working, which was one of the reasons that the government bailed them out. Going forward this should be relatively easy to rectify; recognising that it is the payment system that is crucial, if banks have a contingency plan in the event of their insolvency that the payment system can be isolated and transferred to public ownership, then this system could be made safe from the collapse of supporting banks.

6.1.2 Smoothing Lifetime Consumption

I need a safe place to store any excess income that I might have. I might need some savings for an unexpected purchase or cost that might occur from time to time and some for future purchases or needs. The main feature of a checking account is that savers can have instant access to cash on demand; banks also provide deposit accounts and other products which have a longer waiting time before savers can access their funds. Typically, these functions are fulfilled by a mixture of banks' products, combined with savings from other sources.

People and business also require loans at some point in their life. I might wish to buy a large capital item, such as a house, car or piece of new equipment, which I can only afford if the payments are made over a number of years. Also at a point in my or my company's life expenditure might exceed income, with the expectation that this might reverse at some time in the future. For example, when I was a student, I had a low income but high expenditure; this reversed when I started working, or now that I have children have high expenditure which will (hopefully) reduce when they leave home. When a company is young or expanding it might require a loan, but the investment will be expected to generate enough income to pay back the loan.

6.1.3 Allocation of Savings into Useful Investment

Beyond the needs of individual people and companies, for the overall health and future direction of the economy, banks have a crucial and central role to play. For the economy to function and grow, it requires a balance as to how these loans are allocated; people may require loans to purchase items and smooth consumption, but to generate economic growth, which is needed to pay back the totality of these loans, the economy requires investment. This investment can either be financed from capital markets or from banks. As we saw previously capital markets are not fulfilling this role, are banks?

Practically, all of the money circulating in our economy was created as a by-product of lending by banks. This has two important implications, firstly that banks control the amount of money in the system, and secondly that they decide which sectors of the economy the money goes to.

For their trouble, banks have a massive helping hand from government. Banks have an implicit guarantee. Because of their crucial role in the payment system, if a bank were to fail, it would cause a great deal of collateral damage. It is likely that any bank that is deemed too big, or too integrated into the financial system or too important to fail, will not be allowed to do so by the government. And everyone who deals with the bank knows this, so banks can borrow at a lower rate than they would have done without the guarantees. The bank itself may also be willing to take more risks because of this implicit guarantee.[1]

It is very hard to estimate the value of this implicit guarantee because the counterfactual does not exist; what the banking sector would look like without the guarantee. What is especially hard is that banks would not be so large or be able to engage in certain types of business without the guarantee, and perversely the implicit guarantee may cause banks to take more risks which increases the chance that they will become insolvent and therefore increases the value of the guarantee (called "moral hazard"). Estimates of the value of this guarantee to banks range from £30 billion to over £100 billion, and this does not take into account the expansion of the banking sector due to this implicit guarantee.[2]

6.2 The Creation of Money

6.2.1 How Money Is Not Created – The Economic Explanation

The standard economics textbook argument of how a bank works goes something like this[3]; the central bank or the government has the power to create money. The central bank might issue £1,000 of new money and this finds its

6.2 The Creation of Money

way to an individual. The individual deposits the money in a bank, and the bank lends this out to a business. However, the bank has to keep some money back, say 10%, which is called the reserve ratio. So, the bank can lend out £900 (keeping 10% of £1,000 as reserve). This £900 will eventually find itself to a bank, who can lend out £810 (90% of £900) and so on and so forth until the money system will come into an equilibrium. A relatively simple formulae derived from this process calculates how much money will be generated from new money creation, based on banks' reserve ratio. If the reserve ratio is 10%, the money multiplier will be 10,[4] and therefore for every £1,000 created, the money supply will increase by £10,000.

This account is intuitively simple to grasp and appealing. Within it, it contains the basic function of a bank – to take peoples' savings and loan them out to business. It also contains some assertions; money in circulation is created by government. Although the money supply is increased by the actions of banks, the money supply is determined by how much money governments put into the system and the reserve ratio. The bank is essentially an intermediary, loaning out deposits.

Banks are not like other private businesses, as they have a role in determining the level of the money supply – the government is using banks to get money into the economy, with the implication that if something goes wrong with banks, the system would break down and less money than the government wants will get out into the economy. Additionally, banks have an essential role in the payments system. So, if a business that makes, say, washing machines goes bankrupt, it will cause damage to other business, for example its suppliers, distributors, creditors, etc. But if a bank fails, this means that people cannot pay for transactions and this will do a great deal of damage to the economy. This makes banks more akin to a utility; an electricity supplier going bankrupt will result in people being left without power which is unacceptable in our modern world; the government would have to step in to take over the power company's infrastructure.

If a bank fails, people would lose their savings, so most governments force banks to have mandatory deposit insurance; normally through a levy to a government-owned entity which will cover a proportion of deposits in the event of a bank failure. Now you could argue that it is up to a customer to assess how risky a bank is before she deposits her money with it. But I am writing a book about the finance system, which makes me more likely than the average punter to be able to assess the riskiness of a bank; yet, I would find it almost impossible to make such a judgement and certainly would not have the time to do so. There are ratings agencies that do this job, but we saw in the financial crisis that they may be conflicted and will not necessarily give a reliable assessment.

Banks perform an important role in mediating between different time scales and needs of borrowers and lenders. Maturity transformation is where banks lend out long-term debt (a mortgage could be 15–20 years) but borrow from depositors over the short term. Liquidity transformation is because the borrower wants a long-term debt whereas the lender/saver wants immediate access to his or her money. Both of these make banks vulnerable to bank runs. There is the possible and real risk that savers will decide at the same time that a bank is unsafe and will all try and take their money out. If this were to occur, as the bank's assets are in the form of long-dated loans, it is therefore unable to access these funds to pay back the savers, the bank could have to default. This could be the case even for well-run solvent bank, those whose assets (the value of its loans) are greater than its liabilities (the value of its deposits). Savers are aware of the possibility of a bank run, and so if they think there might be a bank run, it is rational to try and get your money out before everyone else does, and if enough people try and do this, you end up with the bank collapsing. And as we have seen, there will be a great deal of collateral damage if a bank fails, so governments might be particularly keen to ensure that such an event does not occur.

The banking system has evolved whereby the government provides explicit or implicit protection to banks, ensuring that savers' deposits are protected and so is the payment system. Bank runs, as described above, are caused by depositors thinking that the bank will be unable to pay back their deposits. By having a central bank acting as a lender of last resort, banks avoid bank runs. The central bank can always meet the demands of savers, as it can print all of the money that it needs. Because savers know this, they know that a bank – backed by a central bank, will always be able to pay back its savings, and therefore there is never a need for savers to run to the banks to retrieve their savings.

Banks are not like other private, profit maximising companies, they are doing the business of the state; they are distributing and multiplying-up the money supply and are protected by the state for performing this role. The argument that you often see that some banks are "too big to fail" misses the point, it is not the size of the individual banks that means they cannot be allowed to fail, but because of their function in the economy. If you are concerned that a private company is too big to fail, you just have to split it up. But if a company is doing something that would do a great deal of damage if it fails, then the state has to protect it and/or take it over if things go wrong.

Because of this, banks are generally highly regulated. As banks have the central bank standing behind them if they get into trouble, the government has to be assured that they do not behave irresponsibly and therefore regulates banks so that this will not happen.

6.2.2 How Money Is Created

The main problem with this standard economics account of how money is created is that it bears no relation to reality. The account that the Bank of England, for example, gives is as follows[5]: a bank agrees to lend someone money, where someone could be an individual or a company. The bank then opens an account for the individual and deposits money into the account, at the same time creating a credit entry against the individual. Here is the magic trick – the bank creates money out of thin air. The new money then gets spent and finds its way back into another (or the same) bank. The bank holds some of the deposits as central bank reserves, but this does not provide a limit to the amount of money created as the economics text books assert.

The implications of this difference are profound; banks are not intermediaries but are the creators and suppliers of money. Money is created as the by-product of banks' lending decisions and money is therefore entirely debt-based; that is all money has to have an equivalent debt attached to it. Banks also have a privileged position in society, the government has licensed them to create money and decide where that money is allocated. Both the amount of money in the system and where that money is allocated depend on the decision of banks and their employees.

In Britain in the seventeenth century, money was created privately by goldsmiths. People deposited their jewellery or gold with a goldsmith, who gave them a credit note. These credit notes were then used by people as a paper currency.[6] But over time, the state took over this function of responsibility of the creation and distribution of money. Pound notes and coins have pictures of the Queen on them and are backed by the state. In modern times, the state has given away this right to create money to private institutions. These private institutions have privileged position, just as would a private institution that was granted the right to collect tax. If I, for example, were to create and distribute legal tender money, I would be put in prison.[7]

6.3 The Impact on the Economy of Money Creation

Nearly all of the money in the economy is created by banks as a by-product of lending; in fact, 97% of the money in our economy was created by banks via their lending decision; that is of all the money in circulation, 97% is electronic money in bank deposits, and 3% is cash.[8] I am not sure how familiar my reader is with this explanation; but because of organisations such as *Positive Money*, knowledge of bank's role in the creation of money is increasingly widespread. When I first heard this explanation, I was both shocked and disbelieving. However, the implications are subtler than they first appear. It might seem unfair that these *incompetent greedy bankers* have a licence to print money, but they do perform an important function in the economy, and if money was not created in this way, it would have to be created in some other way which could be equally, or more, problematic.

In thinking through the implications, I am heavily indebted (in the intellectual rather than the monetary sense) to the economist Richard Werner who developed the quantity theory of credit.[9]

There are a number of measurements of the amount of money in the economy: M0, MB, M1, M2, MZM, M3, M4–, M4. Werner argues that the reason for this is that economists are not agreed what money actually is. As money is created by banks, he postulates that the money supply is equivalent to the amount of credit in the economy. The increase in credit is equivalent to the increase in the money supply.

Werner splits money/credit into money used for real transactions, for example the purchase of goods and services, and money used for financial transaction, for example the purchase of financial securities. The output of the economy is equal to the amount of money circulating around the system that is the amount of money times the speed (velocity) at which it travels. The output of the economy is the total value of goods and services in the economy, which is the number of goods bought and sold times the price that they are bought and sold at. This is standard economic theory, the extra insight from the quantity theory of credit is that there is an equivalent financial equation; credit times the velocity of money in the financial system is equal to the price times the quantity of transactions in the financial system. This can be summarised in two simple equations:

$$\text{Economic growth (nominal)} = \text{increase}\begin{pmatrix}\text{Prices } (P_R) \times \\ \text{Total Good and services } (Y_R)\end{pmatrix} \quad (6.1)$$
$$= \text{Increase credit in real economy } (\Delta C_R)$$
$$\times \text{ velocity of money in real economy } (V_R)$$

Increase in size of asset market
$$= \text{increase}\begin{pmatrix}\text{Prices of financial assets } (P_F) \times \\ \text{Total financial assets transacted } (Q_R)\end{pmatrix}$$
$$= \text{Increase credit in financial sector}(\Delta C_F)$$
$$\times \text{ velocity of money in financial economy}(V_F)$$
$$(6.2)$$

When banks create money/credit, they increase the money supply, so where this credit is directed makes a difference to what happens to the economy. Werner distinguishes between unproductive credit creation and productive credit creation. The former takes two forms. Lending for consumption increases prices of goods, P_R in Eq. (6.1) which in turn leads to an increase in the size of the nominal economy without an increase in real output – it causes inflation. An increase in lending into the financial economy causes an increase in the price of financial assets or causes an increase in their quantity, both in Eq. (6.2) and results in asset bubbles. In contrast lending to companies that invest causes new goods and services which leads to real economic growth.[10]

Werner's theory is backed up by quantitative analysis. If we start from the premise that banks create money, then Werner's theory passes a common-sense check; there is a limitless demand for money, yet there is not an infinite supply, so money is rationed. As banks are creating the money, where they choose to invest, will determine which areas of the economy will grow.

6.3.1 Lending in the UK

Which sectors are banks lending to? The current situation in the UK is shown in Figure 6.1. The chart shows that loans to non-financial corporations, that is business that might do something productive, is only 17% of overall lending. By far the largest sector is against property which accounts for half of a lending. The second largest sector is lending to other financial corporations. Figure 6.1 provides evidence that nearly all of the lending by banks is not to productive activities.

142   6 A Kind of Magic

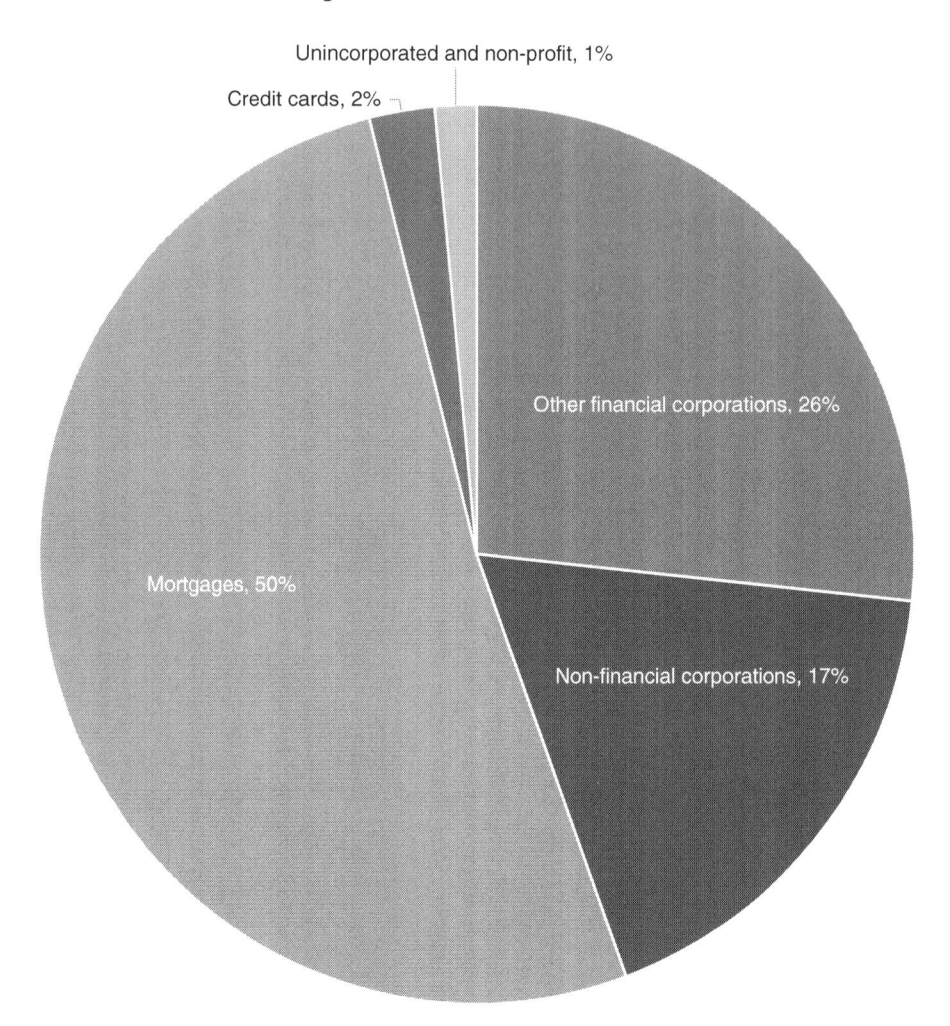

Pie chart showing:
- Mortgages, 50%
- Other financial corporations, 26%
- Non-financial corporations, 17%
- Credit cards, 2%
- Unincorporated and non-profit, 1%

Fig. 6.1 UK Bank lending by sector in 2015
Source: Bank of England Bankstats table A4.1

So why does this happen, why do banks lend into the sectors that they do, which is mostly to property?

The UK high street banks are enormous businesses, so for example Barclays turnover in 2014 was £16 billion for the UK alone. The four large retail banks dominate the UK market, accounting for 74%[11] of lending. Large businesses generally look to achieve economies of scale and reduced costs to maximise profits. Banks can achieve this either by having very large clients or having standardised products which can be rolled out at scale.

A mortgage on a property is very easy to standardise: all you need to do is get a valuation on the property, put a charge on the property and assess your client's income. All of these are relatively cheap and easy to systemise, so banks can scale up mortgage loans relatively easily. In contrast, for bank to lend to a business, the bank manager has to understand the risks of the business, including the capabilities of the people or organisation that the bank is lending to. This is inherently a much more difficult decision and therefore requires a more skilled, and hence expensive, bank manager and has higher information costs; the bank manager has to get to know the local clients and there will be a premium on stability; it will be costly for managers to leave or move.

Added to this, from a manager's perspective lending for investment purposes is inherently more risky than lending against property. If the bank is lending against property, in the event of a default, the bank can repossess the property and then sell it. If the bank is lending to a business for purposes of investment, there may be no asset as collateral, or if there is an asset it may not be ready saleable, or it may only be of value when used in some form of production which might be very specialised.

When lending against property there is much less uncertainty in assessing the value of the collateral, and the future income stream against which the loan is paid. In the case of a mortgage, or personal debt, this is someone's salary, which is easy to assess and is often fairly stable with time. A bank manager does not really have to know the client to assess his creditworthiness. In contrast a company's income is more difficult, especially for a small or new company, and maybe subject to a great deal of fluctuation.

So, all things being equal, the mortgage and personal loans section will grow faster than the bank's lending to companies, until these dominate as is the case now.

However, all things are not equal, because regulation makes it more profitable for banks to lend against property than to companies. Obviously banking regulation is highly complex, but I shall try to explain the appropriate bit here in enough detail so that the reader who is not an expert in bank regulation can understand why.

Banks risk-management practices are regulated by the Basel accords, which are international standard regulation, as well as a great deal of domestic regulation. At the present time, we are between Basel II and Basel III. One of the main levers for regulation is the capital ratio. A bank has to hold a certain amount of capital in relation to its assets, this can be thought of as a buffer to cover losses. The capital ratio is important to a bank's profitability; if the capital ratio is high, this means that the bank has to hold a lot of capital –

on which it cannot earn – compared to its assets, so the income that its assets make is low compared to its capital, and hence the return on capital (think of this as profits) is low. If, on the other hand, the bank can hold a lot of assets for a given level of capital, it can post a high level of profits. Remembering that for a bank, its assets are its loans, a high capital ratio means that the bank can have a large loan portfolio (and hence make a large profit) for a low level of capital.

Under the Basel accords, banks' assets are assessed on a risk weighted basis. That is the loan is multiplied by a number which reflects how risky it is, so a risky loan is multiplied by a 1, and a very safe loan (e.g. a loan to a government) is multiplied by 0. Loans to mortgages are assessed as being very safe and are multiplied by a low number, whereas loans to business are assessed as being risky and are multiplied by a higher number. This means that mortgages are more profitable for a bank than a loan to a company for productive use.

6.3.2 The Morality of Interest

The bible views usury as an evil, and some religions, notably Islam, ban the practice of charging interest. However, in the modern world, we see things a bit differently; if I lend money to a third party, for example through a peer-to-peer lending platform, I am forgoing the use of this money and so you can think of interest as paying me rent for the use of my money.

However, for banks this is not the case – they are creating money out of thin air, so a borrower is not renting money from a bank. An argument for banks charging interest might be that in a free market banks are performing a useful service for which people are willing to pay (interest). But the only reason that a bank can create money out of thin air and not be put in prison for fraud is because the government gives them a licence to do so. This is not a free market, it is a mandate from government to allow privileged actors the right to print money. The bank is therefore providing a service which the government feels is valuable to its citizens, and rather than pay the banks directly for distributing money via loans, it is allowing banks to charge its customers for this service. The government does constrain what banks can charge to some extent.

The revenue that banks make from the ability to create money is calledseigniorage. There is no agreement over how to calculate the value of seigniorage to commercial banks, but I have seen a convincing attempt to quantify it as an average in the UK over the last 20 years of between £18bn and £30 billion – between 1% and 3% of GDP. This is the revenue that is generated by banks from the ability to create money through lending; it is

6.3 The Impact on the Economy of Money Creation 145

essentially the difference between the cost of their funding, which is deposits (less reserve requirements and other costs) and the cost that they would have to borrow money on the capital markets if they were peer-to-peer lenders rather than licensed banks.[12]

If the banking system is not performing its economic function, there is no reason why the government should give it the licences to print money; if the government could come up with an alternative viable technology to create its own money, society could benefit from seigniorage, which could be used to eliminate government debt, reduce taxes or just distribute newly created money, debt free, to citizens.

We have described during this chapter what a banking system is for. To summarise:

- To facilitate the payments system: banks do perform this function. If the government had not stepped in in 2008, the payments system might have collapsed, it is up to the reader to decide whether this is an acceptable risk.
- As a safe haven for people to keep their savings: for most of the time banks do this. If I deposit my money in a bank I am confident that it will not disappear. Again, in 2008 the government had to step in to save the system, and as I write people cannot get their money from the Greek banks, but again it is up to the reader whether this is an acceptable risk.
- The final function is the creation of new money through lending. For the economy to be sustainable that money needs to be directed towards productive use. In this they are totally failing.

I want to explain this last point more fully. Because money is created as a by-product of lending by banks, all the money in the economy has debt attached to it. As the economy grows, debt grows with it. Figure 6.2 shows how debt has increased as a proportion of gross domestic product (GDP) – since 1995 debt has increased from around one and a half times GDP to two and a half times GDP. If financial sector debt is included, the situation is much worse, total debt levels have increased from around twice GDP to five times.[13,14] Remembering that GDP has increased during this time as well – in absolute values the actual debt levels have increased by even more.

As I have explained the reason that banks charge interest is not because they are renting out their money, and not because they are private sector businesses providing people with a useful service, but because governments are allowing them to charge a fee for a useful service to the economy. Because they charge interest, that interest has to be repaid. This means that the economy has to grow

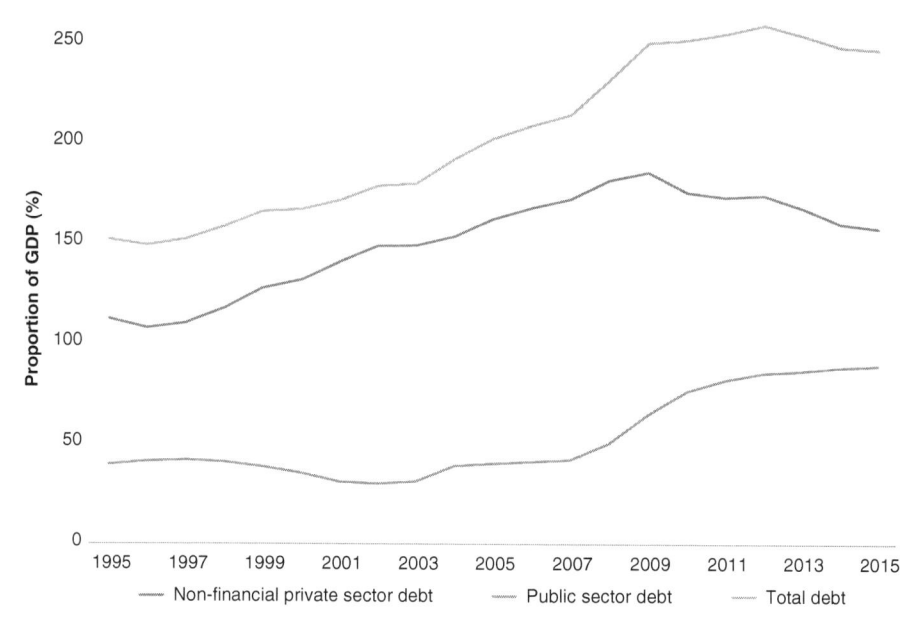

Fig. 6.2 Total UK debt levels

Source: Eurostat
Tables tipspd20 and teina225 http://ec.europa.eu/eurostat/tgm/table.do?tab=table&init=1&plugin=1&language=en&pcode=teina225 and http://ec.europa.eu/eurostat/tgm/table.do?tab=table&init=1&plugin=1&language=en&pcode=tipspd20 accessed 24 January 2017

in total by more than the interest that is to be paid on this debt; otherwise, the income generated by the economy will not be able to service the debt.

For the economy to grow, there must be some level of investment, but we have seen that banks are not doing this; nearly all lending is into the unproductive economy and investment is not coming from capital markets either. The result is Figure 6.2, an increase in debt levels compared to GDP. GDP is only increasing with a greater increase in the level of debt, this situation is clearly not sustainable.

6.4 Property and the Leverage Cycle

The news is often full of stories about the property crisis, how property in the UK, and particularly London, is so expensive, and how first time buyers are desperate to get onto the housing ladder. The government has repeatedly intervened to try to alleviate the crisis by subsidising mortgages.

Figure 6.1 showed us that half of the lending of UK banks is into real estate or property. The numbers are truly remarkable, new loans to property in the UK totalled £45 billion in 2014.[15] Property as an asset class is by far the largest in most countries. In the UK the combined value of residential property is £5.75 trillion (3.6 times GDP)[16] and commercial property is £647 billion (38% GDP). This compares with the market capitalisation of the stock market of £4 trillion.[17]

People need somewhere to live, so does bank lending into the sector provide people with a useful service, allowing them to afford a roof over their head? Does a mortgage allow people to buy property and therefore make it more affordable?

What determines the price of property? Property is two things, an asset and a place to live, so the drivers of the price of property are going to be complex. Property is not a homogenous asset class, what determines the value of an apartment in Manhattan is going to be different from a house in Detroit, or homestead in rural Nebraska.

There are fundamental supply and demand drivers. For example, a lot of people want to live in my home town of London, but there are also strict planning laws which make it difficult, time consuming and expensive to build property fast enough to match demand, which means that property in London is expensive.

However, at least part of the price is driven by the financing of property. If you go to the bank for a mortgage, there are a number of criteria which will affect your ability to get a loan[18]:

1. Affordability: how many times your income covers the loan repayment.
2. Deposit: what proportion of the loan the bank wants you to put down as a deposit.
3. Value of collateral: the higher the value of property, the higher the amount the bank will lend.
4. Loan to value: what proportion of collateral the bank will be willing to lend you.
5. Multiple of earnings: the total value of a loan divided by your income.

For the last 20 years there has been a rapid growth in the buy-to-let market, investors buying properties to rent out.[19] The criteria for getting a loan here are different, in some way simpler; in these cases the bank only needs to look at if the rental income covers the loan, the value of collateral, the deposit and loan to value.[20]

There are a number of observations that we can expect from this:

- The higher property prices, the more banks are willing to lend against property – as loans are a proportion of the value of the property.
- The higher people's earnings, the more banks would be willing to lend, because of both affordability and multiple of earnings cap.
- The lower interest rates, the higher the mortgage will be due to affordability criteria as the annual cost of servicing a mortgage will be lower and hence it will be more affordable.
- The higher rents the more banks are willing to lend against buy-to-let properties.
- Bank's behaviour and regulation: if banks are willing to loan against a lower deposit, a higher multiple of earnings or take a lower margin on affordability, they will be willing to lend more against a property.

Figure 6.1 showed that the vast majority, and an increasing amount, of UK bank lending is into the property sector. From Richard Werner's quantity theory of credit, if lending is into the property sector, this will increase the value of property. But, if the price of property increases, then banks are willing to lend more against property.

We have also seen in previous chapters that the interest rate has fallen persistently over the last 20 years, because of the interaction of governments and the financial markets. All other things being equal, this allows banks to lend more against a property as it makes loans more affordable.

The increase in property prices disproportionately benefits the wealthy; wealthier people are more likely to own a property and therefore they become more wealthy if property prices increase. If you have a higher income, you can borrow more to purchase a more expensive house, which has increased in value. And the banks, estate agents and property investors take a cut of the value of property and hence earn high incomes simply because property prices are increasing, without contributing to the productivity of the economy.

Finally, there is banks' behaviour. Jean Geanakoplos has a neat theory called the leverage cycle.[21] This suggests that the deposit is the limiting factor on people's ability to borrow, so when banks reduce their criteria for deposits, the asset price rises. According to the theory, in good times, the price is driven by optimist/risk takers who borrow as much as they can to purchase assets, which drives asset prices up. However, when the banks get spooked by bad news, they increase the margin call, the amount of deposit required, which means that these marginal buyers have to sell, and the asset price comes tumbling down.

6.4 Property and the Leverage Cycle

Banks make a profit from lending against property. When property prices go up, they are incentivised to loosen their criteria, requiring lower deposits and allowing loans of higher multiple of earnings, therefore further increasing the value of property.

Because interest rates have dropped, mortgages will appear cheaper relative to people's income. Figure 6.3 shows that house prices have increased compared to people's income, more than doubling over the last 20 years and Figure 6.4 that mortgage payments have fluctuated around the same level over the last 25 years. The latter means that, because interest rates have dropped, banks are willing to lend out money at a higher multiple of people's salary.

All of these factors that I have described are endogenous to the finance system. Lower interest rates, higher wealth inequality and the increase in property prices are all caused by the finance system itself, and banks profit from this increased lending into property.

Banks lend against property based on the value of the property and people's ability to pay. People's ability to pay is determined by the interest rate and their income level. People's ability to pay has apparently increased, simply because interest rates have gone down, and banks have been willing to

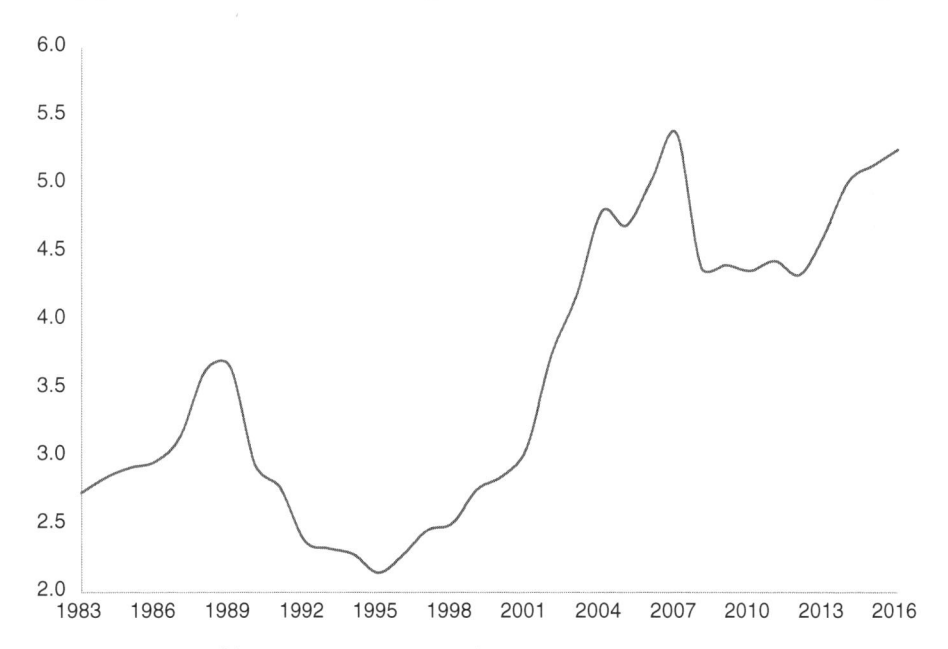

Fig. 6.3 Ratio of house prices compared to income

Source: Nationwide House Price Index
Nationwide House Price Index, figures for first time buyers http://www.nationwide.co.uk/about/house-price-index/download-data#xtab:affordability-benchmarks accessed 20 January 2017

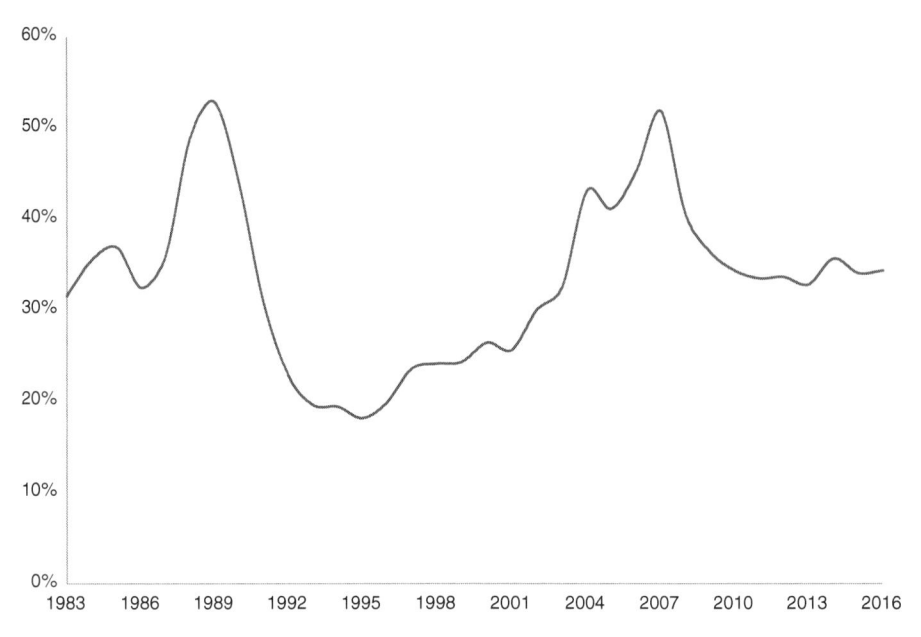

Fig. 6.4 Mortgage payments as proportion of income

Source: Nationwide House Price Index
Nationwide House Price Index, figures for first time buyers http://www.nationwide.co.uk/about/house-price-index/download-data#xtab:affordability-benchmarks   accessed   20 January 2017

lend people greater amounts of money. But banks willingness to lend money against property actually increases the price.

Banks lending to property also decreases the interest rate. More wealth is stored in property and property prices go up because of the leverage cycle. The money creation process does not cause goods inflation as would be expected from the quantity theory of credit. Goods production is offshored and the Chinese central bank has intervened to stop inflation of the price of Chinese goods. Central banks like the Bank of England have asymmetric incentives, if they increase interest rates this will hit property prices, reduce spending and may cause a bank crisis. If they reduce rates it will have no effect on prices of consumer goods, which make up their inflation target. The trend to reduce rates continues, pushing up property prices and increasing lending to real estate.

The set up I have described is almost a ponzi scheme. A ponzi or pyramid selling scheme is whereby I send out a letter to five people asking them to pay me £5; they each send out a letter to five more people, and everyone makes money until the whole thing collapses when you run out of people.

The banking/property ponzi scheme works thus. Banks lend money against property. This property goes up in value, as does the income and wealth of people working in finance, banking and property, so these people can afford to service higher levels of debt. There is more money in the system which can be used to finance deposit. Property prices go up, so everyone wants to be on the housing ladder. Banks profit by lending against property and there is a low level of bad debts because the value of property has increased.

This increases the demand for property and the demand for mortgages, which further increases the price of property. To encourage more people to take on profitable loans banks reduce their rates and deposit requirements and increase the size of loan they are prepared to make. The money created by these loans goes to richer people, who save more into the financial system, causing a savings glut and reducing interest rates, which pushes up the value of property further. This cycle goes on until house prices spiral out of control, increasing by a factor of four over the last 20 years in the UK and in some hotspots by much more – for example sixfold in London.[22]

There is one more possibility though. If we go back to the quantity theory of credit, an increase in credit can lead to an increase in quantity of assets as well as price. There is clearly an increasing demand for housing goods and services, so if lending into the sector causes an increased supply, this would be a productive investment. Unfortunately, the number of houses built in the UK has steadily declined over the last 40 years, from over 350,000 per year in the 1970s to less than 150,000 per year now.[23] There are 25 million homes in the UK, so the current level of building represents only 0.6% of the housing stock. The number of houses have increase, but not as much as required, and only by a tiny proportion of the overall stock. Therefore, according to Werner, credit being created and lent into the housing sector alone will cause prices to rise, which is exactly what has happened.

Half of all bank lending goes towards property. This does not give people access to property services, which could be achieved by increasing the supply of property. However, it does increase the price of property. This has a number of effects:

- Wealth inequality: Lending into property causes the price of property to increase, and more expensive property to increase by more. This increases wealth inequality as people who own property are more wealthy.
- Limiting access to finance: As the wealth of the country becomes increasingly concentrated, those with access to cheap finance are increasingly the property-owning class and high wage earners. Inequality increases as the wealthy have the ability to borrow to purchase assets, whereas the poor cannot.

- Skewing the economy: By lending into the property sector, banks are ensuring that this increases the activity in this sector. The price is important; for example, if a house sells for £100,000 and the estate agent, gets, say 1%, then the agent's fee is £1,000. But if a property sells for £1 million, the fee is £10,000. This means that high house prices cause more economic activity to be property related, but without increasing the supply of housing to the population.
- Growth of banking sector: By continually lending, unnecessarily, against an asset class, a bank expands its own balance sheet and hence its own income. The size of the UK's four large banks compared to the UK economy has grown massively. Debt of the finance sector has quadrupled relative to GDP in the 25 years from 1987. As bank's debt and assets cancel out, this means that they are using the debt to create assets (loans to customers). But we have seen that this is mostly for non-productive activities, the purpose of the lending becomes to increase the size of the banks themselves, as well as, incidentally, the property sector.

Because of this expansion of debt, the economy has to grow to pay off the debt. The economy can only grow if there is investment and this is not happening. More trouble is in store.

6.5 A Different Class of Bank

Up to now I have referred to retail banks, this is the kind of banks that most people deal with on a day-to-day basis.

There is another kind of bank – an investment bank. The difference between an investment bank and a retail bank is that a retail bank can take deposits from the public, whereas an investment bank cannot. This is a crucial difference as only a retail bank can create money as described above.

With the repeal of the Sarbanes Oxley Act in 2002 in the USA, and equivalent legislation in other countries, investment banks and retail banks gradually merged. But the function and character of the two institutions are quite separate. Also, after the financial crises, regulators have been taking action to try and separate the two, and many retail banks are closing down or selling off their investment banking arm, as their dalliance with investment banking has caused them to get badly burned.

What is an investment bank? These are hugely complex beasts, and if the reader would like a full description, I refer her to a textbook such as Fabozzi et al. (2015).[24] A simple explanation is that investment banks mediate the interaction between organisations (which could be a firm, a government or another institution) and the capital markets.

If a company would like to raise funds from the capital markets, or invest in the capital markets or deploy a financial product, for example to manage risk, this is usually facilitated by an investment bank.

If a government wants to raise money on the capital market, it works with an investment bank, who might advise the government, design and structure the financial instrument, such as a bond, advise on price, find buyers and/or underwrite the bond. If a company wants to purchase another company, it will usually work with an investment bank. Investment banks often manage money for institutions or individuals. Their core functions could be thought of as intermediaries; unlike a retail bank, investment banks do not hold the money of their clients.

The key to investment banks' success is information; they are the smartest, best paid guys (yes, usually men), they have all the contacts and all of the information. They know who is buying and selling, as it's their job to know this it is their clients who are doing the buying and selling. They sit at the fulcrum of the financial system.

Sometimes, the terms "buy side" and "sell side" are used. The buy side are the asset owners, and asset managers as described in Chapter 2. Some asset managers are now owned by investment banks.

The sell side, as the name implies, are the organisations, or parts of organisations that put together financial product to sell to the buy side. These could be listed shares, funds (e.g. private equity), securitised bonds or a vast array of products. It is often investment banks who create, put together or sell these products.

The role of investment banks has changed; whilst continuing with their traditional intermediary role, they increasingly act as principle. This has come about in a number of forms and arose out of their more traditional activities. One of the functions of investment banks was to act as broker/dealers. An investment manager might want to buy stock in a company. He will place the order via a broker. To serve their customers, as well as matching buyers with sellers, the broker might hold some stock so as not to affect the market price if there is a big buy (or sell) order. The broker knows who is buying and selling, so he can have an idea of how much stock he needs to hold. But he can also use this knowledge to make money for himself, by buying more stock and selling it at a profit – this is called trading on principle.

Investment banks also work as market makers – in exchange for being allowed to trade, say, government bonds "first" and thus earn extra commissions, they commit themselves to maintain market liquidity in the given security.

Their position of holders of knowledge of markets, and their ability to innovate, has enabled them to develop product where they essentially become more like retail banks (in addition to actually merging with retail banks).

Unlike retail banks, investment banks are only intermediaries, so how can they play the leverage game? Investment banks are in fact at the core of the leverage game. Historically, they were less regulated than retail banks, and culturally they are much more innovative and aggressive in what they do. Retail bankers are portrayed in fiction as dull and solid like Captain Mainwaring or George Bailey; investment bankers like to think of themselves as Christian Grey or Patrick Bateman.

Investment banks are not allowed to take deposits, but there are other ways they can play the leverage game of borrowing short and lending long. An example is through repurchase agreements (repos). The European repo market is worth about Euro 5 trillion.[25] This is where a bank sells a security and agrees to buy it back at a higher price, often the next day. The price differential can be thought of as interest. The bank can use the cash to fund longer term loans. The repo agreement is effectively like a deposit, the bank is taking cash every day from a counterparty, who can choose not to renew the agreement at any time, which is akin to a depositor being able to withdraw their money at any time.

Investment banks stand at the centre of the shadow banking system. This has grown rapidly and is estimated to be larger than the traditional banking system, some estimating the size as $100 trillion.[26] Shadow banking performs the same function as traditional banking via the capital markets. In a simplified form, it works like this: by borrowing on the repo or other "wholesale" markets, investment banks can borrow short-term capital. They use this to buy traditional banking assets, such as mortgage loans, and bundling groups of mortgages into bonds with different risk characteristics, from very safe to very risky, often with extensive use of derivatives to adjust the risk characteristics of the bond. Eventually, after passing through different intermediaries, the bonds are sold to the asset owners described in Chapter 2.[27]

What is the shadow banking process doing? Ultimately, it is taking savings money from asset owners, leveraging it up, and investing the money into a mixture of existing assets, mostly real estate, or complex virtual assets, such as collateralized debt obligations, which pushes the prices of these assets up and allows further lending into these assets. As we have seen money is created as a by-product of mortgage lending, so by pushing the price of assets up, this process increases the amount of money in the system and increases the amount of money that is available to reinvest in financial markets. The next chapter will describe the tools the financial sector employ to maximise their revenue. Through their sophistication and aggressiveness investment banks are at the vanguard of expanding the role of the financial sector.

6.6   Conclusion

Retail banks have a privileged position in society, granted to them by governments. There is a twofold support for banks from the state: because of their crucial role in the economy, they have an implicit guarantee, which is estimated to be worth between £30billion and £100 billion; and their ability to create money is equivalent to an annual average revenue of between £18 billion and £30 billion. These implicit subsidies overlap and there is a wide range in the estimates of their magnitude, but we can say for certain that the subsidy is enormously valuable to the banking sector. In return, banks retail, investment and the shadow banking system are disproportionately lending against assets, the majority is collateralised against real estate. Lending against real estate causes the price of property to increase and the debt levels to increase.

Banks are only lending a very small proportion of loans into the real, productive economy. We have seen in previous chapters that capital markets are not investing into the productive economy either. Retail banks create money as a by-product of their lending activity so money is being directed into these non-productive sectors, and it is also being lent predominantly to the wealthy, boosting the value of their assets. In lending against these assets, the debt in the economy has to be repaid, yet the economy is not investing productively to be able to repay these debts. Also, as we have seen in previous chapters, the workforce is ageing and therefore the debt levels in the economy have to be repaid by a decreasing pool of workers.

Notes

1. Noss, J and Sowerbutts, R (2012) *The Implicit subsidy of banks* Bank of England.
2. Noss, J and Sowerbutts, R (2012) *The Implicit subsidy of banks* Bank of England.

3. This represented the position of textbooks until relatively recently. The latest textbooks for example Sloman, J Garrett, D and Wride, A (2014) *Economics* Pearson; 9th Edition or Krugman, P and Wells, R (2015) *Economics* W.H. Freeman & Co Ltd; 4th Revised edition, still explain the money multiplier story but provide critiques of the theory. They also mention in passing that money is created by banks.
4. The money multiplier is the inverse of the reserve ratio.
5. Mcleay, M Radia, A and Thomas, R (2014) *Money Creation in the modern economy* Bank of England Quarterly Bulletin 2014 Q1.
6. Werner, R (2005) *New Paradigm in Macroeconomics* Palgrave Macmillan.
7. I could, though, create private money, from which I could only profit if I could persuade people to accept it.
8. From Bank of England interactive statistics database data series LPQAUYM and LPMAVAA.
9. For example, Werner, R (2005) *New Paradigm in Macroeconomics* Palgrave McMillan.
10. From lecture by Richard Werner at Robinson College, Cambridge 30 October 2012 https://www.postkeynesian.net/downloads/Werner/RW301012PPT.pdf
11. The Telegraph 6 November 2014 *Full investigation into the dominance of "big four" UK banks confirmed.*
12. Bjerg, O Macfarlane, L Hougaard, R Nielsen Ryan-Collins, J *Seigniorage in the 21st Century: A study of the Profits from money creation in the United Kingdom and Denmark* CBS Working Paper
13. McKinsey Global Institute (2015) *Debt and (Not Much) Deleveraging* McKinsey & Company.
14. There are arguments for or against including financial sector debt. In theory, financial sector debt should net off, all the financial sector does is borrow from one party and lend to another, so including the finance sector would lead to double counting. On the other hand, some of the financial sector debt is outside of the UK. Also, if there is a crisis or downturn, the high finance sector debt will increase the economic damage.
15. Financial Times 22 May 2015 *Lenders pour cash into UK property market.*
16. Savills blog 15 January 2015 *UK housing stock rises to £5.75 trillion* http://www.savills.co.uk/blog/article/185397/residential-property/uk-housing-market-rises-to-5-75-trillion.aspx
17. London Stock Exchange Statistics http://www.londonstockexchange.com/statistics/markets/markets.htm accessed 28 December 2016.
18. For example, TSB Mortgage eligibility criteria http://www.tsb.co.uk/mortgages/guides/mortgage-eligibility-criteria/ accessed 28 December 2016.
19. Buy-to-let mortgages represent around 10% of total mortgages; Council of Mortgage Lenders 14 February 2013 *Buy-to-let lending £16.4 billion in 2012* (https://www.cml.org.uk/news/press-releases/3423/).

20. For example, TSB Mortgage eligibility criteria http://www.tsb.co.uk/mortgages/guides/mortgage-eligibility-criteria/ accessed 28 December 2016.
21. Geanakoplos, J (2009) *The Leverage cycle* NBER Macroeconomics annual.
22. Source: Office for National Statistics accessed 20 January 2017.
23. BBC News 13 January 2015 *Why can't the UK build 240,000 houses a year?* http://www.bbc.co.uk/news/magazine-30776306
24. Frank J. Fabozzi, Franco P. Modigliani, Frank J. Jones (2015) *Foundations of Financial Markets and Institutions (4th Edition)* Prentice Hall.
25. In 2014 International Capital Markets Association *How big is the repo market?* http://www.icmagroup.org/Regulatory-Policy-and-Market-Practice/repo-and-collateral-markets/frequently-asked-questions-on-repo/4-how-big-is-the-repo-market/ accessed 28 December 2016.
26. Fiaschi, D Kondor, Marsili, M (2013). *The Interrupted Power Law and the Size of Shadow Banking* PLoS One 9(4).
27. Palan, R. & Nesvetailova, A. (2014) *Elsewhere, Ideally Nowhere: Shadow Banking and Offshore Finance* Politik, 16(4), pp. 26–34.

7

The Economy's Helminths

How the Finance System Uses Capital to Generate Revenue

Diseases or parasites that kill their host are not very successful. Parasites need a host, a dead host means no home. Bubonic plague was very successful at killing its victims leaving a much smaller, resistant population and no more bubonic plague. There is a lot of common cold or influenza around, these pathogens get the cells of their host to produce more of them, and then to sneeze and cough so that they can be passed on to new hosts, but are very rarely fatal. A helminth is a small worm that lives in animal's gut; it uses your gut as a source of food and shelter. You can live with a helminth without really noticing, although helminths can cause you illness as a by-product of their ability to get your body to behave in a way favourable to their own comfort.

The 1987 film *Wall Street* introduced the character Gordon Gekko, played by Michael Douglas, whose "greed is good" speech epitomised the popular view of 1980s' capitalism. Gordon Gekko was an asset stripper; he would buy a company's shares, break it up and sell off its assets, and if the sum of these assets was worth more than the value of the company, he would make a fortune for himself whilst destroying the host company. But there are no more Gordon Gekkos. Modern financial intermediaries are more like helminths.

Economist Thomas Philippon has shown that the unit cost of financial intermediation has been constant over the last 130 years at around 2%.[1] This is a stunning conclusion given all of the technological advances and improvements in efficiencies that have occurred during that time, many of which have been adopted by the finance sector; yet, the costs of financial intermediation has not decreased.

Figure 7.1 shows that share of GDP of financial services in USA has increased over this time period. This chart actually underestimates the growth of financial services, as many non-financial companies (NFCs) now make a large proportion of their profits from financial activities, which is not captured by the chart. How can there have been such a large increase in the size of finance compared to the size of the economy if the cost of intermediation has not changed?

An economy has a capital stock from which it produces goods and services. This consists of physical assets such as houses, factories, roads and power stations and also social assets such as an intellectual property, knowledge and an efficient tax-collecting regime. In a capitalist economy, the economy's surplus is saved and invested in building up the capital stock.

The finance sector manages part of these savings, for which it receives a fee of a proportion of the accumulated savings/capital, it converts a portion of the stock (the accumulated savings/capital) into a flow (the fee). The justification for the fee is that the finance sector is ensuring the capital stock is managed efficiently and new savings are allocated effectively so that the capital stock can generate more goods and services. The value of this increase should outweigh the finance sector's fee.

This chapter argues that the finance sector manipulates its role of managing savings and capital, to increase its own revenue. It achieves this through leverage, where apparent profit is increased by increasing risk, by creating new artificial financial products which can be bought and sold and by colonising an increasing proportion of the economy out of which revenue can be extracted. The finance sector is supported by an intellectual domination of ideas which come out of financial economics and management theory.

The thesis of this chapter is:

Proposition 1
The purpose of the finance sector is to maximise its own revenue,
Proposition 2
This is achieved by agents in the financial system managing capital stocks and flows in the economy in such a way as to generate revenue for themselves.

Proposition 1 is not controversial. The finance sector is made up of firms, which could be under a variety of different ownership structures.[2] The purpose of these firms and their employees is to make money. If you asked a random sample of finance workers, I would be very surprised if any of them gave a different reason for their work. The view championed by the finance sector itself is that the objective of a firm is to maximise shareholder value.

The Economy's Helminths 161

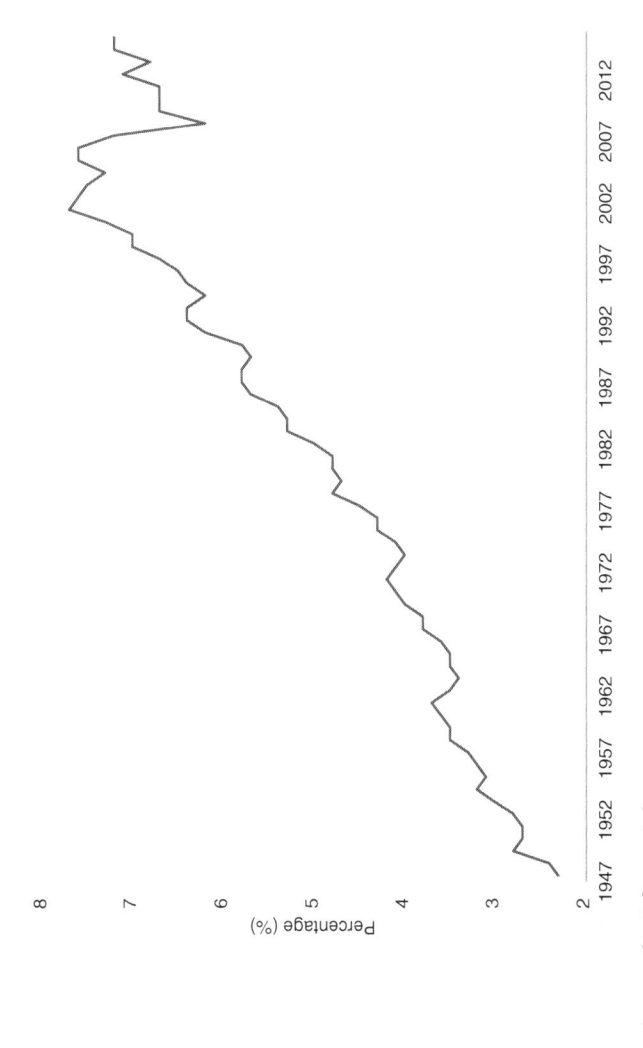

Fig. 7.1 GDP share of US financial sector

Source: US Bureau of Economic Analysis
From https://www.bea.gov/industry/gdpbyind_data.htm accessed 16 January 2017

I have used the word revenue rather than profit as it has been argued that some companies, especially in the finance sector, have been captured by their own senior management, who pay themselves excessively at the expense of the company. Firms either try to maximising revenue for shareholders or they are maximising revenue which is being captured by the firm's employees. Often senior employees are shareholder, so the difference may be academic.

In formulating these propositions, I am not making a moral judgement, finance firms are not looking to do good or bad; they are amoral – a firm is a legal entity, not a moral agent.

Proposition 2 is more controversial and requires justification. Proposition 2 follows logically from Proposition 1; the finance sector has a great deal of influence in controlling where an economy's capital is allocated. If the helminth's aim is to maximise its own revenue and what it does is allocate capital, it will try to allocate capital to achieve its aim, unless it is not allowed to do so by governments, regulators or its clients.

In communist economies such as the Soviet Union, the government or Communist Party was in control of the capital allocation in the economy, so the country developed in a way that reflected these decisions. In our system, capital is allocated in a way that benefits the finance sector; the other outcomes are irrelevant to its decision-making process. Over time the economy and, to some extent, society and the environment, have been shaped in the image of this process. Other institutions also allocate capital, notably corporates and the public sector, but over time these have been to a greater or lesser extent colonised by finance.

The theory behind maximising shareholder value is that if all companies are maximising shareholder returns, then the economy is running efficiently and everyone is better off. How can it be that everyone is not better off if we have a large, thriving, dynamic, profit-maximising finance sector?

The economist William Baumol distinguished between productive, unproductive and destructive entrepreneurship. All societies have entrepreneurs, but the rules under which the society operates determine whether this entrepreneurship is directed to productive or destructive ends.[3]

It is not a good idea for all members of society to be profit-maximising entrepreneurs. If senior members of the government of a country are amoral revenue-maximising individuals, then they will maximise their own revenue by diverting the country's resources into their own Swiss bank accounts. Unfortunately, this has happened very frequently throughout history. For example, former African dictators such as Nigerian President Sani Abacha and Zaire's[4]

Mobutu Sese Seko allegedly stole billions of dollars during their times in office.[5,6] When people are in control of the levers of power of an economy, you do not want them to be able to behave as amoral revenue maximisers.

If people working in finance were amoral and working outside the law, they can divert other people's money to themselves to the detriment of everyone else. An example was Bernie Madoff, a supposedly successful investment manager who was in fact running a Ponzi scheme. When new money came in from investors, he paid it out to existing clients (and himself), apparently generating fantastic returns. Eventually, this scheme came to an end, and Mr Madoff is now languishing in prison. Mr Madoff could do this because he was looking after other people's money; there was an asymmetry of information between him and his investors; they did not know how he was investing his money.

The finance sector has the potential to extract money from people or institutions which it interacts with, and because of this it operates under an extensive set of rules. In the case of Mr Madoff, these rules eventually did what they were supposed to do, as he was ultimately caught and punished. There have also been a number of recent cases where employees of mainstream financial institutions have been colluding to manipulate the market value of indices for their own financial benefit, but to the loss of investors. Again, many of the perpetuators have been caught, the institutions fined and recently, one of the employees has been sentenced to a term in prison.

There is probably much more illegal activity going on where finance employees are enriching themselves illegally, as these crimes are difficult to detect, and therefore, it is likely that the regulator has only managed to prosecute a small proportion of this nefarious activity. But Proposition 2 proposes that the finance sector has managed to divert financial flows for its own use in an entirely legal manner; this is the main problem with the current financial system, not excessive risk taking or criminal activity. It can do this because, for mistaken ideological and practical reasons, governments have delegated the crucial social technology of capital allocation to the finance sector without ensuring that it is allocated broadly where society might want or need it.

7.1 A (Very) Brief History of the Current Financial System

The finance system that we have today is highly contingent on historical events and is also rapidly changing. The system will not last long in its current form; it is like a ship that has hit an iceberg but not yet sunk.[7]

The major factor in the evolution of the current financial system was that a few governments, to solve domestic problems, established the conditions which enabled financial institutions to make a fortune by creating credit on a massive scale.

After the Wall Street Crash in 1929, the US and other governments put in place a number of restrictions on financial activities. The zeitgeist after the Crash was that financial markets were a cause of instability and had to be controlled. So, there was a cap on the interest rate that banks could pay to savers, and there was a separation between different institutions so that each institution could only lend to one sector, for example to households or to corporates. The net effect was to constrain leverage and credit. The US government guaranteed that dollars could be exchanged for gold, which put a cap on the money supply.

In the 1950s and 1960s this era of constrained capital coincided with an unprecedented economic boom in the USA, Europe and Japan, as these economies rebuilt after the war. However, a number of challenges arose which started to undermine the constraints. In the USA, a combination of high inflation and increasingly vociferous demands for resources by different interest groups put pressure on the system. The cap on interest rates meant that periods of high inflation caused income redistribution, as savers were punished by the low interest rates, whilst borrowers were made better off. Because of the cap on credit, the government had to arbitrate on who got this credit, which made the government unpopular, so the US government was incentivised to either find someone else to make this decision and/or increase the available capital so that it was no longer rationed.

Meanwhile, the UK government, which also had credit controls in place, tacitly allowed financial transactions in foreign currencies, pretending that they did not occur in London, and hence getting around its own capital controls. The resultant Eurodollar market became a source of funding for US banks and companies, which could bypass US capital control regulations.

Because of the US governments' increased budget deficits, caused by the Vietnam War and increased domestic spending on social security, the government could no longer afford to support the gold standard, under which it guaranteed that dollars could be exchanged for a predetermined amount of gold.

The outcome of all this was that the US government exited the gold standard in 1973 and progressively loosened and abandoned capital controls. In the 1980s, the European Union instituted the free movement of capital between member states, and the Bank of Japan abandoned its window guidance policies, allowing banks to lend into whatever sector they chose, whereas previously they had been restricted to lending mainly into the export sector.

Other domestic considerations also set the ground work for what followed. In the UK, the government, faced with a declining industrial base, looked to the financial services industry in the City of London to provide economic growth. It progressively liberalised laws, allowing London to eventually become the World's largest offshore financial centre. This was facilitated as London's financial institutions had close connections to Britain's former colonies, which could be used as flags of convenience for transactions which required low levels of oversight.[8]

Many developing countries attempted to increase wealth through export led manufacturing, as the basis of economic development or by exploiting and selling natural resources such as oil. This provided a symbiotic relationship with the US, which was running large government deficits which had to be financed. The export country would produce goods which would be sold into the US markets in dollars. However, if the country sells goods to the US in dollars and does not buy anything in return, this would push up the price of the country's currency against the US dollar. Governments deliberately chose to immunise against this to keep their currencies low; the local government would swap the dollars for local currency and use the proceeds to buy US assets, mainly government bonds which would finance the US government deficit. Americans effectively got access to an unlimited supply of cheap finance, which they could then use to buy more foreign goods.

The countries that pursued these policies were firstly Japan and Germany, then the Asian tiger economies and, now, on an unprecedented scale, China. China now owns approximately $1.3 trillion of US debt (which is ironic, as one of the last purportedly communist countries probably has the ability to bring down US capitalism simply by dumping its US debt holdings).

Another major factor was the actions of two government sponsored enterprises (GSEs) in the USA, Fannie Mae and Freddie Mac. Fannie Mae was established at the end of the great depression and Freddie Mac later, with the purpose of expanding the mortgage market so that more people could afford to buy their homes. They did this through securitisation, packaging up mortgages and selling them into the capital markets, often with a guarantee. Although the GSEs were private companies, they were widely seen as having the backing of the US government, and therefore, these mortgages were thought of as being underwritten by the US government. Both GSEs reached enormous size; when they were nationalised (officially taken into "conservatorship") during the 2007/8 financial crisis, they held or guaranteed $5.2 trillion of mortgage debt.[9]

The situation was set: banks were allowed to create credit and there were loosening controls on their ability to do so. Meanwhile, foreign governments were effectively increasing the supply of savings at an accelerating scale. The barriers on capital movements were coming down, allowing assets to be transferred between jurisdictions and increasing the range of investors. Technology facilitated the increased ability for speedier transactions and flows of information. Finally, a network of financial centres developed with differing regulatory regimes, so institutions had the potential to synthesise virtually any product they could dream up.

7.2 Something Rotten in the State of Finance

Financial institutions found themselves in a position where they could capitalise on the vast increase in the amount of credit and capital flows being created, often by government policy. Globalisation means that there has been a great increase in demand for international financial services, such as currency hedging and international lending. Many countries in the world have rapidly industrialised or reindustrialised since the war, first Japan and Germany, then Spain and Portugal, the Asian tigers, Eastern Europe and now China, India, Vietnam, Malaysia, Brazil and South Africa. Even many of the countries which have not industrialised have still got richer, resulting in a vast amount of new savings that need to be managed, which has created new demand for financial services.

These factors have contributed to a substantial growth in the finance system, especially in international hubs such as London and New York. But this will have only contributed to part of the increase, and as I have argued exhaustively, the finance system only does its job poorly.

Meanwhile, the cost of financial intermediation has remained constant over the last 130 years, despite massive technological improvements, and the share of financial services in GDP has consistently increased, as was shown in Figure 7.1.

Figure 7.2 shows that the profits made by the finance sector more than doubled in the USA between the 1968s and the run up to the financial crisis; it is currently rebounding back towards this level.[10] There may be more need for financial services as there was more international trade and more savings going on. But financial services are meant to be providing a service to the economy; we have shown that this service is not good. So how are they making such an increasing share of profits? Also, by their nature they are providing a service to other industries that actually make or do stuff that people want. Yet, the finance sector takes up to 40% of the profits or real stuff. This is clear evidence of rent-seeking behaviour.

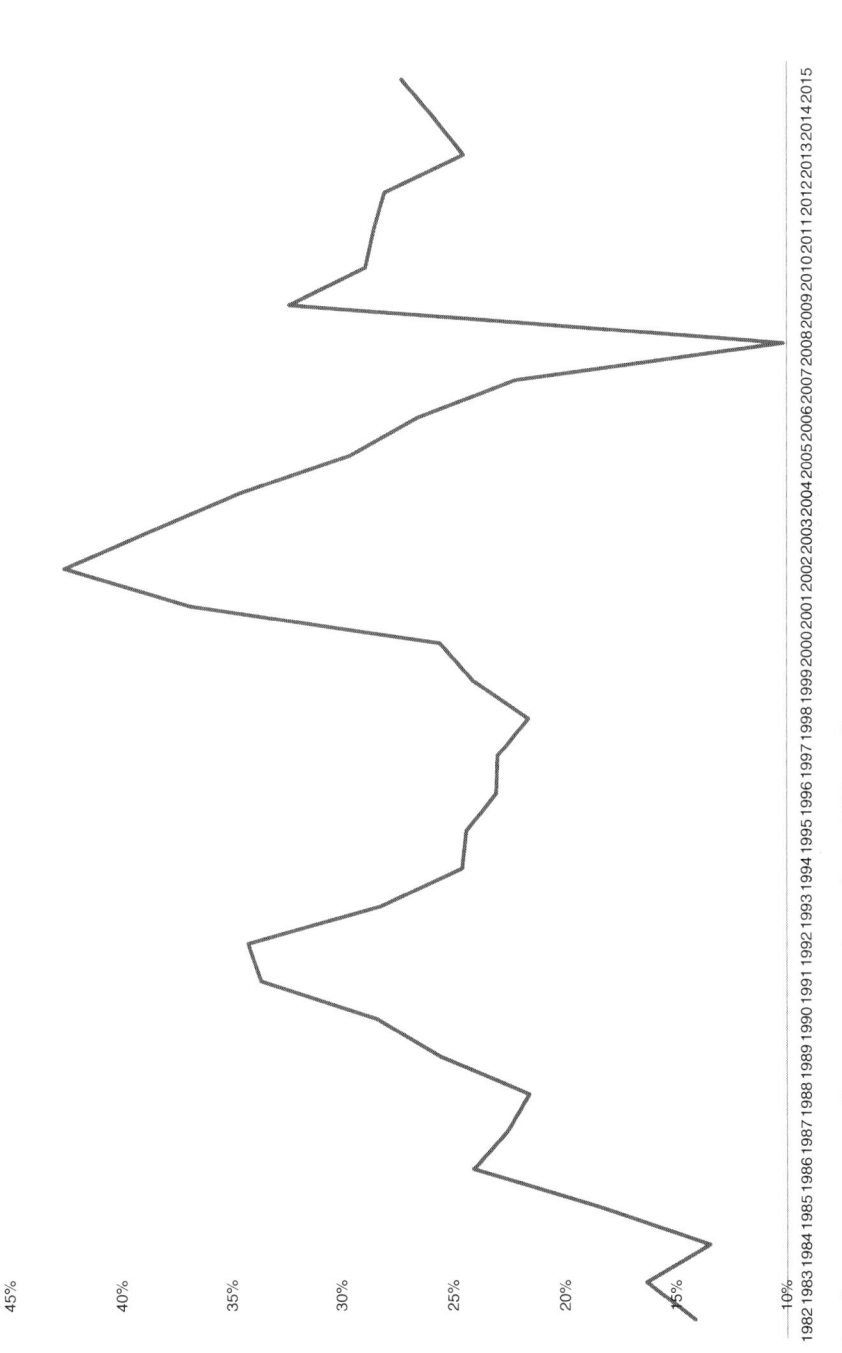

Fig. 7.2 Finance sector profits as proportion of total US profits

Source: US Bureau of Economic Analysis
From National industry data, NIPA table 6.16 https://www.bea.gov/national/nipaweb/downss2.asp accessed 16 January 2017

The finance sector has been accused of being captured by overpaid executives who divert shareholders' funds to pay themselves high salaries. Between the 1940s and 1980s, compensation in finance was similar to other sectors; by 2017 it was four times as high.[11] The excess wages can be thought of as extra profit captured by financial services over and above that illustrated in Figure 7.2. Figure 7.2 also omits many financial firms which are not publicly held corporations, financial operations which are wholly owned subsidiaries of non-finance firms, or firms which are domiciled in tax havens, which together mean that over half of profits are captured by finance. The finance sector is certainly highly profitable for not performing a very good service.

Figure 7.3 shows that the size of the over-the-counter (OTC) derivative markets has multiply by about 100 times in size in 25 years. There is a need for more derivatives then in the past. Derivatives are used to hedge forward prices, so a Brazilian company selling soya beans to the USA can buy derivatives to lock in both the forward price of soya and the exchange rate of the Real against the Dollar, which enables them to not be exposed to large price or exchange rate fluctuations.

Global trade has increased – approximately doubling over this period,[12] but why a 100-fold increase in the derivative markets?

In the 1970s almost all derivatives were based on agricultural products. Derivatives in currency, to allow hedging against currency fluctuations, came in after the breakdown in Bretton Woods when currencies started floating against the dollar; previously when exchange rates were fixed there was no need for currency hedging. Now the vast majority of derivatives are against financial instruments – nothing to do with trade at all.[13]

Derivatives were invented as a risk management tool – a farmer can manage the risk of fluctuating grain prices. Yet, the financial system creates its own risks, caused by the development for complex financial instruments such as derivatives, "financial weapons of mass destruction",[14] as was spectacularly displayed by the financial crisis. What has caused this massive growth in financial market activity, the size, profitability and remuneration of the finance sector?

The options traded in Figure 7.3 have either been created and sold by a financial agent to generate revenue or they are being created as leverage against an existing asset – to increase the return on existing financial assets, so the intermediary can charge more for it or can make increased profit on the performance of the asset.[15]

Figures 7.1–7.3 support Propositions 1 and 2. The finance sector has successfully increased its revenue, at the expense of the rest of the economy,

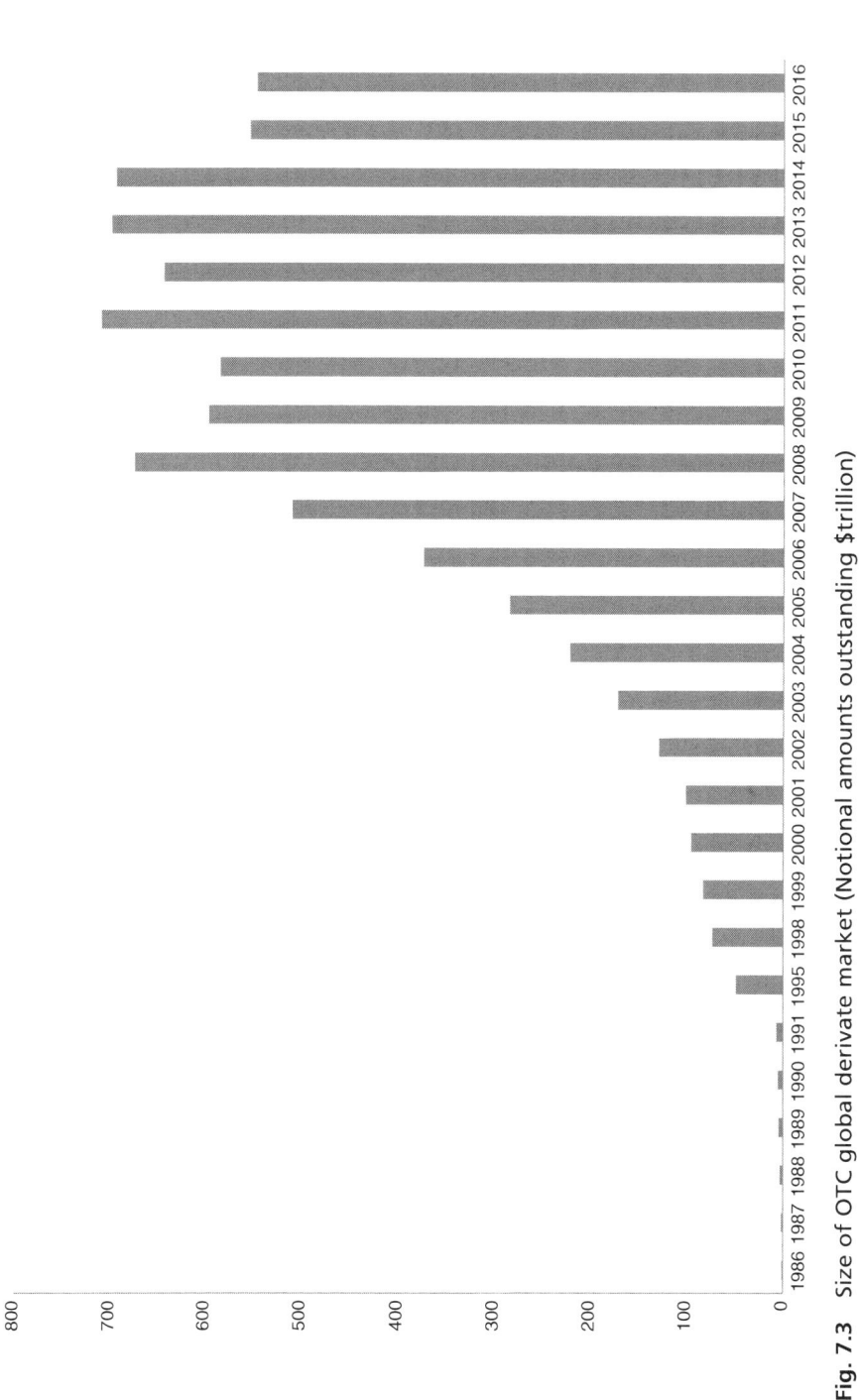

Fig. 7.3 Size of OTC global derivate market (Notional amounts outstanding $trillion)

Source: Bank for International Settlements
Semiannual OTC derivatives statistics http://www.bis.org/statistics/about_derivatives_stats.htm; pre 199 data was quoted in Remolona (1992) *The Recent Growth of Financial Derivative Markets* Federal Reserve Bank of New York accessed 16 January 2017

and it has done so by engaging in activity which is not demanded by the end user, so these activities must be responding to the needs of the finance sector itself.

The core to the finance sector's ability to maximise its revenue is its government-given mandate to allocate capital. This gives the finance sector a great deal of power and information; it is the centre of knowledge of the world's economic activities, which it utilises for its own profit. It uses this power and knowledge to enrich itself. To enhance revenue and entrench its position it employs the following tools:

(1) Leverage – the ability to multiply returns on existing assets;
(2) Abstraction/innovation – the creation of new virtual assets which can be traded generating revenue;
(3) Colonisation – the expansion and capture by finance of non-financial areas of the economy;
(4) Hegemony – the intellectual dominance of financial economics, and the ability to exclude other voices from finance's sphere of influence.

These tools are linked with each other and are dependent upon the capital allocation mandate. Leverage allows the financial sector to increase the revenue it can extract from a pool of assets and stake claims on future revenue. Financial innovation is the development of abstract virtual assets to generate further revenue for financial agents, often by increasing leverage.

Colonisation refers to the process of financialisation, where finance infiltrates into the DNA or control systems of NFCs and governments. Hegemony refers to the intellectual and cultural influence of finance; the development of finance theory has justified finance's dominant position and increased its ability to create financial instruments regulated in the interests of the financial sector. From the sectors of the economy over which finance holds sway, other intellectual disciplines or voices are excluded or even ridiculed.

In suggesting that the finance sector behaves in this way, I am not suggesting that individuals or companies are consciously subverting the economy, but this is the aggregate impact of individual decisions to maximise financial actors' own revenue.

The finance system is a network of agents, and the system has evolved based on the incentives and the constraints under which these agents operate. These incentives and constraints change with time and are influenced by actors in the system. The finance system is bound together by values, the overriding value being to maximising revenue for individual agents and hence the finance sector as a whole. Figures 7.1 and 7.2 show how successfully this has been achieved.

7.3 The Tools of the Finance Trade

The finance system has two main channels for allocating capital. In the deposit channel retail banks create money as a by-product of their lending decision; this created money is lent out into the economy. The economy develops depending on where the loans are allocated.

Banks are profit-maximising entities. They lend where they can maximise their return on capital. Banks prefer lending where the capital requirements are low. Lending products will be developed that can be scaled up at low cost, because the cost of information is low or the perceived risk is low. Banks' activities are concentrated on lending against assets, in particular real estate, which has low capital requirements (because Basel 3 and previous banking regulation view mortgages as low risk), low perceived risk (because the bank can repossess the asset on default) and low information costs (the value of an asset is easy to ascertain).

The effect of lending into real estate is to push up the price of real estate, which means that banks can lend more against these assets. In doing so banks increase the money supply, as money is created to lend against property, increasing debt levels in the economy, because the increase in money supply equates to increased debt.

The impact on the economy is irrelevant to banks, as this impact does not figure in their decision-making process. This is not a free market equilibrium which maximises allocative efficiency, because banks are lending to maximise their own revenues on the back of government-granted powers to create money.

The other channel of allocation of capital is the savings channel via financial markets. People save excess income, and the financial system pools and invests the savings where investment is needed. The mechanism in the savings and deposit channels is different. In the banking sector, lending goes towards inflating an asset bubble. In contrast, in the savings market, savings are transformed into virtual financial assets.

The way I would naively have imagined my pension being invested is that it is invested into the economy, for example by ownership of companies via their shares. These companies use this capital to invest, for example in further production or research and development or to buy kit.

However, my savings are not converted into investment. Instead, they remain as untapped virtual capital, which is used to continually buy and sell shares. This trick is carried out until I draw down my pension when I retire, may be 50 years after I start contributing; the financial system is like a party game of keeping the ball in the air lasting half a century.

By converting financial flows into virtual capital, it is easy for the financial sector to extract rent from my savings. If my savings were used to build a piece of infrastructure, for example fibre-optic broadband, the managers of the infrastructure would pay me a steady return and it would be hard for the financial sector to extract any rent from this. The financial sector also uses virtual financial capital to extract rent from the underlying companies on which my savings has as an ownership claim.

The finance sector uses leverage, financial innovation, colonisation and hegemony to increase its revenue and tighten its grip on the economy. I shall look at these tools in detail to explain how the financial sector extracts rent from the economy.

7.3.1 Leverage

Leverage works to increase the revenue of agents in the financial system. For a given amount of savings, assets and capital in the economy, leverage multiplies the financial return that can be achieved. In doing so financial agents' revenue is increased because they take a cut of those returns and they are paid for structuring the leveraging product. With more leverage, more assets are created, on which financial intermediaries earn revenue.

Leverage refers to the use of borrowing to purchase an asset, the purpose being to increase returns if the asset price increases. This is illustrated by a simple Example 7.1.

Example 7.1 Leverage

I buy a share in Apple Inc. at $100 and sell them a year later for $120; I will make $20 profit, 20% of my initial investment.

If I borrow $90, I only have to put down $10 of my own money, so when I sell the shares and I pay back my loan, and if the interest on the loan was $10, I now have $20 ($120 − $90 − $10), but my initial outlay was only $10 so I have made 100% return.

The downside is if Apple Inc. shares do not go up. If I was not leveraged, I would not lose any money, whereas in a leveraged position I lose all of my initial stake.

Derivatives are a form of leverage; the way they work is almost identical to Example 7.1 as can be seen in Example 7.2.

> **Example 7.2 Derivatives**
>
> I buy a call option for $5 to buy the Apple Inc. shares at $100 in a year's time. At that date, the shares trade at $120.
> If I cash in my option I will now have $15 ($120 − $100 − $5) from a $5 stake, meaning that I have made a 200% return, whereas if I had just bought the stock I would have made a 20% return.
> On the downside if the price of Apple Inc. shares did not go up, I will lose all of my initial stake that is the $5 cost of option.

A bank is a more complex version of this leverage game. In its simplest form, a bank has a layer of shareholder equity, deposits and loans. Its ability to loan is limited by its deposits, but if it can increase its loans compared to its shareholder equity, it can increase its return to shareholders. This is shown in Example 7.3.

Banks are of course constrained by regulation on their level of leverage, and their ability to loan is limited by the level of their deposits.

> **Example 7.3 Bank leverage**
>
> A bank has shareholder equity of $100 million, and loans worth $1 billion making a net return of 1% (the difference between the interest it receives from loans and the interest it pays out to depositors); then its income is $10 million so return on equity (ROE) is 10%.
> If the total loans are $10 billion, then it receives $100 million income and the ROE will be 100%.
> The downside risk is if there are bad loans, and if there are enough of them, this will wipe out the shareholder's equity, as happened in the financial crisis.
> For example, if the bank had 5% non-performing loans which had to be written down to a value of zero, in the first example, the value of these bad loans is $50 million, which reduces the shareholder's capital to $50 million, but in the second example it's worth $500 million, which would wipe out the bank's shareholder capital and the bank would be insolvent.

As we saw, money is created by bank lending, and this money ultimately finds its way back into bank deposits, which allows banks to lend out more. Lending against property pushes up the value of property hence allowing banks to lend even more. Large banks have had an implicit or explicit guarantee from governments, the more they lend, the more they become too big to fail, so if they suffer bad loans they know they will be bailed out.

Banks are public companies owned by asset owners. The investment managers who decide on investing in banks and oversee those investments are incentivised on how the bank's share price performs over the next 3 months. Increasing leverage will increase the return on equity and hence the share price. Bank senior executives are paid in relation to the bank's share price which incentivises them to increase lending. The low probability of a crisis wiping out a bank, especially if it so big that a government is likely to step in to bail it out, is less important to them than increasing short-term earnings, and as bank employees are paid so much that if such a crisis comes they will have earned enough not to care. This model of banks expanding for ever broke down in the financial crisis, and the weakness of banks is at the forefront of investor's minds. It remains to be seen what new model for profitable banking emerges.

Although banks are constrained by regulation in the lending that they can make, Basel III bank regulation specifies that the leverage ratio, the ratio of shareholder capital to total loans,[16] has to be 3% or more; this is still a very high leverage ratio without much room for bad debts. Through financial innovation, creative accounting and regulatory arbitrage, banks had previously been able to increase this ratio, although regulators are now attempting to clamp down on methods of getting around regulation, even so banks are still highly leveraged. By increasing leverage, banks increase return on equity and increase the remuneration of their employees.

Investment banks cannot take deposits but they are at the core of the leverage game as was described in Chapter 6. Just before it collapsed in 2008, the investment bank Lehman's had a debt-to-equity ratio of 60 to 1,[17] an enormously leveraged position. Investment banks stand at the centre of the so-called shadow banking system. This is larger than the traditional banking system, some estimating the size as $100 trillion.[18]

Shadow banking is taking pooled savings from asset owners, leveraging it up, and creating loans against existing assets, which could be real estate or financial assets; this increases the prices of these assets and allows further lending against these assets. This process creates more debt in the economy; mortgages are packaged up by banks and sold to investors in the form of bonds. The banks that sold off the mortgages can now lend out more into real estate, creating more money in the process.

As well as creating leverage, financial intermediaries can also trade on that excess revenue generated by leverage, and because of their privileged position in receiving information on who is buying and selling, this information is utilised and combined with the ability to create financial assets to earn further revenue. The information might only give the trading intermediary a small advantage, but via leverage, for example through using derivatives, he can turn the small advantage into a large gain using only a small amount of capital.

The leveraging of an asset, as has been described for real estate, also increases the value of that asset as the increased price increases the ability to leverage the asset which leads to a positive feedback loop. The level of leverage in the economy drives down interest rates; interest rates are the inverse of the price, so by pushing up the price of all assets, leverage lowers the yield of these assets and hence reduces the interest rate. It also means that you need less capital to generate returns so the price of money falls. This reduction in interest rate further perpetuates the process, borrowing becomes cheaper, and hence, more money can be directed towards asset purchases.

This process cannot continue indefinitely, as at some point the mismatch between the price and the value of the underlying asset will catch up. This is the process famously described by the economist Hyman Minsky,[19] the time that the market realises the price is wrong is called the Minsky moment. At this point there will be a dramatic fall in the market. However, the agents in the financial system are asymmetrically rewarded. The upside of the leverage cycle can last a long time; the crash is usually short and sharp. During the upside, the agents are rewarded on performance, everyone does well as assets are going up and this is what everyone believes is normal. The crash affects everyone, but as pay cannot be negative the downside loss does not match the upside gain as the gains have already been taken. The financial system is often bailed out when there is a crash so that the loss is socialised; the rest of society pays the bill. There have been moves to claw back bonuses for excessive risk-taking or fraudulent behaviour. However, what I have described is not risk taking or fraudulent, everyone is just doing their job; everyone does badly at the same time, so no one can be blamed.

In summary, leveraging works by directing lending and investment towards assets which can be collateralised, such as real estate or financial assets, and away from real investment. This happens because financial agents have the ability to create leverage to direct financial flows and these agents get paid more the more leverage there is.

7.3.2 Abstraction/Innovation

Financial innovation is the process by which financial agents create products which abstract existing assets, allowing further leverage of the assets and rent extraction by the finance sector.

A simple form of abstraction occurs when I buy a company share. In this case I am buying ownership claims on the company, the underlying company owns a bunch of assets, but I own a share of the legal structure which owns the assets. As I argued in Chapter 5, this is a form of virtual capital; the shares are bought and sold, with the money rarely or never being drawn down by the company. Every time the shares are bought and sold, a financial intermediary is making money. As the assets are traded on an exchange they have a price and I am charged a brokerage fee in relation to this price.

Derivatives are a further abstraction from real assets. Financial agents can create, buy and sell derivative, thus multiplying the number of virtual assets and transactions that can be made for a given underlying asset.

The shadow banking system contains a slew of abstracted assets, with names such as collateralised debt obligations (CDOs), credit default swaps and synthetic CDOs. Abstracted assets are created on the back of primarily abstracted assets (such as mortgages) which sit on the real, physical asset of real estate.

The abstracted assets can be traded, and hence, financial intermediaries can make money from buying and selling these assets. Abstracted assets also increase leverage, as has already been discussed; hence, the fees that can be extracted are of a higher order than for the underlying assets. Because of this leverage, financial agents can use the abstracted financial instrument to game the system further.

The strategy employed by high-frequency traders (HFTS) is an example of gaming. HFTS employ a number of strategies but typically exploit information which gives rise to temporary arbitrage opportunities. HFTS buy and sell large volumes of stocks very rapidly, typically in fractions of a second, to exploit the arbitrage opportunity. HFTS detect the volumes of trades and uses this information to buy up stock and quickly sell on, thus making a small profit. As volumes are large and HFTS do this repeatedly, they can make a large profit. However, this profit ultimately comes from the asset owner who pays more for their stock purchases.[20]

Abstraction/innovation allows the financing of assets which have not been financed before. For example, the financial crisis of 2008 was triggered by the collapse of the sub-prime mortgage market. Sub-prime mortgages were loans taken out by people with poor credit rating. The financial innovation was bundle up mortgages into different risk tranches which then could be sold into the capital markets at elevated ratings and prices. The result is that a new asset class has been brought into the financial system, out of which financial intermediaries can generate income.

7.3.3 Colonisation

Colonisation refers to the increasing influence of the finance sector over other parts of society and the economy through the process of financialisation. The finance sector has used its control over capital to colonise non-financial corporations and the government.

Chapter 5 detailed how asset managers use their delegated ownership of companies to change company behaviour in the interest of asset managers. The aim of asset managers is to boost short-term share performance. By linking senior management pay to share performance gives rise to a cascade of effects resulting in companies being run to increase income for asset managers and corporates' senior executives.

One effect is the financialisation of non financial corporations (NFCs). NFCs increasingly play the leverage game. Financial assets relative to sales of NFCs increased from 27% in 1971 to 46% in 2011 in USA,[21] and income from financial activities relative to non-financial incomes went up fourfold over a similar period.[22] This has coincided with reduced corporate investment.[23] The increased financialisation allows NFCs to leverage themselves and thereby boost short-term profits. For example, General Electric, USA's largest industrial group, actually made over half of its profits from financial services, in the run up to the financial crisis.[24]

As well as reducing investment and leveraging financial assets, another way of increasing short-term profits is to lower employment costs, by laying off staff, offshoring production and capping salaries. Chapter 8 will detail the resultant stagnation in wages.

Companies try to squeeze more money out of customers and suppliers. The extensive use of advertising, especially involving psychological techniques, leads to customers increasingly getting into debt to buy products they cannot really afford and don't need or are actually harmful, reducing "everything that is human…to that of a consumer",[25] exactly what is needed to increase company earnings. The debt is often supplied by the corporates who are increasingly acting as banks through the financialisation process.

Companies pass on their costs to society. Employees who are laid-off do not pay tax and have to be supported by the state until they can get another job. Corporates spend a huge amount of money on lobbying; the fossil-fuel industry alone spent $350 million in lobbying in 2013/2014 in the USA, in return they receive $42 billion in subsidies[26] (a 120% return on this investment) as well as weaker regulation allowing them to pass on pollution cost to society. And as we will see in the next chapter, pharmaceutical companies spend even more on lobbying, in the USA to $3 billion over the last 18 years.[27]

Another way of boosting profits is through tax avoidance; this is made possible because different countries have different tax regimes, so multinational companies can book profits to low tax environments. This is of course aided and abetted by the financial sector, which can shift transactions across borders and advise on minimising tax payments.

The financial services industry itself engages in a great deal of political lobbying; the US finance sector spends $1.4 billion in lobbying in 2013/14.[28] This is one of the ways that finance has colonised the government.

As finance colonises the economy, governments become reliant on finance. Governments look to the finance sector for expertise; this could range from Greece employing the investment bank Goldman Sachs to use interest rate derivatives to suppress the reported cost of public debt so that it could enter the Euro,[29] or the revolving doors between regulators, public prosecutors and financial services firm. The journalist Matt Taibbi has documented how relatively lowly paid regulators and prosecutors are greatly in demand for highly paid jobs in financial service firms.[30] These regulators are disinclined to be overly aggressive with their future employers, and it means that regulation is sympathetic to financial services firms. Revolving doors also means that the more complex the regulation is, the more demand there is for regulatory experts, and the more opportunity for gaming regulation.[31,32]

Senior-level politicians and office holders often have a background in investment banking; the influence of Goldman Sachs alumni is legendary, ranging from current and former US secretaries of the Treasury to the current Governor of the Bank of England. The combined effect is to embed the importance of financial markets, the thinking of financial markets actors and sympathy with the finance sector within government. Because most of the people who understand the complex details of finance, work in finance, because of the resources that the finance sector can deploy towards political lobbying, and because of the revolving doors of regulators, financial regulation is crucially influenced by financiers, not surprisingly in their own favour.

The finance sector has grown over the years as we have seen, and as we have seen NFCs are increasingly turning into financial companies. The finance sector has channelled capital towards virtual financial assets or real estate. With the growth of the finance sector, its highly paid staff and its profits, government are increasingly reliant on tax receipts from the finance sector. The economy is increasingly dependent on high price levels of houses and other assets and is increasingly indebted and so more reliant on the financial sector. As wealth is tied up in housing and the stock market, if these go down in price, people would not be able to borrow money and will therefore spend less – the economy will tank.

The helminth has become too big, any medicine strong enough to control the helminth will damage the host, which is the whole of society.

Finally, governments have become increasingly reliant on the finance sector to raise debt via the bond market. I have argued that this is unnecessary, if the government stopped subsidising finance there would be much reduced need for government debt. Large bond investors have a great deal of influence with governments, as they can sell bonds and cause the cost of borrowing to go up. Finance ministries have to court bond investors and to some extent dance to their tune.

This is worse for smaller countries, especially ones that are heavily indebted. Countries which are in a particularly bad state, such as Argentina, lose access to capital markets and have to deal with the IMF. When a country has a debt crisis and looks like it will not be able to pay its debts, investors sell its bonds and the cost of borrowing increases, making the situation worse. The IMF then steps in by lending large amount of capital to the country, usually to stop capital flight and tries to stabilise the situation. This bails out the investors, not the country.

7.3.4 Hegemony

The concept of hegemony was a concept developed by the Italian philosopher Antonio Gramsci (1891–1937), who proposed that the ruling elite propagate a hegemonic culture which becomes the norms under which society operates.[33] Decisions are made, for example by governments and corporations, within a rational framework which has internalised the intellectual hegemony of the time.

The hegemony of finance is based on two groups of theories, modern portfolio theory (MPT) of financial economics and shareholder value in management theory. These are centred on a worldview where free markets bringing about prosperity often described by its critics as neo-liberalism.

The finance sector influences theory in a number of ways. Financial institutions often fund academic institutions, but probably more importantly they recruit most of their employees from university finance and economics courses. Hence, universities will be more successful if they are useful to potential future employers of their students, and faculty often get lucrative jobs or consulting work in the finance sector, so they are incentivised to do work which is useful to finance. The capital markets regulation is highly influenced by finance theory, so the markets operate in a way that finance theory would suggest, because that is the way they are set up, and this is what academics study.

There is an ethical underpinning for all of this, formalised by the Arrow-Debreu model; under certain assumptions, complete and competitive markets deliver a pareto-efficient outcome; no one can be made better off without making someone else worse off; free markets are the best of all possible worlds. By expanding free markets, we move towards greater efficiency, and hence prosperity for all, so it is incumbent on governments and regulators to ensure as free and complete markets as possible.

Financial economics contains a suite of theories which are widely used in finance, MPT, the efficient market hypothesis (EMH), the capital asset pricing model (CAPM) and the Black-Scholes model for pricing options.

The EMH is that all relevant information is contained in the price of an asset; the market price changes when new information comes in; prices follow a random walk and it is impossible for an investor to beat the market. The price of an asset is therefore equivalent to its value.

This theory is important for the ideology of the market; if it is true that the price of the stock market tells you real information about the state of the economy, financial institutions should report solely on the market value of their assets and liabilities, you are better off investing in assets which are easy to buy and sell (i.e. financial assets), short-term performance is important because the price is the true value of the asset and the price of the stock market reflects the underlying health of the economy.

This philosophy has even more profound importance for the "real" world outside the market. Stuff which is hard to value, such as a forest, the climate or society, becomes periphery, an afterthought, an externality. "Non-financial" concerns are only considered when the real business of the market has been done.

If EMH does not hold, I will defer why it does not until Chapter 9, then the world looks rather different.

MPT and Black Scholes are crucial to finance in different ways; they allow products and regulation to be constructed in a rational way. MPT allows investment managers to construct portfolios around an index and define how risky the portfolio is, convincing the world that they can invest in that portfolio and measure its risk. Derivative markets were devised by their participants in the image of Black Scholes theory and regulators were persuaded that the trading of derivatives can help manage risk and was not a form of gambling because of the Black Scholes Model. The derivatives market is an example of performativity of theory – where reality is based on economic theory.[34]

Shareholder value aligns with MPT; the main or sole purpose of a company is to maximise its value to its shareholders, where value is equated to the price of its shares. This gives license to reward company directors in relation to the share price who are then incentivised to do everything they can to push up the short-term market value of the company's shares.

7.3.5 Where the Rent Comes from

The helminth makes its revenue by taking a share of the activities of the economy. The economy's assets are a stock which has been built up over a long time through its surplus, which is recycled back into the economy as savings.

The finance sector makes its revenue by taking a fee for the management of a proportion of these assets and the flow of savings that is being allocated to different investments. The fee taken is a proportion of the market price of these assets. The fee is a charge to society for the efficient management of assets which can then produce a greater quantity and quality of goods and services.

The finance sector can increase its revenue by increasing the market price of underlying assets, increasing the share of assets that it manages or by charging a higher management fee. The tools of the finance trade are used to achieve these ends.

It has also been argued by two Nobel Prize-winning economists, no less, that much of the profit from financial activity is basically legal fraud, persuading people to buy financial assets which they do not understand and therefore pay too much for.[35] Financial innovation and complexity greatly enhance this process, as the more complex financial products are, the easier they are to misprice. The revenue from this activity is a direct transfer from the economy's savings pool.

Even if this is so, rather than focus on these mis-selling cases I want to focus on how the finance sector extracts rent when everyone is doing their job in apparent good faith. The market price is key. EMH claims that the price is the same as the value, but this is absurd, as I will explore further in Chapter 9; if the stock market were to go down 40% one day, as it has done (or indeed in the "flash crash" some shares lost most of their value for a few minutes), the day after the crash the companies that make up the stock market can produce the same amount of goods and services as the day before, has their value really gone down by 40%?

The price of all financial assets has been boosted by the continuing decline in interest rates, which as I have argued is endogenous to the financial system.

The price of individual companies' shares has been boosted by share buy-backs, reduced investment and reduced staff costs.

Because the price of assets has been on a general upward trend due to the decreasing interest rates, this allows the finance sector to create virtual financial assets such as derivatives, which leverage the increase in price to generate more revenue for the helminth. Virtual financial assets absorb some of the savings directly, for example via hedge funds which buy and sell derivatives. As well as benefiting from the leverage of derivatives, hedge funds' fees are leveraged; they typically take 20% of the gain. Financial assets can be used to generate revenue indirectly, for example derivative traders are making money from price fluctuations which is ultimately paid for by the asset owner.

The increase in price itself generates increasing financial flows through a number of channels: savings are attracted into financial assets by the lure of good returns; charges are masked by these high returns. The increase in price fools governments into believing that the country's wealth is increasing who increase support the finance system, which increases the need to bail it out when things go wrong. The increase in the price of assets causes more inequality; the wealth of those that have assets increases and they can borrow against that wealth cheaply. Richer people spend less of their extra income than poorer people, so as the benefits of growth go to the wealthy, the amount of savings ploughed back into the financial system increases.

The increase in price and hence revenue from the finance sector means that finance can attract the cleverest people in society, who then turn their brains to engineering increased revenue for finance rather than generate real wealth for the economy.

The range of assets managed by the finance sector has been increased through financial innovation. For example, mortgage-backed securities enable the finance sector to generate revenue from housing stock. The sub-prime mortgages which triggered the financial crisis were leveraging previously un-financeable housing stock and ascribing them an artificially high value.

These processes are aided and abetted by colonisation and hegemony. Governments and companies act in a way to help the finance sector. Regulators and governments support the financialisation of assets. Central banks continually reduce interest rates and recently have used unconventional techniques to reduce them further. Governments bail out the system. Companies increasingly embrace financialisation and the use of financial tools such as derivatives.

7.3 The Tools of the Finance Trade

I will illustrate the process by some simplified examples to look at how the finance sector increases its revenue and where that money comes from.

> **Example 7.4 – Bond fund**
>
> A simple bond fund holds just one 10 year UK Government bond (£100 million par value; 5% coupon) and charges 1% AMC. Currently bond yields are 1%.[36]
> The value of the bond is £140 million and the income is £5 million; the annual fees are £1.4 million.
> In the early 1990s when bond yields were 9%, the market price of the same bond would have been £70 million and hence, the fees will have been £0.7 million.

Solely by virtue of interest rates being lower, the fee collected by the fund manager is twice what it would be with higher interest rates, £1.4 million compared to £0.7 million. In both cases, the bond pays £5 million per year. The excess income of the investment manager comes out of the income that the bond is generating; the fund is only receiving £3.6 million compared to £4.3 million at higher rates. If rates were higher, the excess would have been paid to the investor. It is true that the price of the fund is higher when interest rates are lower, but if the investor were to sell to cash in her return, she would have to buy another asset which would also have a higher price and hence lower yield.

> **Example 7.5 – Mortgage-backed securities**
>
> A bank collateralises a book of sub-prime mortgages which are ultimately sold to a pension fund in the form of mortgage-backed securities. The mortgages are split into tranches which are sold via a number of bonds with different risk characteristics. The underlying risks are adjusted by the use of complex structures involving derivatives. In the 2008 financial crisis some of the bonds halved in value.

The structuring of mortgage-backed securities allowed an asset which was not part of the finance system to be brought into it and given an inflated value. Having sold off the book of mortgages, the bank has spare lending capacity to lend to another group of sub-prime borrowers.

The inflated value is caused because people can borrow money against the house which they were not previously able to do. The mortgage-backed securities are overvalued because the underlying property is overvalued and the complex derivative structure does not reduce the risk of the investment. The finance sector has opened up a new asset class, of which it either receives interest or an intermediation fee.

The chain of intermediaries is receiving its income from the borrower paying interest. If this was not available, she would still need a roof over her head so she would pay rent. Here, the finance sector's income is diverted from another sector. The initiator bank can lend against a new group of houses, which it would not have been able to do without the securitisation process, as it would have to keep the book of mortgages on its balance sheet. As money is created during the lending process, the extra lending equates to an extra tranche of money created against real estate with the associated increase in debt. Because the mortgages are sub-prime, the lender can charge a high interest rate than.

The increase in debt in the economy is caused by the pension fund lending against housing. The pension fund could have lent money to someone else, for example government debt, but it could also have invested in something useful, like infrastructure.

To securitise the mortgages required a complex of intermediaries; the fees are relatively high, and these fees are a transfer to the finance sector. The complex financial products which were created allowed the mortgages to be sold at a high price as the buyer thought he was buying a risk-free product, which ultimately turned out not to be so, and when this was realised the mortgage-backed security returned to a more realistic price.

Fees are taken by the finance sector up front, out of assumed future revenue. These mortgages went wrong in the 2008 financial crisis, so the future revenue never materialised; yet, the intermediaries received their fees and bonuses. The end owner of the mortgage-backed security, or the government whole bailed out the system, took a loss which was the previous fees taken by the intermediaries.

The housing stock already existed so the excess savings that the pension fund used to buy the assets were not used to build up more capital stock of the economy.

Example 7.6 – Hedge fund

A hedge fund, managing pension fund money with a 2/20 charging structure, buys a call option on a company. The company announces that it has restructured by reducing its staff cost, reducing R&D spend and will engage in a share buy-back. The price of the company's stock jumps 20% on the news.

The option is leveraged, so as we saw in Example 7.2, a 20% increase in share price could correspond to a 200% increase in option price. The hedge fund takes fees of 20% of the increase that is 20% of 200%.

Where does this money come from? Savings from the asset owner invested in the hedge fund are diverted to a virtual financial asset, a derivative. The share price increased because the company is reducing wages and investment in the future and using the money to buy-back its shares. The money is therefore being partly diverted away from accumulation of future capital stock and partly transferring future wages to capital. The hedge fund is capitalising the present value of a future stream of payments (less wages) in advance; this is money that would have gone to pay staff more.

The net result is more inequality as the highly paid hedge fund and company management get paid more whereas the company staff get less, and partly a reduction in the future capital stock; the company is spending less on R&D.

As the asset owner is investing in a derivative, it only has to invest a smaller amount to make the same gain from price movements; it can thus spread its investments around more assets. However, because of the leveraged position, if the underlying stock goes down, the asset owner loses all of his money, compensated by the higher gain if it goes up. By contrast the hedge fund still makes a fee whatever happens but makes a very high fee if the investment goes up. Ultimately, the asset owner is paying much more in fees and taking more risk than if he just invested in the underlying asset.

These examples are gross simplifications of what actually happens. However, the more complicated the processes involve more intermediaries, more complex products and hence more rent extraction by the financial sector.

These examples demonstrate the financial sector increasing its revenue by altering asset prices, extending into new assets and increasing its fees. It does this through leverage – the hedge fund is leveraging the increase in price in the asset; financial innovation – the creation of mortgage-backed securities; colonisation – company management engaging in behaviour which suits the finance sector; and the central bank dancing to the tune of the finance sector by reducing interest rates. All of this is underpinned by hegemony; EMH justifies the payment of fees in relation to the price of an asset and MPT allows for the structuring of mortgage-backed securities; the company management is behaving in a way justified by maximising shareholder value.

With this leverage of the whole economy: the increase in the combined market value of financial assets, through the various methods described in this chapter, means that the finance sector's revenue is increased because it is taking a slice of the assets managed and that slice goes up with the value of the assets managed. The finance sector's revenue is real money, which is either spent in the economy or reinvested in (financial) assets. This leads to further inequality or reduces the well-being of everyone else as the relative price of goods changes to reflect the money being spent by the finance sector or its employees. The financial assets in the system, though mostly abstracted assets, can be sold and converted to real money, so more of this potential future money is directed to finance sector employees, whose spending of it prejudices everyone else's.

Another couple of points to note thrown up by these examples. The revenue of the finance sector is counted as economic output/GDP, as if they have created revenue, whereas actually they have diverted savings to themselves. From the government's perspective this looks good; the prejudice to future growth is hidden. The financial intermediaries are also paid by capitalising future revenue; the economy has to pay back the debt that has been created, but a proportion of the fees are paid up front. This capitalisation is booked as economic output, without a negative loss of future revenue being accounted for in the national accounts.

Finally, the whole economy is leveraged through the increase in debt that has been created. This debt has to be repaid out of a declining capital stock, as savings have not been invested to build up this capital stock. The increase in leverage also increases the risk to the economy and means that the government and central bank are more likely to intervene as the damage from a crisis will be greater.

7.4 How Do They Get Away with It?

"What is the robbing of a bank compared to the founding of a bank?"[37] Finance is the control centre of a capitalist economy; the keys to the control room have been handed to the finance sector. Actors within the finance sector have used their ability to harness these controls to enhance their own revenue, as you would expect them to do given that they are profit maximisers. They have enhanced their revenues through leverage, financial innovation, colonising other sectors of the economy and through intellectual hegemony. How have they got away with it for so long?

We live in a free-ish world, so if someone is selling oranges or iPads or gives yoga classes at an extortionate price I can find someone else to provide these goods or spend my money on something else. However, crucially in finance there is limited competition, as the government has ensured that only certain entities can provide these services. The most extreme example of this is banks; they have a government-given mandate to create money. If I set up a rival bank creating money cheaper than banks, I would be put in prison. I could apply for a banking license, but this is very difficult and expensive. The mandate for pension providers and insurers is not as blatant as for banks, but it is still there, only certain entities which have certain characteristics can provide these services, and financial flows are directed towards them by governments. We saw in chapter 2 the massive concentration of assets with a small number of super-large asset managers.

The nature of the goods and services supplied by financial services is different from other goods and services, it gives the supplier a great deal of power. If someone sells lots of oranges or yoga classes, they might get rich and have a certain market power over their customers or suppliers. But they do not have the ability to direct flows of capital so that the citrus fruit or meditation industries grow, they cannot get into the DNA of companies and get them to behave differently. As finance directs the flow of capital towards itself it also becomes large and powerful, it can influence policy and regulation.

If I buy an orange or take a yoga classes, I can quickly tell if the orange is rotten or the yoga class is rubbish and it is easy for me to understand how much I was charged. This is not true for financial services, the cost is hidden and if I leave my money in a bank or give it to a pension provider, unless the bank goes bankrupt I can't tell how good it is; until I get my pension in 40 years time I have no idea if it is sufficient. In fact this asymmetric information extends to government and society as well, finance is complicated; in the 10 year run up to the financial crisis, everyone thought how wonderfully well the finance sector was doing, it appeared to be managing risk and making large profits, risks can take a long time to manifest by which time it is too late.

Finally, the finance sector has not got away with it. If we continue the brief history from Section 7.2 we had 10 or so good years, the great moderation, years of low inflation and high growth. During this time the finance sector increased dramatically in size, as well as profitability, employment and products offered. And then we had the crash in 2008, followed by 8 years of ultra-low interest rates, low growth and a declining finance sector.

The financial crisis has damaged the banks, both financially and reputationally. There has been increased scrutiny and legislation, and a raft of fines for banks – $139 billion between 2012 and 2014[38] – and ultra-low interest rates make it hard for them to profit. Their profitability has been damaged and they have pulled out of a lot of previously profitable activities. This is at a time when there is competition from outsiders such as challenger banks and peer-to-peer lending platforms, which are genuine threats to existing business models.

The impact on asset management is slower and more subtle. Investment managers did not have to be bailed out in the financial crisis. However, with ultra-low interest rates it makes it harder for them to maintain their fees. Active managers have been hit by poor performance and are faced with increasing competition from passive managers offering much cheaper services. Their judgement day is arriving, slowly.

Does this matter? We have a dysfunctional finance system, but how does this impact the real world? The next chapter will detail *collateral damage*.

Notes

1. Philippon, T (2014) *Has the U.S Finance industry become less efficient?* American Economic Review Volume 105.
2. Such as public corporations, private companies or partnerships.
3. Baumol, W (1990) *Entrepreneurship: Productive, Unproductive, and Destructive* Chicago Journals.
4. Now democratic Republic of Congo.
5. *Late Nigerian Dictator Looted Nearly $500 Million, Swiss Say* The New York Times. 19 August 2004. Retrieved 9 April 2010.
6. Business Pundit 28 March 2011 10 *Politicians* Who Stole Fortunes http://www.businesspundit.com/10-politicians-who-stole-fortunes/
7. This section is Largely taken from Krippner, G (2011) *Capitalizing on crisis: the political origins of the rise of finance* Harvard University Press 2011.
8. Shaxson, N (2011) *Treasure Islands* The Bodley Head.
9. W. Scott Frame, S Fuster, Tracy A and Vickery, J (2015) *The Rescue of Fannie Mae and Freddie Mac* Federal Reserve Bank of New York Staff Report No. 719.
10. Cohen, S and DeLong, B (2016) *Concrete Economics* Harvard Business Review Press.
11. Cohen, S and DeLong, B (2016) *Concrete Economics* Harvard Business Review Press.
12. WTO data.
13. Commodities Futures Trading Commission, annual reports.
14. Warren Buffet; quoted by BBC News 4 March 2003 *Buffett warns on investment "time bomb"* http://news.bbc.co.uk/1/hi/2817995.stm accessed 10 December 2016.
15. Some of this increase was also due to regulation, forcing banks/companies to hedge financial risks, but probably only a small share.
16. It is more complicated than this in reality.

17. https://hbr.org/2009/09/lessons-from-lehman.
18. Fiaschi, D, Kondor, I and Marsili, M (2013) *The Interrupted Power Law and the Size of Shadow Banking* arXiv:1309.2130.
19. Minsky, H (2008) [1st. Pub. 1986] *Stabilizing an Unstable Economy* McGraw-Hill Professional, New York. ISBN 978-0-07-159299-4.
20. Lewis, M (2914) *Flash Boys* W. W. Norton & Co.
21. Davies, L (2013) *Financialization and the nonfinancial corporation: an investigation of firm-level investment behavior in the U.S., 1971-2011* UNIVERSITY OF MASSACHUSETTS AMHERST Working Paper 2013.
22. Krippner, G (2005) *The financialization of the American Economy* Socio-economic review 173–208.
23. Davies, L (2013) *Financialization and the nonfinancial corporation: an investigation of firm-level investment behavior in the U.S., 1971–2011* UNIVERSITY OF MASSACHUSETTS AMHERST Working Paper 2013.
24. New York Times 18 July 2015 *General Electric reports rise in industrial profits* http://www.nytimes.com/2015/07/18/business/ge-q2-earnings.html.
25. Hayko, G (2010) *Effects of Advertising on Society: A Literary Review* Hohonu volume 8.
26. Oil Change International *Fossil Fuel Funding to Congress: Industry influence in the U.S.* http://priceofoil.org/fossil-fuel-industry-influence-in-the-u-s/ accessed 12 December 2016.
27. OpenSecrets.org https://www.opensecrets.org/lobby/top.php?showYear=a&indexType=i accessed 12 December 2016.
28. America for Financial Reforms 18 March 2015 *Updated AFR Report: Financial Sector Lobbying and Campaign Spending Top $1.4 Billion for 2014 Election Cycle – $1.9 million a day* http://ourfinancialsecurity.org/2015/03/afr-report-financial-sector-lobbying-and-campaign-spending-top-1-2-billion-for-2014-election-cycle-1-8-million-a-day/
29. Der Spiegel 8 February 2010 http://www.spiegel.de/international/europe/greek-debt-crisis-how-goldman-sachs-helped-greece-to-mask-its-true-debt-a-676634.html.
30. For example Rolling Stone 17 August 2011 *Is the SEC Covering Up Wall Street Crimes?* http://www.rollingstone.com/politics/news/is-the-sec-covering-up-wall-street-crimes-20110817.
31. Although this is not unique to finance; the same regulatory capture occurs in many industries.
32. Admati, A (2016) *It Takes a Village to Maintain a Dangerous Financial System* Forthcoming in Just Financial Market: Finance in a Just Society, Lisa Herzog, Editor, Oxford University Press.
33. Gramsci, A (1992), Buttigieg, Joseph A, ed., *Prison notebooks* Columbia University Press.
34. MacKenzie, D (2008) *An engine not a camera* The MIT Press.

35. Akerlof, G and Shiller, R (2015) *Phishing for Phools: The Economics of Manipulation and Deception* Princeton University Press.
36. As at November 2016.
37. From *The Threepenny Opera* (1928) by Berthold Brecht.
38. The Economist 1 May 2015 *What's wrong with finance*.

8

Collateral Damage

Impact of the Financial System on the Real World

About 250 million years ago, the two supercontinents, Gondwana and Laurasia, started breaking up. Gondwana and Laurasia contained virtually all the world's land mass; Gondwana in the South was made up of what is now Australasia, India, Africa, Antarctica and South America, and Laurasia in the North was made up of Eurasia and North America. It is thought that the splitting up of these continents gave rise to a great deal of volcanic activity. Another theory is that a meteorite may have hit the earth at this time, but if it had done any evidence has been buried by over 200 million years of continental drift.

Whatever the cause led to a massive amount of volcanic activity, probably in what is now Siberia. This pumped out carbon dioxide and methane into the atmosphere on a massive scale, causing global warming, which triggered the release of huge amounts of methane stored in the ocean. This in turn was converted to carbon dioxide, and oxygen levels in the atmosphere reduced to only 7%.

The result was that most of life on the planet was wiped out over a relatively short period, where relatively short means tens of thousands of years; 97% of marine invertebrates – which was most of life at the time – became extinct, as did 57% of terrestrial vertebrates; this was the greatest mass extinction event in the earth's history; life took around 10 million years to fully recover, and all current life on earth has evolved from the survivors of this catastrophe.[1]

More is known of the events of 65 million years ago. A massive meteorite, measuring 30 km wide and travelling at 100,000 miles per hour crashed into what is now the Yucatan peninsula in Mexico, later home to the Mayan civilisation, forming a crater 200 miles across. This immediately spewed out debris which killed anything in its path and ignited the forests in North America. It caused massive earthquakes and tsunamis 1–2 km high cascaded over the oceans. The impact led to a great deal of dust in the atmosphere for about 10 months, resulting in a nuclear winter lasting about 10 years. Shockwaves from the impact were transmitted to the other side of the planet, leading to large scale volcanic activity in what is now India. This led to rapid global warming and increased dust particles in the air.

The result was another mass extinction – this time three quarters of all plants and animals, most famously the dinosaurs, were wiped out. In human time, as opposed to geological time, the event lasted a long time, with some populations of dinosaurs surviving a hundred thousand years after the event before eventually disappearing.[2]

The third event of planetary mass extinction is happening now. The event that triggered it was far less dramatic than the other two, but the impact is similar, indeed it is actually playing out more rapidly. A series of periods of global warming and cooling caused deforestation and reforestation in some parts of Africa. This led to a great deal of evolutionary pressure on the ape populations, favouring larger brains. In one period of deforestation, an ape evolved adapted for living in the plain, it was hairless, walked on its hind legs, had a particularly large brain and refined vocal chords allowing far greater communication than any previous animals.

The ante was really upped around 10,000 years ago when this ape learned to farm, and then over the last 200 years after industrialisation.

It has been estimated that we have wiped out 7% of species and are on track for one half of earth's higher life forms being extinct by the end of the century. The rate of species extinction is 100 to 1,000 the normal rate, this is a rate 10 to 100 times greater than previous episodes of mass extinction.

The World Wildlife Fund produces a survey of the state of the world's biological diversity, called the Living Planet Index. Their latest report has found a nearly 60% decline between 1970 and 2012 42 of wild animal populations in the world. Compare this to the Cretaceous–Paleogene mass-extinction event (the one that wiped out the dinosaurs), which took 100,000 years to wipe out three quarters of all plants and animals. Although not all of these animals in the current mass-extinction event are extinct, yet.

For our economy, and by implication finance system, to be sustainable, resources have to be invested at such a scale as to transform our economy to halt and reverse this third mass extinction.

8.1 What Is Sustainability?

Definitions of sustainable development usually refer to the 1987 report of the Brundtland Commission,[3] a body set up by the United Nations to get countries to work towards a sustainable future:

"Development which meets the needs of current generations without compromising the ability of future generations to meet their own needs."

This is not a bad definition, but I do not think it is adequate when faced with the full extent of human's impact on the living planet. You could imagine a scenario where the mass extinction of most of the species of the planet is sustainable in line with the Brundtland Commission's definition, provided future generations could meet their own needs. If we were to move towards a technological future where humans were entirely self-sufficient in food, if food could be produced entirely artificially, and because future people will have no experience of nature, they will no longer have a "need" for it, then the development path of destroying nature is sustainable under the Brundtland Commission's definition.

I propose to define the sustainability of a system as

> The ability of a system to maintain itself indefinitely without a high risk of it dropping to a lower level of complexity.

A system is made up of a network of agents, for example a brain where the agents are the neurones, or an ant colony where the agents are the ants. The complexity of the system is essentially the number of connections between the agents. My definition is necessarily subjective in what is meant by a "high" risk. Living with a low risk might be acceptable or reducing the risk beyond a certain threshold may not be achievable or outside the control of the system. For example, there is a risk that human civilisation will be wiped out by another giant meteor hitting the earth or by alien invasion, but this does not mean that civilisation is unsustainable. Also, it is subjective as to how much less complexity would be acceptable.

The current global situation is clearly not sustainable; human activity is wiping out large numbers of species. All species live in some form of ecosystems, because of the extinction or large depletion of non-domesticated species, these systems are suffering from a reduced level of complexity. Current human development, which is destroying these ecosystems, is not sustainable.

8.1.1 Global Trends

Sustainability has to be considered in the context of how large the human economy is becoming, and how its geographic distribution is changing. The main challenge going forward is not that the population is growing, population growth is slowing, but that the majority of people in the world in aggregate are becoming rapidly richer and therefore consuming more resources.

If we take a long view of human population growth, it does not look sustainable. The human population reached 1 billion people in 1800, in the nineteenth century it increased by an unprecedented 60%, in the twentieth century it increased by 400% (Figure 8.1).

The rate of population growth is declining. The population of the world is projected to peak at around 9–10 billion people by the middle of the century.[4] That is 50% more than the population at the turn of the century.

The overall trend masks large regional difference. In demographic theory, the first demographic transition is where death rates fall because of better diets and healthcare and the population expands rapidly. This occurred in Europe and North America in the nineteenth century, causing a 60% rise in population, and occurred in most of the rest of the world in the twentieth century, hence the fourfold increase in global population.

Many emerging economies are entering what is called the second demographic transition; this is where fertility rates[5] drop, populations expand but at a decreasing rate until birth rates are approximately the same as death rates, resulting in a stable population. Europe and North America have reached the end of this transition, achieving stable populations by the middle of the twentieth century.

Most Asian countries are already at the end of the second demographic transition too, their birth rates have overtaken the death rates causing declining populations. For example, South Korean women have on average 1.24 children during their life, which is below the replacement rate – the birth rate required to maintain the current population. Even in India, which might be expected to be a high fertility rate country, women now have only 2.59 children on average – just above the replacement rate – but this rate is declining rapidly. In contrast, in Africa, birth rates are still high; the fertility rate in Kenya it is 4.68 (although down from 8 in 1970[6]).

Most of the future population growth in the world will be in Africa, by the end of the century there will be 3.5 billion Africans, which will make up over 40% of the world's population, compared to around 1 billion today (Figure 8.2).

8.1 What Is Sustainability? 195

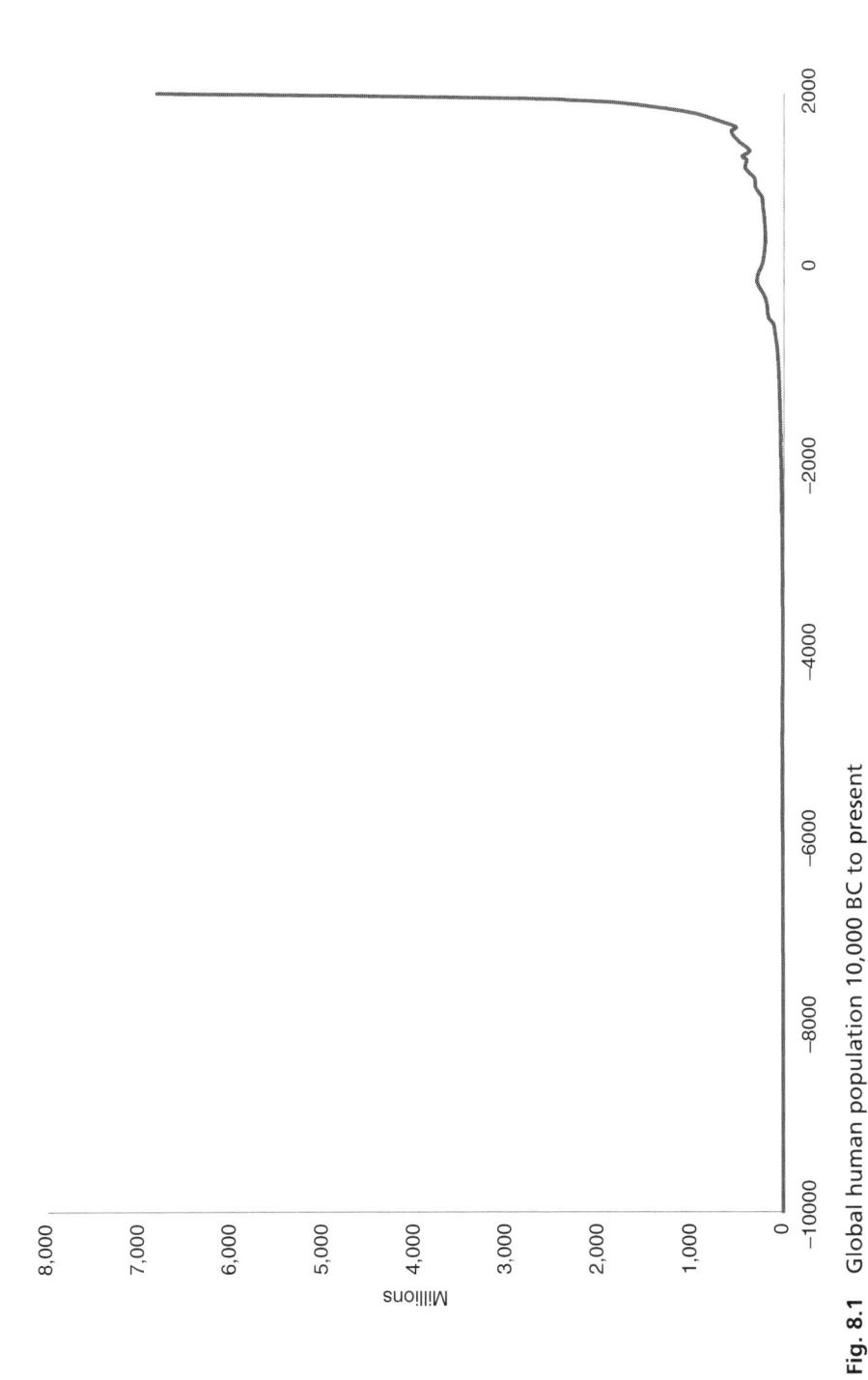

Fig. 8.1 Global human population 10,000 BC to present

Source: United States Census Bureau and United Nations Population Division
United States Census Bureau up to 1950 https://www.census.gov/population/international/data/worldpop/table_history.php and United Nations Population Division *The World at Six Billion* for subsequent dates http://www.un.org/esa/population/publications/sixbillion/sixbilpart1.pdf accessed on 20 January 2017

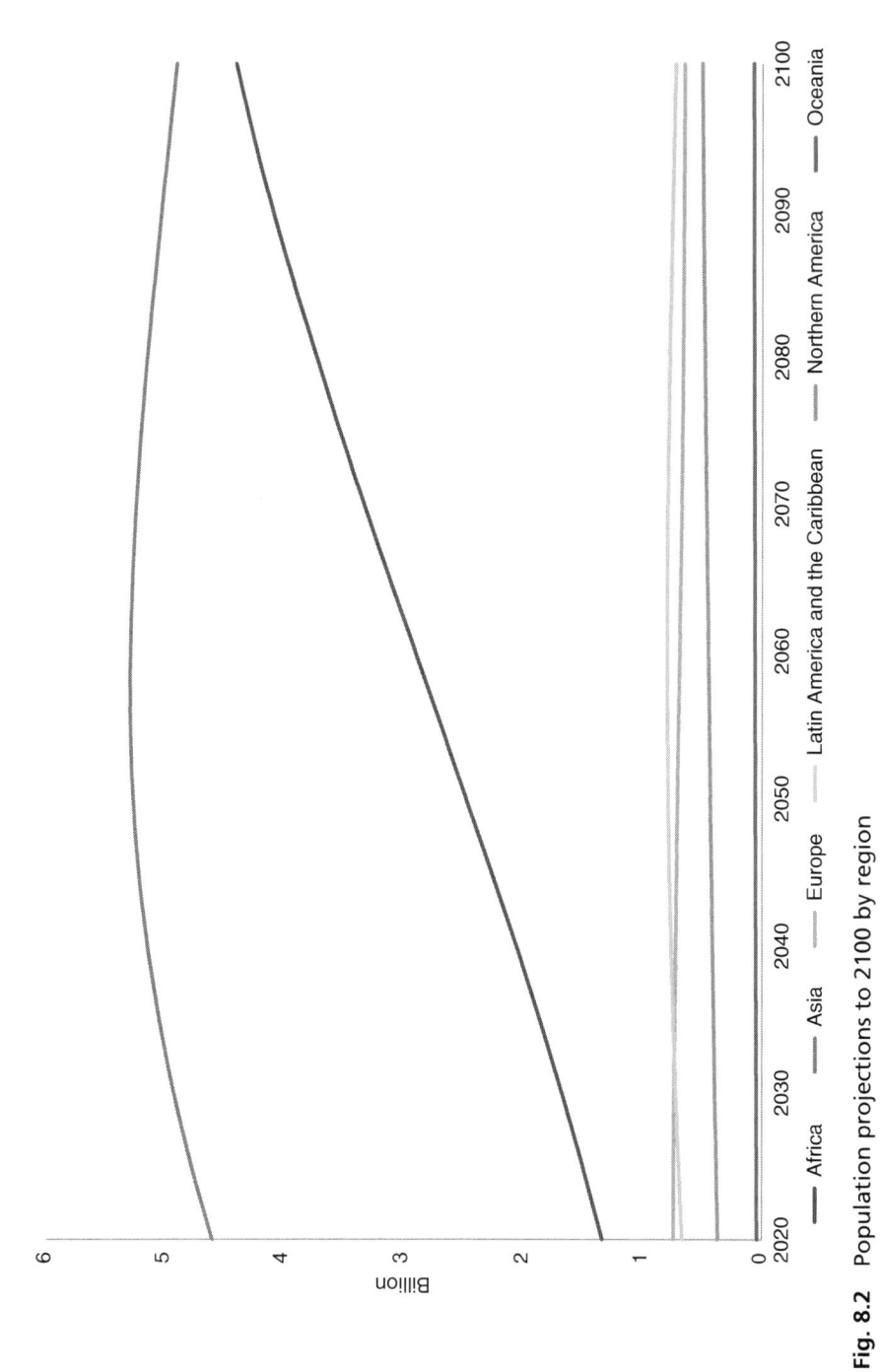

Fig. 8.2 Population projections to 2100 by region

Source: World Bank
From http://blogs.worldbank.org/opendata/future-world-s-population-4-charts accessed 20 January 2017

Whilst population growth is projected to tail off, the global economy is projected to grow exponentially. The economy has already grown from global GDP of $2 trillion in 1900 to $70 trillion now.[7] The OECD project that the economy will be between $355 trillion and $1,200 trillion by 2100. This is obviously a very wide range; but even at the lower end of the forecast, the global economy will grow by 5 times from its current size, at the top end of its projection it will have grown 600-fold between 1900 and 2100.[8]

Because of the different rates of population growth, the balance of power within the world will change, as is implied by Figure 8.2. Currently, though the population of Asia is many times larger than all other regions, and Africa is slightly larger than Europe or the USA, this is not translated to economic power, as these regions are much poorer than their European and North American counterparts. Figure 8.2 shows that the population gap between Asian countries and the West will widen, and Africa will catch up with Asia. If the African and Asian economies continue to close the income gap with the West, then Figure 8.2 makes it clear that the world economy will be dominated by Asia and Africa.

Up until recently, the majority of trade was around and across the Atlantic, between and within Europe and North America, but these projections imply that over the course of this century the Atlantic economies will become a relative backwater, with most trade moving first to the Pacific and then the Indian Oceans. These trends represent tectonic shifts in the world economies. It also means that future financial systems will be dominated by Asian models of finance, which are not imitating the shareholder finance model described in this book.

8.1.2 Underlying These Trends

Underlying these trends in demography and the economy are a number of factors, specifically political and technological. The major factor was the decision by China, which at the time had 1/6th of the world's population, to pursue a developmental state model of growth. This has been spectacularly successful, meaning the Chinese economy has grown by nearly 10% per annum since 1978, its economy increasing in size by 60-fold in this time.[9] The ability of China to pursue its growth strategy based on exports has been facilitated by other countries willing to buy Chinese imports, and to allow the growth of credit to finance these purchases. The rapid rate of growth has also been facilitated by technology, for example rapid advancements in communication technologies and shipping infrastructure.

The resultant rapid industrialisation of China has had a number of consequences for the rest of the world, but specifically China has required a huge amount of raw materials. This has caused many of other economies, such as Brazil and South Africa, to also grow rapidly. The growth of China has coincided with a number of other countries choosing to embark on a similar developmental path. The fact that China is now running out of spare workers – its growth has been predicated on mass urban migration bringing former subsistence farmers into the workforce, a trend that may have run its course – and that China has become much wealthier, means that companies are searching out other countries such as Bangladesh and India for production, leading these countries to embark upon a path of rapid industrialisation.

The result is that large chunks of the planet which was previously populated by very poor subsistence farmers are being brought into the global economy and are rapidly transitioning to enjoying something approaching a Western lifestyle.

This has been facilitated by the widespread availability of mobile technology, which enables even poor farmers in Africa to access a wide range of services and information which they were previously unable to access. This includes things that we would take for granted, for example access to the price of non-local goods, access to a means of payment, basic savings products and knowledge about the rest of the country and world.

It appears inevitable that most people in the world will gradually or rapidly transition from a traditional lifestyle to a modern one with all that entails.

This represents a massive increase in the size and complexity of the global economy.

8.1.3 Planetary Boundaries

The massive increase in the size of the economy is presenting and will increasingly present a massive burden on the environment. Some argue that growth in the size of the economy can be decoupled from environmental damage. Figure 8.3 compares GDP growth with carbon emissions since the 1970s.

It is true that as countries get richer, they often manage to reduce localised environmental damage. For example, in London the River Thames was highly

8.1 What Is Sustainability? 199

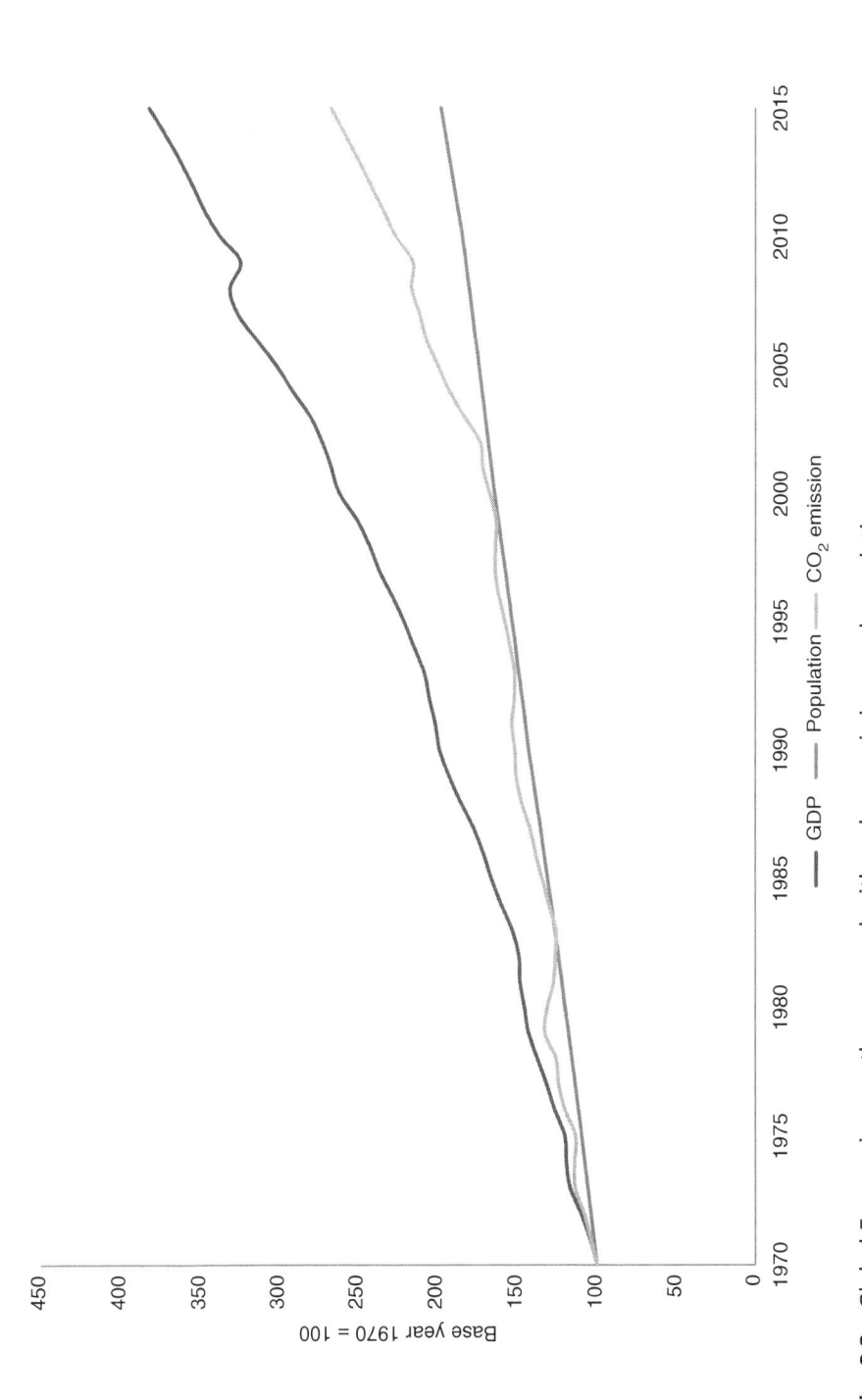

Fig. 8.3 Global Economic growth compared with carbon emissions and population

Source: UN (population) Carbon Dioxide Information Analysis Centre (CO_2 emissions) and World Bank (GDP) For CO_2 data Boden, T.A., Marland, G., and Andres R.J. (2015). Global, Regional, and National Fossil-Fuel CO_2 Emissions. Carbon Dioxide Information Analysis Center, Oak Ridge National Laboratory, U.S. Department of Energy for population http://www.un.org/esa/population/publications/sixbillion/sixbilpart1.pdf accessed on 20 January 2017

toxic 40 years ago, whereas now it is clean enough to swim in. Some global environmental problems have been addressed; for example the Montreal Protocol banned gasses which damage the ozone layer which seems to have been broadly successful.

However, some of the achievements of local environmental clean ups have been achieved through off-shoring – by moving dirty industries to poorer countries with less environmental controls. You cannot offshore the damage caused by global environmental damage, for the foreseeable future we only have one planet to work with.

The best analysis of planetary boundaries that I have seen is developed by the Stockholm Resilience Centre. They have identified a number of thresholds which, if crossed, could flip planetary systems irreversibly into a different state with uncertain consequences (Figure 8.4). The graph shows how close we are to the boundaries; the boundary for genetic diversity has already been breached because of the massive reduction of populations of animals and plants, as has the boundary for phosphorous and nitrogen pollution, because of the extensive use of these chemicals in farming. We are approaching the boundary for land-system change and climate change.

The concept of a planetary boundary is the level at which human impact pushes natural systems irreversibly into a different state. The boundaries are interlinked; for example climate change is caused by an increase in carbon dioxide and other GHG emissions. As well as causing warming, carbon dioxide is absorbed into the oceans causing acidification. Coral reefs are damaged by both warming oceans and ocean acidification, as well as pollution from biogeochemical flows, another planetary boundary.

All the planetary boundaries have the same ultimate cause; a growing number of people consuming more stuff. The process of making, transporting, consuming or disposing of the stuff causes pollution or uses land and resources. The human economy is becoming large compared to the planet that we live on, so its resource use, and its use of natural systems to dispose of waste is damaging those systems.

This is more than an ethical problem of caring for the environment, because we live on a planet and use its natural systems to provide things that we rely on to live, such as water, air and food. If any or many of the natural system flip into a different state, we have little idea of what that new state might mean for us.

All of human civilisation has flourished during a period of relative stability. Figure 8.5 shows the temperature record calculated from an ice core drilled at the Vostok station in Antarctica over the last 100,000 years. It shows that the past 10,000 years, the entire period of settled agriculture and human

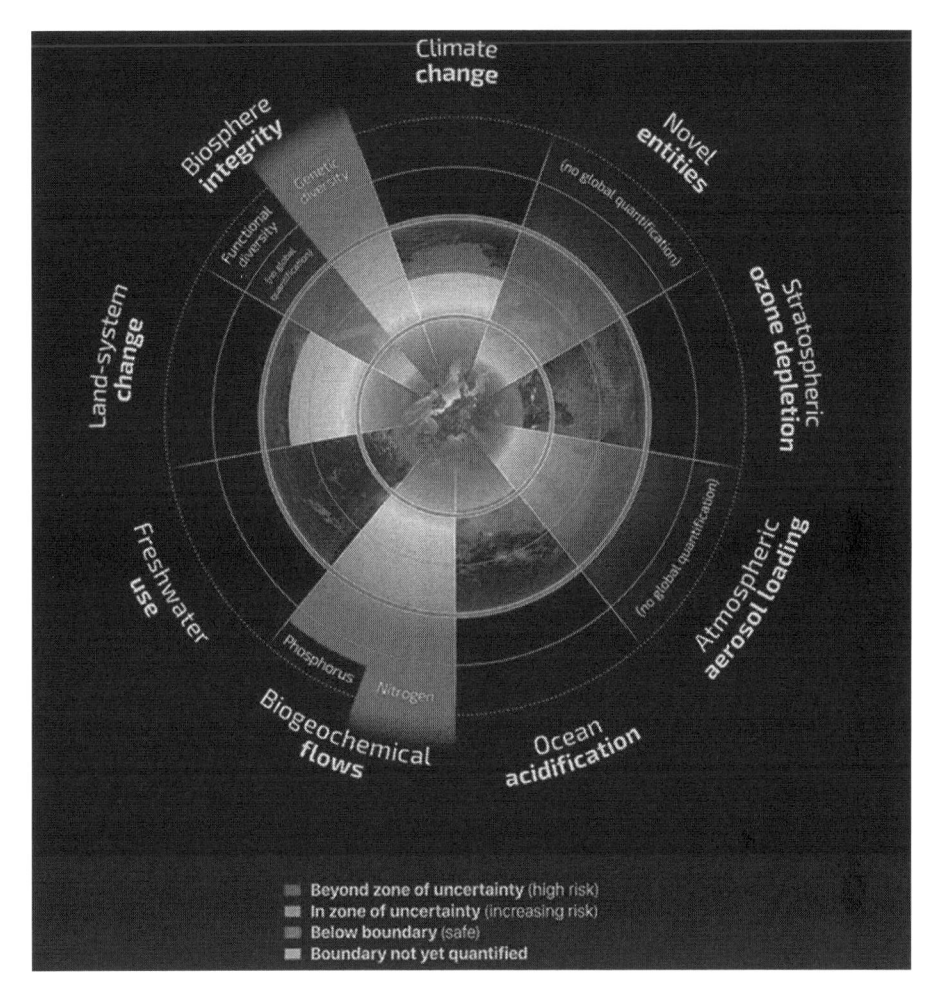

Fig. 8.4 Planetary Boundaries
Illustration: F. Pharand-Deschênes/Globaïa
From http://www.stockholmresilience.org/research/planetary-boundaries.html

civilisation, has had an anomalously stable climate. Before this, the climate fluctuated wildly, and before this there were no great civilisations and the human population numbered less than 2 million. Returning to this volatile state could happen if we breach the climate change boundary.

Saying that, some environmental problems are being addressed, just not quickly or forcibly enough. Take climate change, for example; in Paris in 2015, all of the governments in the world agreed to try to limit GHG emissions to such an extent that global warming would be kept to below 1.5°C above the pre-industrial average, which they agreed is a dangerous level. To achieve this,

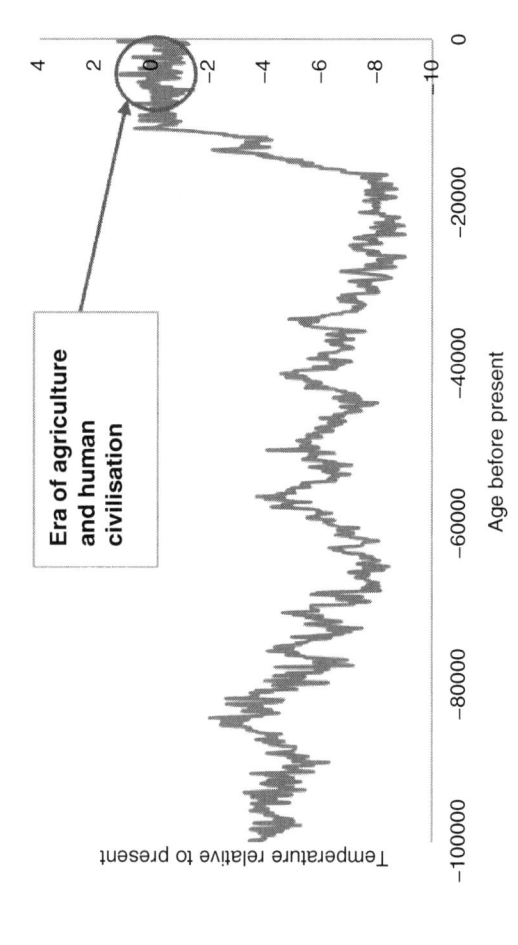

Fig. 8.5 Global temperature over last 100,000 years

Source: Climate Data Information
Source Vostok ice data http://www.ncdc.noaa.gov/paleo/indexice.html accessed 22 January 2017 from http://www.climatedata.info/proxies/data-downloads/

GHG emissions will need to be almost totally terminated within 30 years, and that is if emissions peaked around now, which is just not happening.

8.2 What Has Finance Got to Do with This?

To transform the global economy into a resource-efficient, low-carbon economy will require a new, global industrial revolution much greater in size than previous industrial revolution. The required investment is immense.

The current financial system has very little to do with this – and that's the problem. Finance's main crime is that it is blind to the catastrophic environmental problems we face and has no concern about them. Whatever system of finance that we have, the human economy, if allowed to grow unchecked will continue to wreak environmental damage, as it has done in the past. Environmental damage is not confined to capitalist systems, the damage inflicted on its environment by the communist Soviet Union was immense, including the post-apocalypse landscape that used to be the Aral Sea, or the Chernobyl nuclear disaster.

The shareholder finance system does have negative impacts, which I will outline below, but more important is it's capture of the allocation of capital and therefore block on the economy's ability to transform itself. Capital cannot be allocated into the green economy because it is being harnessed for such vital uses as credit default obligations or to finance the next housing bubble.

The finance sector's main concern is to enrich itself, and whether or not it can do so with a green economy it is of no concern. Many actors in the finance sector have actually been quick to engage with the "green economy", seeing it as an opportunity to make money.

It is estimated that $93 trillion needs to be invested in low-carbon infrastructure over the next 15 years.[10] This compares with current actual investment levels of about £150 billion per year into renewables, an impressive amount but an order of magnitude too low.[11]

This is to address climate change alone, the discussion earlier showed that climate change was one of many planetary boundaries that we are reaching. To date climate change has only been a minor contributor to the third mass extinction currently occurring, although it has the potential to be the major cause. To achieve a genuinely sustainable economy would require the redesign of our industrial organisation; I cite climate change alone as this is the area where investment needs have been researched in detail.

The scale of the environmental crisis we have is unprecedented, yet we understand the problems, we know and have available the technical means to avert them and we are awash with savings waiting to be invested, so we have a unique opportunity to put the global economy on a sustainable path. Effecting this transformation will impact economic growth; it should massively increase growth which is suffering from "secular stagnation"; a lack of demand,[12] and a sustainable industrial transformation will boost that demand immeasurably. Yet why don't we do it? Because we have handed the controls of the economy to the finance sector, and in so doing they have made themselves all-powerful and now dominate the political discourse to such an extent that the environmental destruction of the planet is rendered unimportant compared to such issues as ensuring investments are liquid.

8.2.1 Negative Impacts of Finance

The negative impacts of finance can be deduced from the discussions in previous chapters. The helminth's main concern is to extract revenue for itself out of economic activity. One by-product of this activity is creating an economy with increasing debt and leverage, which makes the whole economy, including governments, companies and individuals much more vulnerable to short-term downturns. Governments, companies and individuals are therefore desperate to constantly boost short-term income and economic activity by whatever means possible, which normally means increasing debt levels and consumer spending. Much of this consumer spending is into physical stuff, which uses up resources and causes pollution.

Another by-product, which complements the impact of debt and leverage, is the compulsion of corporate executives to boost shareholder value, manifest in a constant attempt to meet quarterly earnings targets, an incentive set on the behest of asset managers. To achieve this, companies are incentivised to engage in activities which are harmful to the environment; the incentives are to cut costs on R&D, for example on improving efficiency, to sell more products through extensive use of advertising, therefore promoting harmful consumerism, and to try and pass on externalities to society; large corporates spend huge amounts on lobbying, as has already been documented, part of which is to weaken environmental legislation. Another way of increasing environmental damage is to offshore to countries where it is cheaper to produce, and one of the reasons it's cheaper to produce is these countries have weak environmental laws.

8.2 What Has Finance Got to Do with This?

Even without the influence of the finance sector, corporates engage in these environment-destroying activities. Many countries with large coal mining industries keep these alive from union and worker pressure as much as from corporate pressure. The influence of the finance sector is to magnify the natural tendency of companies to engage in environmentally destructive activities.

All this is as naught compared to the helminth's interception and use of savings for its own benefit, as described in Chapter 7. The world is awash with savings, we have a saving's glut which is the subject of much angst amongst economic policymakers. Yet this is not translated into sustainable investment. Why not? Because the controls of society's investment are in charge of the helminth, for whom it is more profitable to create artificial assets then it is to actually make investments.

We saw in Chapter 5 how less than 5% of savings is actually invested; the remainder is diverted into financial assets – why? so that these assets can be bought and sold so that the intermediaries can take a profit. The regulation that ensures this happens is drafted in the context of a hegemonic discourse dominated by finance. The purpose of savings is for investment in the economy, investment that is desperately needed to convert our economy into a sustainable economy. The investment that is occurring into the green economy, all £150 billion per year, either comes out of the less than 5% which is actually invested or is directly invested by the public sector.

A metric used by company executives to measure success is return on capital, which is the ratio of profit to capital, companies seek to maximise this ratio. To maximise return on capital you could increase profits, but you could also reduce capital used, for example by returning capital to shareholders. This is actually a measure of how good you are at sweating your assets, rather than making new investments, you want to try and squeeze profits out of existing assets, by selling more of the same stuff or by reducing staff costs. But why is return on capital so important, when savings are not scarce and there is a need for investment?

Chapter 6 described how banks do not lend into the real economy either, but instead choose to blow property bubbles, lend for consumer spending or lend to each other, despite their massive balance sheets and government-mandated ability to create money.

This consumer spending is to buy goods which use resources and create pollution in the production process. Companies persuade people to buy goods that they do not need through advertising.

Attempts to address environmental problems through the finance system have generally end up being co-opted by the finance sector through the hegemony of ideas as illustrated by two supposed successes of the environmental lobby: the carbon markets and the carbon bubble.

The **carbon markets** were the creation of the Kyoto Protocol, an international agreement in 1997 between 192 national governments to limit GHG emissions. Although nearly all countries signed up to it, a few, most notably the USA, never ratified the agreement.

Under the Kyoto Protocol, countries which did not meet their agreed targets were allowed to purchase emissions permits from countries which exceeded their targets. Within countries, emitters were allocated permits to emit GHGs which they could trade with other emitters or purchase off-sets from projects in developing countries. The whole scheme was trumpeted as a great success but was actually an unmitigated disaster; global GHG emissions reached record levels during the operation of the carbon markets, and large carbon emitters made windfall profits, as did traders in carbon permits.

A far better, easier, fairer, more effective system would be for countries to have taxed carbon emissions. Yet this was rejected out of hand for a market solution, because financial markets are efficient and know best.

Stranded fossil-fuel assets or the **carbon bubble** is the idea that fossil-fuel companies might be overvalued, because to meet our climate change targets most fossil-fuel reserves will have to be left in the ground. This argument has gained quite a lot of traction, for example the G20 – the grouping of the world's 20 largest economies, set up an organisation called the Financial Stability Board, which in turn has set up a task force to develop climate-related financial risk disclosure.[13]

The environmental movement considers the carbon bubble being taken seriously in the financial world as a great achievement. However, if we examine what this argument is saying, that the calamity of one of three mass extinctions in the billions of years that life is on the planet is only important in so much as it might have an impact on financial markets, and institutions should therefore, but only if they want, tell us what risk this entails for their shareholders. Financial economics holds illimitable dominion over all.

Finance has a claim on those stranded assets; they have to be burned. If we were to move to a low-carbon economy, the net result is we will probably be financially better off, once renewable energy is up and running; when the sun shines or the wind blows, the energy produced by solar or wind energy costs nothing to produce. All of the fossil-fuel reserves will become valueless, so those with financial claims on the reserves will do their damnedest to see that this does not happen. The lobbying power of corporates, overseen by asset managers, is mobilised to do everything to stop this happening.

8.3 Impact on Society

8.3.1 Inequality and Growth

Beyond the impact on the natural world, how does finance impact society? A couple of years ago, everyone was talking about – well, perhaps not everyone – a very long economics textbook called *Capital in the Twenty-First Century* by the French economist Thomas Piketty.[14] The 600 pages can be summarised thus: R>G; the return on investments is greater than economic growth in advanced economies, meaning that people who have assets (the rich) receive returns in excess of economic growth whereas the poor do not have assets and therefore do not benefit from these returns, and hence inequality has increased through time.

You might ask, so what? True, there are downsides to inequality, the poorer get jealous and unhappy, and there are many social inequities associated with inequality such as increased crime and depression.[15] Also, Piketty makes the point that some people who own capital might have worked hard to earn that capital, but others might have just inherited it, which is not fair and is not good for the reward system of our society.

The main argument justifying inequality is that if everyone is better off by virtue of increased inequality, then it is more important that large chunks of the population are better off than that the population as a whole is unequal.

However, Figure 8.6 presents a different picture.

Figure 8.6 shows that households below median income have not increased their real income in the United States since 1967, and the earnings of those in the fourth quintile (the 20th to 40th highest earners out of every hundred) have barely increased at all.[16]

This is actually worse than it sounds. Anyone who watched the TV series *Mad Men*, or was alive at the time, will know that women in 1967 either had very lowly, poorly paid jobs such as secretaries or were unpaid housewives. When women got married, they often gave up their jobs. Although there is still a gender pay gap, it is much lower than it was in 1967, and far fewer women are housewives. A typical household nowadays will have two wage earners earning similar salaries, as opposed to in 1967 where the man would work, with maybe a much smaller addition from the woman. I am not for one moment suggesting that this was a good thing. But when we compare 1967 with today, the household earnings today should be almost twice what they were in 1967 simply

Fig. 8.6 Real income growth in USA

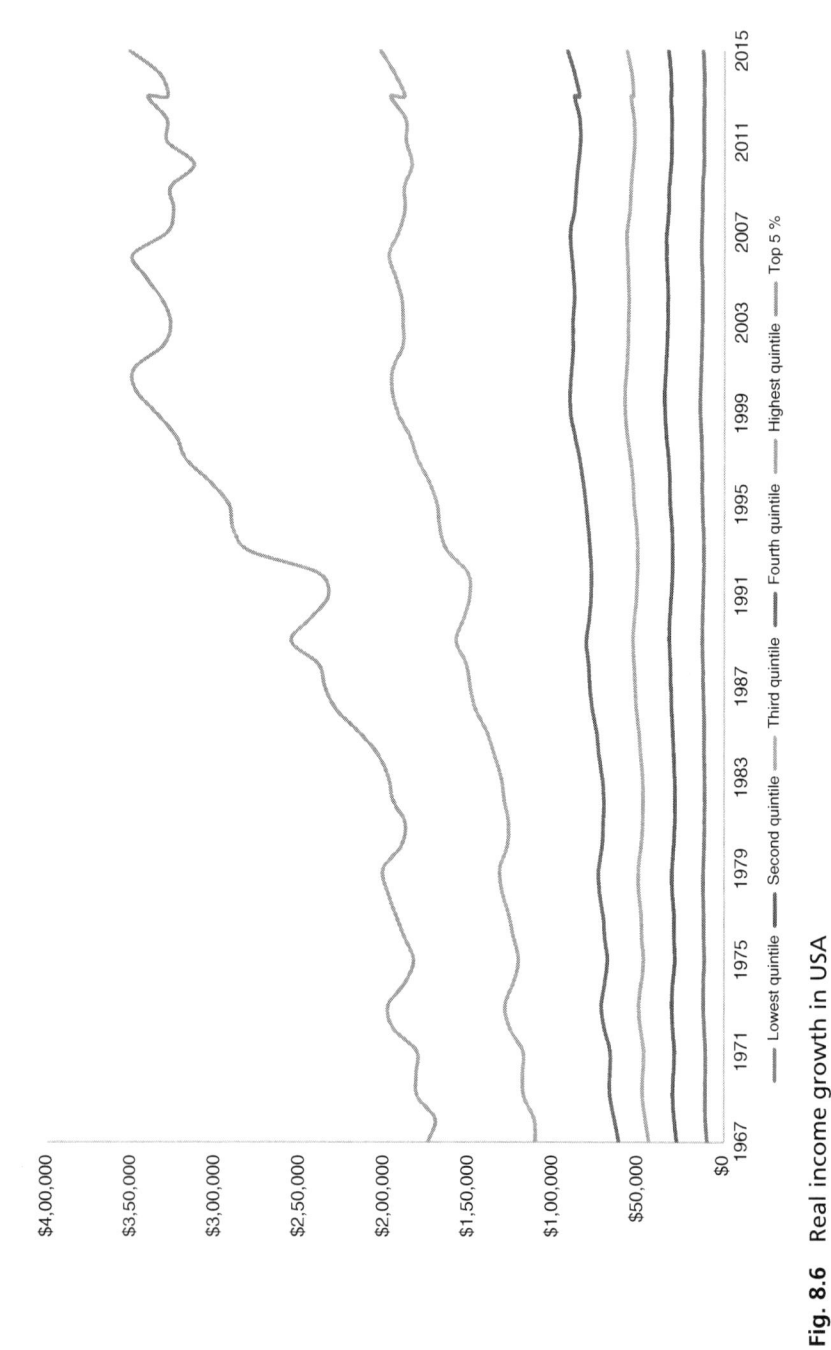

Source: United States Census Bureau
The chart show the mean within each quintile band so the 3rd quintile is approximately the population's median in 2015 prices. Table A-2 from http://www.census.gov/data/tables/2016/demo/income-poverty/p60-256.html accessed 22 January 2017

because today a household comprises two workers, compared to effectively one in 1967.

In this period the US economy has increased considerably in size, the GDP per capita has more than doubled since 1967 in real terms.[17] This means that the United States has been very successful in growing its economy, but all of this excess growth has gone to the wealthiest in society.

If we judge the success of economic growth in the USA because it delivers improvement in the lives of most people, on this score it has failed. The secondary considerations of fairness and unhappiness caused by inequality outweigh the non-existent improvement in welfare brought about by economic growth.

Not only are the vast majority of people in the USA not better off than 40 years ago, they are actually worse off. This is because debt levels have increased over this period – they have more than doubled compared to both income and assets in that time.[18] Access to credit is a good thing, it allows people or companies to have the opportunity to buy a house, a car or start a business. But high debt levels are not a good thing, if I earn $40,000 I am better off if I have debts at the 1967 level of $40,000, then if I have current debts of $80,000.

Finance has contributed to all of these factors, increased inequality, the stagnation of wages and the increase in debt levels. As described in the last chapter, the finance sector increases debt and leverage in the economy as this is how it increases its profits. Through colonisation, the finance system increases the range of assets that it has a claim on and hence increases the potential debt levels in society, as more assets are used as collateral against debt.

The cult of shareholder value, to be described in more detail in the next chapter, has caused companies to cut staff costs, reducing wages for almost everyone except key staff and company executives. Company executives' pay has been linked to share price, in the interest of asset managers, massively increasing their pay. The finance system has grown as have the wages of those in finance. The increase in the pay of those at the top – finance professionals and company executives – does not correspond with better company performance, it does not create value[19] but has been achieved by cutting the pay of everyone else.

Another modern trend is off-shoring, the location of factories in jobs where wages are lower. The next section shows that this is not necessarily such a bad thing for labourers in developing countries, but it is generally disastrous for those in the countries from which jobs have been offshored.

8.3.2 Global Inequality

The global picture is a bit more complicated than the USA and other developed economies, and the role of the finance sector is more ambiguous. The global picture is characterised by the "Elephant curve" represented in Figure 8.7. This shows the growth in global incomes over the last 20 years split by income distribution.

The two groups of people that have benefited most are the global "middle class" and the very wealthy. The ones who have lost out are the very poorest and those in the 80–95% bracket.

The global middle class by Western standards are not rich at all, they earn between $3 and $16 a day, which would be on social assistance in rich countries. These are mostly people in Asia who have benefited from the growth of China and India and are typically people who have migrated from rural areas to urban areas.

The people who have lost out are the middle class in Western countries. These have seen jobs migrate to developing countries which has put downward pressure on their wages, the wealthy within their county benefit from the higher returns to capita brought about by this globalising trend. The current wave of populism is attributed to this phenomenon; the middle class are seeing the wealthy pull away from them and are being threatened by cheap competition from Asia.

The number of very poor people in the world living in extreme poverty has reduced considerably over the last century (Figure 8.8) and this is largely seen as a success of capitalism. At the start of the twentieth century, nearly everyone in the world was extremely poor. During the course of the twentieth century this proportion has steadily reduced, with an acceleration of this reduction over the last 30 years, with the proportion on less than $1.90 per day around 10% of the world's population.

This book is a critique of the shareholder finance system, not capitalist economies. Much of the reduction in absolute poverty has been down to a different kind of capitalism, take the example of China which has successfully lifted about 500 million people out of absolute poverty since 1981.[20]

The financial system designed and deployed by the Chinese government is very different to the West's system (there is also a great deal of variation between Western countries). The Chinese have followed a developmental state model of financial development. This is a model first employed by the Japanese government after the Second World War (or arguably developed by the USA in eighteenth century, and Germany in nineteenth century), which

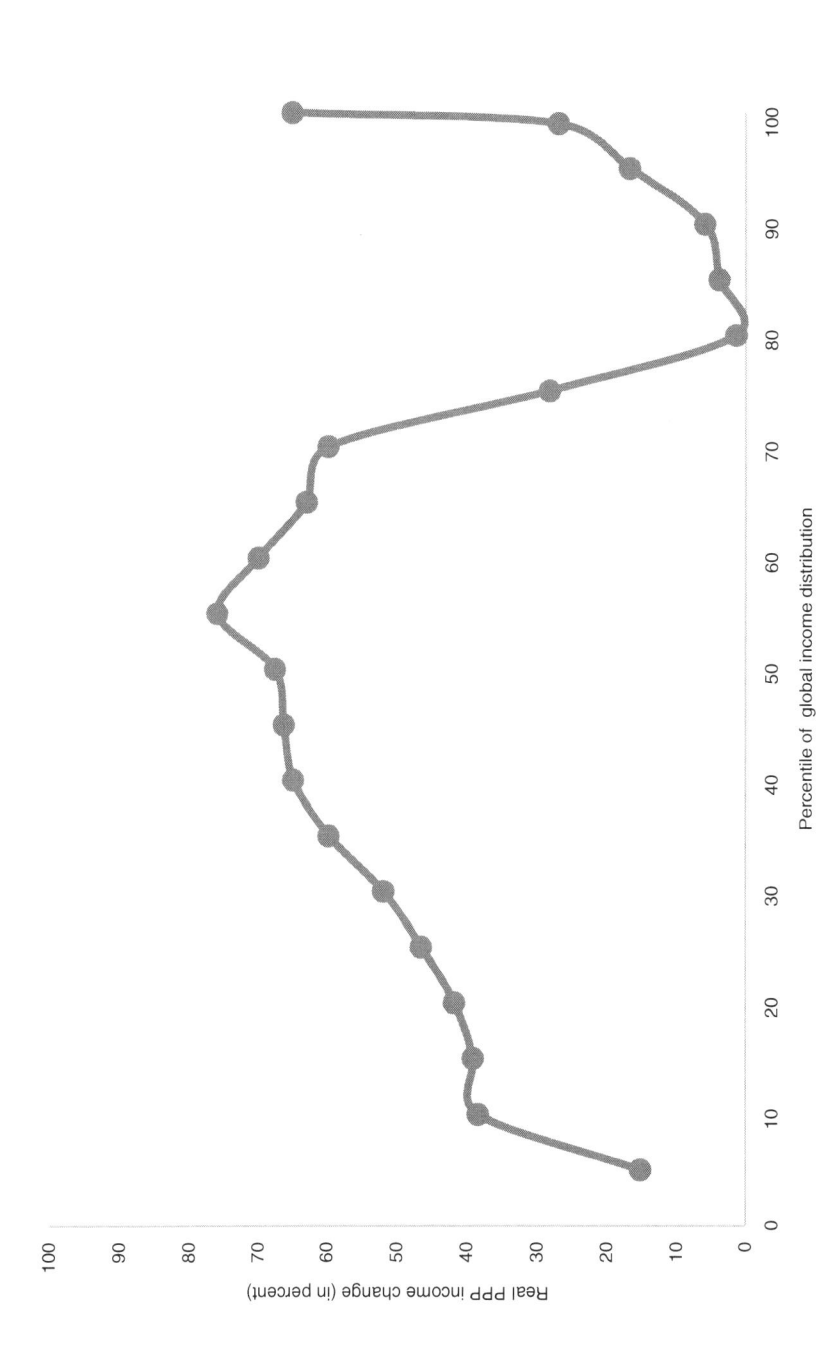

Fig. 8.7 Change in real income between 1988 and 2008 at various percentiles of global income distribution (calculated in 2005 international dollars)

Source: Branko Milanovic
Milanovic, B (2012) *Global Income Inequality by the Numbers: in History and Now* World Bank

212   8 Collateral Damage

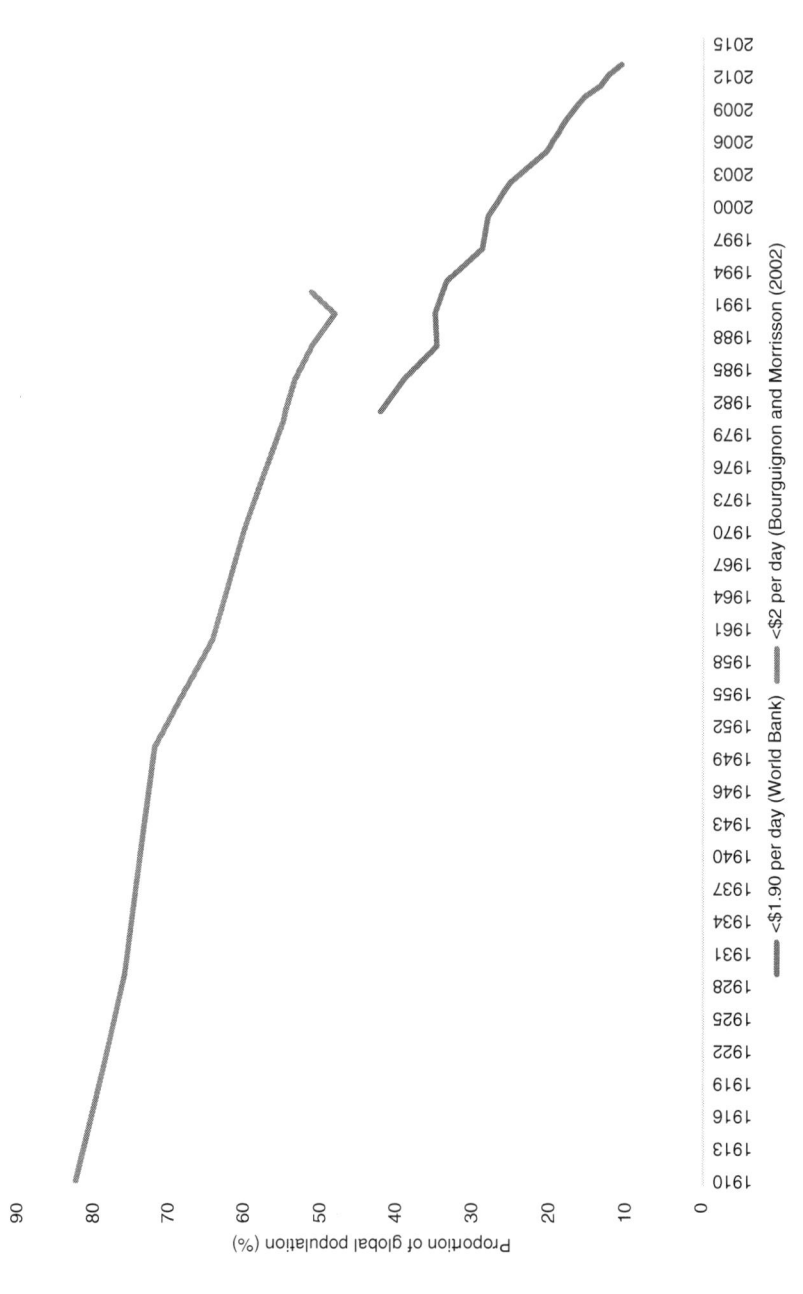

Fig. 8.8 Proportion of global population living in extreme poverty

Source: World Bank, Bourguignon and Morrisson (2002)
The recent data series from 1981 onwards was from the World Bank World Development Indicators; this uses $1.90 per day as definition of poverty, the older data series from early twentieth century up to 1992 was taken from Bourguignon, F and Morrisson, C (2002) *Inequality among World Citizens: 1820–1992* The American Economic Review, Vol. 92, No. 4 both accessed 23 January 2017

was copied by the Asian tiger economies (Hong Kong, Taiwan, Singapore and South Korea) in the 1980s and 1990s.

The characteristic of this development path is the state promotes favoured industries for the specific purpose of developing the country's economic base. These countries have high savings and investment rates often enforced and directed by the state, with a concentration of effort on rapidly developing an export manufacturing sector, the state uses a variety of tools including favourable tax and regulatory regimes; national and local governments are co-opted into helping businesses in this sector. Selective tariffs are also employed, to protect favoured domestic industries. Finance is largely state directed, via the banking system. The central bank instructs banks as to which sectors they will lend to, with the emphasis being on export-focused manufacturing. Finance is almost entirely via banks as opposed to capital markets. The central banks often manipulate their currencies; because of the large trade surplus generated by the export industry, the currency should appreciate, making exports more expensive. To stop this, the central bank buys foreign assets, normally US Treasuries, to keep the currency low and exports competitive.[21]

The developmental state model has been highly successful, achieving extraordinary levels of economic growth. For example, China's GDP per capita has more than doubled in the last 10 years,[22] the four Asian tigers are now four of the richest countries in the world, whereas in the 1960s they were as poor as African countries.

The growth of China, in particular, has contributed to the reduction in global inequality. China is now home to approximately a seventh of the world's population, most of who were very poor up until the 1990s. A large number of Chinese have become much richer because of industrialisation and economic growth, although Chinese society has become more unequal in the process. And as a seventh of the world's population who used to be very poor are entering some kind of middle class that means the world is less unequal than it used to be.

Where is the financial system in this development and poverty-reduction story? You would have thought that capital should flow from countries with older populations and developed capital basis, to countries with younger populations and low capital, that is from developed countries to developing countries. In fact, the flows are the other way. The picture as to why this happens is complicated but the rapid development of some economies has little to do with international financial flows, countries which export capital have a better growth record than those that do not.[23] The Chinese government, for example, forces people to save and exports capital to keep its currency low to promote exports. This manifests itself in the Table 2.4 which shows that China is home to four of the largest SWFs.

The claims of the promoters of free financial markets, as discussed in detail in the next chapter, are that free markets cause an efficient allocation of resources. However, for the very poorest in the world, the world of finance has got very little to do with them. The 3 billion people living on less than \$2.50 per day[24] are not touched in any way by global finance. Admittedly that is probably not the finance sector's fault, the lack of investment in poor countries is caused by poor institutions within those countries.[25]

Where large numbers of people have been brought out of poverty, it is because the government of the country they live has decided to pursue policies that will achieve rapid economic growth. Countries like China have used the international financial system as part of their plan; they have used it to buy up foreign assets to keep their currencies competitive to boost their exports. This is anathema to the design of the finance system, in which free markets allocate capital effectively, the actors in these free markets are not supposed to be the communist government of the world's largest country buying up asset to manipulate the value of their currency.

8.3.3 Health and Happiness

The finance sector negatively effects people's health and well-being both directly and indirectly.

The direct method is debt. The finance sector makes money through issuing debt, the more debt there is, the greater its revenue. The process of financialisation boils down to companies making money through credit instead of selling people products. Debt makes people unhappy, it causes them stress, increases the incidence of mental illness which in turn makes physical illness worse.[26]

The debt, or leverage, of the whole economy brought about by the finance sector also causes people poor health outcomes and unhappiness. As we have seen, the financialised model of economic growth has been one corresponding to increased debt levels and stagnating wages. When inevitable recessions occur, the impact of the recessions is magnified by the debt levels leading to more redundancies and bankruptcies. These, in turn, cause large amounts of stress, as does the insecurity of knowing that this may occur, which again causes poor mental and hence physical health outcomes.[27]

The indirect channels are through advertising and lobbying. Advertising persuades people to buy stuff that they don't want. For the last 60 years, since Sigmund Freud's nephew Edward Bernays introduced ideas discovered by his uncle into the world of public relations psychological theory has been ubiquitous in advertising.[28] The purpose is to get messages into people's heads to get them to part with their money often by incurring more debts. A single advertising campaign is merely to get you to buy a particular good. However, the combined effect of all advertising campaigns is to turn citizens into consumers, to make people feel they are lacking something, something which you can buy, and buying that something will make you happy.

Buying a product gives you an instant hit of happiness, but that happiness rapidly fades, leaving you empty till the next hit. Memorable experiences and meaningful relationships give you longer lasting happiness.[29] The pervasiveness of advertising is focusing on the same false message, meaning that people will pursue false goals to try and make themselves happy.

Pharmaceutical companies spend a huge amount on lobbying, in the USA $3 billion over the last 18 years.[30] The reason is to keep very strong patent laws, so they can charge highly for medicines over a long-time period, and so that the USA's public health institutions are not allowed to negotiate drug prices; the result is to boost these companies' profits at the expense of tax payers and people who need medication[31]; the people who can no longer afford the medication and the worsening of the USA's healthcare system means that citizens are less healthy as a result of the lobbying activity.

Meanwhile, the world is rapidly running out of effective antibiotics, because pharmaceutical companies have cut research into new ones as this research is not profitable in the short term, even though the lack of antibiotics could be "apocalyptic".[32]

Companies may very well engage in lobbying and advertising without the intervention of the finance sector. The incentives set by the finance sector make the pressure on companies to do so stronger. The aim of maximising return on capital means that rather than waste capital developing new products and developing new drugs, it makes more sense to try and sell existing products, or variants or upgrades of existing products, and to lobby governments to maximise your revenue for existing products, and to pass on externalities to society. The focus on short-term shareholder value means that companies are looking for quick wins, such as advertising and lobbying, rather than investment that might only be profitable in the long run, such as in research into antibiotics.

8.4 Fiddling While Rome Burns

The finance sector may not have actively caused these underlying problems which threaten our way of life but it is a major factor in our failure to take the kind of evasive action that humans have managed to organise before. In the same way, it may not have caused the inequality which currently threatens our political institutions – though it has been partly responsible – but it now undermines our ability to tackle it effectively. We have unfortunately created a financial system in the name of efficiency and progress, but – as it has developed – it seems to be undermining our ability to take imaginative or innovative action.

Some common themes emerge in the discussion of the impact of the finance sector on the environment and society. The themes are debt; the finance sector looks to increase debt and leverage as this is how it makes money. Increasing levels of debt are bad on a personal, societal and planetary level. On the personal level, they cause insecurity, anxiety, reduce happiness and increase incidence of mental illness. On societal level, it means that when the economy goes into recession, the damage is magnified, which means that companies and governments take short-term action to try and perpetually keep the economy growing. This normally means boosting consumer spending and further increasing debt, causing more resource use and environmental damage, as well as the other negative societal consequences of higher debt levels.

Corporates pursuing quarterly targets and worrying about return on capital seek to sweat assets; they prefer to get the maximum return out of their existing capital stock rather than invest to create new capital stock. This means that fossil-fuel assets have to be burned rather then left in the ground, externalities are passed onto society; lobbying is a tool to reduce environmental legislation, off-shoring to avoid environmental and labour laws, tax avoidance to avoid paying dues to society and extensive advertising to turn people into consumers to get them into debt to buy stuff they don't need, all with resultant environmental damage.

Lobbying, tax avoidance and off-shoring are also linked. Corporates lobby selected governments to give them favourable tax treatment and regulatory environment so that they can situate some of their activities in these countries, allowing them to escape the regulation and tax of other countries, predominantly the USA which is many companies' largest market. Corporates lobby hard on trade deals so that their interests are served. And companies look for countries with poor or non-enforced environmental and labour laws to situate production at least cost to themselves.[33]

Corporates would probably do all of this anyway without the intervention of finance, but the finance sector, by linking executive pay to share price, makes the focus of corporates more short term and the incentives for this behaviour stronger. The hegemony of financial ideas and influence means that corporates, governments and even the environmental movement buy into this agenda.

Nicholas Stern has said that the two defining challenges of our century are poverty and climate change.[34] I would add to that climate change is only one aspect of the third mass extinction that is happening now. The finance sector is largely conspicuous by its absence from these challenges, which gives a lie to its defining justification that society's capital is allocated efficiently making everyone better off (see next chapter). Underinvestment in poor countries is because of poor institutions in those countries[35] and this is not the finance sector's fault, indeed some of the tools of finance; professionalism and transparency could have a role to play in improving these institutions.

Another big theme is the use by China and the Asian Tigers of the West's financial system, a development path that could be copied by other countries. These countries are now the major population centres of the world and are fast becoming the major economic centres. What growth path will China and other developing countries pursue, will they follow the mass consumption model of the West or some other model? Up until now China has been growing by increasing industrial production for export, financed by high savings and investment without increasing domestic demand. The Chinese government is now pursuing policies of both stimulating demand and trying to make her economy more resource efficient. However, China already faces spiralling levels of debt. This is a crucial question for the planet's future.

Notes

1. Stearns, Stephen C. and Rolf Hoekstra (2005) *Evolution: An Introduction*, 2nd ed. Oxford University Press.
2. Stearns, Stephen C. and Rolf Hoekstra (2005) *Evolution: An Introduction*, 2nd ed. Oxford University Press.
3. Brundtland Commission (1987) *Our Common Future* Oxford University Press.
4. See United Nations (2004) *World Population to 2300* United Nations Department of Economic and Social Affairs.
5. That is the number of children a woman has during her lifetime.
6. World Bank data collated by Google https://www.google.co.uk/publicdata/explore?ds=d5bncppjof8f9_&met_y=sp_dyn_tfrt_in&hl=en&dl=en accessed 1 January 2017.
7. All figures in current $dollar terms.
8. OECD (2012) *Long-Term Economic Growth and Environmental Pressure:*

Reference Scenarios for Future Global Projections OECD Environment Directorate
Environment Policy Committee.
9. *Source*: World Bank data collated by Google, accesses 30 December 2016.
10. Global Commission on the Economy and Climate (2014) *Better Growth, Better Climate: The New Climate Economy Report.*
11. IEA (2012) *Special Report: World Energy Investment Outlook* International Energy Agency.
12. Summers, L (2016) *The Age of Secular Stagnation* Foreign Affairs March/April 2016.
13. See https://www.fsb-tcfd.org/ accessed on 31 May 2017.
14. Piketty, Thomas (2013) *Capital in the Twenty-first Century* Éditions du Seuil, Belknap Press.
15. Wilkinson, R and Pickett, K (2009) *The Spirit Level* Allen Lane.
16. The fourth quintile has increased less than 50% in nearly 50 years, a real increase of 0.8% per annum.
17. Multpl: http://www.multpl.com/us-real-gdp-per-capita accessed 1 January 2017.
18. Federal reserve Bank of San Francisco 18 January 2011 Economic Letter Mian, A and Sufi A (2011) *Consumers and the Economy, Part II: Household Debt and the Weak U.S. Recovery* http://www.frbsf.org/economic-research/publications/economic-letter/2011/january/consumers-economy-household-debt-weak-us-recovery/ accessed 1 January 2017.
19. Li, W and Young, S (2016) *An Analysis of CEO Pay Arrangements and Value Creation for
FTSE-350 Companies* CFA Society.
20. World Bank China Overview http://www.worldbank.org/en/country/china/overview#3 accessed 21 December 2016.
21. Cohen, S and DeLong, B (2016) *Concrete Economics* Harvard Business Review Press.
22. Trading Economics: http://www.tradingeconomics.com/china/gdp-per-capita accessed 1 January 2017.
23. See for example Gros, D (2013) *Why does capital flow from poor to rich countries?* CEPR and Prasad, E and Rajan, R and Subramanian, A (2007) *Foreign Capital and Economic Growth* Brookings Papers on Economic Activity, Economic Studies Program, The Brookings Institution, vol. 38 (2007–1).
24. World Bank data: http://www.worldbank.org/en/topic/poverty/overview.
25. Alfaro, L Kalemli-Ozcan, A and Volosovych, V (2008) *Why Doesn't Capital Flow from Rich to Poor Countries? An Empirical Investigation* Review of Economics and Statistics Vol. 90.
26. Drentea, P and Lavrakas, P (2000) *Over the limit: the association among health, race and debt* Volume 50, Issue 4.

27. Burgard, S Brand, J and House, J (2009) *Perceived job insecurity and worker health in the United States.*
Soc Sci Med.
28. See for example Ferrier, A (2014) *The Advertising Effect: How to Change Behaviour* OUP Australia & New Zealand.
29. Haidt, J (2006) *The Happiness Hypothesis* Basic Books.
30. OpenSecrets.org https://www.opensecrets.org/lobby/top.php?showYear=a&indexType=i accessed 12 December 2016.
31. Goldacre, B (2012) *Bad Pharma* Fourth Estate.
32. BBC News 24 January 2013 *Antibiotic "apocalypse" warning* and Bloomberg News 30 June 2016 *There's Big Money Again in Saving Humanity With Antibiotics.*
33. *Power and Inequality in the Global Political Economy* Lecture by Nicola Phillips 9 November 2016 http://www.lse.ac.uk/website-archive/newsAndMedia/videoAndAudio/channels/publicLecturesAndEvents/player.aspx?id=3653.
34. Speech given by Nicholas Stern in Paris on 26 August 2015, quoted 26 August 2015 by Grantham Institute http://www.lse.ac.uk/GranthamInstitute/publication/negociations-climatiques-developpement-durable-et-croissance/
35. See Notes 26 and 28.

9

On Value and Values

The Value Embedded in the Financial System and the Values That It Could Embody

Once upon a time, 24 stockbrokers got together under a buttonwood tree outside 68 Wall Street and formed the New York Stock Exchange. A century earlier, merchants used to meet at the Lloyd's coffee house in the City of London to agree how to share risk, and started the London insurance market that bears the same name. Then, the big bad government came along and started interfering with these free markets and messed everything up…

The financial system operates on a set of norms which equate all human values with financial value, where value is the market price. This is proving catastrophic for the economy, society and the planet. The New York Stock Exchange/Buttonwood creation story is part of a myth wherein financiers see themselves as free market entrepreneurs, embodying something natural and spontaneous, and should be left alone by governments to create wealth. But as we saw in Chapter 3, they work in Potemkin markets, every aspect of which is dominated by government. The markets-as-nature is a myth, yet governments and regulators believe the myth, so the irony is that they heavily regulate the markets to get them to behave as close to the regulator's image of how a free market should behave.

In this chapter I investigate the values embedded within the financial system. Up to now I have argued that the financial system is not achieving its purpose. To decide on purpose we need to take a view on whether the purpose is worth while; the judgement on what is worthwhile is an ethical question.

A famous ethical problem is the trolley problem: an out of control trolley is charging down the railway track and is going to crash into five people and probably kill them. You can pull a lever to switch the trolley onto a side track, but there is someone on this track, so in doing this you will save the five people but almost definitely kill this one person; is pulling the lever the right thing to do?[1] Or the variation I like is if there was a fat man standing next to you, would you push him on to the track to stop the trolley and save the five people?[2]

Philosophical problems like this are specifically designed to isolate the ethical issue in question, in this case, is it OK to deliberately kill one person to save five people? If this were a real-world situation, you would also have to ask another question, would pushing the fat man onto the track stop the trolley and save the five people? If it didn't, it would be wrong to push the fat man whatever the ethical question was as you would be killing one and not saving the five.

So far in this book I have argued that the financial system is not doing what it is supposed to be doing, by operating the levers it is not saving the five people. I have also articulated what the financial system is supposed to be doing.

In this chapter I look at what ethics the financial system embodies. The financial system is hugely complex, and therefore it is challenging to summarise its ethical position. This chapter argues that the ethics of finance can be summarised in the concept of financial value. The aim of finance is to create and maximise market value. The ethical justification for this is that the price of an asset, the market value, corresponds to the asset's actual value. In maximising market value, the finance system is optimising the economy, and as those assets are optimised, the economy can run efficiently at its full potential. The economy's assets are used to generate return and economic output hence everyone is materially better off compared to some other system of asset allocation.

Like the trolley problem, there is an ethical question; is everyone being materially better off desirable, and a practical question; does pulling the lever of the finance system make everyone better off? More specifically, this chapter considers the following questions:

1. Is market value the dominant value within shareholder-capitalism finance?
2. How do theories of finance embody this value?
3. How does finance theory determine market practice?
4. Is the objective correct, is optimising economic activity a worthwhile objective?
5. Does finance theory work theoretically and in practice?
6. What would an alternative set of values look like?

As we have seen, free capital markets are not possible and do not exist in the real world, and the current non-free capital markets set-up is highly problematic because it largely allocates capital to activities that are at best useless and at worse harmful to the environment and society. Because society's capital is allocated by the finance sector, we get an economy and society which are the outcomes of this capital allocation.

The economy could grow and develop in different ways depending on where capital is allocated. The current system we have allocates capital in a specific way, which is a by-product of the incentives on those that allocate capital – the financial intermediaries who allocate capital to maximise their own revenues. There is no guarantee that this will be in the best interests of society or the economy, in fact I hope that this book has shown that it is not.

This chapter critiques the values that are embedded within the financial system. These values are important to the operation of the system because they give the financial system intellectual justification, which is why governments support and protect the system, the values are embedded in regulation, and in the behaviour and culture of the firms and individuals that operate the system.

9.1 Hegemonic Theories

Chapter 1 introduced the notion of shareholder finance, the form of finance practiced most notably in Anglo-Saxon economies, such as the USA, the UK, Canada and Australia, but also in countries such as Chile, Holland and Ireland. Shareholder capitalism also holds dominant sway in the Bretton Woods institutions such as the World Bank and IMF.

The objective of shareholder finance is to make everyone materially better off, and this is achieved through free markets.

Figure 9.1 is a schematic picture giving an overview of the process by which ethical values are translated into economic outcomes.

The Buttonwood myth and others like it imply a situation whereby financial markets are somehow natural, as Adam Smith wrote it is in man's nature to "truck, barter and exchange",[3] and if men are allowed to pursue these natural tendencies, an invisible hand makes everyone better off.

The actors within the finance system behave, and often justify their activities, by reference to an ethical framework, for example Lloyd Blankfein, the

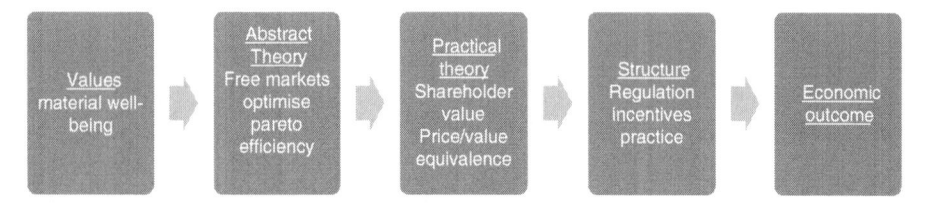

Fig. 9.1 How values translate to economic outcome

CEO of Goldman Sachs, famously stated, "I'm doing God's work".[4] For the centuries since Adam Smith, economists have been beavering away devising theories that justify why a market economy achieves a beneficial outcome.

With a Potemkin market view of the world, governments have designed, participate in and regulate markets based on a specific theoretical framework; shareholder finance is not the only way to run financial markets; there are different possibilities of managing financial systems which are also capitalist, such as the developmental state or stakeholder capitalism as described in Chapter 1. These forms of capitalism are not necessarily better or worse than shareholder finance, but their existence shows that societies have to make a choice as to how their financial systems work.

Theoretical justification that free markets result in making people materially better off is formalised by the Arrow-Debreu model. Under certain assumptions, complete and competitive markets deliver a pareto-efficient outcome; which means that no one can be made better off without making someone else worse off.[5] This simple result has widespread implications. If you create a free market and allow people to trade, people will be better off or at worst they will be in the same situation. If everything can be traded, then people will make welfare-improving trades, until the economy achieves its maximum overall utility.

Because of this economic orthodoxy, the aim of governments (in shareholder finance countries), the central bank, regulators, the World Bank and IMF is to encourage free and complete capital markets.[6]

Arrow-Debreu is a theoretical justification that a free-market economy is the best form of economic organisation. However, other economic theories are required to apply the philosophy of free markets into tools that can be used to regulate and practice finance. Within finance, capital is allocated at two levels. At the portfolio level, asset owners, as described in Chapter 2, delegate their portfolios to asset managers who then allocate assets on their behalf. The theoretical framework for how they do this is a suite of financial economics theories; the EMH, MPT, the Black-Scholes model and the capital asset pricing model (CAPM).

The second level of capital allocation is where company management makes investment decisions involving the assets of companies. The dominant framework of shareholder value was developed by business schools and management consultants. Shareholder value and MPT are aligned; they are both based on the presumption that maximising market value is an overriding objective, and asset owners, investing in line with MPT, have influenced companies to maximise shareholder value.

9.1.1 Standard Finance Theories

I describe here a suite of theories that were developed within the academic discipline of financial economics. They are important as they form the basis of financial regulation and practice. A full discussion of the evidence as to whether or not these theories are correct would require a whole book in itself. In this section, I briefly describe how these theories form the basis for decision-making in financial markets.

The basic theories that make up MPT are[7]:

- EMH: Under certain assumptions, a market reflects all relevant information. The corollary is that it is impossible to beat the market, except by taking more risk, unless you have some (illegal) insider information. Market movements follow a random walk caused by new, unpredictable, information being received by the market.
- MPT: An investor can construct an optimal portfolio maximising his expected return for a given level of risk, where risk is defined as volatility. The theory describes a concept called an efficient frontier which is the maximum expected return for any given level of risk. The theory assumes that all investors are risk averse, which leads to the conclusion you cannot increase expected return without taking on more risk.
- CAPM: This theory allows investors to evaluate a security. The expected return on an asset is what is termed the risk-free rate plus a risk premium, adjusted by what is termed Beta which is a measure of the volatility of the security compared to the volatility of the market. This Beta is synonymous with risk.
- Black-Scholes model: This is a model which provides a methodology for calculating the price of an option and is widely used within finance to do so.

The above suite of theories form the basis of the framework by which investors make decisions. As described in Chapter 2 an institution, usually with the advice of an investment consultant, will decide on asset allocation into broad asset classes such as equity and bonds. Once assets have been allocated, the institution appoints an asset manager to allocate the assets within each asset class (smaller institutions may appoint one investment manager for all of their assets, large institutions may appoint multiple managers).

Typically, the mandate of a manager will be to invest against an index, with a specification of a target to outperform the index for a given level of risk. The index is a weighted average of all of the stocks or bonds which constitute the market; this means that the asset manager will as a default buy all of the securities that make up the asset class in the same weighting as the index, and then take relatively small positions which diverge from that index.

This framing of a mandate comes straight out of MPT. The index is a weighted average of the investment class, so this represents an efficient frontier as defined by MPT. Outperformance can only be achieved by taking a risk against this portfolio, a mandate will specify what this risk is and hence the expected outperformance. There is an internal contradiction here, by EMH even a skilled asset manager can only beat the index by taking more risk, any attempt to invest in a stock because it is cheap and the market has mispriced the stock is futile, according to EMH.

The ultimate expression of MPT is an index tracker fund, alternatively known as a passive fund. As the market is efficient, by holding a weighted average of all stocks, the investor is maximising return whilst minimising risk. As all the fund has to do is track the index, a computer can do this better than a human, the fees are driven down to a minimum as computers are paid less than expensive human asset managers. Table 2.5 shows that Vanguard, the pioneer index tracker, is the second largest investor in the world and 40% of US equity are managed passively. Vanguard's business model was explicitly based on MPT.[8]

Some funds pursue alternative strategies, for example aiming for total returns, where the aim is to achieve a targeted absolute level of return, whatever the market does. A hedge fund can achieve this through short selling, if the stock goes down the hedge fund will get a positive return if it holds a short position. This strategy is inherently based on the proposition that EMH is not correct, it is possible for a clever hedge fund manager to beat the market. But these strategies are defined as being alternative to the mainstream, which invests in line with MPT.

Another strategy now in vogue is called smart beta. Certain characteristics of stock have been noticed to persistently outperform the market, so a smart beta fund will invest passively in a way that takes into account these market-beating characteristics. Smart beta is based on the premise that markets are not efficient, otherwise these persistent factors would not exist whilst paradoxically using the language (Beta) and methodology (risk-weighted return against an index) of CAPM and MPT.

The predominant manifestation of financial economics on regulation is mark-to-market accounting. All financial institutions have to produce accounts at some time or other, and at the date of the accounts they have to state the value of the assets and liabilities. The value that is used is the market value in line with the EMH; the market value reflects all available information and thus represents the actual value of the underlying asset. Accounts are produced every 3 months by asset managers and investment consultants, appointed by asset owners, monitor these quarterly performance figures. This puts a huge pressure on asset managers and by inference underlying company executives to meet quarterly performance targets.

The reader might think that mark-to-market is the obvious thing to do and you don't need EMH to justify using the market value. However, market value is potentially problematic. If we take an extreme case; in the 2010 flash crash some stocks of major companies stock fell to 1 cent per share for a few minutes, before recovering to their usual price.[9] The price for these few seconds clearly did not reflect the underlying value of these shares. Under more usual circumstances, some assets, for example a piece of infrastructure, do not necessarily have a market price if they are not traded, and some assets' market prices might be distorted on the date of the valuation. For example, during the financial crisis no one wanted to buy mortgage-backed securities, so either there was no market price at all or it was anomalously low. Institutions have had to liquidate their assets at times of crisis because of having to report the market price, whereas a more sensible strategy might be to hold onto the assets until the crisis passes. If you are a pension fund who doesn't have to pay out pensions for many years, the daily, monthly or even annual market fluctuations should not be important, but mark-to-market accounting makes these fluctuations important, and it also encourages funds to hold assets which can be bought and sold quickly, which might not be the best strategy to pay your pensioners in 50 years' time.

All of the standard models of financial economics rely on unrealistic assumption, for example the assumptions of CAPM are that there are no transaction costs, information is costless, investors have homogenous expectations or interpret information the same way, investors are rational and risk averse, investors can lend and borrow unlimited amounts at the risk-free interest rate and investors aim to maximise utilities and are price takers.[10]

Clearly, many of these, or indeed all of these, are not true in the real world. It has been shown that investors are not rational, and this can lead to asset bubbles and then the market overcorrecting.[11] If EMH were true, it would suggest that there is no need for a financial services industry, or at least such a large one – if the market knows best I could get a monkey to invest for me and she should do as well as an asset manager, as all pricing information is already in the market.

Even so, there is an element of truth in these theories. Even if the market were not efficient, it does not mean it is easy to beat, to which anyone who has tried to make money on the stock market will attest. MPT implies that an investor should diversify, spreading her risks as widely as possible, trying to invest in assets which are uncorrelated with each other. This passes a common-sense test, a poor performing asset should be balanced by other assets doing well, if they are truly uncorrelated. And if I am entirely ignorant of the future, it would not be a bad starting point to invest in a weighted average of the entire market, in doing so I am piggybacking on the knowledge of the other market participants.

Despite focussing mostly on technicalities of the markets, these financial economic theories also embody a set of values, but those values are not immediately apparent. The price is right, the price reflects the underlying value of a security, this price signals useful information about the asset, in fact all there is to know about the asset, it embodies all current knowledge of what will happen to that asset in the future. The process of investing is therefore scientific, its success and risk can be measured and that investing in such a way is efficient, and this efficiency is a good thing.

If the price of an asset reflects all available information, then the price embodies our best estimate of what might happen in the future, it is the best estimate of the value of a financial asset. By using market price as an indicator, capital is being allocated efficiently and the price is providing valuable information about the real world. Other, non-financial values, are not as important, the non-financialness means that in taking these into account, efficiency is undermined, the economy will not be running at full potential and overall welfare will be reduced. The non-financial consideration has to be very important indeed to justify lowering overall welfare.

These standard finance theories translate these ethical values into a framework which can, and is, used by participants in the financial market and regulators to make investment decisions.

9.1.2 Shareholder Value

The concept of shareholder value is that you can assess the value of a company by the value of its shares, and indirectly by assessing the discounted cash flows generated by its future revenue. The goal of a company, it is argued, is to maximise shareholder value, and therefore the company's decisions should be made on this basis. "An activity only made sense if capital employed by it made a decent return, judged by its cash flow relative to a hurdle rate (the risk-adjusted return its providers of capital expected)."[12]

The promotion of shareholder value goes back to an article by the economist Milton Freidman, who argued that the sole purpose of a company was to make money and any executive who didn't were "unwitting puppets of the intellectual forces that have been undermining the basis of a free society these past decades".[13] The ethical and ideological background is clear, both from what Friedman wrote and from his background of advocating free market policies. The approach was popularised by the influential CEO of GE, Jack Welch, and formalised into a useful set of tools by a textbook *Valuation: Measuring and Managing the Value of Companies.*[14]

A company should make rational decisions based on optimising its return on investments for a given level of risk. Many of the malpractices of modern corporate behaviour have been blamed on the cult of maximising shareholder value, but financial engineering to boost paper profits in theory should not change shareholder value. Reducing investment and returning money back to investors through share buy-backs should reduce shareholder value if the investment had a positive cash flow. Similarly, reducing pay and using market power to exploit customers or suppliers may undermine shareholder value if this leads to poor industrial relations or relations with other shareholders.

However, if we combine maximising shareholder value with EMH, we get an alignment of interests between company management and asset managers. If a company returns money to shareholders and this boosts the share price, as it would because the asset managers are most interested in quarterly performance, according to EMH the value of the company has increased, therefore this action has indeed increased shareholder value. Company executives should be paid in relation to their share price as the efficient market's valuation of the company is its actual value. Governments act in line with the enactment of shareholder value, and this directly affects company behaviour. For example "in 1993, Congress amended the tax code to tie executive pay to 'performance' metrics. In 1991, average CEO pays at large public firms was 140 times that of average employees. By 2003, it was approximately 500 times. Whereas equity-based compensation at such firms was 0% in 1984, it climbed to 66% by 2001. The percentage of CEO pay from stock option grants rose from 35% in 1994, to 85% by 2001."[15] And the perverse incentives extend well beyond just boosting the share price: research shows that corporate executives reject profitable projects if it would make them miss the next quarter's earnings targets.[16]

Legally, corporations are not owned by the shareholder, it is up to the directors of a company which objectives to pursue. Shareholders are a diverse group; some shareholders hold a company's shares for microseconds and some for many years. HFTS are interested in making a very fast arbitrage profit, a pension fund is interested in the company generating a revenue to pay pensioners in many years' time. Maximising shareholder value for different groups of shareholders with different objectives may not be possible in reality.[17]

It has been empirically shown that the widespread objective of maximising shareholder value has caused companies to engage in increasingly short-term behaviour, in ways that I have documented in this book, at the expense of long-term performance. The mantra of shareholder value has actually caused a reduction in shareholder value for long-term investors.[18]

9.1.3 Sugar and Spice

I have set out how finance theory translates the values of finance into practice, in the words of sociologist Donald Mackenzie economic theory is "an engine, not a camera",[19] meaning economic theory creates reality rather than observes it.

This finance theory is not applicable; it applies to free markets where the actors are profit-maximising individuals. It does not apply to Potemkin markets which are set up by governments, regulated by governments, the dominant players are governments and the price is largely influenced by governments.

Furthermore, finance theory does not reflect how a market actually works.

I will briefly describe an agent-based model called Sugarscape. Sugarscape is an experiment which suggests that the market value of an asset reflects information which is of little use in determining the asset's value. Most of the information embodied in the price reflects the structure of the market and the interaction of market participants. As financial markets are Potemkin markets so the market value reflects how governments have set up the market and interfere in it.

Sugarscape is an agent-based model, a computer simulation which models a much-simplified version of the real world and populates this world with virtual agents who follow rules on how to behave. The model is run over multiple time periods to see what happens when these agents interact. In Sugarscape, the agents need to consume a certain amount of two commodities, sugar and spice, to survive. There are two mountains of each commodity on the island where the agents live (i.e. there are four mountains). Agents are placed randomly on this island, some on top of the sugar or spice deposits and some not, so some agents have endowments of the resources and some do not. The agents can see a certain distance, in each time period they can move a certain distance and they can trade with other agents nearby.

When the model is run, the way this mock-up world develops is recorded; how much spice and sugar are traded, at what price and how sugar and spice end up being distributed between agents. You can do this for yourself online.[20] The output is surprisingly realistic; trade routes develop between spice and sugar mountains. The wealth distribution of agents looks very much like the real world; the majority of agents end up being poor, and some agents end up very rich through trading. This is not because the poor agents are lazy and the rich agents are clever and hardworking; they are all computer simulations and this is the inevitable outcome of trade and initial proximity to resources.

The relative price of sugar and spice in each time period is shown in Figure 9.2. The equilibrium line shows what the price should be, given the relative availability of sugar and spice, whereas the actual price jumps around all over the place, though it does, roughly, follow the line of the equilibrium price; Figure 9.2 resembles a real market. Figure 9.2 looks like a random pattern, but it is generated by deterministic rules; the behaviour of each agent is specified, there is no randomness in the model.

The Sugarscape model shows that trade causes the price to follow what appears to be a random distribution. The price does give information of the value of the asset, the relative value of sugar and spice, but variations in the price are driven by the structure of the market and the behaviour of the actors in the market. This has been confirmed by many other agent-based models attempting to model more realistic markets.[21] The financial markets are many times more complex than Sugarscape, so we can expect this effect to be amplified not lessened.

It is hard to overstate how central the concept that the price is equivalent to value is for financial regulation and compensation. For example, asset managers are paid in proportion to the market value of their funds. But if the market value does not reflect the underlying value is this appropriate? Also, financial institutions' assets and liabilities are valued using the current market

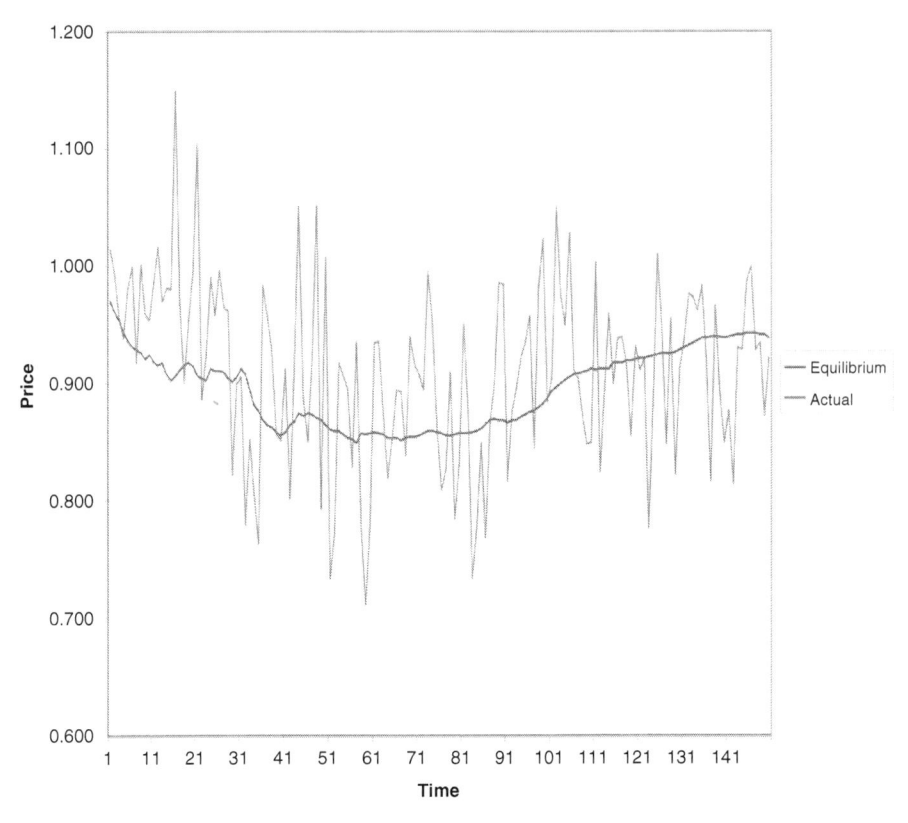

Fig. 9.2 The price of sugar and spice in Sugarscape

Source: Palin et al. (2009)
Taken from Palin, J Slater, A Smith, A and Silver, N (2009) *Complexity Economics: Application and Relevance to Actuarial Work* FIRM Conference. The chart was created from a simulation of Sugarscape

price. If this price largely reflects the structure of the market this is not really a useful measure of solvency. It is true that using some alternative metric to market values does present problems. But if we were presented with Figure 9.2 without any preconceptions and asked to design regulatory regime, one based on market values would not be the obvious choice

What does Figure 9.2 tell us beyond developing a regulatory framework? The motivation behind outsourcing society's investment decisions to the finance sector is so that capital will be managed efficiently. The information inherent in the price provides information and motivates the investment manager to allocate these assets efficiently. However, the information in the price is information about the structure of the market and the behaviour of the actors in that market. The useful information is hidden by these drivers of price fluctuations. Much of the information is about how the governments have structured the market, what the regulation is, what central banks are going to do regarding interest rates and how governments might spend their money. It has very little to do with whether capital is being managed efficiently.

Governments and central banks pay a lot of attention to the market value of equity markets, the market value of bonds and interest rates, the value of their currencies, and the price of commodities. Governments or central banks often react to movements in these markets, for example by reducing interest rates if the stock market falls. But if this fall is caused by the internal dynamics of financial markets, should policy not be driven by anticipating that financial markets inevitably rise and fall, and insulating the economy from any impacts that it will do so?

9.1.4 The Best Possible World

The ethical basis of free financial markets is that the size of the economy is optimised, because capital is allocated efficiently, and this capital allocation produces the maximum amount of economic activity.

The credo of politicians, business leaders and economists is that we need to generate economic growth. Arrow-Debreu show that free markets allocate capital efficiently, precious capital is allocated to its most efficient users, this allocation will then optimise economic activity and generate the optimum level of economic growth.

If we were to accept that the current financial system optimises capital allocation to achieve growth, contrary to all the evidence presented in this book; is economic growth itself a desirable objective, is making everyone in aggregate materially better off what we, as a society, should be aiming for? Or in other words, is the ethical basis on which financial markets constructed worthwhile?

Economic growth refers to the year on year increase in GDP. This is the total of the number of monetary transactions in the economy of goods and services. There are lots of sources of wealth that are not captured by GDP, but generally it is a good measure of how rich a country is; I am always struck by how, on arriving in a country, I can guess what a country's GDP per capita is from certain tell-tell signs; for example a country above a certain level of GDP will have well-maintained roads with markings and signs; whereas poorer countries don't have these.

A mainstream economic assumption is that economic growth is a good thing, because it makes all people richer, and if people are richer, they are better off. Sweden is richer than Nigeria, so it can afford not only road signs and markings but also decent schools and hospitals. If Nigeria grows rapidly, it will eventually reach something like Sweden's income levels, and most citizens will be able to afford good diets and smartphones, as well as having access to better medical care and education, either privately or because the government can raise enough tax from its citizens to be able to build and staff decent schools and hospitals.

The counter argument is that once countries achieve a certain income level, which studies have shown is around $15,000 per capita, often described as "low developed country level" economic growth no longer makes the population any happier.[22] Nigeria should aim for economic growth, but once it's GDP has hit around $15,000[23] policymakers could make their citizens better off by concentrating on well-being rather than only on economic growth.

Proponents of growth and proponents of well-being argue at cross-purposes. When policymakers talk about the need for growth they mean two things. Firstly, long-term growth is needed so that people become materially better off. Secondly, the economy needs to grow in the short term, because if it doesn't then we go into a recession, the definition of which is that the economy is not growing. And as we all know a recession is a bad thing.

The proponents of "growth doesn't make us happier" are only talking about long-term growth. However, when politicians worry about growth it is the short-term variety that they are most worried about. This is again because of incentives and measurement. It is not obvious how to get an economy growing in the long term, and even if it were, it is not possible to measure if we are on a long-term growth path. For example, it might be reasonable to assume that a massive investment in education might lead to long-term growth. But this will not manifest itself until current school pupils are in employment, so the boost in economic growth might not occur for another 10 years. And at this time, it would be very difficult to discern whether the increase in education spending caused the increase in growth and also none of the politicians who made the decision would still be in office. To pay for the increase in spending, the government may have had to increase taxes, reducing the short-term growth and the popularity of the politicians.[24]

Why are politicians terrified of a recession? The UK's GDP is $41,787.47[25] per capita. If it grows by 3%, then the GDP per capita would be $43,041.09, if it shrunk by 3%, it would be $40,570.36. Next year I would prefer my income to be $43,041.09 than $40,570.36. If it were the latter, I would have to cut down my spending a bit, but it would not be disastrous. However, if the economy as a whole grew by 3% this would be an excellent result, whereas if it declined by 3% this would be catastrophic – why is this?

The reason is that we have a highly leveraged economy, a situation brought about by the finance sector, as described in Chapter 7. If the economy grows, the money supply grows and hence debt increases. So, for example the UK total debt (public and private) is about five times GDP[26]; debt levels and interest payments become a significant burden on an economy if it shrinks in the short term, especially because the debt is not evenly distributed. People and companies' expectations change in a recession, more so because of their own debt burdens, and they cut down on spending and investment. This leverages the effect of the recession, making the outcome worse. Especially if, as often happens, this coincides with interest rates rising, making the cost of debt higher.

When an economy goes into recession, people do suffer genuine hardships, with consequences for their happiness and voting decisions. Heavily indebted companies may go bankrupt, meaning their former workforce will be unemployed and their debts unpaid. This cause a knock-on effect through the economy, where banks, faced with bad debts, become more conservative in their lending, companies faced with a lack of demand reduced investment and lay-off staff, and people who are indebted and lose their jobs cannot repay their debts, people and companies have to make forced sales of assets, reducing asset prices, with further negative feedback loops making the situation worse.

In the long run people and organisations get better at doing things and there is technological progress which results in economic growth. However, the trend is not in a straight line, the rate of growth will inevitably fluctuate around this trend.

Figure 9.3 indicates that there is not too much that individual governments can do to avoid recessions, as they happen at the same time across countries. It has been argued that the long period without a recession before the financial crisis of 2008, caused the resultant recession to be worse.[27]

Figure 9.3 shows the GDP growth rate of USA, UK, Japan and France over the last 45 years. In all four countries, growth is usually between 2% and 4%, but there have been four periods of recession. The periods of growth and recession correspond between the countries, indicate the cause is likely to be external or common to those economies.

Recessions are necessary for the effective functioning of capitalism because they clear out the dead wood: capitalism is about creative destruction, in good times anyone can make money, but in bad times the inefficient companies are wiped out.

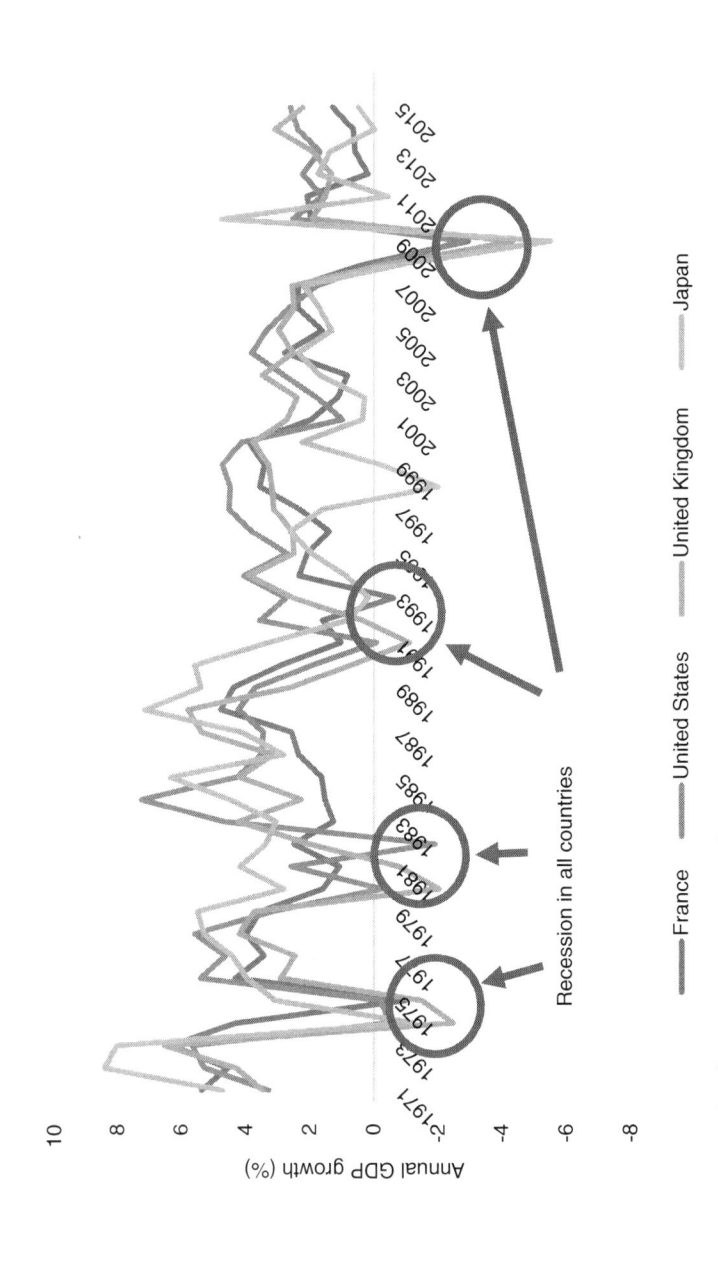

Fig. 9.3 GDP growth of USA, UK, Japan and France

Source: World Bank

I have used these four economies as they have been rich, developed countries for most of the period so have comparable economic records. Source: World Bank http://data.worldbank.org/indicator/NY.GDP.MKTP.KD.ZG accessed 23 January 2017

Recessions are inevitable, unavoidable and maybe necessary for the economy as a whole. The impact of recessions on individuals and society can be harmful, but this harmful impact is also predictable (increased unemployment, lower asset prices and increased bad debts). So surely a wise economic policy is to prepare for inevitable recessions and try to minimise their harmful impacts?

I will briefly review what kind of growth is actually delivered by shareholder capitalism embodied in the Potemkin markets, as has been previously discussed in Chapter 8:

- Debt: debt is endogenous to the finance sector, the finance sector creates debt in the money-creation process, and it uses leverage to maximise its own profits. Economic growth is accompanied by growth in debt cause by the finance sector. As described above, high levels of debt and leverage in the economy makes the damage caused by recessions worse than an economy with low debt. High debt levels are bad in themselves; it means that governments are forced to pursue austerity programmes, cutting back on welfare spending. And financial hardship easily translates into real hardship – Individuals with high debt have higher stress levels, worse health outcomes and often suffer from mental illness and poor well-being outcomes.[28]
- All growth goes to top 20%: In Chapter 8, Figure 8.8 showed that in the USA since 1970, real wages have only increased for the top 20% of the population. Economic growth is often compared to a pie; with economic growth, the pie gets bigger so everyone can eat more. Figure 8.8 demonstrates that though the pie is indeed much bigger, around 10 times bigger[29] than in 1970, 80% of the people are eating the same amount, with all the rest being eaten by the top 20% and most by the top 1%. The actual growth generated might make consumption in aggregate increase, the vast majority of the population only get a few leftover crumbs.
- Environmental destruction: Chapter 8 showed that the increase in size of the global economy is causing the destruction of much of the planet's ecosystem, so this growth, which has accrued to only a few people, causes a massive negative impact. The impact on humans is already apparent, but as much of the destruction is being done to the planet's operating systems on which humans rely to survive; the majority of the damage will only be manifest at some future date.

In summary, the ethical objective of free capital markets is to maximise economic output, and make everyone better off. However, people are not necessarily better off through maximising economic output, the resultant increase in economic activity causes environmental destruction, the benefit of the increase accrues to a small proportion of the population and the financial system generates large quantities of damaging debt in achieving this growth.

I want to stress that economic growth is not bad per se, except that the growth that has been delivered is bad. Rather than worrying about economic growth, governments could try to reduce debt levels in the economy, minimize environmental destruction and address inequality, there is no definitive argument either way whether these policies would positively or negatively impact long-term growth. In contrast, during recessions, governments often pursue policies which make these factors worse and negatively impact long-term economic growth, typically trying to boost spending by increasing debt levels.[30]

9.1.5 The Ethics of Capital Markets

Shareholder value combined with standard finance theories provide the practical tools for regulation and practice in capital markets. Employing finance theory, an investor can put together a portfolio of assets which optimise returns for a given level of risk, ensuring that capital is invested with the most efficient users of that capital. At the individual company level, companies themselves make investment decisions to maximise shareholder value. Therefore, investors are optimising returns for savers, and they are investing in a way which will maximise returns; capital is being allocated efficiently by investors into companies and by the companies themselves. The outcome is a win-win scenario, savers are benefitting from the maximised return and companies, and hence the economy, are achieving optimal investment levels and hence growth potential. The outcome for society is that everyone is better off, the economy produces its optimum outcome.

However as none of this is true; there is no intellectual basis for savings and investments to be made in this way. The Buttonwood story is part of a myth that capital markets are free and spontaneous – they are not; they have been created, arbitrarily to match this economic theory and its implied values. They could equally well be created in the image of different economic theories, and different sets of values.

Ethical questions framed within the mainstream economics are generally along the lines of: free capital markets make the economy as a whole better off, does this outweigh the possible negative consequences, such as inequality and passing on negative externalities to society?

Nicholas Stern, author of the Stern Review on climate change famously said that Climate Change was "the greatest market failure the world has seen."[31] The market is failing because climate change is not valued by the market. This is a fundamentally flawed identification of the problem; capital markets prioritise financial value above all other human values. Values such as caring about the environment or future generations are ignored because they are hard to convert into a product that can be traded.

If you have a resource such as an oil reserve, or a forest, or a social relationship; by turning it into something that you can trade, like petrol, or wood or a sales channel adds financial value, so capital markets will seek to exploit these resources, justified by the massive added value of doing so.

However, the contention of this book is that capital markets are not free, they are Potemkin markets and they do not optimise capital allocation, as control of the capital is captured by the intermediaries for their own benefit. Capital markets, as constructed by governments, generate a great deal of wealth for the few, and leave the rest of the economy mired in debt and lead to environmental destruction. The compression of values into value does not bear up to any scrutiny, so is not a worthy objective on which to organise society and must be abandoned. The problem of climate change is not a market failure, it is an intellectual failure that instead of basing decisions on a sound ethical basis we have chosen to default to making decisions based on the flawed ethics underlying the organisation of the financial system.

If governments have set up the financial system in this way to do their bidding, and this has not worked, how should capital markets be set up? I attempt to answer these questions in Chapter 10. First, we need to discuss what values finance should embody.

9.2 What We Talk About When We Talk About Flourishing

There is a strong ethical argument behind the current architecture of free markets, namely that in achieving economic growth we are making everyone better off, and by having complete and free financial markets, capital is allocated efficiently and economies will achieve their growth potential.

Neither of these statements is true; capital is not being allocated efficiently and once people have achieved a level of income above poverty economic growth does not make people better off.

What is an alternative ethical vision and how might this be achieved? Over the years many people have tried to impose their ethical visions on society, usually with disastrous consequences and a lot of people dying. Compared with Hitler, Stalin, Mao, Mussolini and the like, the financial system that we have are benign indeed. It's just we could do better, and with the impeding environmental catastrophe that we are creating, we need to do better.

The Arrow-Debreu argument applied to finance is that we should strive to make capital markets competitive and complete, because then capital will be allocated efficiently. My proposal is that financial markets should allocate capital to enable people to flourish.[32]

It is problematic to outline what it means to flourish, because my idea of what flourishing entails is likely to be different to everyone else's. However, what I have tried to do is outline some concepts which are concrete enough to be goals that we can strive for, but general enough that it would be difficult to construct an argument against, whilst allowing that people can pursue their own version of a good life with these factors in place:

1. *Health:* People are better off if they are healthy then if they are not, and, even if they are entirely selfish, are better off if other people are healthy as well. Health refers to both physical and mental, with poor mental health being one of the main reasons of lack of happiness.[33]
2. *Dignity:* Adam Smith put it well "A linen shirt, for example, is, strictly speaking, not a necessary of life.…But in the present times…a creditable day-labourer would be ashamed to appear in public without a linen shirt…Under necessaries, therefore, I comprehend, not only those things which nature, but those things which the established rules of decency have rendered necessary to the lowest rank of people".[34] Smith's insight is that people need and are entitled to, not only the basic necessities of life, like food and shelter, but also other stuff, which are social requirements for dignity. In Smith's day, these were a linen shirt and leather shoes. Nowadays, or in different countries these adornments may differ and change through time. Also, what represents dignity might be immaterial, for example paid work might be one, but the general point is that all people should be entitled to at least the basic requirements of dignity.
3. *Healthy environment:* There are many ethical formulations that looking after nature is a good thing. A deep green environmentalist might argue that nature and other animals have their own rights to flourish, the

Judaeo-Christian tradition that man was given stewardship of the planet by god and therefore entrusted to look after it, a utilitarian that nature provides humans with useful goods and services. People might disagree on the extent to which humans should exploit or conserve nature, but all would agree that all other things being equal, a healthy natural world is better than an unhealthy one.

4. *Autonomy:* This is about people having the ability to make their own decisions and pursue their own interests without interference. I think there will be universal agreement that this is a good thing in itself, but there will be violent disagreement about what this entails. A libertarian might advocate that everyone can do almost whatever they want, without interference from a government (which runs into problems in extremis, as some people might then take power and enslave other people, which I am sure is not what libertarians want). At the other extreme you have forms of socialism, which sees an active role for the state. People might have theoretical political freedom, but are unable to exercise it due to a lack of economic freedom. For example, if some people cannot afford a decent education, they cannot have effective autonomy as adults. Most people will disagree on what freedom means, but I think it is fair to assume that most people agree that freedom to go about your lives and make choices, as long as these choices do not harm others, is a worthy objective.

5. *Security:* There are many risks that people can manage for themselves, such as driving carefully, not smoking, eating a healthy diet, etc. There are, however, many external risks that are more difficult, for example being invaded by a foreign army or terrorist attacks. There are also many risks that involve conflict of interest between parties, such as property disputes or environmental pollution. Again, most people would agree that living in security is better than not living in security, but there will be disagreement over what this entails and the pay-offs with other objectives. So, for example ensuring security from terrorists might entail some loss of autonomy.

6. *Fairness:* Most people would prefer to live in a world, where either certain sectors of society are not privileged with arbitrary power over resources or denied access to these resources. Similarly or aligned, no groups or individual within society should be above the law or conversely targeted by law enforcement, and everyone should have as equal or fair access to opportunities as possible. Again, there will probably be a great deal of disagreement as to how this should be achieved.

7. *Pursuit of good life:* There are a number of other factors that have been identified by philosophers from Aristotle onwards, such as ability to pursue personal fulfilment, authenticity, pursuit of practical wisdom, interpersonal connectedness, civic engagement and transcendence.[35] I consider these as subsidiary to autonomy, whereby people can pursue their own version of the good life. But a flourishing society might encompass all of these factors.

There is of course disagreement over where resources should be allocated within these different groupings and how best to achieve outcomes. So, for example some people believe that protecting the environment is very important and some people might describe themselves as anti-environmentalist. Even someone who described themselves as anti-environmentalist would probably not see environmental destruction as a good thing, per se, they would just see it of not such importance compared to other factors, or see themselves as against the environmental movement.

However, just because these ethical choices are difficult to make, does not mean that we should not make them. At the moment, as we have seen, resources are allocated based on a flawed ethical argument; the ethical argument over capital allocation needs to be made explicit, so society can decide on what ethical path it should follow and then develop a financial system which embodies this path. This too will be problematic, the least bad way of deciding this will be through the democratic process, which, in the famous words of Winston Churchill "is the worst form of government, except for all those other forms that have been tried from time to time."[36]

9.3 The Economy We Have Compared to the Economy We Want

The economy could grow and develop in different ways depending on where capital is allocated. The current system we have allocates capital in a specific way, which is a by-product of the incentives on those who allocate capital, the financial intermediaries who allocate capital to maximise their own revenues. There is no guarantee that this will be in the best interests of society or the economy, in fact it is likely that it will not be.

The financial markets are not responsible for all of the factors that influence human flourishing. Some of these are in the control of the political

9.3 The Economy We Have Compared to the Economy We Want

and legal system, or civil society. For example, the financial system does not really have much influence on whether there is freedom of speech or equality before the law in society.[37]

However, there are elements of our system which are contrary to human flourishing. If we consider health, the finance system is biased against investing in infrastructure in general which would include health infrastructure. Companies are incentivised to reduce R&D spend, including in medical research. Big pharma companies maximise shareholder value by intense lobbying, in the USA alone spending $3 billion over the last 18 years.[38] The reason they do this is to keep very strong patent laws, so they can charge highly for medicines over a long-time period, and so that the USA's public health institutions are not allowed to negotiate drug prices, and for laxer prescription rules leading to opioid epidemics. Companies reducing staff costs means more unemployed (who have worse health outcomes) and increasing debt levels in the economy leads to worse physical and mental health.

Finance impacts people's dignity by increasing levels of household debt, incentivising companies to reduce staff costs, creating inequality, rationing credit so that it is harder and more expensive for poorer people to get credit. We dealt with the massive environmental impacts in the last chapter. I believe that the financial crisis played a large part in the rise of populism that we are currently experiencing in politics, as it highlighted the unfairness in our society. Extremely highly paid financial intermediaries, entrusted with society's assets, messed up on an enormous scale, yet were bailed out by governments and got to keep their jobs and high salaries. Hardly anyone was punished. Everyone else got austerity. This was unfairness writ large, it was obvious for all to see.

Can the values of human flourishing really be encapsulated within finance? I believe they can. There are a number of practices which already seek to integrate these concept in their operation, from the most unlikely sources:

- Industry: The **circular economy** seeks to provide goods and services with minimal us of resources and waste.
- Accounting: **Triple bottom line** and **six capitals** are alternative accounting conventions which seek to account for environmental and social impact.
- Investment: impact investment is a form of investment which seeks to make positive environmental and social returns in addition to financial returns.
- Green investment: Investment into sustainable infrastructure seeks to transform the economy from its current high resource use to a sustainable,

low carbon economy whilst delivering the goods and services that we need to flourish.

In the next chapter I will seek to address solutions to the current shortcoming of the finance system, and outline how finance could make a positive contribution to human flourishing.

Notes

1. Foot, P (1978) *The Problem of Abortion and the Doctrine of the Double Effect* Virtues and Vices (Oxford: Basil Blackwell, 1978) (originally appeared in the Oxford Review, Number 5, 1967).
2. As described in Singer (2005) *Ethics and Intuitions* The Journal of Ethics.
3. Smith, A (1776) *An Enquiry into the nature and Causes of the Wealth of Nations* William Strahan, Thomas Cadell.
4. Quoted in Dealbook (2009) *Blankfein Says He's Just doing "God's Work"* New York Times November 9 http://dealbook.nytimes.com/2009/11/09/goldman-chief-says-he-is-just-doing-gods-work/?_r=1.
5. Arrow, K Debreu, G (1954) *Existence of an equilibrium for a competitive economy Econometrica*. **22** (3): 265–290. https://web.stanford.edu/class/msande311/arrow-debreu.pdf
6. Turner, A (2013) *Economics after the crisis* MIT Press.
7. Fabozzi, F Modigliani, F Jones, J and Ferri, M (2010). *Foundations of Financial Markets and Institutions*, 4th ed. Prentice Hall.
8. Mackenzie, D (2006) *An Engine, Not a Camera* MIT Press.
9. Wall Street Journal 9 May 2010 *Dow Takes a Harrowing 1,010.14-Point Trip.*
10. Fabozzi, F Modigliani, F Jones, J and Ferri, M (2010). *Foundations of Financial Markets and Institutions*, 4th ed. Prentice Hall.
11. See for example Shiller, R (2005) *Irrational Exuberance* Princeton University Press.
12. The Economist 2 April 2016 *Analyse This* http://www.economist.com/news/business/21695940-enduring-power-biggest-idea-business-analyse.
13. Quoted in Forbes 26 June 2013 *The Origin Of "The World's Dumbest Idea": Milton Friedman.*
14. Copeland, T Wessels, D Koller, T and Goedhart, M (1990) *Valuations* John Wiley & Sons.
15. Stout, L (2012) *The Shareholder Value Myth* Berrett-Koehler Publishers.
16. The Economist 1 May 2015 *What's wrong with finance.*
17. Stout, L (2012) *The Shareholder Value Myth* Berrett-Koehler Publishers.
18. Stout, L (2012) *The Shareholder Value Myth* Berrett-Koehler Publishers.
19. Mackenzie, D (2006) *An Engine, Not a Camera* MIT Press.
20. The Sugarscape: http://sugarscape.sourceforge.net/

21. ABM have failed to replicate an actual markets (see, e.g., E. Samanidou, E. Zschischang, D. Stauffer, T. Lux (2007) *Agent-based Models of Financial Markets* arXiv:physics/0701140) but this is not the point, they demonstrate the dynamics of a market. An actual market is more complex than any model, and because it is a complex system, the precise interaction of the agents determines the precise outcome of the market.
22. Easterlin, R (2005) *Diminishing marginal utility of income?: Caveat emptor* Social Indicators Research, 70: 243–255.
23. It's currently around $3,000, so it has a way to go.
24. This argument really applies to rich countries. There is a well-trodden model whereby poorer countries can and have industrialised and thereby rapidly grow; the developmental state model. Here, countries direct finance and provide government support for key industries, at the same time putting up tariff barriers to protect these industries; and then gradually move the economy up the value chain. So initially the industries chosen are ones that the country has an advantage because of cheap labour. As time goes by the country supports more advanced technologies which can make use of an increasingly educated work force. See for example Cohen, S and DeLong, B (2016) *Concrete Economics* Harvard Business Review Press.
25. In 2013.
26. Economics help website: http://www.economicshelp.org/blog/4060/economics/total-uk-debt/ accessed 8 December 2016.
27. Bean, C (2009) *The Great Moderation, the Great Panic and the Great. Contraction* Speech given at the Schumpeter Lecture, Annual Congress of the European Economic Association, Barcelona 25 August 2009.
28. Sweet, E Nandi, A Adam, E and McDade, T (2013) *The High Price of Debt: Household financial debt and its impact on mental and physical health* Soc Sci Med. 2013 Aug; 91: 94–100.
29. Source: Google, World Bank.
30. See, for example Chapter 9 of King, M (2016) *The End of Alchemy* W W Norton and Company.
31. Quoted in the Guardian 29 November 2007 *Stern: Climate change a "market failure".*
32. I am indebted to my friend Mishko Hansen for the concept of flourishing, and his unpublished thesis Hansen, M (2015) *Subjects of value: Consumption and the Ethics of Business* Cambridge University.
33. Layard, R (2011) *Happiness: Lessons from a New Science* Penguin.
34. Smith, A (1776) *An Enquiry into the nature and Causes of the Wealth of Nations* William Strahan, Thomas Cadell.
35. I owe this formulation to Bess, M (2016) *Make way for the Superhumans* Icon Books Ltd.
36. Quoted by The International Churchill Society http://www.winstonchurchill.org/resources/quotations/the-worst-form-of-government.

37. All though Taibbi, M (2014) *The Divide: American injustice in the age of the wealth gap* Spiegel & Grau argues that finance and inequality does pervert the course of justice.
38. OpenSecrets.Org Lobbying: https://www.opensecrets.org/lobby/top.php?showYear=a&indexType=i accessed 12 December 2016.

10

A Financial Renaissance?
Some Modest Proposals to Create a Flourishing Financial System

I have spent the last few years trying to move the financial system to get capital invested at scale into the low carbon economy so that we can avoid dangerous climate change. I thought this was a good use of my time because the financial system is the control centre for allocating capital in the economy, and if you want to try and transform the economy to avoid environmental catastrophe, the financial system will have to allocate capital in a different way. Whilst working on this problem, I came to the realisation that this was not what the financial system is for, the finance system does not do investment, its purpose is to feed the helminths.

I hope the reader will by now be convinced that the finance sector does not provide the services to the economy that it is there to do, instead most of its activity is to extract rent from the rest of the economy. Getting finance to help humans flourish would first involve getting finance to do its job properly.

And yet there are a lot of good parts of the finance system. Shareholder finance is much better than systems of allocating capital that has prevailed for most of human history, a big man and his advisors deciding on who gets what. It is also much better than the crony capitalism infesting many parts of the world today.

The attractive features of our financial system are transparency, the rule of law and professionalism. These are great achievements and not to be undervalued; any change, however dramatic, should not throw these babies out with the bathwater.

In this chapter I propose a number of potential solutions. But why should anyone listen to me, and what chance is there of reform against such a powerful vested interest in keeping things the same?

Change is inevitable. The current finance system is broken in many ways. If we consider banks, banks were bailed out in the financial crisis, but they now face a slew of new regulations, most of which are aimed at the wrong problems, but cumulative weight of this regulation makes many banking activities non-viable, in turn making it harder for banks to make a profit.

The constant stream of fines imposed for criminal behaviour further eats into profits and makes banks risk averse. This and bank-bashing in the media affects morale and makes being a banker a less attractive career option. Low interest rates also make it harder for banks to make money.

Low interest rates also make it harder for asset managers and other financial intermediaries to make money – if returns are 10% and costs are 3%, an average investor is still seeing a 7% return, but if returns are 2% she is receiving a negative return and will start asking hard questions. Constantly reducing interest rates is the consequence of the current financial set-up.

These difficult conditions are coming at a time when there is new competition from genuinely disruptive business models. At one end of the scale is peer-to-peer lending, a saver can lend money directly to a borrower cutting out the banker. On the other end of the scale are index tracker funds which charge a lot less than traditional funds and have outperformed them too.

Finally, new technology, including social technology, makes many of the incumbents of the financial system redundant, they just don't know it yet.

An important question is who delivers the required change. Unfortunately, though I believe in human agency and that solutions should come from the ground up, in this situation a lot of the impetus has to come from government; governments created the mess so they have to clean it up.

By governments, here I mean the core governments of financial capitalism, namely the UK and the US government. I am also referring to central government, even though it may act via other agencies such as the central bank.

The first and most important thing governments have to do is to withdraw support for the failed financial sector and thereby stop it causing more damage. This is easier said than done, government support will have to be phased out over time to avoid large shocks. The savings channel should present the lesser problem; governments should stop mandating or auto-enrolling people into a pension and remove any tax-breaks on savings. Even this, though, will be met with howls of protest by the finance industry and their supporters in the media. However, as people realise they are contributing into a Sisyphus savings system which cannot deliver a decent income when they need it, the support for the current system might evaporate.

Banking is more problematic as we need to replace the current system with something that works, and all monetary systems that have been tried to date have been problematic. With the development of electronic money, a viable alternative does exist which avoids many of the past problems of monetary systems. For my libertarian friends, we could even have a system with no government involvement at all.

However, beyond removing support for finance, is there a more positive role for government? In this chapter I look at two problems. The first is how to solve the technical problems that the current finance system is failing to do. However, delivering people with a decent pension in our current economic paradigm will not necessarily save us from continued global environmental destruction, or deliver an economy that allows people to flourish.

In writing this chapter I am faced with a genuine dilemma. Governments plus the finance system has screwed up to such an extent, should governments try and use the finance system to solve these problems? If governments withdraw support for finance, do they need to replace it with something else?

I believe that that they should for two reasons. Governments can easily provide a savings system which works, which I shall outline in Section 10.1; this savings system is tried and tested in Sweden. People do look to government to provide a functioning money system, if you did away with fractional reserve banking you would probably end up with chaos and panic, so a credible alternative supported by the state is required.

Secondly, the current economic system has done such a great deal of damage to society and the environment that it needs to be put right, we need what amounts to a new industrial revolution, which will not just happen by itself. When the UK and USA faced the threat from Nazi Germany, they could not just leave it to the market to produce tanks and airplanes, they needed more involvement from government than this.

Figure 10.1 presents a schema of the measures proposed in this chapter. The first level is for the government to actively end its support for the current system; by removing bank's licence to print money, ending fractional reserve banking; to stop incentivising savings or pensions via the financial markets, to reduce the activity of the financial sector through a financial transaction tax (FTT) and to reduce the size of SWFs by reducing the demand for oil.

250 10 A Financial Renaissance?

Fig. 10.1 Towards a flourishing finance system

1. Remove support for failing system
- End fractional reserve banking
- Remove pension incentives
- Drain swamp of petrol $
- Financial transaction tax

Banking/money
Savings/investment

2. Develop systems which serve purpose
- Swedish critical health insurance
- Electronic money
- House building
- Pawnbroker for all seasons

3 Promote flourishing Utilise financial tools for sustainable economy
- Development banks
- Limited fractional reserve
- Buffer funds
- Incentives for impact investment

The second level is to replace the current failed systems with ones that actually work; this can be achieved through introducing electronic money, stimulating housebuilding and introducing an adapted version of the Swedish pensions system. The third level of support is to move the economy to a truly sustainable economy which promotes human flourishing, the use of local development banks and not-for profit banks to finance poor regions and sustainable businesses and to utilise investment mandates to incentivise sustainable investment with a positive societal impact.

Many of the tools of finance have been developed over many years and have been proved immensely powerful, they have just been pointed in the wrong direction. We have great social and environmental problems, and if solutions do not come from finance and the private sector, the alternative is direct government provision, which is immensely problematic.

If governments attempt to provide all the solutions directly, they run the risk of taking away human agency, and as identified by Friedrich Hayek, they run into information and coordination problems, with the end result being the risk of a totalitarian state.[1] The problems I have identified in this book are that there is too much government involvement in finance, or the wrong sort of involvement, or misguided involvement. If my proposals were carried through there would ultimately be less government involvement in the economy, it would be more capitalist if you like, just a capitalism that meets the needs of its citizens.

Most of the proposals I make in this chapter are based on solutions that are already in use in some part of the world or have been suggested and developed by leading experts in their respective fields. I do not give detailed implementation solutions; other people have developed functioning solutions, to which I refer in the text.

10.1 Getting Finance to do what it's Supposed to do

10.1.1 Scandi-Style Pensions

Just as Scandinavians do the best furniture, knitwear and TV detective series, they also have developed the only pensions system that actually works.

In thinking about the design of a pension system there are two elements, what is the best design for a system to provide people with a decent pension, as discussed in Chapter 4, and how should savings be managed to foster sustainable development of the economy, as discussed in Chapter 5. The two are obviously related, an unsustainable economy cannot pay a decent pension. The Swedes have cracked the first problem, which I describe in this section, the chapter will then discuss sustainable finance and will come back to answer the latter question.

In many countries, pensions have been outsourced to the private sector from the state sector for a good reason, the state system was not working. State systems are usually PAYGO, which simply means that workers pay a contribution which entitles them to a benefit; the contributions are used to pay the pensions of people who are currently retired. The problem with this system is that if you have an ageing population, there will be fewer tax payers and more pensioners, so either tax has to go up or pensions have to go down.

Worse, politicians have incentives to make short-term decisions at the expense of long-term costs. Governments generally are tempted to reduce the contributions into the system and promise increased pensions, making the system ever more unsustainable, for example as this book is being written the Polish government is in the process of doing this.[2] Workers can pay low contributions when there are lots of workers compared to the number of pensioners, which will easily cover the pensions of the small number of retirees. Governments can also promise high benefits as these will not be paid until the current workforce retires. Both measures are popular with workers – they are going to have a big pension and don't have to pay much for it, so they are happy with the government. If there is a big population bulge of people in their 40s, which there currently is in many countries, the funding problem that this causes will not manifest itself for 20 years. A government may be in power for 4–5 years, and a minister for even less time so funding problems will not manifest themselves until they are long gone, by which time there will be someone else to take the blame.

Anticipating these problems, or with the encouragement from the World Bank, many countries have abandoned PAYGO systems over the last 20 years and have moved to a private funded system along the lines described in Chapter 4.

The problem with most PAYGO systems is the fault of the design and governance, not with the concept. Sweden has successfully overcome these design problems and has implemented a sustainable system, demonstrating that PAYGO can work and providing a model which other countries can follow.

It works as follows: workers contribute into the system and they are awarded a notional pension pot. The value of this pot is determined by the contributions that they pay in plus an interest rate determined by the pensions agency. When members retire, their pot is converted into an income stream which the pensions agency is responsible for paying. The pension is subject to a minimum level for poorer people.

The fund is administered by an independent pensions agency who have a mandate to pay people a pension that they can live off. The money that comes in from contributions is partly used to pay pensioners and partly goes into one of five buffer funds which are invested in capital markets.

The agency periodically reviews whether the total of future contributions plus the buffer funds is large enough to pay pensions; it can adjust the pension age, the contribution level and the increase in level of pensions to make the fund balance.

Workers also pay a proportion into an extra funded pillar, which works like a normal DC pension pot.

The Swedish PAYGO model works because it is outside political control, the pensions agency's incentives are to keep the fund in balance. The ability of the agency to adjust benefits means that the scheme remains solvent when economic or demographic circumstances change, and the buffer funds mean that the scheme always has liquidity.

Compared to the funded system run by the private sector in the UK and other countries, the Swedish model has far less friction costs; the costs of the staff running the system are minimal compared to the fees deducted by investment managers, as described in Chapter 4. The system delivers a pension that workers can live off, unlike the private system, and it delivers this to all workers, not just the rich. The various risks that are inherent in the private system are mitigated, such as poor investment performance, bankruptcy of sponsoring employer and increasing life expectancy.

Unlike the private pension system, the Swedish System does what it says on the tin; it provides people with a pension and reduces the government's fiscal burden, at a fraction of the cost of the private system. The cost of the Swedish pension system is relatively modest, at 7.4% of GDP,[3] for which Swedes get a decent and sustainable pension.

It also does not give intermediaries such a great deal of power and money to allocate the country's capital, although the five buffer funds and the extra funded pillar do resemble conventional pension funds; they are public entities with a mandate to invest funds to maximise return at a low level of risk.[4] The funds represent a key design element of the system, as they provide liquidity and allow the system time to adjust should market or demographic developments adversely affect the system. For example, if life expectancy is found to have increased by more than anticipated, the future costs of the system will increase. The system does have brake mechanisms so that benefits can be reduced, but it would not be equitable between generations if they were suddenly applied. The buffer funds allow the brake mechanisms to be adjusted more slowly over many years by running down the funds and then increasing them again once the system has adjusted.

The buffer funds mean that the system does to some extent have to rely on the capital markets which the rest of this book has suggested have served us so poorly. Should we trust the financial sector to manage these funds, given its high costs and the damage it inflicts on society? The idea of spreading the risk of the system by having these buffer funds is sound. The main flaw in the system is the management of these funds, which are managed in line with flawed ideas of MPT and shareholder value. I will discuss later in this chapter how the funds could be managed to promote sustainable outcomes.

The setting up of a government agency to run the pension system would appear to involve more government interference in the market. However, the current pensions and savings system involve a huge amount of government interference through regulation and the actions of the central bank. Once the agency is set up it only performs a very simple administrative function; all it does is collect contributions and pay out pensions, whilst ensuring that the pension system is solvent; there is low risk that it would turn into a monster like the GSEs in the USA. Once the agency has been set up, central government can mostly withdraw and let the thing run itself.

10.1.2 Who Needs a Pension, Anyway

A story I have heard as to why many countries have a retirement age of 65 is too good not to relate, even though it is only partially true. Otto von Bismarck, the Prussian chancellor in the nineteenth century, found out from his statisticians that people die by 65, so he promised his people a fantastic pension from age 65. This set the retirement age, which other countries have largely followed.

The original idea of a pension was that in a world where people did hard physical labour in factories, when they could no longer work, they received a pension and most of them died soon after it started.

Now the world is different. Life expectancy in most developed countries is over 80 and increasing. Some people do manual physical labour, but most people work in offices. As well as living longer, older people are getting healthier. In a knowledge economy, older people have a lot of knowledge that they could impart to younger people or could use to continue working

10.1 Getting Finance to do what it's Supposed to do

and earning. Pensioning them off at an arbitrary age like 65 loses this valuable resource. When people retire, their health and happiness has been shown to reduce.[5]

The Swedish pensions model might work well in delivering a pension at low cost but is a pension what people and society want or need? Does it help people flourish? A pension is not equitable; it favours people who live longer and people who live longer are generally wealthier. If someone is poor and does a physical, and possibly dangerous or unhealthy job, they may not be able to work much beyond retirement age, whereas a wealthier person doing a high-status job would have a much longer life expectancy and could probably work long beyond retirement age.

A better alternative, would be for people to work in jobs that they found fulfilling and did not want to retire. They might want more flexible working conditions, such as having more time off, and the ability to work from home. Sufferers of chronic degenerative illnesses such as Alzheimer's, who can no longer work and need care, do not require a pension, they require critical health insurance, something that pays their medical bills and provides an income when they can no longer work. This arrangement would be an improvement of health, well-being and the productive capacity of the economy to the current situation.

Instead of providing a pension, the system should provide compulsory critical health insurance and a voluntary savings arrangement. There are a number of potential problems with this system, but if designed correctly these problems could be minimised. Firstly, with health insurance there is always the problem of adverse selection; an unhealthy person knows they are unhealthy so is more willing to buy insurance. However, if insurance is mandatory, everyone would have to pay throughout their career so adverse selection problems are removed. As poorer people are more likely to get ill earlier and unable to do their jobs, this compensates for them losing out as they do not live as long (on average) as richer people.

There is also a problem in assessing whether or not people are critically ill; there is even an incentive for corruption – if a doctor certifies someone to be ill, then this is very valuable to the patient. Here the governance of the agency running the system is critical, with a dual mandate of serving their beneficiaries and being financially sustainable. The criteria and implementation for paying out is then crucial but can be adjusted by the agency, who can with time develop strategies for avoiding false certification.

It will be in the agency's interest to promote healthier life styles and provide palliative care if they can do so cheaper than the alternatives. I will discuss how this might be achieved when discussing the buffer funds.

10.1.3 Draining the Sovereign Wealth Swamp

Chapter 2 described how some of the largest asset owners in the world are SWFs. The way to reform these institutions is to eliminate them; the savings/investment system is serving no purpose, so they are doing no good by recycling their reserves into financial capital.

Of the 10 largest SWFs of Table 2.4, half of them derive their income from oil.[6] Why should it be that some governments receive a huge revenue from the rest of the world, often for a very small population, just because they happen to be home to fossil-fuel reserves? Especially as the utilization of those reserves contribute to climate change. This is to pass no moral judgement on the countries that happen to be oil rich; those oil reserves need to stay in the ground if we are to avoid dangerous climate change, and the world would be fairer if wealth was not being transferred to a very few just for having these reserves.

If the demand for oil is destroyed, these governments will receive little income from their reserves and will cease to accumulate funds, in fact they will have to draw them down to invest in their economies' transition away from fossil fuels, which will ultimately be good for those societies. The fiscal-break price of oil is the price of oil required for the governments of these countries to be in surplus; if it is below these levels, they have to start drawing down their SWFs. Currently, for Qatar it is $55, UAE $73, Saudi Arabia $106 and Norway $70.[7] The price of oil as at the end of 2016 is $53,[8] so all of these countries are running budget deficits. These are estimates based on cost of extraction and fiscal policy at the moment.

Sixty-four per cent of oil consumption is in the transport sector,[9] of this over half is used by light vehicles, that is cars.[10] With the rapid improvement and decline in price in electric cars, there is at last an alternative to petrol cars. However, only half a million electric vehicles are sold annually[11] compared to the total car sales of 70 million,[12] so it would take a long time to scale up the production of electric vehicles 100-fold and then to replace the billion motor vehicles in use in the world.

However, an opportunity does present itself. Cars are typically idle for 23 hours a day, so if all private vehicles in cities were replaced with carpools of self-driving vehicles, 90% of vehicles could be removed from cities, at the same time reducing journey times. Self-driving electric vehicles are incredibly cheap to run, as fuel costs are very low and you don't have to pay a driver, so transport costs would be massively reduced too. There would be many benefits of moving to this transport system, reduction in carbon emissions, elimination of exhaust pollution and virtual elimination of road deaths and accidents. A study showed that journey times could be reduced by 40%, and journey costs could be a quarter of current costs of using a car.[13]

Self-driving carpools could be rapidly implemented at scale as only 10% of the existing stock of cars need to be replaced; petrol demand from motor vehicles, over 30% of oil use, could be virtually eliminated, which would progressively and permanently reduce demand for oil. Further cuts could be made by enforcing vehicle standards on trucks and shipping. With the progressive reduction in demand for oil as these policies were implemented, the price of oil would progressively decline, meaning that oil exporting countries would no longer have spare reserves with which to build up SWFs and have to diversify their economies.

For the first time, it is technically possible to destroy demand for oil, and this has to be done to reduce GHG emissions and hence the damage from climate change. To speed up the transition will require Western Governments to reduce their citizens' free agency, in that it will have to start phasing out the use of petrol cars. However, the current situation has an impact on many aspects which are detrimental to human flourishing, including free agency. Much oil in the world is in the control of countries who are members of the OPEC. Although I said that I was not passing any moral judgement on the governments of oil-rich countries, it cannot be overlooked that many of the OPEC countries are dictatorships with appalling human rights records. Since the 1970s, OPEC, and in particular Saudi Arabia, has had a great deal of influence over the price of oil, the world's largest traded commodity and hugely important to Western economies. Western governments have kowtowed to this medieval monarchy, which has practically no rights for women, practices public beheadings, has been accused of funding some of the world's most extreme terrorist organizations and of committing war crimes in neighbouring Yemen.[14]

Many of the West's military interventions since Second World War have been in the Middle East, because of the importance of oil, most of which have been disastrous and at huge financial cost to the West and human tragedy in the Middle East. The West's involvement in the Middle East over a prolonged period of time to secure it's oil supply has been one of the major causes, if not the main cause, of the current wave of international terrorism. Russia is another fossil-fuel-based economy with an unpleasant government which likes to throw its weight around with damaging consequences.

If the West weened itself off oil now, unfortunately terrorism would not go away, but it would take away the long-term cause. Our military involvement in these areas and the resultant terrorism causes a great deal of loss of free agency and is the cause of a great deal of government intervention in our lives, including by OPEC and the Russian government. Phasing out the use of petrol would therefore temporarily increase benign government intervention in one section of our lives, at the same time reducing malign government intervention in other aspects of our lives.

This intervention, whether it is by governments or cities, is indeed taking away people's agency, their agency to be stuck in slow moving traffic in their own cars. Once the city or state has intervened and the result is a clean, pollution-free city where you could actually move around, private enterprise will provide the carpooling; ultimately, there will be less state involvement than there is now.

If countries act unilaterally and reduce demand and hence the price of oil, there is a risk that others, for example developing countries, could step in to utilise the cheap oil and take up the slack in demand. I do not think this likely though; China is leading the way in electric car use; the large increase in demand for electric vehicles should reduce their price too, continuing the existing trend. Many developing country cities have chronic traffic problem and are highly polluted; the solution I have outlined offers them a way out of the mess, and hopefully poorer countries could skip a technological step and move straight to electric vehicles.

The non-oil SWFs are as a result of the Chinese government's policies of accumulating foreign reserves to promote their exports. Unfortunately, there is nothing that can be done about these, but the Chinese government has already started moving away from this policy.[15] These funds should be run down with time, especially as China faces an ageing population, meaning that the Chinese government will have to spend more on social security and pensions.[16]

10.1.4 Financial Transaction Tax

FTT or Tobin tax (named after the economist who thought of the idea) is an idea which has been doing the rounds for a long time. As the name suggests, this is a tax on all financial transactions. The purpose of the tax, and it would only have to be very small, would be to make the unnecessary churning carried out by financial agents unprofitable. The EU has been, largely unsuccessfully, trying to introduce a FTT.[17]

Unsurprisingly, there have been howls of protests from the financial services industry whenever the FTT is proposed, as a large proportion of its income, and hence a large proportion of the rent extracted from the economy, comes from financial transactions or creating unnecessary financial products that can be bought and sold. The FTT would seriously curtail this activity, which, as I have argued, is mostly useless and harmful.

There are two arguments against the FTT; the main one is that it would curtail liquidity. All liquidity means is that there are people who buy and sell stuff to each other, and as we saw in the financial crisis when you actually need them they go away. Most asset owners would do better if they had to hold onto their assets for longer periods; they would not have to pay so many transaction fees and would have an incentive to ensure that their assets are better managed long term. The FTT would encourage them to do so, as it would be more expensive for them to sell out of positions. The FTT would also destroy the business models of blatantly rent extracting activities, such as high-frequency trading (HFT). The other argument is if any government introduced an FTT, the trading would just go elsewhere. This is a major problem for economies such as the UK, which are so heavily reliant on financial services. But we have to make a choice: Do we want to be so dependent on this one industry, or start to ween ourselves off it?

10.2 Money Trouble

Money has always caused trouble. Throughout history monetary systems have flipped between those based on credit and those based on specie. Credit proceeded money; in tribal societies where people repeatedly interact and live amongst the same people, people exchange goods based on mutual obligations. For example, I would say to a neighbour "hey, I like those oranges" and he would be obliged to give me one; at some later date he would tell me that he liked my shoes, and I would be obliged to share those with him. Over the course of our lives these would approximately cancel out.[18]

When people started to live in towns and cities, their economies become too complex for these informal arrangements to work. The earliest forms of writing developed in Mesopotamia were accounting systems to record a debt-based money system centred around the temple/state.[19]

Debt-based money became problematic in the time of empires. Soldiers had to travel around to conquer, rape and pillage. They could not be paid on credit, as it would not work in the different locations that they plundered, so they had to be paid in precious metals, which could be easily transported and was valuable everywhere. Emperors found it useful to standardize these coins by stamping their portrait on them as it increased their power, prestige and legitimacy.

Since then historical eras have alternated between increasingly complex versions of the debt and specie-based money depending on the needs of society. The last flip was in the early 1970s, when the USA abandoned the gold standard and the world moved to a system of debt-based money based on fractional reserve banking.[20]

The problem with debt/credit-based money is that it relies on trust, in fact credit is derived from the Latin word "credo" which means faith. There is a brand of people, often labelled "gold bugs" who argue for a return to the gold standard; their argument is that fiat money is in the hands of the government, who are always incentivised to print more money and thus debase the currency. This will ultimately lead to the erosion of trust and hence collapse of the system. As governments are in charge of the money system, and they need to raise tax and spend money, they face the temptation to resort to printing money, of which QE is the latest iteration.

On the other hand, the problem with specie money is that the quantity of money is arbitrary and fixed. When economic activity increases, there was more need for money than the actual availability of precious metal, which resulted in deflation leading to economic damage caused by debt-deflation. If you have a debt worth $100, and the value of money increases, the value of the debt increases and hence your ability to pay it decreases.

Gold bugs' motivation is suspicion of governments. However, in our current credit-based money system as we saw in Chapter 6, 97% of money in circulation was created by banks. The problem of the modern economy is that banks, not governments, have been using their power to create money and using it to boost asset prices and hence their own revenues. Now that banks have become risk averse after the financial crisis, they are not lending enough, and when they are lending it is to the wrong sectors.

The problem that we are trying to solve, therefore, is we want a money system that provides trust and cannot be gamed by whoever is in charge of the virtual printing press, be it banks or governments. We also want a system that is flexible so that the money supply can expand and contract in line with the needs of the economy.

For the first time the technology is available to achieve this goal. With 97% of money being electronic, it should be possible to monitor all transactions, or at least approximate to the level of transactions. Transactions in physical money are at such a low level that they can be easily adjusted for, and as argued by Kenneth Rogoff, higher denomination notes should be withdrawn anyway to reduce criminal activity and tax evasion.[21]

If money transactions increase, there is a need for more money, so the central monetary authority should create the required additional money. As this money is the property of society, it can be distributed equally to all members of society; new money created paid into all citizens' bank account in equal measure. It is more politically troublesome if money needs to be taken out of the system, then the central monetary authority will need to find someway of withdrawing money equitably.

The money creation process also needs some adjustment mechanisms; for example, in a recession, where economic transactions reduce, you would not want to take money out of the economy to encourage people to spend. On the other hand, when the economy is overheating, money creation can be less than that implied by the increased activity in economic activity to dampen the system.

Such an electronic system has been in use by Bitcoin, which makes use of a technology called blockchain. Blockchain is a methodology for recording the history of each unit of electronic money; the recording is distributed across the computers of people who use Bitcoin, so it is resilient and resistant to hacking (a hacker would have to hack all the computers that are running blockchain). Bitcoin and other cryptocurrencies have their advocates and critics, as does blockchain technology. A national electronic currency would not necessarily look like Bitcoin, but a government introducing such a currency would have the cryptocurrency experience to draw upon.

An electronic monetary system would be problematic and it would probably not work perfectly immediately. There would be problems in estimating or recording the number of transactions and the adjustment mechanism may cause unforeseen problems. But the algorithm that would control the system could be improved with time. People who might argue that this system would place even more power with government are mistaken; all government do is oversee the algorithm and make sure there is no fraud. Bitcoin is an entirely privately run version of this system, the only reason I am proposing the government is involved is that they are ultimately accountable and going to be around for a long time. I am guessing that people will trust a government currency over a private one, but I am not dogmatic about this, if a private money system came along which was more trustworthy than the government one, there is no reason why it should not be used if it was generally accepted. This is effectively what happens in many African countries, where people use mobile phone credits as money; they trust the mobile money more than the national currency which has been manipulated and mismanaged over the years.

The benefits of seignorage are distributed evenly to the people, which is fair, and this system would take the power of money creation away from banks, who have proved themselves not worthy of this privilege.

The linkage between debt and money creation would be broken, so the economy would no longer be doomed to perpetually accrue more debt with all the misery that entails. The ledger system of blockchain could potentially reduce the risk of failure of the payments system, as all money transactions are recorded, so claims on any given unit of electronic money are recorded and the payment system should be simple to reform after a crisis, even if an institution fails.

In this section I am not proposing one technological solution, but outlining that electronic money could potentially solve past and current problems with money. For a country to adopt such a system would be risky and would have to be constantly adjusted; however, the system we have is a proven failure and electronic money system has the potential to work. If all this seems very far-fetched, the reader might like to know that such radical organisations as the Bank of England, The People's Bank of China and the Riksbank (Swedush Central Bank) all have research programmes on the adoption of national digital currencies, which are generally very positive towards the idea.[22]

10.2.1 What to Do About Banks

The creation of electronic money does away with the need for fractional reserve banking, the algorithm creates money, banks can only lend out money that already exists and is deposited with them.

A radical alternative to fractional reserve banking has been suggested by economist Laurence Kotlikoff which he calls narrow purpose banking,[23] variations of which have gained quite a lot of support. It views banks as essentially investment funds, so if you put your money with a fund in a bank, you know exactly where the money is going, the job of the regulator is merely to judge how risky each fund is.

The problem with narrow purpose banking is that it overlooks the role and risks involved that banks achieve through maturity and liquidity transformations; I mostly leave money in a bank account as opposed to a savings product because I might need it at short notice, whereas borrowers from banks usually want long-term loans. This always leads to the risk of bank runs, if there is even a rumour of trouble; everyone would want to get their money out at the same time, causing the bank to fail. Narrow purpose banks are immune to failure, but they do not perform a maturity transformation, either the lender is locked into lending his money out over the long term or the borrower can only take out a short-term loan.

Mervyn King, the former governor of the Bank of England, came up with what I think is a more realistic solution which he calls "pawnbroker for all seasons". Under this system, banks pre-agree with the central bank how much their assets (the loans) should be discounted in the event of a crisis, depending on how risky they are. In the event of a crisis, the central bank lends against these assets at the pre-agreed rate; banks are therefore not only safe but also penalised for taking risks.[24]

There is no reason that his pawnbroker needs to be a government entity; the Bank of England started out as a private institution and could be so in future, as long as we could be sure that the private entity did not game the system by becoming too important to fail, and therefore benefiting from an implicit government guarantee.[25]

The current system of fractional reserve banking has proved itself adept at lending to certain sectors; should it be employed to enhance sectors of the economy that promote flourishing? We shall return to this question later.

10.2.2 Housing Trouble

As we saw in Chapter 6, much, or even the majority of banking activity in the UK, is concerned with financing housing. Yet, the current system is simply leveraging up existing assets. If there is a shortage of housing the only answer is to increase the supply. I do not think it controversial to say that having a decent and affordable place to live is one of the requirements of human dignity, and hence a necessity of human flourishing.

A simple, no costs solution is simply to ease planning restrictions; which has been shown to increase inequality[26] and remove tax on housebuilding. Governments, or cities, could take a more active role, they could embark on their own social housing or they could work with developers at boosting the supply or provide incentives for developers to build.[27] Governments such as the UK can currently borrow money at around 0%, so the financing cost of building social housing is virtually nothing. The aim should be to stop house prices increasing and therefore capping the debt levels on the economy and making housing affordable, avoiding the currents spiral of increased property prices, increased debt, unaffordable housing and increased inequality.

This is such a simple, common-sense solution to our current housing crisis, which is almost daily in the news and the popular press, that it demonstrates the hegemony of financial economics in political discourse that it has not been adopted.

10.3 Sustainable Finance

There are a number of cool innovations that have been made in the financial and business worlds. But as finance does not do sustainability and compresses all values into financial value, they are currently used only at the margins.

However, if we are going to reimagine the financial system, these off-the-shelf sustainability tools could be rapidly deployed at scale. They have been developed by finance professionals with a deep understanding of the financial system and its flaws; the tools have a track record and a history of development, which has allowed the practitioners to learn from real-world scenarios and resolve some of the problems that would beset untested pilot projects.

The technology is available to cure many of our environmental and social problems. For example, to address climate change, we know how to completely decarbonise our electricity grid by a combination of energy efficiency, renewable energy and even a bit of nuclear power, and we could replace a large portion of our transport network with electric vehicles. This section shows that the social technology is also available to invest in the transformations that are required. So why are we not using them?

10.3.1 Accounting

The first of these, and may be the most important, is from the unlikely world of accounting. The basic concept is that if companies report profits on their accounts, why not get them to use the same techniques to measure social and environmental impact?

A number of people thought of this idea at the same time, and there are a number of different accounting standards and organisations promoting these standards.

- *Triple bottom line accounting* is an accounting system for organisations to not only report on profit but also their impact on people and the planet; this has been taken up by the United Nations and a number public sector bodies in their reporting standards.
- *Carbon disclosure project* is an investor-led initiative which gets companies to report on their GHG emissions. Related to this is the Carbon

Disclosure Standards Board, which is an accounting standard for reporting on GHG emissions. Many governments are considering making GHG reporting mandatory.
- *Integrated reporting* a framework for companies to report on value creation, where value has a much broader definition than just financial value, employing the concept of the six types of capitals: financial capital, manufacturing capital, human capital, social and relationship capital, intellectual capital and natural capital. "All organizations increase, decrease or transform capitals through activities", and the idea behind integrated reporting is to capture an organisation's use of and effects on this capital.[28]

There are also a slew of other initiatives which are variations on these themes such as *The Prince's Accounting for Sustainability Project, the Global Reporting Initiative* and *Circles of Sustainability*.

There are problems with all of these standards. Unlike financial accounts, you cannot reduce concepts such as sustainability into a set of numbers, to do so is to lose the essence of sustainability, which is an appreciation of the complexity of things. However, if the reporting is more subjective then comparison becomes more difficult. The fact that there are a number of different approaches reflects this difficulty.

These approaches are inherently reductive; they are all attempts to reduce nature or society to a value. The value reported is not simply a financial value, which is an improvement on financial value, but it is still a value expressed as a number rather than an ethical structure of values.

The main problem as it stands, though, is even if companies report their triple bottom line or their carbon emissions or produce integrated reporting, there is no motivation for them to do anything about it beyond their moral choice, and companies are legal entities, not moral agents.

10.3.2 Investment

There are a number of innovations which have come out of the investment world, the same world I have been disparaging throughout this book, which have the potential to have a genuinely positive impact on society. I will briefly describe a couple of these.

10.3.2.1 Impact Investment

The aim of impact investment is to create a positive social and/or environmental impact in addition to a financial return. The majority of impact investors aim to achieve a return equivalent to what they would have received for a non-impact investment; the remainder are willing to sacrifice some financial return for increased environmental or social impact. The size of the impact investment market is tiny compared to conventional investment, but at around $70 billion it is not insignificant.[29]

A motivation behind impact investing is getting away from the philanthropy model of wealthy people giving money to charity for good causes. It is centred on a belief that to scale an investment, the underlying investment has to be able to generate its own revenue; if it can generate a revenue it will grow or be copied, and thus, the impact will be greater than if it just absorbs grant money. Impact investment is premised on the belief that efficient decision-making by professional investors is more beneficial than arbitrarily giving out grants (although sophisticated philanthropic organisations would argue that their decision-making process is not arbitrary). The impact investor will make decisions on a rational basis and therefore allocate capital to users who are both doing "good" and will be effective agents of change.

By investing and receiving a return, the impact investor can make better use of limited resources compared to a grant making body which cannot reuse money that it donates. Philanthropic organisations, the donor community and international financial institutions such as the World Bank, make use of impact investment, as well as asset owners that we have already come across such as pension funds and family offices. The accounting frameworks described above are used by impact investors to measure performance.

Most impact investments have achieved the returns that they were expecting.[30] And as the majority of impact investments are aiming for market returns, why cannot non-impact investment invest in these? We have seen in Chapter 5 that non-impact investors are not investing at all, so perhaps it is a case that profit-seeking impact investors are what normal investors *should* look like. Impact investment has been criticised as it ends up being an expensive form of finance for genuine projects that help the poor; poor people do not have much money so cannot pay much in the way of returns. If the investment is something that helps poor people get richer, such as microcredit, it takes a long time for them to get richer, during which time they will not be able to pay commercial returns, and the returns that are paid back to investors are taking money away from the poor. As we have seen investors' time horizon is short, and with the insistence on constant monitoring, the time frame for getting a decent return on investment could be much longer than the patience of the asset owner to see results, whether these results are financial gain or non-financial impact.

10.3.2.2 Green Investment

What I have termed green investment is investment where the use of proceeds is invested directly into the "green" economy. As can be imagined, the first problem is what on earth is the "green" economy. My organisation, the Climate Bonds Initiative, has addressed a narrower problem and isolated investments into a climate-resilient economy. A climate-resilient economy means one that reduces the risk of climate change by reducing our GHG emissions to avoid dangerous climate change, and investing in resilient infrastructure, which will be resistant to the impacts of the climate change that will inevitably occur. The climate-resilient economy will still have to provide the goods and services which people need and desire.

We do not know what the future economy will look like and what the best way of achieving a climate-resilient economy is. It is not obvious what an investment in this economy will look like. Renewable energy, such as solar power, obviously contributes to a low carbon economy. But to be climate resilient, we need energy in other areas which are more controversial. For example, an energy efficiency investment will reduce GHG emissions, but if the investment is in the wrong form of energy efficiency it could lock in a higher level of energy usage then a better investment. Also, the guiding principle of climate finance is the use of proceeds of the investment which must be used for reducing GHG emissions; typically, energy efficiency is part of a much larger investment, for example part of a refurbishment project; if only a small proportion of the investment is in the actual energy efficiency, is this investment green? And beyond this there are much more controversial areas, for example is nuclear energy green?

Climate Bonds Initiative has put together panels of experts to design standards which are effectively taxonomies of what represents climate-resilient investment so that these issues can be navigated. Their process for deciding is transparent, so anyone can comment. To qualify for a certified climate bond, the use of proceeds needs to be audited to ensure that the investment is definitely being spent on the investment. The standards need to change with time as science and technology develop.

To get from where we are at a climate-resilient economy requires a huge investment, equivalent to a new industrial revolution, an estimated that $93 trillion needs to be invested in low carbon infrastructure over the next 15 years.[31]

So far there are $694 billion of climate aligned bonds that have been issued[32]; an impressive amount but 100-fold increase is needed to change our economy.

Most green or climate bonds have been oversubscribed, even though they generally are low yielding. The reason is that they have a captive audience of socially responsible investors, who currently face a shortage of investment grade "green" assets. However, if the climate bond market did grow towards the size that is required, it would rapidly use up all socially responsible investment; people would have to find another reason to invest in them.

The two innovations that I have described approach the challenge of investing sustainably from different angles; impact investing is a ground-up solution which finances projects or organisations that can create social and environmental benefits, whereas green bonds are an attempt to shift conventional investment into sustainable infrastructure at the scale required for a climate-resilient economy.

Both encounter the problem that the financial system is based on the premise that investing based on financial value is inherently in the best interest of society meaning that anything that is not captured by the financial value proposition is peripheral to the process.

10.3.3 Industry

The concept of the **circular economy** has been developed to try and move industrial organisation away from a linear process of extracting resources, turning them into manufactured goods, and then disposing of the resultant waste. The circular economy uses waste as input and tries to minimise its resource use throughout the production and life of a product, ultimately reusing the material of the product at the end of its life.

There are related concepts that are being developed such as **biomimicry**, which is a form of industrial organisation which attempts to learn from nature; natural systems are in some sense a circular economy which ultimately receive energy for sunlight and recycle organisms back into the ecosystem when the organism dies. **Cradle-to-cradle** is a concept whereby products are designed specifically to incorporate the sourcing of resources and energy and reusing or repairing products and/or materials.

These concepts predate the development of the **sharing economy** which is currently in vogue and has been made possible by technological developments and the widespread use of the internet. We need or want an outcome but we do not necessarily need to own something to achieve this. For example, we might want to get from A to B, safely, comfortably and cheaply, but this does not mean that we necessarily need a car to do this; it might be much easier and cheaper to join a car pool.

With the development of the sharing economy, there needs to be a lot less production of physical products, as "consumers" are sharing products; in the example of cars that I gave above, only 10% of the cars currently in use are required. This in turn means that the pressure on resources is lessened compared to the current owner/user economy.

The business world, and even its theoreticians, seems to be noticing the change. The latest developments in business schools and management thinking are moving beyond shareholder value in a helpful way. Shareholder value is based on the premise that consumers want a product which they purchase from companies. New thinking is based on the insight that value is created by the interaction of customer and firm in an experience, which is a co-creation between company and consumer. For example, a car only produces value if someone drives it. This leads to the concept of service-dominant firms which add value by having an ongoing relationship with customers.[33]

This view of companies is much more sympathetic to the sharing economy and hence the circular economy than shareholder value. If companies are providing experiences and have ongoing relationships with customers, sharing products rather than exchange and ownership keeps that ongoing relationship. If companies are managing a relationship with a customer, providing services over an extended time period, the company retains control of the physical products which provide these services and therefore reusing and maintenance become much more integral to the service, then if the product is simply sold to the customer who then owns and is responsible for it.

This section shows that as well as the technology being available to organise a sustainable society, the social and financial technologies also exist as do theoretical frameworks. So why haven't they been enacted? There are two main reasons; there is a huge amount of inertia in the economy, capital has been accumulated over a long period of time and is sunk in the "old" economy. Shifting would make that old capital worthless – like the capital sunk into a coal mine or an oil rig. Ideas take a long time to seep into the political and business discourse; existing incumbents – who want to protect the value of their assets – are powerful and block change. As we have seen, the finance system diverts investment into financial assets, which increases the inertia in the system as there is less renewal from new capital investment.

Secondly, there is no incentive to enact any change to a circular economy because the incentives in the financial system are based on a flawed financial value paradigm. I will explain how the new paradigm could be brought about in the last section of this chapter, after taking a brief diversion into FinTech.

10.4 FinTech

FinTech is the great white hope. In 2015 FinTech start-ups raised $19 billion.[34] FinTech is the use of new technologies to provide financial services; quite a few applications of FinTech have already been described in this book; HFT and blockchain technology being examples. Passive or index tracker funds may have been around for a while, but they are essentially replacing people with computers who make investment decisions so could also be described as FinTech.

It is generally accepted that FinTech is already disrupting business models within the financial system and will continue increasingly to do so. FinTech could potentially impact on all of the four functions of the finance system, the payment system, smoothing lifetime consumption, risk management and allocating savings into investment, in fact it already does all of these things.

For example, the mobile phone network M-Pesa in Kenya allows people to pay each other using mobile phone credits (payment system), Vanguard, as we have seen, allows people to save directly into a market index (smoothing lifetime consumption), there are a large number of start-ups which allow insurance pooling between groups of users (risk management) and market place lending (peer to peer) allows individuals to lend to each other (allocate savings into investment).

These innovations tend to replace the intermediary, in the examples the bank, the insurance company, the asset manager and the broker/dealer. As we have seen throughout the book, the current financial sector is charging too much for these services, and it is not delivering a good service. At the very least, with FinTech these services are being delivered cheaper and more effectively.

A FinTech-dominated financial sector cannot game the system to extract rent in the same way as the current financial system. For example, if banks are largely replaced by market lending platforms, where one individual just lends to other individuals, all the platform does it to take a facilitation fee. Under this model, the platform cannot leverage itself up and become too big to fail.

There are, though, opportunities to game the system in other ways. For example, HFT extracts rent by buying up securities faster than normal investors. Much of their rent is gained at the expense of traditional broker dealers. Also, HFT can be easily stopped by introducing a small FTT.

So generally, FinTech should make the financial services sector smaller and more efficient, which was one of the aims of this chapter.

Will FinTech ensure a better outcome for society and the environment? Because FinTech is cheaper, it can improve access, M-Pesa has brought banking services largely to rural Africans who previously had no access at all, so this is inherently more inclusive than current finance. People and business that are financed via marketplace lending platforms are often ones that cannot borrow from banks.

However, there is no guarantee that lending will be any more sustainable than before. Let me give two examples:

Alipay: Many of the students at the university I teach are Chinese; none of them have a bank account with a traditional bank, they all have bank accounts with Alipay which is part of Alibaba, a giant company which is the Chinese equivalent of Amazon, the online shop. If a company like Alibaba replaces banks, it might be able to offer a cheaper service than traditional banks, but it will have similar or even greater market power, it will also present systemic risk; it will be too big to fail; and its incentives may be different, but not necessarily better than traditional banks.

HNW Lending: a friend of mine has set up a peer-to-peer lending platform. Someone approaches HNW Lending to borrow money, HNW Lending offers them terms (an interest rate, level of security and term) and matches the borrower with a lender like myself. HNW Lending takes a cut. The advantage to the borrower is that he can access funds much quicker than via a bank, the advantage to the lender is that I receive a higher interest rate than I would in a bank deposit as the middle man (bank) is replaced by HNW Lending who is more efficient and hence takes a lower intermediation fee.

When faced personally with the lending decision, I come to the same conclusions as a high-street bank, I lend against good collateral, which is easy to value and to put a charge against, i.e. real estate. And hence, the problem to the economy would be the same if companies like HNW Lending replaced banks; individuals would mostly decide to lend against real estate than to business because each loan against real estate appears safer.

There are advantages to peer-to-peer lending over banks; firstly, there is less systemic risk, if my loan defaults the damage is just to me, HNW Lending is not systemically connected to other market place lending; HNW Lending does not lose any capital if the loan defaults. Secondly, HNW Lending cannot leverage up its loan book, it does not possess the ability to create money to invest against property, pushing up the price of property. Any asset bubbles that were blown by peer-to-peer lending platforms should be much more limited than the ones blown by banks. On the other hand, the lender is taking the risk on the loan, if it defaults they are the ones that risk the loss and could have their savings wiped out.

Finally, neither Alipay nor HNW Lending contributes anything to the environment or society, especially at the level that is required to transform the economy. Their main attraction is they do less damage than the current incumbents.

10.5 Could Finance Be Sustainable?

Reader, I am faced with a dilemma. A drain-the-swamp strategy, whereby governments removes support and replaced the functions of the helminth with better alternatives, would create a smaller, efficient finance system, which would cheaply, effectively and safely be able to deliver what it is supposed to do, especially when supported by the FinTech revolution. On the other hand, we need an industrial revolution to transform our economy into a sustainable economy, and what I have described will not deliver this transformation.

There are financial tools available which could be utilised to bring about the rapid change that we need. However, if these are empowered by government, there is the risk that this will give rise again to all the problems of the current system:

- Regulatory arbitrage: Whenever governments introduce financial legislation, this creates the opportunity for the finance sector to arbitrage the regulation; that is to game the regulation to make money for itself.
- Inequality: Any support for finance enriches the rich and the finance sector itself. For example, if savings are encouraged by tax benefits, it is only the rich who save and benefit from these tax breaks.
- The return of the helminth: Replacing the existing set of financial tools with others will create opportunities for leverage, financial innovation, colonization of other areas of the economy and creating a powerful lobbying group that could subvert regulation in its own interest.

On balance, though, the finance required for a transition to a sustainable economy is so great that I think we have to take the risk. If we want this transformation, there are not really any viable alternatives. If we take private finance out of the equation, it would leave government to do the bulk of the investing, which has its own dangers. Also, if we drain the swamp of government-backed finance, people still need to save, and the way they will do it will be as I have outlined, via property or very large enterprises like Alibaba.

I will outline how we could power up the tools of finance, and let the reader decide if the risks are worth it.

10.5.1 The Buffer Fund

The design of the Swedish pension system included five buffer funds and an additional DC fund into which savers contribute. The number of funds is somewhat arbitrary, but the concept of having buffer funds is integral to the system. They allow smoothing if changes in benefit levels are required and can potentially reduce the cost of the fund if returns are good.

The main flaw with these funds is their mandate, which is to maximise return for a level of risk, based on the misguided values implied by MPT and its accomplice shareholder value.

Instead the funds could be run with a mandate based on a set of values to enhance human flourishing. The buffer funds do have to generate returns to make the payment of pensions cheaper, but they also have to help the economy grow sustainably so that the economy can generate enough income for workers to pay pensioners; a flourishing mandate is much more in keeping with their purpose.

There are a number of tools which the funds could use, some may work and some may not, but as there are five funds, they could be given complementary mandates, for example:

- Sustainable infrastructure fund: Infrastructure should be thought of for what it does rather than as large kit. For example, we need transport infrastructure to get us from A to B or health infrastructure to cure us from illnesses. This does not necessarily mean building roads and hospitals, it could be investing in drone technology so goods could be transported off the road network or preventative health so that people would not need to go to hospitals. A taxonomy of sustainable investment could be developed as has been developed for climate change by the Climate Bonds Initiative.
- Venture capital into circular economy: This will fund businesses with circular economy principles such as cradle-to-cradle manufacturing processes.
- Triple bottom line/six capitals investment: This would be investment into existing companies, with the aim to make them more sustainable. The fund would act as an active investor, engaging with management, setting appropriate pay structure for executives, and the fund would be compensated on the improvement of underlying investee companies.
- Impact investment fund: As described above.

- Health/Reducing liabilities: My preferred option would be for a critical health insurance system rather than a pension system. If this were the case, the liabilities would be reduced by improving the health of the population and reducing the cost of providing palliative care. The purpose of the fund would be to invest in better health outcomes, this could be medical research or the building of care homes, or investment in adult education so that people could retrain to do jobs that they find more fulfilling and would be better motivated to work later in their lives.

The powerful and proven investment tool that would make these funds effective is the mandate. The mandate is the target set by asset owners for their asset managers. Standard practice is to base this on MPT – to beat an index at a given level of risk. Even though this is a self-contradictory mandate – MPT is based on the premise that you cannot beat an index – it has proved immensely powerful in aligning the incentives of companies with the interests of the asset manager who invest in them.

The sustainable mandate can instead be set against a different incentive structure; for example, to maximise triple-bottom line returns. In this case the asset manager would be rewarded if he could maximise the fund's profit, environmental and social impact, with appropriate weightings. As discussed, this does have the downside of trying to reduce complex concepts like society and sustainability to a simple metric, but the mandate setting could be transparent and subject to feedback from stakeholders; it could have built-in mechanisms which ensured that outcomes improved with time.

10.5.2 Preferencing

The buffer funds are an essential design feature of an effective pension or critical health insurance system. Should we go further than this; should savings be encouraged into a sustainable economy? The main incentive that governments use for savings/investment is tax incentives. And the problem with these is that they are highly regressionary; the rich benefit and the poor do not. Also, these incentives present a high risk that regulations will be gamed, wealthy people employ smart advisors to use the regulations for their own benefit rather than for what they were intended, which means that more regulation is drafted to try and stop the abuse, which gives rise to more opportunities for gaming, and the system becomes increasingly complex and inefficient, losing its original purpose, as has happened with the current pensions/savings/investment system.

For this reason, I would not be inclined to introduce tax breaks to encourage savings, even into sustainable areas. However, there are legacy funds; if we are shutting down the current system, it would not be fair to take away tax incentives on current savings; people have saved in good faith in the assumption that these savings will not be taxed until they retire. What could be changed is that any tax advantage could be given only if the funds are transferred, over time, into sustainable funds. This could be direct investment in sustainable infrastructure, or it could be an impact investment-type fund. If the latter, the government could give tax rebates for the societal and environmental benefits of these funds, which would align the incentives of the investor with society.

The other policy leverage tool available to governments relates to capital requirements. Financial institutions such as banks and insurance companies have to hold assets in financial instruments to meet their liabilities. These reserve assets must cover the liabilities and have a buffer in case things go wrong. Sustainable assets could be preferred in these solvency requirements. Chapter 2 explained briefly how these requirements work; different asset classes are given different weightings so if institutions hold more risky assets, they have to hold more of these to compensate for the risk. Mortgages and government bonds are given very low weightings as they are considered low risk, so institutions are encouraged to hold a lot of these.

If the weightings are biased in favour of sustainable investments such as green bonds, it would encourage institutions to hold more of these assets. There is a precedent to doing this, German banks are encouraged to hold Pfandbrief, or covered bonds, which are bonds securitised against long-term assets. These are given a low-risk weighting and hence, German banks hold more of these assets.

10.5.3 Banking

In my proposal to reduce the power of banks, I suggested the introduction of electronic money could mean that fractional reserve banking was no longer required. However, we have seen from the damage it has done, what a powerful tool fractional reserve banking is – it has the power to cause huge investments at scale into an asset class, real estate. This is because it is incentivised to invest in that asset class, as described in Chapter 6.

My most dangerous proposal is therefore to allow fractional reserve banking in certain favoured sectors of the economy, as this would drive finance into these sectors. These sectors would be the very ones that are least served by the current banking sectors, the poor, the unbanked, small businesses and companies involved in sustainability.

How would this work? Fractional reserve banking is the way all banks work today; they create money in the lending process. Under the system of electronic money, this would not be allowed. However, governments could give special mandates to fractional reserve banks as long as they were below a certain size and as long as they were mission driven, where that mission conformed with some of the aspects of human flourishing. Democratic society should decide on what that criteria is and one of the accounting systems described above could be employed to measure the impact.

Another innovation in the banking system that could be employed is development banks. There are international development banks such as the World Bank, or national such as KfW in Germany. In some ways, a development bank acts like an investment bank, it mediates access with the financial markets, although it also helps its client structure deals and often provides funding itself. As their name suggests, they use these investment banking tools to help countries develop and to help bring people out of poverty.

Development banks could be set up and deployed at a much more granular scale. For example, many regions of the developed world have suffered from globalisation as production has moved to developing world countries. Regional development banks could be set up in these locations, to give preferential finance to businesses in these regions allowing the regions to rapidly redevelop.

There could be development banks set up for the purpose of promoting certain sectors, such as the circular economy. Expertise would be centred within these development banks in the sector. An example of this is the Green Investment Bank, set up by the UK government to lend into the "green" economy but was later neutered by the Government for ideological reasons.

10.6 Summary

Government could reverse a lot of damage that has been done by the financial sector simply by withdrawing its support. However, as the financial system is so central to our economy, it is incumbent on governments to set up other structures which provide the services that finance is failing to provide. Fortunately, a working model for a pensions/savings system works in the form of the Swedish system, and with electronic money the current system of fractional reserve banking can be replaced.

To reverse the environmental damage caused by the current economic and financial system would require the equivalent of a new industrial revolution. The technology to bring about this revolution is in place, but the finance system is a blockage to change. However, removing the current financial system will not be enough to get transformation at the scale that is required. I believe it is worth taking the risk of redeploying the tools of finance to bring about a sustainable, capitalist, industrial revolution.

Notes

1. Hayek, F (1944) *The Road to Serfdom* Routledge Classics.
2. See for example Reuters 4 July 2016 *UPDATE 2-Poland announces big shakeup in pension system*.
3. OECD Data: https://data.oecd.org/socialexp/pension-spending.htm accessed 9 December 2016.
4. Severinson, C and Stewart, F (2012), "Review of the Swedish National Pension Funds", OECD Working Papers on Finance, Insurance and Private Pensions, No. 17, OECD Publishing.
5. See for example Department of Health (2016) *Health of the "baby boomer" generation* UK Government.
6. And the Qatar Investment Authority from natural gas as well.
7. CNBC 3 December 2015 *Oil prices and budgets: The OPEC countries most at risk* and Bloomberg 12 December 2014 *$70 Oil Is Norway Break-Even Point, Central Bank Chief Says*.
8. Brent crude as at 15 December from OilPrice.com.
9. International Energy Agency (2016) *Key World Energy Statistics 2016*.
10. International Energy Agency (2016) *World Energy Outlook 2011*.
11. Cobb, J (2016) *Top Six Plug-in Vehicle Adopting Countries – 2015* HybridCars.com.
12. Statista *Number of cars sold worldwide from 1990 to 2016 (in million units)* https://www.statista.com/statistics/200002/international-car-sales-since-1990/accessed 13 December 2016.
13. Integrated Transport Forum (2015) *Urban Mobility System Upgrade* OECD.
14. For example; Human Rights Watch 13 October 2016 *Yemen: Saudi-Led Funeral Attack Apparent War Crime*.
15. Financial Times 14 December 2016 *Managing the inevitable decline of the renminbi*.
16. Banister, J Bloom, D and Rosenberg, L (2010) *Population Aging and Economic Growth in China*
    PGDA Working Paper No. 53 and The Atlantic June 2016 issue *China's Twilight Years*.

17. Financial Times 5 June 2016 *EU financial transaction tax progress stalls.*
18. Graeber, D (2011) *Debt: The First 5000 Years* Melville House Publishing.
19. Graeber, D (2011) *Debt: The First 5000 Years* Melville House Publishing.
20. Graeber, D (2011) *Debt: The First 5000 Years* Melville House Publishing.
21. Rogoff, K (2016) *The curse of cash* Princeton University Press.
22. See, for example Barrdear, J and Kumhof, M (2016) *The Macroeconomics of Central Bank Issued Digital Currencies* Bank of England Staff Working Paper 605 and Tolle, M (2016) *Central Bank Digital Currency: Th End of Monetary Policy as We Know it?* Bank Underground https://bankunderground.co.uk/2016/07/25/central-bank-digital-currency-the-end-of-monetary-policy-as-we-know-it/
23. Kotlikoff, L (2010) *Jimmy Stewart is Dead* Wiley.
24. King, M (2016) *The End of Alchemy* Little, Brown Book Group.
25. Congdon, T (2009) *Central Banking in a Free Society* Institute of Economic Affairs.
26. See for example The Atlantic 23 November 2015 *How Zoning Laws Exacerbate Inequality.*
27. Hilber, C and Vermeulen, W (2012) *The Impact of Supply Constraints on House Prices in England* Spatial Economics Research Centre Discussion Paper 119.
28. Integrated Reporting (2013) Capitals: *Background Paper for <IR>.*
29. Global Impact Investing Network (2016) *annual Impact Investor Survey.*
30. Global Impact Investing Network (2016) *annual Impact Investor Survey.*
31. Global Commission on the Economy and Climate (2014) *Better Growth, Better Climate: The New Climate Economy Report.*
32. Climate Bonds initiative (2016) *Bonds and Climate Change The state of the market in 2016.*
33. Vargo, S. and Lusch, R (2008) *Service-dominant logic: continuing the evolution* Journal of the Academy of Marketing Science(36): 1–10.
34. Castilla-Rubio, J Zadek, S and Robins, N (2016) *Fintech and Sustainable Development: Assessing the Implications* UNEP.

11

Epilogue: Twilight of the Gods of Finance

The book has argued that the current financial markets we have are the creations of governments and society. They have overreached their original purpose, to efficiently invest the surplus of the economy; this function is only a minor sideshow to the main activity of extracting rent from the rest of the economy. The impact on society and the environment is corrosive; the financial system causes inequality and debt, encourages short-term behaviour and is a block to how we need to transform the economy to avoid impending environmental and societal crisis. As government and society created this system, they have every right to take it apart and set up a financial system which does what society wants and needs.

There is much angst about risk in the current system, but the greater risk is that the current system survives then it collapses in a future financial crisis.

This is the current state, but what of the future?

The original purpose of capital markets was for companies or governments to raise a lot of capital to build stuff, for example a government might need new battleships or a company might want to build a car factory. The company would employ people in the resultant factory to build the cars, and as Henry Ford famously put it he wanted to pay his workers enough so that they could buy his cars. The factory took raw materials or components and turned them into physical goods which it could sell at a profit. Workers could purchase goods made in factories out of their wages, maybe with the help of a loan from a bank. Excess income could be saved via the financial system which was invested in other companies who made stuff. When the workers got old they retired and lived off their savings.

Obviously, we do not know for sure what is going to happen in the future, but the way things are going suggests that the world does not look like this anymore, and in the future increasingly less so. Companies produce digital goods rather than physical goods, which don't require a factory to make. Companies do not require large numbers of staff to produce these goods. There will be far fewer people employed, and they will have no money to buy goods that companies produce, and these goods cost nothing or relatively little to produce. As we have seen in this book, people cannot save in the financial markets and expect to receive a pension. People will not have a career path where they work and then retire, as there will be a diminishing number of jobs, they will spend a lot of time out of work, and people will live longer and healthier meaning that there is no need to retire when they are old.

I will justify each of these claims in turn.

11.1 Companies Don't Need Large Amounts of Capital

An increasing proportion of goods in the economy are non-rival. A rival good, like a car, means that if I buy the car someone else cannot. Possessing a non-rival good does not take away the use of the good from someone else, so for example if I download an app onto my iPhone, it does not stop someone else from downloading the app. Typically, the marginal cost of the app is zero or very low; it doesn't cost the app provider anything to sell another app once it has been written.

To produce the app does require some capital, but not much compared to what you need to produce a car; and companies that produce apps are typically not funded via capital markets. It is true that some of these companies eventually list on a stock market, but this is to reward the owners, not to raise more capital.

Although an increasing proportion of goods are non-rival, there are still many goods which do need to be made in a factory, for example Tesla, the electric car manufacturer, is currently building a massive factory in the Nevada desert to make batteries for their cars, expected to cost $5 billion.[1] Even non-rival goods such as apps require a physical good, such as an iPhone to use them.

As I argued in Chapter 10 with respect to transport, we would be better off moving to a sharing economy, which would only require 10% of the current

11.1 Companies Don't Need Large Amounts of Capital

number of vehicles. In such a world, most of the value in transport by private vehicles would be captured by car-sharing platforms such as Uber. You would still need car factories, but they would only need to make 10% of the cars that are made today.

In the case of the iPhone, which is an expensive physical good, Apple subcontracts the manufacturing of the phone to other companies. These companies only receive about 30% of the value of the iPhone; Apple gets the remaining 70%.[2] This means that most of the value of the iPhone is captured by the design and marketing, processes which do not need large amounts of capital. In fact, companies like Apple are massively cash rich; they have no need to raise money from financial markets.

These are all developments that are happening now. Slightly more speculative is the impact of 3D printing; that is if you want a good, you download the design and print it yourself. This may only be viable for simple goods such as toys, but it reflects a world where consumers pay more for the non-rival design rather than the manufacturing of physical goods.

There is still a need for some companies to raise large quantities of funds. For example, recently, the American pharmaceutical company Eli Lilly's new drug Sola, which was intended to slow the progression of Alzheimer's, failed its trial.[3] It has been estimated that the cost of developing a new drug is $2.6 billion,[4] which would have just been written off because of the failure.

Capital markets do not like the sort of risk represented by developing a new drug, where it costs a huge amount of research and development to develop a new product, with the possibility of total failure. We saw in Chapter 5 how the financial sector encourages companies to reduce their spending on research and development, which in the case of pharmaceuticals could have catastrophic consequences because of the lack of development of new antibiotics. Also, as we have seen, to recoup the cost of development, pharmaceutical companies spend a huge amount on lobbying with the intent of keeping the price of the drug high for as long as possible, which is not ideal for the sick people who need the drug, especially if they have not been working for a large proportion of their lives and will not be able to afford them. Drugs are not non-rival goods, but they resemble non-rival goods because the marginal cost is very low, all the cost is in the fixed cost of developing the intellectual property.

It has also convincingly been argued that research which requires large amounts of capital has been directly or indirectly funded by the state not the capital markets; the state is effectively acting as a venture capital fund.[5]

11.2 Companies Don't Employ Many People

Table 11.1 shows the price paid for recent tech firms compared to how many people they employ. Despite the huge amounts of money involved, these companies don't employ many people.

One of the sectors that is being hardest hit by technology is finance, for example the number of jobs in financial services in New York has declined by about 10%, with much of the decline driven by automation – 70% of equity trades are now carried out by algorithms.[6]

The replacement of people by machines is not a new occurrence, famously looms being smashed up in the 1810s by the followers of "Ned Ludd". And at every historical instance that this has happened, although workers have been displaced by machines, the economy as a whole has always managed to generate more jobs doing something else. In the past, when people have been replaced, machines (normally with the aid of people) are doing something more efficiently than was done previously by people alone. Because this function becomes more efficient, it is also cheaper, so people can afford more of the output. Hence, the economy produces more goods in total and creates more jobs than were lost.

Studies predicting the loss of a large number of jobs because of technological progress should therefore be treated with a great deal of scepticism. Artificial intelligence (AI) is different to previous waves of technology, as it attempts to replicate aspects of what is special about humans. In contrast an automated loom substitutes for humans doing mechanical operations.

A current example of AI is the driverless car. Google has done almost a million miles of road testing its driverless car; so far it has only had one accident when a human-driven car crashed into the back of a stationary driverless car. Effectively, all jobs which require a human to drive could be replaced using current technology or very near-future technology. Driverless cars replacing human drivers would remove human error, meaning that 1.2 million people per year globally would not die in car accidents. There would be massive savings in hospital costs, reduced journey times, reduced haulage costs, energy efficiency savings, traffic policing and insurance.

Table 11.1 Recent tech-firm takeovers

Year	Purchaser	Company	Price	Number of employees	Price per employee
2006	Google	YouTube	$1.65 billion	65	$25 million
2012	Facebook	Instagram	$1 billion	13	$77 million
2014	Facebook	WhatsApp	$19 billion	55	$345 million

Tonev, A and Jose, D (2016) *The Nomadic Investor* HSBC Global Research

If it were just drivers that were being replaced, we would still expect the economy to generate many more jobs than had been replaced by driverless cars. But it is not just drivers that will be replaced, there will be a tsunami of AI-job replacement. A recent paper suggests that 47% of current jobs in the US are susceptible to be replaced by computer.[7] The authors find that in the past, routine jobs, both cognitive and physical, have tended to be replaced by machines. However, at present it is non-routine jobs that are now susceptive to be replaced. Jobs for humans that will be created will be where there are bottlenecks, which computers currently cannot do, mainly jobs that require social skills, creativity or human relationships. The frontiers of technology are not fixed; there is no reason to assume that AI will not be able to penetrate further. Just recently, I was arranging a meeting with a friend via his personal assistant, Amy. On meeting my friend, and expecting to meet Amy, I was somewhat surprised to find out that she was an AI!

For people who use the services performed by computer rather than by humans, they are getting the same or better service cheaper and more efficiently. Why would we not want driverless cars if they are cheaper and safer? Why would you use a GP rather than Dr Watson, the AI doctor with a better diagnostic record than a human doctor – no more having to wait at the doctor surgery or visits to Accident & Emergency in the middle of the night when your own personal physician is loaded onto your smart phone.

A lot of jobs that are being created are what anthropologist David Graeber calls "bullshit jobs".[8] When Graeber and I were young, our parents had their car washed by a machine. Now, they are washed by hand, because people are cheap enough to replace the car-wash machine. Car-washers will never earn enough to be able to buy a car or save their excess in the capital markets – in effect they are not meaningful jobs.

Even a best-case scenario from a jobs perspective would involve a constantly changing jobs markets, with some jobs being wiped out by AI or new technology-enabled business models on a continual basis. The worst case is that large chunks of human employment are permanently replaced by computers, with far fewer jobs being created to take their place leading to decreasing levels of employment.

11.3 People Living Longer and Healthier

Life expectancies in both developed and developing countries have been increasing rapidly. For example, the life expectancy in Japan is well into the 80s. In developing countries like China, life expectancy is catching up – increasing from 60 to 75 in the last 20 years.[9] Girls born in the UK now are expected to live to 94.[10] The current trend is also that people are healthier for most of their retirement period.[11]

Future medical advances will be concentrated on the elderly, both reducing mortality at higher ages and providing an increasingly healthy life in old age. "Scientists now understand aging as a process involving a wide array of interacting cellular and metabolic mechanisms, and they are zeroing in on strategies for altering these mechanisms, one by one, in ways that could cumulatively have a dramatic impact in the average human health span."[12] It is entirely feasible that life expectancies for some people could double this century, to around 160. If this happens, it is likely to coincide with most of that life extension to be healthy and active – there would be little demand for life extensions which kept people in care homes for 80 years.[13]

Even if we ignore the possible of dramatic life extension, the typical life of a person living in a developed country entails her being educated into their twenties, retiring in her 60s and living until 90. In this model, she is working for, say, 42 years and not working for 48 years. If we combine this model with the insight that AI will replace many jobs on a rolling basis so that people will be frequently and for long periods out of work, in education or retraining, it is likely that for most of a person's life they will not be in formal employment. The model of having one career during your working life and an old age when you are retired on the proceeds of your employment no longer fits. It is more likely that people will have an extended working life during which they will have periods of employment, extensive periods of part-time work and of unemployment and retraining. The last few years of life will have high expenses when care and medical assistance are required.

11.4 What Is to Be Done?

What impact will all this have on capital markets? If companies no longer need to raise money, there is no need for them to use capital markets. If there are fewer workers, there will be less people to buy these goods, so companies cannot make a profit, and non-employed workers will have no excess money to save via the capital markets. Capital markets as they are today and much of the finance sector will therefore become redundant.

The basic model of capitalism is changing or has already changed. I hope that I am not sounding like Karl Marx again, who said that capitalism would eventually break down and lead to revolution; I am sure that we will stick with capitalism and I do not believe that the lumpen proletariat will rise up in revolution. But the current financial setup where our excess savings finance business investment is over.

What do I think the future of finance will look like? To be honest, I really don't know, although as I outlined in Chapter 10, traditional finance is already being replaced by alternative FinTech models such as marketplace lending.

More importantly is how will people live if there is no work? The problems that result from lack of income are probably the easiest to solve. As machines replace people, goods will become cheaper to produce. That means the economy as a whole has the potential to generate more goods; the problem will be lack of demand as there will not be workers to buy the goods. People will need a universal income, an income large enough so that they can live with dignity irrespective of whether they work or not. The owners of the capital will have to agree to this, as otherwise there will be no one to buy their goods and the system, which they are heavily invested in, will collapse. The universal income will have to be sufficiently high that people are reasonable comfortably off. It must also be remembered that many goods will become cheaper as they are produced by machines and not people, and increasingly goods will be have zero or negligible marginal cost to produce.

If these goods are given away for free, there are problems of copyright; people would not be motivated to invest in research, development or production if they were not going to make any money from producing new goods. Under our current system, we get round this by charging people for these non-rival goods. An alternative would be for the government to pay producers of patented goods a fee for the number of people who use it, with maybe an adjustment for social good (e.g. this would help with development of medical research).

The less easy problem to solve caused by the lack of work is what will people do all day? How are they to live meaningful lives and not spend their days becoming depressed and watch day-time TV (or whatever virtual-reality entertainment replaces it, I shudder to think). The social stigma of unemployment needs to be removed; if someone wants to work and is lucky enough to find employment, this should be seen as a privilege. Government's focus could be to find meaningful activities for people who are unemployed rather than trying to get them to do meaningless bullshit jobs. For example, adult education could be free, volunteering and civic participation should be encouraged to revive civil society.

Finally, what should finance professionals do? I must admit that I do feel a twinge of guilt as I have denigrated the work of my fellow finance professionals, many of whom are hard-working decent people, and many of whom are my friends. It is hardly a consolation that they are not even bloodsucking vampire squids, but like worms that live in your gut and are just agents of a system governed by wrong incentives which control their lives. Oh, and they will soon be redundant.

But finance is a powerful technology and you, the finance professionals, are the keepers of its lore. Finance can be used as a positive force to improve people's lives and to help solve the environmental crisis that we face. It is up to you smart, talented and conscientious people, who hold the detailed knowledge of the system, to change the system from within so that it can become a force to enhance the beautiful things in life; nature, social relations and human flourishing, rather than engaging in a futile and mis-guided attempt to reduce all that is good to a financial value.

Notes

1. Bloomberg 27 February 2014 *Musk's $5 Billion Tesla Gigafactory May Start Bidding War.*
2. The Economist 10 August 2011 *Slicing the Apple.*
3. Financial Times 23 November 2016 *Alzheimer's drug failure deals blow to US drugmaker Eli Lilly.*
4. FT Magazine 23 November 2016 *High stakes: Eli Lilly's hunt for an Alzheimer's drug.*
5. See DeLong, B and Cohen, S (2016) *Concrete economics* Harvard Business Review Press and Mazzucato, M *The Entrepreneurial State: Debunking Public vs. Private Sector Myths* Anthem Press.
6. Bloomberg Markets 19 February 2015 *The demise of Finance jobs in New York City.*
7. Frey, C and Osborne, M (2013) *The Future Of Employment: How Susceptible Are Jobs To Computerisation?* Oxford Martin School.
8. Graeber, D (2013) *On the phenomena of bullshit jobs* Strikemag.
9. World Bank data.
10. Office for National Statistics Life Expectancies.
11. BBC News 10 April 2012 *Life expectancy: How long will you Live.*
12. Bess, M (2016) *Make Way for the Superhumans* Icon Books.
13. Bess, M (2016) *Make Way for the Superhumans* Icon Books, citing Post, S and Binstock, R (2004) *The Fountain of Youth: Cultural, Scientific, and Ethical Perspectives on a Biomedical Goal* Oxford University Press.

Index

3D printing, 281

A
Abacha, Sani, 162
ABM, 245n
abstraction, 170
   finance trade tools, 175–176
Abu Dhabi, 53–55, 71
Abu Dhabi Investment Authority, 31, 37, 56, 60, 71
Abu Dhabi National Oil Company, 37
academic literature, 24
access to finance, 151
accounting, 243, 259
   carbon disclosure project, 264
   integrated reporting, 264
   sustainable finance, 264–265
   systems, 275
   triple bottom line, 264
activist investors
   pensions, 125–126
actuaries, 43–44
Administradoras de Fondos de Pensiones (AFP), 56–57
adult education, 285

advertising, 204, 214–215
   spending, 19
Aegon, 31, 60
aerospace and defence, 63
affordability, 147
Africa, 7
   deforestation, 192
   fertility rates, 194
   mobile technology, 198, 261, 270
ageing population, 80–82, 91–92, 116, 258
agriculture, 200
AIG, 31, 59
Airbnb, 21
Alibaba, 270–272
Alipay, 270–272
Allianz, 31
Alzheimer's disease, 255
Amazon, 124, 271
Amundi, 45
Annual General Meetings (AGMs), 28, 118–119, 124
annual management charge (AMC), 46, 93
Antartic, 3
anthropology, 283

288 Index

antibiotics, 215, 281
anti-environmentalism, 242
apes, 192
Apple, 47, 64–65, 172–173, 281
Aral Sea, 203
Aristotle, 242
Arrow-Debreu Model, 180, 224, 233, 240
Artificial Intelligence (AI), 282–284
Asian crisis (1997), 91
Asian tiger economies, 22, 165, 213
  industrialisation, 166, 217
asset class, 226
asset liability model (ALM), 43–44
asset managers, 19, 23, 28–29, 33, 35, 116–120
  largest global, 45
asset owners, 30–43, 224
  endowments and family office, 39
  global, 31
asset pricing, 228
asset values, 222
asymmetric information, 74n
atmospheric aerosol loading, 201
austerity, 109, 243
Australia
  Anglo-Saxon-style finance system, 97, 223
  economic growth, 10
  mandatory pension contributions, 32, 83
  shareholder capitalism, 21
authenticity, 242
auto-enrolment, 58, 73, 83, 95, 249
automation, 282–283
automobiles, 256–257, 279–280
  see also driverless cars; electric vehicles; transport sector
autonomy, 241–242
Aviva, 31
AXA Insurance, 31, 60
AXA Investment Managers, 45

B

BAE systems, 63, 71
Bangladesh
  industrialisation, 198
bank-bashing, 23–24, 248
Bank of England, 90, 108, 121, 133, 139, 150, 178, 205, 262
banking sector
  growth of, 152
  sustainable finance, 275–276
Bank for International Settlements (BIS), 62
Bank of Japan, 164
bank leverage, 173
  see also leverage
bankruptcy, 61, 214, 253
banks, 133–155
  equity market, 63
  fines, 187
  government bail-outs, 28
  lifetime consumption, 135
  money, 262–263
  payments system, 134–135
  savings and investment, 135–136
  types, 152–155
bank transfers, 7
Basel II, 143–144
Basel III, 134, 143–144, 171, 174
Baumol, William, 162
Bernays, Edward, 214
BHS (British Home Stores), 31
billionaires, 4
Bill and Melinda Gates Foundation, 38
biodiversity loss, 3
biogeochemical flows, 201
biological diversity, 192
biomimicry, 268
biosphere integrity, 201
Bitcoin, 261
Black Rock, 45, 48, 124
Black-Scholes Model, 180, 224, 225
Blankfein, Lloyd, 223–224
blockchain technology, 261, 269

BNY Mellon Invest, 45
bonds, 39–41
   asset allocation, 103
   funds, 183
   global invested capital, 40
   market, 62–63
   pensions, 105–109
  see also government bonds
BP (British Petroleum), PLC, 46, 121–123, 126
Brazil
   industrialisation, 166, 198
Brecht, Bertolt, 24
Bretton Woods institutions, 168, 223
Brexit, 4
British Empire, 72
brokerage function, 49
brokers, 48–49
Brundtland Commission, 193
bubonic plague, 159
buffer funds, 254, 255, 272–274
  see also sustainable finance
Buffett, Warren, 38, 118
buyers, 56–62
buy-to-let market, 147
buy-side, 48, 79, 153

C

Caisse de dépôt et placement du Québec, 57
California State Teachers' Retirement System, 57
California Teachers' Pension Fund, 127
call option, 110
CalSTRS (California Public Employees' Retirement System), 34, 56–57, 71, 73
Canada
   Anglo-Saxon-style finance system, 223
   independent ratings agents, 40
   pension funds, 57

Canada Pension Plan and CPP Investment Board, 57
Canary Wharf, 1–2
capital, 14–16
capital asset pricing model (CAPM), 180, 224, 225, 227
capital control, 164
capital gains tax (CGT), 108
capital goods, 91
Capital Group, 45
capitalism, 21–22, 53, 59
   1980s, 159
   21st Century, 126
   capital stock, 160
   citizens, 251
   'crony' 247
   developmental state, 22, 245n
   financial, 248
   Marxist, 284–285
   poverty and, 210
   rentier-capitalist class, 83
   shareholder, 21–22, 223, 237
   stakeholder, 22, 224
   US, 165
capital markets regulation, 179–180
   origins and future prospects, 279–280
  see also Potemkin markets
capital stock, 160, 216
capital types, 265
carbon bubble, 206
  see also collateral damage
carbon dioxide, 3, 191, 200
carbon disclosure project, 264
Carbon Disclosure Standards Board, 264
carbon emissions, 265
   global economic growth, 198–199
   vehicles, 256–257
carbon markets, 206
  see also collateral damage
car-sharing platforms, 281
cartels

cartels (*cont.*)
  oil, 69–70
cash, 42
Catherine the Great, 53
central banks, 68–70
Central Provident Fund, 57
CEOs (Chief Executive Officers), 119, 128, 229–230
challenger banks, 187–188
charity, 266
Chernobyl nuclear disaster, 203
Chile
  AFP, 71
  employees, 38
  mandatory pension contributions, 32
  privately run funds, 56–57
  shareholder capitalism, 21
  shareholder finance, 223
China
  asset ownership, 31, 60
  debt levels, 217
  developmental state capitalism, 22, 197–198, 210
  electric cars, 258
  export-led growth, 70–71
  foreign reserves, 258
  GDP per capita, 213
  goods production, 150
  government influence, 56
  industrial production, 217
  industrialisation, 69, 166, 198
  life expectancy, 283–284
  ownership of US debt, 165
  pension funds, 34, 57
  poverty, 210, 213
  SWFs, 37, 213
China Investment Corporation, 31, 37, 60
Chinese Central Bank, 89
Churchill, Winston, 242
Circles of Sustainability, 265
circular economy, 243, 268–269, 273

City of London, 165, 221
civic engagement, 242
Civil Service Retirement and Disability Fund, 34, 57
civil society, 285
clean energy, 15
Climate Bonds Initiative, 267–268, 273
climate change, 3, 14, 122, 200–201, 203, 217, 239, 247, 256–257, 264, 267, 273
climate-resilient economy, 267–268
Clinton, Bill, 115
CNP Assurances, 31
coal mining, 205
collateral damage, 18, 191–217
  carbon bubble, 206
  carbon markets, 206
  finance and, 203–206
  global inequality, 210–214
  health and happiness, 214–215
  impact on society, 207–215
  inequality and growth, 207–209
  negative impacts of finance, 204–206
  see also planetary boundaries; sustainability
collateralised debt obligations (CDOs), 176
colonisation, 17, 170, 172, 272
  finance trade tools, 177–179
commodities, 112–113
Common Agricultural Policy (CAP), 63
communism, 22, 162
Communist Party, 162
consumerism, 204
consumer spending, 204, 205
copyright, 285
corporate debt, 62–63, 109
covered bonds, 275
cradle-to-cradle processes, 268, 273
credit cards, 13
credit default swaps, 176, 203

Cretaceous–Paleogene mass-extinction
    event, 192
Crimea, 53
criminal acts, 23–24
Cuba, 53–55
currency manipulators, 69–70

D

debt, 18–19, 237
    levels, 209, 214, 216, 243, 263
debt-based money, 259–260
debt-to-equity ratio, 174
Deepwater Horizon spill, 121
deforestation, 192
demographic theory, 4, 90, 194
Denmark
    pension fees, 97
deposits, 147
deposit and savings channel, 23, 27–28
derivatives, 42
    leverage, 173
    OTC global markets, 12, 25n, 168
Deutsche Asset & Wealth
    Management, 45
developing countries, 209
development banks, 275–276
dignity, 240, 243
dinosaurs, 192
discount rates, 65–66
diversity, 24
dividends, 41
Douglas, Michael, 159
driverless cars, 282–283
Drucker, Peter, 83
drugs, 281

E

earthquakes, 192
Eastern Europe
    industrialisation, 166
East India Company, 72
economic growth, 237–238

economic theory, 24, 230
economy's helminths, 17, 159–188
    abstraction, 175–176
    bond funds, 183
    colonisation, 177–179
    dysfunction of the finance system,
        186–188
    hedge funds, 184
    hegemony, 179–181
    history of the current financial
        system, 163–166
    innovation, 175–176
    leverage, 172–175
    mortgage-backed securities, 183
    revenue, origins of, 181–186
    unethical behaviour, 166–171
ecosystems, 193, 268
'the edge' 49
education, 15, 234, 241
    training and, 122–123, 284
efficient market hypothesis (EMH), 47,
    51n, 180–181, 185, 224–229
electric vehicles, 264
    cars, 258, 280
electronic money, 249, 260–262,
    275–276
Elephant curve, 210–211
Eli Lilly, 281
Elizabeth II, queen of England, 139
emerging markets savings glut, 91
Employees Provident Fund, 57
Employees' Provident Fund
    Organisation (EPFO), 57
employment, 282–284
    company requirements, 282–283
    future for finance professionals,
        284–286
endowments, 38–39
entertainment, 285
entrepreneurship, 162–163, 269
environment
    damage, 198–200, 203–205,
        216, 276

environment (cont.)
  destruction, 237–238, 242
  finance, economy and society, 4
  law, 204, 216
environmental, social and governance (ESG), 123, 126
equality before the law, 243
equality of opportunity, 241
equity, 41
  asset allocation, 103
  investment, 103–105
  market, 6, 63–64
ethics, 242
  of capital markets, 238–239
  questions, 222
  values, 228
  vision of society, 240
Etihad, 54
Euro area, 178
Eurodollar market, 164
European Union (EU), 122
  European post-war economic boom, 164
  free movement of capital, 164
  FTT, 258
  fuel, 124
  Solvency, 2
  regulation, 35–36, 61
evolution of man, 192
exchange traded fund (ETF), 112
extinction, 191–192, 203, 217
ExxonMobil, 124

Facebook, 21, 110, 282
fairness, 241
family offices, 38–39
farming, 192
Federal Home Loan Mortgage Corporation (Freddie Mac), 62, 165
Federal National Mortgage Association (Fannie Mae), 62, 165
Federal Old-age and Survivors Insurance Trust Fund, 34, 56–57
fertility rates, 80, 194
Fidelity Investments, 45
fiduciary duties, 59
finance and economics courses, 179
finance sector
  developments and crises, 9–14, 20–21
  finance, impact of, 6–9
  tools of, 171–186
financial corporations, 13
financial innovation, 17
financial intermediation, 159–160, 174–175, 183–186, 223
financial legislation, 272
financial sector debt, 152, 156n
Financial Services Authority (FSA), 133
financial system
  history of, 163–166
  unethical behaviour, 166–171
financial technologies, 20
Financial Times, 63, 121
financial transaction tax (FTT), 249, 258, 270
fines, bank, 187
Finland
  government spending, 72
FinTech, 20–21, 269–272, 285
First World War, 5
flash crash (2010), 227
flourishing financial system, 250
  see also FinTech; money; sustainable finance
flourishing markets, 239–242
  see also values
food and beverages, 63
Ford, Henry, 279
fossil fuel, 14, 124, 177, 206, 216, 256–257
foundations, 38–39
fractional reserve banking, 275
France

Index 293

asset managers, 45
asset ownership, 31, 59
eighteenth century, 72
GDP growth rate, 235–236
government bond yields, 68
PAYGO system, 97
pensions, 77
Franklin Templeton Investments, 45
fraud, 144, 175
free capital markets, 223
freedom, 241
  of speech, 243
freshwater use, 201
Freud, Sigmund, 214
Friedman, Milton, 229
FTSE 100 index, 94
FTSE All share index, 42, 44, 46, 117
funded schemes, 80–82
  see also pensions

G
G20, 122
gaming regulation, 178
GDP (Gross Domestic Product), 145–146, 186, 233–235
  US, 160–161, 166
Geanakoplos, Jean, 148
gender, 24
  pay gap, 207
  women's rights, 257
General Electric, 177
General Insurance, 31
Generali Insurance, 59
General Organization for Social Insurance (GOSI), 31
genetic diversity, 200
Germany
  asset managers, 45
  asset ownership, 31, 59
  banks, 275
  covered bonds, 275
  developmental state capitalism, 210

economic policy, 165
independent ratings agents, 40
industrialisation, 166
Nazi/WW2, 249
pensions, 77
stakeholder capitalism, 22
gilts, 65
Glazer family, 104
global economy: growth of, 197–199
global financial crisis (2007–8), 5, 9, 13, 20, 63, 67, 70, 89, 106, 133, 135, 138, 176, 177, 187, 248
global invested capital, 40
globalisation, 10, 166, 276
The Global Reporting Initiative, 265
global warming, 3, 192gold bugs, 260
Goldman Sachs, 178, 224
Goldman Sachs Asset Management Int., 45
goldsmiths, 139
Gondwana, 191
good life *see* pursuit of good life
Google, 47, 72, 124, 282
Gordon Ramsey, 54
government bonds, 22, 59
  see also bonds
Government Employees Pension Fund (GEPF), 57
government intervention, 82
government investment, 91
Government Pension Fund Global, 31, 37, 60
Government Pension Fund of Norway, 34, 56–57
Government Pension Investment Fund, 31, 34, 57, 60
Government of Singapore Investment Corporation, 37
Government of Singapore Investment Fund, 37
government-sponsored enterprises (GSEs), 62, 165, 254
Graeber, David, 283

294 Index

Gramsci, Antonio, 179
Greece
  banking crisis, 145, 178
green bonds, 267–268, 275
green economy, 203, 267, 276
green environmentalism, 240–241
greenhouse gases (GHGs), 122, 124, 200–203, 206, 257, 264, 267
green investment, 243–244, 267–268
  see also investment
Green Investment Bank, 276
Greenland, 3
Greenspan, Alan, 69, 88–89
Greenspan Put, 69, 88–89
Gucci, 54

H

happiness, 214–215, 235
  see also collateral damage; health
Harvard University endowment, 38
Havana, Cuba, 54
Hayek, Friedrich, 251
health, 15, 214–215, 234, 240, 243, 255, 273, 283–284
  see also collateral damage; happiness
healthy environment, 240–241
hedge funds, 42, 69, 185
  economy's helminths, 184
  pensions, 110–111
hegemonic theory, 17–18, 170, 172, 216–217
  finance trade tools, 179–181
  shareholder value, 229–230
  standard finance theories, 225–228
  values, 223–244
helminths, 159
  see also economy's helminths
high-frequency trading (HFT), 176, 230, 259, 270
Hitler, Adolf, 240
HNW Lending, 271
Holland

pension fees, 97
shareholder capitalism, 21
shareholder finance, 223
Hong Kong
  capitalism, 213
Hong Kong Monetary Authority Investment Portfolio, 37
household income, 207–209
housing
  bubbles, 203, 205
  housebuilding, 263
  money trouble, 263
  see also mortgages; property
HSBC Private Bank, 38
human civilisation, 200–201
human society, 3–4
Hungary, 4

I

Icahn, Carl, 125
immigration, 80
impact investment, 265–266
  fund, 273
  see also investment
impatience, 65–66
implicit guarantees, 136
income levels, 207–209
'incompetent greedy bankers' 140
increased spread, 91
independent ratings agents, 40
India
  colonial history, 72
  fertility rates, 194
  industrialisation, 166, 198
  pension funds, 57
industrialisation, 22, 166, 192, 198, 245n
industrial revolution, 203, 277
industry, 243
  sustainable finance, 268–269
inequality, 4, 14, 91–92, 185, 238, 263, 272

global, 210–214
growth and, 207–209
wealth, 151
see also collateral damage
inflation, 32, 65
infrastructure
pensions, 112
ING Group, 31, 59
Initial Public Offering (IPO), 41, 104–105, 113
innovation, 170, 172, 182, 272
finance trade tools, 175–176
insolvency, 133, 135, 173
Institute and Faculty of Actuaries (UK), 24, 43
institutional investors, 28
insurance
bankruptcy, 60
buyers, 59–61
captive insurers, 50n
companies, 34–36
household, 60
liability, 60
marine, 50n
monoline, 36
motor, 60
premiums, 60
integrated reporting, 265
intellectual property, 160, 281
interest rates, 64–70, 87–92
central bank rate, 88–90
low, 248
morality of, 144–146
natural rate, 90–92
ultra-low, 92, 188
intermediaries, 43–49
see also financial intermediation
international investment
pensions, 112–113
International Monetary Fund (IMF), 37, 73, 179, 223–224
internet companies, 20

interpersonal connectedness, 242
Invesco, 45
investment
green, 243–244, 266–268
impact, 265–266
sustainable finance, 265–268
investment/asset managers, 44–46
investment banks, 48–49
retail banks vs, 152–155
investment decisions *see* actuaries
investment management and capital markets, 27–50
see also asset owners; intermediaries
investment performance, 253
investments, 39
investment styles
active and passive, 46–48
iPhones, 64–65, 280–281
Ireland
economic growth, 10
shareholder capitalism, 21
shareholder finance, 223
irresponsible investment
pensions, 122–126
Italy
asset ownership, 31, 59
fertility rates, 80

J

Japan
asset ownership, 31, 59
developmental state capitalism, 22, 210
domestic markets, 71
economic policy, 165
GDP growth rate, 235–236
industrialisation, 166
insurance regulation, 35
life expectancy, 283
pension funds, 34, 57
post-war economic boom, 164
joint stock companies, 72

J.P. Morgan Asset Management, 45
Judaeo-Christian tradition, 241

K

Kay, John, 6, 121
Kay Review, 6, 117
Kazakhstan
    pension funds, 59
Kenya, 194
    mobile technology, 270
Keynes, John Maynard, 38, 69, 118
KfW, 276
King, Mervyn, 263
knowledge economy, 130n
Kotlikoff, Laurence, 262
Kuwait, 37
Kuwait Investment Authority, 37
Kyoto Protocol, 206

L

land-system change, 200–201
Laurasia, 191
Legal & General Group, 31, 59
Legal & General Investment
    Management, 45
Lehman Brothers, 174
leverage, 17, 170, 272
    bank, 173
    cycle theory, 148
    derivatives, 173
    finance trade tools, 172–175
    property, 146–152
    ratios, 134
leveraged buy-out (LBO), 111–112
libertarianism, 241, 249
LIBOR, 134
life expectancy, 32, 253
    impact on finance industry,
        283–284
lifetime consumption, 7–8, 77–78, 270
    banks, property and money, 135
liquidity transformation, 138

Living Planet Index, 192
Lloyd's Insurance, 221
Lloyd's of London, 60
Lloyd's syndicates, 50n
LMX spiral, 60
loans, 8–9, 143–144
    affordability, 147
    deposits, 147
    loan-to-value, 147
    multiple of earnings, 147
    value of collateral, 147
loan-to-value mortgages, 147
lobbying, 19, 124–125, 177–178, 204,
    206, 215–216, 272
London Stock Exchange, 28, 63, 104
long-term growth, 234
long-term investment, 120
low-carbon economy, 203, 206,
    244, 247
LTCM, 69
low global growth, 90

M

Mad Men (TV series), 207
Madoff, Bernie, 163
Malaysia
    employees, 38
    industrialisation, 166
    pension funds, 57
management theory
    shareholder value, 179–181
Manchester United Football Club
    (MUFC), 104
Mao, Zedong, 240
marketplace lending platform, 20, 285
mark-to-market accounting, 227
Marks and Spencer's (M&S), 111
Marxism, 22, 54
Marx, Karl, 22, 83, 284
maturity transformation, 138
Mayan civilisation, 191–192
    pyramids, 1–5

medical research, 285
    see also health
mental health, 240, 243
meteorites, 191–192
MetLife Insurance, 31
Mexico
    Yucatan peninsula, 191
middle classes, 210
Middle East
    military and political intervention, 257
Military Retirement Fund, 34, 57
mining, 63
Minsky, Hyman, 175
mobile phones
    credits, 261, 270
    monetary transfers, 25n
    technology, 198
    see also smartphones
modern portfolio theory (MPT), 179–181, 185, 224–228, 254, 272–274
money
    banks, 262–263
    creation of, 136–146
    economic explanations, 136–139
    housing trouble, 263
    impact, 140–146
    'magic' of money creation, 139
    morality of interest, 144–146
    trouble, 259–263
    UK lending, 141–144
monoline insurance, 36
Montreal Climate Pledge, 123–124
Montreal Protocol, 200
Moody's and Fitch, 40
moral hazard, 136
mortgages, 8, 13, 143–144
    mortgage-backed securities, 49, 182–185
    mortgage-related debt, 62–63
    see also housing
M-Pesa, 270

multifamily offices, 38
multiple of earnings, 147
Mussolini, Benito, 240
Myners, Paul, 28–29, 121

N

narrow purpose banking, 262
National Pension Service (NPS), 34, 56–57
National Social Security Fund of China, 34, 37, 56–57
Natixis Global Asset Management, 45
natural environment, 19
natural interest rate, 90–92
natural world, 3–4
Nazism, 5, 249
Ned Ludd, 282
neo-liberalism, 179
NEST (National Employment Savings Trust), 72, 83, 95–96
Netherlands
    asset ownership, 31, 59
    pension funds, 34, 57
New York Stock Exchange, 104, 221
New Zealand
    auto-enrolment, 33
Nigeria, 162
    income levels, 234
    insurance regulation, 35
    mandatory pension contributions, 32
Nippon Life Insurance Company, 31
Nobel laureate, 247
Nobel Prize, 181
non-financial companies (NFCs), 13, 62, 160, 170, 177–178
non-governmental organisations (NGOs), 125
non-profit organizations, 13
Northern Trust Asset Management, 45
Norway
    asset ownership, 31, 59

Norway (cont.)
  oil, 256
  pension funds, 34, 57
  SWFs, 37
Norwegian Pension Fund, 127
novel entities, 201
nuclear power, 264
nuclear winter, 192

O

ocean acidification, 201
off-shoring, 200, 209, 216
oil, 37, 54, 63, 124, 249, 256, 258
  cartels, 69–70
Ontario Teachers' Pension Plan, 57
Organisation for Economic Cooperation and Development (OECD), 122, 197
Organization of Petroleum Exporting Countries (OPEC), 63, 70, 257–258
over-the-counter (OTC), derivative markets, 168–169
ozone layer, 200

P

pandemics, 122
pareto-efficiency, 224
passive index-tracking fund, 20
patents, 285
'pawnbroker for all seasons' 262–263
pay-day loans, 8
PAYGO, 80–82, 97, 252–253
payments system, 145
  banks, property and money, 134–135
peer-to-peer lending platforms, 188, 248, 270–271
Pension Benefit Guarantee Corporation (US), 59
Pension Protection Fund (UK), 59

pensions
  activist investors, 125–126
  aging population, 80–82
  alternatives, 110–112
  annuities, 60
  'asleep at the wheel' 116–122
  asset allocation by funds, 102–103
  auto-enrolment, 33, 58, 73, 83, 95, 249
  benefits, 114–126
  bond investment, 105–109
  buyers, 56–59
  commodities, 112–113
  cost of, 85–87
  deal, 101
  defined benefit (DB), 30–33, 85–87
  defined contribution (DC), 30–33, 85–87
  equity investment, 103–105
  fees and charges, 92–96
  funded schemes, 80–82
  funds, 30–34
  future prospects, 96–97
  government intervention, 58–59, 82
  government regulation, 32–33
  hedge funds, 110–111
  individual and state functions, 79
  infrastructure, 112
  international investment, 112–113
  irresponsible investment, 122–126
  limitations, 102–114
  market performance, 94–96
  mark-to-market, 118
  national purpose, 80
  PAYGO, 80–82
  private equity, 111–112
  productive investment of funds, 113
  property, 110
  proportion of productive investment, 113
  Scandi-Style, 251–259
  structure of schemes, 33–34
  tax benefits, 33, 58

The Unseen Counter-Revolution, 83–85
see also Sisyphus savings system
Pensions Policy Institute (UK), 108
People's Bank of China, 37
performativity of theory, 180
personal fulfilment, 242
petrol, 256–258
Pfandbrief, 275
pharmaceutical companies, 178, 215, 243, 281
philanthropy model, 266
Philippon, Thomas, 159
philosophy, 222, 242
Piketty, Thomas, 207
PIMCO, 45
Pitt-Watson, David, 93
planetary boundaries, 4
 schema, 201
planetary damage, 198–203
 see also collateral damage
Poland, 4
 pension funds, 59
pollution, 19, 177–178, 200, 241, 257
ponzi schemes, 150–151, 163
population growth, 4, 194–197, 201
 history of global human population, 195
 projections to, 2100 by region, 196
populism, 4, 210
Portugal
 industrialisation, 166
Positive Money, 140
Potemkin markets, 16, 21, 53–73, 127, 221, 230, 237, 239
 implications, 71–74
Potemkin, Prince Grigory, 53
poverty, 4, 210–214
 global levels, 78, 212
Pramerica Investment Management, 45
preferencing, 274–275
 see also sustainable finance
price

interest rates, 64–70
The Prince's Accounting for Sustainability Project, 265
principle/agent problem, 59
private equity, 41
 pensions, 111–112
property, 13, 109
 leverage cycle, 146–152
 loans, 147
 pensions, 110
 see also housing; mortgages
prudence, 59
Prudential Financial Inc, 31, 59
Prudential (UK), 31, 59
psychological theory, 214–215
public sector, 55, 205
pursuit of good life, 242
pursuit of practical wisdom, 242
put option, 110
Pyramid of the Magician, Uxmal, 1–5

Q

Qatar
 oil, 256
 SWFs, 37
Qatar Investment Authority, 37
Quantitative Easing (QE), 89, 108, 260
quantity theory of credit, 140–141, 148, 150

R

real estate, 17, 40–41, 62, 147, 271
real estate investment trust (REIT), 41
recession, 234, 235, 237–238
reduced investment, 91
reduction of liabilities, 274
redundancies, 214
reforestation, 192
regional development banks, 276
regulatory arbitrage, 272
renewable energy, 206, 264, 267

rent-seeking behaviour, 166
repurchase agreements (repos), 154
research and development (R&D), 185, 204, 243
retirement, 279–280
  age, 254–255
return on capital, 205
return of the helminth, 272
risk, 65–66, 193, 225
risk management, 7, 143–144, 270
Rogoff, Kenneth, 261
Roman Empire, 3
Royal Society of Arts (RSA), 92, 98n12, 99n18
Russia, 258
  18th Century, 53
  fossil fuels, 257

S
S&P, 500 Index, 99n19
SAFE Investment Company, 31, 37
SAMA Foreign Holdings, 31, 37
Santiago Principles, 37
Sarbanes Oxley Act, 152
Saudi Arabia
  asset ownership, 31, 59
  oil, 70, 256–257
  SWFs, 37
savings
  allocation into useful investment, 135–136
  channel, 27–30, 248–249
  emerging markets, 91
  glut, 90, 205
  industry see Sisyphus savings system
  pension costs, 85–87
scandals, 23–24
Scandi-Style pensions, 251–259
  FTT, 258–259
  radical alternative, 254–255
  SWFs, 256–258
Second World War, 22, 72, 210, 257

secular stagnation, 204
securitisation process, 184
security, 241
seigniorage, 145, 262
self-driving vehicles, 256–257
sellers, 61–70
sell-side, 48, 79, 153
service-dominant firms, 269
Sese Seko, Mobutu, 162–163
shadow banking system, 154–155, 174
Share Action, 125
share buy-backs, 41, 125
shareholder finance, 22, 223, 247
shareholder value, 209, 215, 225, 229–230, 238, 254, 268–269
  see also hegemonic theory
sharing economy, 268, 280–281
shocks, 248
shopping, 53–54
short-term growth, 234
Singapore, 70
  capitalism, 213
  pension funds, 57
  SWFs, 37
smart beta, 226–227
smartphones, 234, 283
  see also mobile phones
Smith, Adam, 223–224, 240
social housing, 263
socialism, 22, 241
socially responsible investment (SRI), 123, 267
social security funds, 56–57
social technology, 6–7, 248, 264
Society of Actuaries (US), 43
sociology, 230
Sola, 281
Solvency Capital Requirement (SCR), 36
Solvency II Regulation, 35–36, 61
Somalia, 3
South Africa
  civil servants, 38

industrialisation, 166, 198
pension funds, 57
South Korea
   capitalism, 213
   fertility rates, 194
   pension funds, 34, 57
Sovereign Wealth Funds (SWFs), 36–38
   buyers, 56
   oil, 70
Soviet Union, 162, 203
Spain
   government bond yields, 68
   industrialisation, 166
Stalin, Joseph, 240
standard finance theories, 225–228
   see also hegemonic theory
Standard and Poor's (S&P), 40
Starbucks, 124
State Street Global Advisors, 45
Stern, Nicholas, 217, 239
Stern Review, 239
Stichting Pensioenfonds ABP (ABP), 34, 57
Stichting Pensioenfonds Zorg en Welzijn, 57
Stockholm Resilience Centre, 200
stratospheric ozone depletion, 200
sub-prime mortgages, 176, 182–184
subsistence farming, 7, 8
Sugarscape model, 230–233
   price of sugar and spice, 232
sustainability
   banking, 275–276
   Buffer Fund, 273–274
   definition and types of, 3–6, 193–198
   ecological, 5
   economic, 5
   of finance, 271–276
   financial system and, 24
   global trends, 194–197
   preferencing, 274–275
   self, 5
   societal, 5
   underlying factors of trends, 197–198
   see also collateral damage
sustainable finance, 264–276
   accounting, 264–265
   industry, 268–269
   investment, 265–268
sustainable infrastructure fund, 273
Sweden
   buffer funds, 273
   income levels, 234
   mandatory pension contributions, 32
   pensions, 276
   savings systems, 249
   Scandi-Style pensions, 251–254
Swensen, David, 38
SWIFT transfer, 134
Swiss bank accounts, 162
Switzerland
   government spending, 71
synthetic CDOs, 176
Syria, 3

T

Taibbi, Matt, 178
Taiwan
   capitalism, 213
   fertility rates, 80
Tajikistan, 7
taxation
   avoidance, 124–125, 178, 216
   breaks, 272
   incentives, 106, 108–109
Tax Research UK, 108
tech firms
   takeovers, 282
technology, 166, 197–198, 248, 282
   growth, 10–12
temperature

temperature (*cont.*)
  global history, 202
terrorism, 241, 257, 258
Tesco, 55
Tesla, 280
Thamotheram, Raj, 121
Thrift Savings Plan (TSP), 34, 57
TIAA-CREF, 45
Tobin tax *see* Financial Transaction Tax (FTT)
'too big to fail' 138–139, 173, 270–271
totalitarianism, 251
trading on principle, 49, 153
transcendence, 242
transport sector, 256–257, 273
triple bottom line accounting, 243, 264, 273–274
trolley problem, 222
Trump, Donald, 4
  Trump effect, 99n19
tsunamis, 192
Turkey, 4

U
Uber, 21, 281
unemployment, 285
unincorporated organizations, 13
United Arab Emirates (UAE), 53–55
  asset ownership, 31, 59
  oil, 256
  SWFs, 37
United Kingdom (UK)
  ageing population, 82
  Anglo-Saxon-style finance system, 18, 97, 223
  annual government subsidy of finance, 108
  asset managers, 45
  asset ownership, 31, 77
  auto-enrolment, 33
  bank lending by sector (2015), 13, 142
  bond market, 105–106
  Brexit, 4
  capital control, 164
  capitalism, 248
  contribution rates, 86–87
  debt of the finance sector, 152, 156n14
  debt levels, 145–146, 235
  economic growth, 10, 152, 164–165
  equity, 42, 44, 117
  equity funds, 98n12
  equity market, 94–95, 112–113
  fertility rates, 80
  financial assets, 73
  GDP growth rate, 235–236
  government bonds/gilts, 65–66, 72
  government bond yield curves, 66–68
  government deficit, 105–106
  government influence, 55–56
  green economy, 276
  history of currency exchange, 139
  history of net borrowing, 107
  institutional investment, 121
  IPOs and rights issues, 113
  lending, 141–144
  mortgage payments as proportion of income, 150
  occupational pension schemes, 34
  pension guarantees, 59
  pensions sector, 96–97, 102
  private pension system, 253
  projections of support ratio, 80–82, 86
  property sector, 152
  ratio of house prices compared to income, 149
  shareholder capitalism, 21–22
  tax savings benefit on pensions, 83–84
  Treasury, 122
  WW2, 249
United Nations Principles of Responsible Investment (UNPRI), 123–124

Index

United Nations (UN), 193, 264
United States (US)
  Anglo-Saxon-style finance system, 18, 97, 223
  asset managers, 45
  asset ownership, 31, 59, 77
  bond market, 61–62
  capitalism, 165, 248
  CEO to worker compensation ratio, 119
  company profits, 126
  corporate debt, 109
  corporate profits, 10–11
  debt-based money, 260
  debt holdings, 165
  debt levels, 209
  Department of Business Innovation and Skills, 122
  developmental state capitalism, 210
  domestic markets, 71
  economic growth, 209
  employment, 282–283
  equity, 226
  exports, 165
  Federal Reserve, 69, 89, 114
  fertility rates, 80
  finance sector profits, 166–167
  financial assets, 73
  fuel, 124
  GDP growth rate, 235–236
  GDP share of financial sector, 9–10, 160–161
  government bond yields, 68
  government influence, 55–56
  GSEs, 254
  healthcare system, 215
  income growth, 207–208
  indices, 99n19
  insurance regulation, 35
  Kyoto Protocol, 206
  legislation, 152
  NFCs, 177
  pension funds, 34, 57
  post-war economic boom, 164
  privately run funds, 56–57
  public health institutions, 215, 243
  ratio of investment to shareholder funds, 120
  real income growth, 14
  share buy backs, 109
  shareholder capitalism, 21–22
  Treasury, 71, 178, 213
  wage increases, 237
  WW2, 249
universal income, 285
Universities Superannuation Scheme, 34
The Unseen Counter-Revolution, 83–85
  see also pensions
urban migration, 198, 210
utilities, 64
utility maximisation, 224

V

value of collateral, 147
value of financial assets, 64
values, 21, 221–244
  best possible world, 233–238
  economic development, 242–244
  economic outcome, 224
  ethics of capital markets, 238–239
  flourishing markets, 239–242
  hegemonic theory, 223–244
  sugar and spice, 230–233
Vanguard, 20, 124, 226, 270
Vanguard Asset Management, 45
venture capital, 273, 281
Vietnam
  industrialisation, 166
virtual capital, 172
virtual reality entertainment, 285
volcanic activity, 191–192
von Bismarck, Otto, 254
Vostok station, Antarctica, 200

W

wage stagnation, 4, 18, 214
Waitrose, 54
Wall Street Crash (1929), 5, 164
Wall Street (Film), 125, 159
wealth inequality, 151
  see also inequality; poverty
Weimar Republic, 5
Welch, Jack, 229
welfare, 228
Wellington Management, 45
Werner, Richard, 140–141, 148, 151
wisdom, 242 *see* pursuit of practical wisdom
women's rights, 257

World Bank, 58, 73, 122, 223–224, 252, 266, 276
World Wildlife Fund, 192

Y

Yale University endowment, 38
Yemen
  war crimes, 257

Z

Zaire, 162
zero sum game, 128
Zuckerberg, Mark, 104